Literacy Learning and Teaching

Language as Social Practice in the Primary School

Literacy Learning and Teaching

Language as Social Practice in the Primary School

Edited by **LEN UNSWORTH**
THE UNIVERSITY OF SYDNEY

M

Copyright © Len Unsworth and contributors 1993

All rights reserved
No part of this publication
may be reproduced or transmitted
in any way or by any means
without permission

First published 1993 by
MACMILLAN EDUCATION AUSTRALIA PTY LTD
107 Moray Street, South Melbourne 3205
6 Clarke Street, Crows Nest 2065

Associated companies and representatives
throughout the world

National Library of Australia
cataloguing in publication data

Literacy learning and teaching.

Includes index.
ISBN 0 7329 0517 6
ISBN 0 7329 0516 8 (pbk.).

1. Language arts (Primary). 2. English language — Study and teaching (Primary). 3. Children's literature — Study and teaching (Primary). 4. Literacy. 5. Children — Books and reading. I. Unsworth, L. (Len), 1950– .

372.6044

Typeset in Sabon by Superskill Graphics Pte Ltd, Singapore
Printed in Hong Kong
Jacket cover design by Maria Fontana
Illustrated by Joe Szabo

Contents

List of Contributors vi

Introduction vii

1 The Social Construction of Literacy in the Primary School 1
   Alan Luke
2 Children's Literature: What to Look for in a Primary Reading Program 55
   Maurice Saxby
3 Beginning Reading with Children's Literature 93
   Len Unsworth and Mary O'Toole
4 Managing the Language Program: Children's Literature in the Primary Classroom 145
   Len Unsworth
5 Using Systemic Grammar in Teaching Young Learners: An Introduction 197
   Geoff Williams
6 The Language of Social Studies: Using Texts of Society and Culture in the Primary School 255
   Bill Cope, Mary Kalantzis and Peter Wignell
7 Choosing and Using Information Books in Junior Primary Science 297
   Len Unsworth
8 Resourcing Children's Learning 349
   Keith Pigdon and Marilyn Woolley

Index 414

List of Contributors

Bill Cope	Senior research fellow, Centre for Workplace Communication and Culture, University of Wollongong and University of Technology, Sydney
Mary Kalantzis	Director, Centre for Workplace Communication and Culture, University of Wollongong and University of Technology, Sydney
Allan Luke	Reader in Education, Faculty of Education, James Cook University, Townsville, Queensland
Mary O'Toole	Primary school teacher, Ministry of Education, Victoria
Keith Pigdon	Senior lecturer, Institute of Education, University of Melbourne
Maurice Saxby	Formerly Head of Department of English, Kuring-gai College of Advanced Education
Len Unsworth	Senior lecturer, Faculty of Education, University of Sydney
Peter Wignell	Lecturer, Faculty of Education, Northern Territory University
Geoff Williams	Senior lecturer, Faculty of Education, University of Sydney
Marilyn Woolley	Senior lecturer, Institute of Education, University of Melbourne

Introduction

What can student teachers and experienced classroom practitioners in infant and primary schools expect to find in another text on literacy development and schooling? In this book there is certainly a coherent practical and theoretical framework for classroom work with children's literature and for developing literacy and learning in key learning areas. But this book also has a distinctive orientation to literacy development, learning and teaching as interconnected social processes. What is on offer is access to the detailed practical ramifications of new theoretical understandings concerning the *social construction of literacy*, the importance of *functional grammar* in understanding language as a meaning-making resource, the relationships between *learning and teaching and classroom management*, and the role of *visual literary and informational texts* in constructing different forms of knowledge. This book seeks to engage teachers in a critical review and constructive reorientation of practices associated with 'whole language', 'natural learning' and 'literature-based language programs' towards a theoretically coherent, socially responsible, language-based pedagogy.

The social construction of literacy as discussed by Allan Luke in the opening chapter emphasises our view of the complete interconnectedness of learning and linguistic and social processes. The individual chapters explicate this in relation to different aspects of the curriculum including early reading development (Chapter 3), children's literature at all levels in the primary school (Chapters 2 and 4) as well as social studies (Chapters 6 and 8) and science education (Chapters 7 and 8). An understanding of this interdependence of learning, linguistic and social processes depends on knowledge of how language functions as a meaning-making resource (Chapter 5). It is this kind of technical knowledge of functional grammar — of the linguistic technology of meaning making — which is of great practical value in understanding the role of language in learning and designing effective learning experiences. The introduction to functional grammar (Chapter 5) emphasises its practicality for primary teachers, drawing on aspects of children's literature and literacy development from the early chapters of this book and introducing some issues in curriculum area learning taken up in the following chapters. The consistent perspective developed across the range of key learning areas can be seen in the following recurrent themes:

- Since learning and literacy are socially constructed, the 'what' of our learning cannot be separated from the 'how'.
- Since different key learning areas and social contexts have their own dominant grammatical and generic forms (text types) and grammatical structures, we need to abandon the notion of a singular basic literacy in favour of the development of multiple literacies.
- Since language is not an inert container for meaning, it is our selection

Introduction

- of particular grammatical and generic structures that constructs particular meanings.
- Since children's access to the linguistic system and to different forms of knowledge is a function of their position in the social system, there needs to be a strategic link between explicit teaching and opportunities for children's independent learning.

Socially Constructed Literacies

The kinds of readers, writers and learners children become — what they think is entailed in comprehending and composing texts — depends on the kinds of texts to which they have access and the kinds of interaction they experience around those texts. To develop the multiple literacies and critical perspectives essential to productive participation in cultural life, children, from the beginning of their schooling, need to have critical involvement with, and enjoyment of, children's literature and informational texts of science, society and culture. If young children are introduced to reading with children's literature, then their reading and understanding of literary texts will begin simultaneously. The only way to learn to comprehend children's literature is to engage directly with such texts with the support and guidance of a more experienced reader. Literary texts for beginning readers contain multiple semiotic cues, assisting inexperienced readers to attend to grapho-phonic relationships and at the same time provoking them to construct multiple interpretive 'readings' of the textual information. Without this kind of access to such texts, children cannot become active interpretive readers of literary texts. How children are taught to read, throughout the primary school, determines what they think reading is. It is from this position that Maurice Saxby discusses what to look for in a primary reading program (Chapter 2) and the chapters on beginning reading with children's literature (Chapter 3) and programming with children's literature in the primary school (Chapter 4) deal with the details of classroom implementation.

Critical Literacies Across the Curriculum

The grammatical and generic forms of scientific reports and explanations, historical accounts, procedural texts, persuasive and analytical expositions and other genres children will encounter both inside and out of school are very different from the narrative forms of children's litera-

Introduction

ture. Through their experiences of reading and writing, children should be systematically introduced to the range of genres which construct and communicate knowledge and simultaneously construct views of children and their roles within school and broader social contexts. Approaches to doing this are detailed in the second half of the book, beginning with Geoff Williams' account of the significance of grammatical understanding in appreciating how particular language forms are essential to the construction of particular meanings (Chapter 5). This is taken up in the next two chapters. Bill Cope, Mary Kalantzis and Peter Wignell show how different kinds of meanings in social studies rely on the use of particular grammatical forms and from this perspective they show how children can be helped to develop a critical perspective on *texts of society and culture* (Chapter 6). Similarly Chapter 7 demonstrates the importance of information books in learning how to construct and communicate scientific understanding. A variety of ways of *resourcing the curriculum,* using print, film and technological media, are then detailed by Keith Pigdon and Marilyn Woolley (Chapter 8) to extend the curriculum focus on science (Chapter 7) and social studies (Chapter 6).

The Integration of Linguistic Form and Meaning

Language is not a neutral conveyance of meanings. It is not like an inert pipe for channelling meaning from one person to another (Reddy 1979). Rather language form is active in the construction of meanings because the language we use is our selection from a system of interrelated grammatical choices for making meaning (Halliday 1984). What we can mean depends on our access to the linguistic system. In other words, learning in science or social studies, or any other curriculum area, necessarily involves simultaneously learning the language forms that construct knowledge in those discipline areas. Understanding 'uncommonsense' or specialist knowledge means gaining access to the technical vocabulary as well as the grammatical and generic structures that construct and communicate that knowledge. This means that in addition to developing learning via oral language interaction, teachers need systematically to teach children the forms of written language which distinguish the specialised ways of documenting and explaining the world from the perspective of disciplines such as science and social studies. Chapter 5 introduces the basic grammatical knowledge underlying this task and then in 'Choosing and Using Information Books in Junior Primary Science' (Chapter 7) and 'The Language of Social Studies' (Chapter 6) the theoretical and practical bases for undertaking classroom work are detailed.

Introduction

Balancing Explicit Teaching and Independent Collaborative Learning

There is no place in the classrooms of the 1990s and beyond for the sterile traditional teaching of the past with its mechanistic transmission of knowledge and passive, receptive learning. We do need to develop active, critical learners who will take the initiative in extending their knowledge of the world. However, in determining our role as teachers in bringing this about, we need to bear in mind that children's access to the linguistic system and to different forms of knowledge is a function of their position in the social system. An overemphasis on making children individually responsible for their own learning through their own choice of learning materials and tasks, such as selection of books to read or the form of text to write, may well mean that children's learning experiences are being restricted to the choices that they see as possible for them in the light of what they currently have knowledge and experience of. For example, if children continue to read only 'choose your own adventure' books or humorous short stories and avoid more demanding children's novels, they may need to be shown how to read such books by being taught how such texts make meanings. This may well involve allocating a book to be read and prescribing supportive reading-related activities. Similarly some children may need to be taught quite directly how to 'read' the complex interaction of linguistic and visual texts in information books for various curriculum areas. Such direct intervention may also be needed to ensure that children can write the forms of text which will function as indices of their learning and progress in the school system.

This kind of sensitive intervention in a class of 20 or 30 children requires careful planning. There needs to be a strategic link between explicit teaching and opportunities for children's independent learning. Highly routine learning tasks (such as completion of cloze texts or drawing a 'wanted poster' of a book's main character) must give way to activities designed to develop children's understanding of particular text forms and particular concepts. Similarly, allocation of children to fixed groups within classes or *laissez-faire*, opportunity group allocation needs to give way to strategic, flexible and functional grouping of children according to their experiences of the task at hand. In 'Beginning Reading with Children's Literature' and 'Managing the Language Program: Children's Literature in the Primary School', sample programs have been included to provide detailed illustrations of how this approach might be implemented. Sample learning tasks and programming strategies are also included in the chapters dealing with science (Chapter 7), social studies (Chapter 6) and alternative ways of resourcing the curriculum (Chapter 8).

Introduction

Just the Beginning!

The issues dealt with in this book are fundamental to the teaching of critical social literacies in the primary school. Although selected key learning areas have been discussed in some detail, a conscious decision was made not to attempt the kind of panoramic survey of all of the topics that are embraced by the primary language program. What we have gained is a thorough introduction to new, informing theoretical understandings and detailed accounts of their impact on practical planning of day to day classroom activities. Much more work is needed. It is hoped that teachers will regard this book as a beginning to their participation in both a critical review of literacy pedagogy and the practical development of a language-based theory of learning.

Len Unsworth

References:

Halliday, M.A.K. (1984) *Language as Social Semiotic: The Social Interpretation of Language and Meaning*, Edward Arnold, London.

Reddy, M.J. (1979) 'The conduit metaphor: A case of frame conflict in our language about language', in *Metaphor and Thought*, ed. A. Ortony, Cambridge University Press, Cambridge.

1
The Social Construction of Literacy in the Primary School

Allan Luke

Contents

Shaping Literacy in Schools: An Introduction   3

Literacy as a Social Semiotic Technology   7

Literacy and Social Power: Regulating the Word   11

Literacy and Equity   14

Selecting and Constructing Literate Traditions   18

Before Schooling: Language Socialisation   22

Literacy Events in Homes and Communities   26

Literacy as Curriculum   32

What's in a Story?   35

Constructing Literacy in Classroom Talk   41

Critical Social Literacy in the Classroom: A Beginning   46

Notes
References

Shaping Literacy in Schools: An Introduction

Many teachers have become accustomed to media declarations that schools are failing and that standards of literacy and language are deteriorating. Unfortunately, schools are easy targets for political criticism in the midst of alleged declines in literacy, and in the face of economic and social uncertainty. As philosopher Jurgen Habermas (1976) notes, during the periodic economic and political 'crises' endemic to contemporary capitalist societies, high-profile institutions like schools, churches and corporations become the focus of efforts to rebuild social solidarity, legitimacy and loyalty. Claims that schools should return to the teaching of the universal 'basics' take diverse forms, varying from 'correct spelling', 'knowledge of literary classics', and 'the ability to sign one's name' to 'finding the main idea' and the 'ability to read a basic consumer text'. A 'return to the basics', the popular wisdom holds, would address a range of youth, educational and ultimately economic and social problems.

These basics are often affiliated with discipline, respect for authority, allegiance to country and, what in the late 19th century were called the '3 Rs', reading, writing and arithmetic. Yet the very diversity of versions of the 'basics' in public debate points to the varied, conflicting political forces at play. These criticisms of educational standards frequently reflect the concerns of conservative social forces, from corporations and employers, to elite classes whose privilege is tied up with the maintenance of mainstream, dominant cultural traditions.

In other words, 'back to the basics' is not just a disinterested call for specific skills or curricula. It builds and connotes a selective, interest-bound version of culture. It typically harks back to a mythical era prior to an alleged breakdown of school, teacher and principal authority. Sometimes this vision is captured in the nostalgia for 1950s childhood and community life, for a postwar white-picket fence era without crime, migrants, media violence, budget deficits, drugs and so forth. Then, the claim goes, standards of learning, discipline and institutional order were maintained. Then, the story goes, all children left school able to perform the 'basics' of good spelling, handwriting and so forth. But there is *no* evidence that such an ideal educational era existed (Luke 1988; Cope 1990). Student populations and the very aims and methods of schooling change in response to emergent and, at times, conflicting, educational agendas and political imperatives. Likewise, standards and practices of literacy shift over time, in accordance with changing practical demands and cultural contexts for the use of written language.

In this light, many criticisms of schooling would be more accurately viewed as expressions of larger societal conflict and economic change — they should rightly be read, heard and analysed as polemical aspects of the public, political discourses on schooling. At the same time, I do not want to suggest that all is well with schooling and literacy. Across

Western nations there is an increasing recognition among members of working class, migrant and aboriginal communities that schools are failing to provide systematically the competences needed by their children to excel and succeed (e.g. Delpit 1988; Delgado-Gaitan 1990). There is compelling historical and contemporary evidence that, the best intents and efforts of many teachers notwithstanding, many school systems are not providing equitable access to powerful literacies (e.g. Gee 1990). This is an ongoing story tied up with schools' historical role in the production of sociocultural *in*equality. Across Western nation-states, schools have evolved as institutional sites for the reproduction of stratified social systems. At the same time, in many locales in Australia and other countries, teachers, teacher educators and curriculum developers are attempting to remake literacy in primary classrooms for children in ways that increase and enhance children's powerful participation in literate culture. This chapter is part of that effort.

Literacy is a dynamic, evolving social and historical construction. It is not a fixed, static body of skills. Standards and practices of literacy are contingent on the agendas and power relations of institutions and communities, governments and cultures. That is, literacy refers to social practices that are put to work in institutions such as the family and community, school and workplace according to stated and unstated rules. It is shaped and used in institutional *sites* and *events* — whether the classroom lesson or bedtime story, the social encounter or political meeting, the retail sales transaction or legal briefing. Its possession and use is part and parcel of what makes these occasions and situations, institutions and participants' identities what they are.

In this way, literacy is constructed by individuals and groups as part of everyday life. At the same time literacy also is constructive *of* everyday life. In literate societies it becomes a crucial element of one's cultural 'tool kit' (Bruner, 1991) for doing social relations, work, and for handling economically valuable and culturally significant information. But how it is 'done', by whom, when, with what texts — and how much latitude and free play individuals and groups exercise — are influenced by the institutions, ideologies and interests operant in these societies. For many children, this formal shaping of the possibilities and limits of literacy begins in the primary school classroom.

Literacy education is about the distribution of knowledge and power in contemporary society. Who gets what kinds of literate competence? Access to texts? Where and to what ends? Who can criticise? How? To what extent? These issues are significant not only for students' lives and economic destinies, but also for the overall distribution of competence and knowledge, wealth and power in a literate society. My aims in this introductory chapter are twofold. First, I want to explore how, where and in whose interests literacy is constructed. Second, I want to frame key choices and decisions teachers face in appraising and building selective traditions of literacy in reading, language arts and literature programs.

At issue here is a reassessment of what is at stake in the teaching of literacy in schools, a reassessment which goes considerably beyond 'back to the basics' rhetoric and the prevailing wisdom of many curriculum packages and in-service programs. Reading and writing are so deeply ingrained in post-industrial cultures that they appear 'natural' and invisible aspects of everyday life. We seldom stop to inquire about what reading and writing are, who has which capabilities with and access to texts, and how reading and writing are shaped by and shape our social and economic paths. This is risky for the teachers and university students who comprise the historical 'winners' of school literacy instruction. Teachers are part of the 3 per cent of the Australian workforce with university training and therefore will have had training with specialised kinds of literate practice (e.g. essay and report writing, reading academic texts). The very stock and trade of education is tied up with the use of language and literacy, and the 'making' of literate students. To enter the profession of teaching — to act as guides for successive generations' entries into literate culture — requires literate competence which is at once wide ranging and extremely specialised.

As members of this group, it is at once convenient and perilous to develop programs and approaches to teaching based on 'self-reproductive' assumptions: that is, assumptions which unquestioningly mirror and produce for the next generation aspects of our own childhoods and educations. These might include beliefs that how we learned literacy is best for all children; relatedly, that the values and attitudes we had towards literacy and book culture as children are the 'norm' against which we can judge and assess our students. Yet these reconstructions of the socioeconomic and educational 'facts' of our childhoods are often romanticised. The danger here is that we will judge our students against these benchmarks, this despite the fact that in the 15 or 20 years that have lapsed, the student clienteles of schools, the life experience and cultural background of primary school students have changed in profound ways. These are different children from us. This is, in many substantive respects, a different, multimediated literate culture, a different job market and economy, and a different polycultural social environment. Given the crucial place of teachers' work in shaping literacy, literate culture and the child literate, it is imperative that we know more about literacy in contemporary society.

Many current and aspiring teachers begin from contemporary 'literacy myths' (Graff 1987): for instance, that literacy necessarily makes you more intelligent or more morally worthy; that literacy consists of individualised, basic psychological skills; that working class children inherently are not as good at learning literacy; that girls are 'naturally' taken by romance reading; most recently, that learning literacy is a 'natural' and 'spontaneous' process for all children; and that there is a single, optimal formula for teaching literacy, one which if properly applied will 'solve' the problem of student literacy once and for all. These are all instances of ideology in action, that is, of situations where the consequences of history, culture and social relations are interpreted as the effects of 'nature', as 'the ways things are', or as innate to the child, childhood, and literacy itself. Educators can, through the 'message systems' of curriculum, instruction and evaluation (Bernstein 1990), *construct* particular consequences and effects — for instance, girls' taste in romance novels, Aboriginal children's dislike of reading, or a preoccupation with particular kinds and contents of literature — and then construe these as natural or somehow intrinsic to the child.

These are not simple matters for individual opinion or commonsense. They are far too crucial to be left to this and, as I will show here, there is a powerful popular ideology tied up with treating literacy as a matter of individual difference and aesthetic taste. How schools, curricular programs and classroom instruction construct literacy for students and parcel out entry into different career and life trajectories needs to be defined and tabled for debate.

Schools and teachers frame and distribute varying kinds and levels of literacy as *cultural capital* (Bourdieu 1990), credentials or 'identity papers' to be taken out into marketplaces of jobs and social relations. In this way, who gets what kinds of competence — and the relative equality or inequality of access — has a significant impact on students' life trajectories. Their eventual career paths, their participation, status and ultimate 'power' as citizens and workers are influenced by the distribution of cultural capital in the school. These patterns of unequal access, achievement and outcomes begin in the earliest grades. There, stratified differences in reading and writing development are not wholly attributable to 'individual difference' but rather fall along the historical grids of social class, ethnicity and gender (Cook-Gumperz 1986; Anyon 1981; Sharp and Green 1975). I begin here from the supposition that *social class, ethnic and gender stratification of achievement in reading, writing and affiliated school subjects is at least in part produced by inequitable and inappropriate teaching, texts and assessment.*

Teachers make daily decisions about what to teach, to whom, when and how. This requires expert knowledge and competence: familiarity with a range of literary and functional texts; technical and theoretical understandings of how language and literacy are learned, how texts work, how textual language is different from oral language, and the specific textual configurations and demands of school subjects (Carter 1990; Christie *et al.* 1992). But there is more to it than this. If indeed literacy is a social practice which figures significantly in children's political, economic and social participation, then the teaching of literacy requires an understanding of how texts and literate competence fit into larger patterns of community culture and social structure. 'Reading' and 'writing' are transitive verbs: learning to read and write always entails 'reading and writing the world' (Freire and Macedo 1987). If literacy is always about knowledges and values, ideologies and world views, then indeed teachers also need to have a reading of how literacy constructs and shapes the social world. Furthermore, if literacy is a form of cultural capital built and distributed in schools and classrooms, then literacy education is by definition a political enterprise — entailing the making of social and economic power and relations. Not to address this explicitly and consciously, as Freire (1968) argues, is to default to someone else's political agenda.

This chapter is an introduction to literacy as a social construction. My central claim is that the teaching of literacy requires social and cultural analyses of literacy in contemporary society and, crucially, of how it is part of the lived experience and futures of children and their communities. In what follows, I will begin from definitions of literacy, looking at how schooling entails a *selective tradition* about what will count as reading and writing, and at how educators' decisions about how to shape literacy in the classroom invariably reflect contending interests, ideologies and politics.

I will then outline various community and cultural resources which shape what children bring to the classroom, and how children conceive of the possibilities and potentials of literacy. These knowledges and competences may or may not assist children when they encounter school-based versions of literacy in the classroom. Here we can trace classroom instances of the social construction of literacy, where teachers select and frame texts, genres and events. I will conclude with a discussion of the possibilities for teaching children a *critical social literacy*, framing key questions we can ask of the literate traditions forged in classroom lessons and texts.

Literacy as a Social Semiotic Technology

Some starting points are in order. Literacy is at the heart of cultural and economic life in information-based, late-capitalist societies like Australia. Written language is a central mode for daily economic transactions, social relations and labour. Rudimentary textual competence is required for even minimal participation, much less powerful control over the texts of everyday life. More versatile and critical competence is needed for occupational mobility, informed civic participation and, quite simply, to avoid being exploited as a worker, citizen and consumer.

But beyond these broad claims, the place of literacy in the current educational landscape is disputed. Here I want to define literacy education in relation to ongoing debates with an eye towards a more realistic assessment of what active participation, and even basic survival, will require of today's students. Critical and informed participation in Australian society requires that students be given equitable access to functional, academic and critical capacities with text. This *critical social literacy* includes:

1. versatile and flexible competences to contend with diverse texts, genres and discourses in various social contexts — occupational, academic and community — and in various media, including print, electronic and visual;
2. the capacity to use text as a means for learning and decision making in periods of continual and new education across life cycles; and
3. the capacity to use text as a means to critically assess and to influence their positions in changing economic, occupational and social conditions and relations.

What is central to this definition is that *literacy and education are means for access to cultural knowledge and social power.*

The experience of reading and writing literature indeed may lead to 'personal power' and 'creativity', 'individual growth' and heightened 'self-esteem', as many teachers and researchers claim (cf. Gilbert 1990). But in a society where significant work and social relations are undertaken via communications media including print, any assigned, personal value of literacy is contingent on its use and worth in social and cultural contexts. Recall my earlier explanation that literacy is a social practice which is 'done'. It is not an internal possession, but rather it is a form of human labour, a means for the production of and engagement with cultural artefacts and social relations. To undertake literate labour, all readers and writers engage with codes for language and text — even if and when their aim is to dispute or contest them. In this sense, reading and writing are never truly solitary or individual. Despite their varying uses of literacy in public and private domains, the journalist, the teen-romance reader, the romantic poet and the priest all operate on the basis of conventions for reading and writing learned as part of her or his *interpretive community* (Fish 1980). Without knowledge of such conventions and, relatedly, participation in the textual rituals of these communities, the literate wouldn't know where to begin and finish, what to enjoy and to dislike, how to agree or disagree with text.

Children master the codes and conventions of their community's language system. Language consists of signs and symbols used by human beings to construct meaning: it is thus a *social semiotic system* (Halliday 1978). Literacy refers to the social practices that have developed with the material technology of written language. These practices involve the use of language in a dual sense. First, the reading and writing of texts makes use of linguistic and symbolic codes shared by communities of readers and writers. The technology of writing makes possible the representation and reiteration, interpretation and transformation of cultural patterns, knowledges and practices. Whether with quill or ballpoint pen, on tablet or magnetic disk, writing makes texts and meanings semi-permanent and portable, recoverable and readable across space and time. Second, in institutions such as families, schools, churches, workplaces and mass media, using literacy involves a variety of goal-oriented interactions around texts in social situations.

To reiterate: literacy is about cultural knowledges and social power. To become literate, children must master conventionalised linguistic and symbolic codes for constructing and deconstructing meanings with and around written texts. That is, they must develop both implicit and explicit, tacit and active *knowledge* of how written language works and its possibilities for access to and the representation of culturally significant ideas, concepts and beliefs. But to use literacy to realise sociocultural *power*, they also need to deploy language to conceptualise and realise goals and alternatives in specific social relationships and situations. One always reads and writes in cultural contexts and social situations — and it is in these contexts and situations where relations of power are constructed, deployed and waged.

Despite 19th century Romantic associations of literacy with solitary, individual reading and writing and intimate access to the 'self', literacy entails social activity: goal-seeking and purposive, situated and local. Its use occurs in *institutional sites*, where specific text types or *genres* have been developed to do 'work' in those sites (Kress 1985). Here I define institutions in the broadest sociological terms — to include not only those formal organisations like schools, churches, governments, corporations, but the family, mass media and other sites of socialisation as well. In literate and information societies, entire institutions may be constructed around and through texts, textuality and textual work: newspapers are built around the representation of 'reality' and the production of specialised genres (Fowler 1991); the stock exchange is little more than a site for the circulation of information and symbolic capital (Harvey 1987); a significant majority of the economic resources and work of schools are devoted to text-based activities and the production of the literate. Literacy, then, is more than a skill used in institutions. In post-industrial societies the very activity of representation is an economic activity *par excellence*. The production of text, information and image is as significant as the production of manufactured goods (Poster 1990), yielding both symbolic and financial capital. At the same time, the institutions of everyday life are not just places where discourse, text and literacy occurs; these very institutions are shaped, constructed and 'made up' by written language.

The uses of literacy may range from the study of a religious text to negotiation over a loan contract, from writing a reminder note to filling in applications and forms. In these sites social relations of power are waged (e.g. between minister and lay person, bank loan officer and client, parent and child, employer and employee, teacher and student). There, literate culture is played out according to both stated and unstated rules, where writing and reading are used to shape and construct one's social identity, to assemble one's identity papers (Gee 1990; cf. Shotter and Gergen 1989). In a literate society, how and what one reads and writes is interpreted as a significant marker of class, gender and even ethnicity.

Social institutions and communities utilise the printed word for a range of social and linguistic purposes, tied to intellectual work, to information exchange and to identity formation. In her ethnographic study of three communities in the southern United States, Heath (1986a, p. 21) described seven observable 'functions and uses' of literacy in daily life:

1. Instrumental. . . . information about practical problems of daily life (price tags, checks, bills, . . . signs . . .).
2. Social interactional. . . . information pertinent to social relations (greeting cards, . . ., letters, recipes).
3. News-related. . . . information about third parties or distant events (newspaper items, political flyers . . .).
4. Memory-supportive. . . . a memory aid (messages . . . on calendars . . .).

5. Substitutes for oral messages . . . when direct oral communication was not possible or would prove embarrassing (messages left . . . for child. . . , notes explaining tardiness to school).
6. Provision of permanent record . . when legal records were necessary or required for other institutions (birth certificates, . . ., tax forms).
7. Confirmation. . . . support for attitudes or ideas already held . . . (advertising brochures. . . , directions. . . , the Bible).

Heath studied three communities — working class Afro-American, working class white American, and middle class mixed Afro-American and white — in order to analyse the complex interrelationships between community cultural traditions, social class and work, and schooling. She found that their uses of literacy depended greatly on diverse patterns of work, leisure, child-rearing and family relations.

As ethnographic description these categories are not meant to be exhaustive or universal. The functions and uses of literacy vary according to the *division of literate labour* in local cultural and economic practices. This division, as we will see, is tied to the stratification of wealth and power. To take a comparative example: in the South Pacific island of Tuvalu the primary function of vernacular literacy is the reading of religious texts and the writing of emotion-laden personal letters (Vetter 1992). Among the West African Vai in Liberia, adult males become literate in three languages, each of which is used for highly specialised social functions (Scribner and Cole 1981). Classical Arabic is used to study the Koran, Vai for some business transactions and personal letters, and English for schooling and formal governmental business.

In any community, competence in literacy thus not only entails how to read and write identifiable genres of texts. It also requires strategic knowledge of how to 'read' social situations and institutional rule systems and act effectively in order to conceptualise, articulate and achieve social goals, actions and alternatives (deCastell, Luke and MacLennan 1986). Becoming literate, then, not only involves learning how to make sense with the lexicogrammatical patterns of textual language but also entails learning a schema for what literacy is, how to use it, when, where and to what possible ends. For example, a young male Vai literate not only learns by rote aspects of Arabic vocabulary, grammar, the generic structures, stylistic and prosodic features of Quranic verse, but at the same time learns when and where to use Classical Arabic for religious purposes. Its inappropriate use — for instance, its use to write a personal letter — would be shunned by those religious and community authorities who see themselves as guardians of Quranic literacy.

Further, Quranic literacy is not taught to girls. In this way cultural boundaries and institutions shape literacy — and literate labour — as gendered work. This is a crucial point, for children in primary schools are not only learning the skills and metaknowledges of reading and writing English, for example alphabetic knowledge, phonemic awareness, word attack skills, knowledge of syntactic and generic structures, spelling patterns and subject-related vocabulary. They also acquire from teachers, master literates, attitudes and knowledge about access to, the limits and possibilities of the technology — senses of the (school) authorised uses and contexts, purposes and goals for reading and writing.

Literacy thus is a model emergent social technology: it changes the cultures and environments which it appears in, and it is a means for shaping how people conceive of themselves, their identities and their environments. A critical literacy entails not only a rudimentary control of the linguistic and semiotic codes of written text, but also understandings of the ways in which literacy has shaped the organisations and values of social life, and of the ways in which the texts of everyday life influence one's own identity and authority. Literacy is therefore as much about ideologies, identities and values as it is about codes and skills. But an accurate assessment of the literacy needs of contemporary Australian students and workers requires that we consider literacy in a broader historical and socioeconomic context. There we can see the changing relationships between literacy and power in action.

Literacy and Social Power: Regulating the Word

Since the Protestant Reformation, schools have been charged with the selection and framing of practices, texts and contexts thought to be worth teaching. The evolution of alphabetic literacy in the 4th century BCE in Greece was predated by various writing systems in the Middle East and Asia. Since their inception, writing systems have been used for the storing, recovery, critique and analysis of various knowledges, quite literally as memory aids for keeping kinship, agricultural, legal and literary/historical records. The movement from oral to literate cultures was far more gradual and less dramatic than many earlier accounts would have us believe, spanning centuries (Graff 1987). The transitions from written to oral cultures are evidenced in hybrid literary genres — in conventional forms of written poetry which are extensions of spoken genres (e.g. epic, lyric poetry), and in forms of speech which are strongly influenced by written genres (e.g. the lecture, the political speech).

An economical, precise, portable technology for the inscription, elaboration and transmission of messages across space and time enabled the development of a range of social institutions: from commercial and agricultural enterprises to religious establishments, from the emergence of disciplines of analytical sciences to new means of government surveillance and monitoring of the populace, from the development of new and hybrid genres of literature to the mass dissemination of 'how to' manuals and popular texts.

Throughout its early evolution, literacy as a technology of social development and control remained in the hands of a patriarchal elite. Those who could read and write — male clerics, scribes, court members, merchants, members of the aristocracy — acted as gatekeepers of scientific and religious enlightenment, cultural history, government and trade and even kinship records. To be literate was to have access to and control of dominant patriarchal knowledges and cultures. Thus, while the records, culturally significant knowledges, laws and histories of oral cultures might have been 'embodied' in the memories of (male) tribal spokespersons, chiefs, shamen and poets and the (musical, poetic and dramatic) spoken texts that they generated, that information passed into written archives in literate cultures. This did not necessarily democratise access to culturally significant or powerful information. In fact, quite the opposite occurred: prior to Protestant literacy campaigns, literacy education was restricted to elite male groups. The regulation of information became a crucial element in governmental and religious control of a populace, an issue highlighted by continuing debates over censorship and freedom of information laws. Even with the introduction of compulsory state schooling for literacy in countries like Germany and England, textbooks and teaching methods were seen by Luther and reformation colleagues as a means of maintaining religious conformity and orthodoxy (Luke 1989). There is evidence that in Catholic jurisdictions like France, the introduction of schooling for literacy was seen as a similar mechanism for control of religious belief and everyday reading practice (Davis 1987).

The movement for universal literacy can be traced back to the Protestant Reformation, when Luther argued that expanded access to the ability to read the Bible was a prerequisite for spiritual salvation and social participation in the seminal German state. At this point as well, the emergence of the printing press in Europe enabled the mass publication and dissemination of literature both spiritual and mundane, representing both the dominant culture and the forces of sedition and protest. As an aspect of popular and educational culture, then, mass literacy has been a 'double edged' sword (Graff 1987): it can be used as readily to enlighten as to indoctrinate, to emancipate as to constrain, to transform as to conserve. Like later developments of new communications technologies, the printed word was greeted as a vehicle for critical social and scientific inquiry, for personal and community enlightenment on the one hand, and for control, surveillance and indoctrination on the other.

In Western countries, we have come to assume that literacy is a universal 'right', guaranteed in constitutions of nation-states and human rights declarations of UNESCO, Amnesty International and other bodies (Freebody and Welch 1992). But the call for 'universal literacy' for woman as well as man, layperson as well as cleric, black as well as white, working class as well as ruling class, slave as well as landholder, is relatively recent. To this day, a significant number of countries bar women and children from subcultural and ethnic groups from access to literacy. The Vai, as noted, do not introduce women to Arabic or Vai literacy — effectively excluding them from significant religious, cultural and mercantile practices. Similarly, in the African country of Malawi, many boys learn Arabic literacy in village religious education, while girls are relegated to domestic work such as food preparation. In the Guatemalan highlands, indigenous Indian peoples are effectively excluded from state-run education systems and thereby are unable to participate in voting, public meetings and business transactions. These require a basic knowledge of Spanish and some degree of literacy.

The enforcement of *il*literacy thus remains a powerful tool for economic and political exclusion and domination, for relegating people to what Freire (1968) has called 'cultures of silence'. In so-called 'developing' and 'late-capitalist' countries alike, inadequate educational provision of literacy for girls and women, rural peoples and urban lower socioeconomic classes, aboriginal and migrant groups is an effective means for disenfranchising people from powerful cultural texts and knowledges, and from reappraisals of their economic and political conditions and possibilities (Arnove and Graff 1987). Despite stated intents of 'equality of educational opportunity' and 'universal literacy', many of these same patterns are at work in our communities and schools. The central issue for teachers is this: how literacy's potential is realised depends on what social institutions teach, encourage and enable people to do with it.

From this historical perspective, we can look again at calls that we should go 'back to the basics'. As I noted, educational 'crises' in general and 'literacy crises' in particular tend to surface at times of economic, moral and political change and instability. The most recent foregrounding of the need for investment in education as 'human capital' in Australia and other Western countries reflects the structural reorganisation of global economic relations and markets (cf. Porter *et al.* 1992). As Australia's role in a transnational economy changes, moving away from traditional commodities and resources exported to other sectors, the tendency has been for governments and business to look towards educational institutions to 'lead' structural socioeconomic change by reorganising and retraining a workforce. But whether an economic system can be led by institutions like schools is problematic. Just as blaming schools for economic decline is spurious, to look to schools to solve systemic and transnational economic patterns is, at best, questionable.

This is not to dismiss the fact that a significant percentage of the adult population of Australia and other late-capitalist countries have real problems managing print in everyday situations (Wickert 1990). These problems contribute greatly to economic, political and social exclusion. While difficulties in measuring levels of literacy make exact estimates problematic, there is little doubt that enhanced access to and competence with literate practices provide individuals with increased economic and political engagement with mainstream Australian culture. What is needed is a sustained, informed revaluation of the place and potential of literacies in Australian life and work, not the expectation of educational, social and economic panaceas. Many of the current claims and controversies over literacy which teachers must address are premised on assumptions about the social consequences of literacy for students, communities and nations. I here want to reconsider a central element of the current debate in Australia: the role of literacy and education in achieving social equity.

Literacy and Equity

'More' literacy does not necessarily equate with 'more' social power. This depends on what kinds of practices and texts we are speaking of, and on the actual uses and assigned statuses of these in characteristic social contexts. Becoming literate in and of itself does not necessarily lead to increased social power, personal enlightenment, cognitive development and so forth (Scribner and Cole 1981). As we have seen, there are ample historical and contemporary instances where 'making people literate' has been a key means of standardising and regulating their beliefs, practices and values in the interests of dominant groups (Oxenham 1980).

Language, like all 'open semiotic systems', is 'goal-seeking' (Wilden 1982; Halliday 1978). All discourses, texts and genres have been specialised to achieve social and intellectual purposes. Some discourses, texts and genres are more widely distributed and more readily accessible than others; some have been assigned more cultural capital than others. In light of this, the selection and spread of reading and writing practices by schools is not arbitrary or inconsequential. Children's differing levels of achievement of literacy are key factors in unequal educational and occupational outcomes. Hence, Michel Foucault's (1972) point: that schools both 'permit *and* prevent' access to language and discourse, that schooling is as much a system of exclusion as of inclusion. But who gets included and excluded and from what discourses, texts and genres?

Since the advent of literacy, differing kinds of competence with texts have been deemed by dominant (literate) groups and classes to have differing kinds and levels of value. In some cases, this is because practices bear utilitarian value. Consider, for instance, reading to carry out a job or conceptualise a task, or writing to make a recoverable record of a procedure or event. These literate practices would have significant value in many work settings and, hence, might be a prerequisite for access to and effective performance at specific jobs.

In other cases, displays of kinds and levels of literacy have little utilitarian value but are used as markers of cultural status, worth and group membership. Some employers, for instance, repeatedly emphasise 'correct spelling' as an essential aspect of job performance, even in job contexts where little writing or spelling is required. Knowledge and discussion of 'quality' literature, to take another example, serves negligible informational purposes for an estimated 10 000 purchasers of each new release of 'quality' contemporary literature in Australia. Arguably, such 'literary' literacy might serve learned intellectual and emotional purposes for members of a largely university-educated, upper and middle class audience. Nevertheless, the reading of 'quality' literature is an acquired leisure activity displayed in public and private settings as a marker of class membership (Bourdieu 1986). In other communities, specific literate tastes and practices are stigmatised as signs of undereducation. Heath (1983) and Christian-Smith (1992), for instance, stress that in some working class US communities the reading of romantic fiction was considered aberrant behaviour by groups within the community. In these cases, a similar literate practice, solitary reading of fiction, may be valued in some communities and shunned in others. Who reads what kinds of literature, where and when is thus a marker of boundaries of class and gender.

The claim that literacy is a form of cultural capital has several dimensions. The term 'cultural capital' refers to acquired knowledge and competence which can be translated into status, wealth and mobility in a class-stratified society (Bourdieu and Passeron 1990). As noted, schools produce differing kinds and levels of literacy — ranging from rudimentary competence at decoding text, to HSC essay production, from job-related skills to personal journal writing. Further, genres and texts read and written have varying degrees of cultural capital in particular social and linguistic 'markets' (Mey 1985; Bourdieu 1990). In current educational debates over literacy, four overlapping kinds of textual practice can be distinguished on the basis of the institutional 'markets' where they are used and valued:

1. Those practices which are specialised primarily for academic purposes for learning but also have demonstrable applicability in contexts of work and community life (e.g. reading to recall information, writing recounts).
2. Those practices which are specialised for schooling, but have questionable 'transfer' to community and occupational activities (e.g. test-taking, worksheets).
3. Those practices which have specialised vocational and community purposes, but which are typically omitted in school curriculum (e.g. reading signs, instructions, writing personal notes).
4. Those practices which primarily function as status markers for class membership in both public and private settings (e.g. rote knowledges about authors, recitation of literature).

These categories are provisional. As Edelsky (1991) points out, the differences between 'meaningful' and 'meaningless', between educationally significant and senseless activities need further definition and exploration. Many worksheet-style activities, for instance, are simulations of teaching and learning which may have little affiliation with a 'literacy in use' in community, occupational or even subsequent academic activities. Such literate practices have more to do with school procedure and ritual than educational value. Clearly, the relationships between the social function and institutional status of genres and discourses need to be the subject of further linguistic and sociological theory and analysis (e.g. Threadgold 1989; Martin 1992). But the matter of selecting what is 'useful' and 'powerful' for students may be less obvious and self-evident than is supposed in many school-based programs. With 'empowerment' the new cliché of 1980s education (Cook, Homer and Nixon 1991), it is crucial to recognise that power is relational and contextual (Gore 1992). Power is not a static feature or possession of a text or individual, but is enacted in social relations and work with other human subjects in institutional contexts.

Differing kinds of textual competence have different 'payoffs' for children in institutional sites. For example, the working class white children Heath (1983) studied began school proficient at 'fill in the blanks' activities; their community and church pre-school socialisation has built a model of literacy as a sequence of skills. Moving into the linguistic 'market' of the skill-based primary program, they did quite well until middle primary, when comprehension and composition activities became focal in the curriculum. We might similarly trace skills learned in literature and job-skills-based English programs out from the high school into tertiary and occupational sites. One of Heath's (1986a) key findings was that many of the genres and competences emphasised in schooling had minimal 'transfer' to occupational and community life (e.g. expository writing, literature study). Conversely, those functional literacies 'done' in community and occupational contexts, and even those required for further training and education, tend to be neglected in school curricula, especially in primary school. Diehl and Mikulecky (1988), for instance, argue that the verifiable transfer of training of reading competence from school to occupational contexts is low. The question of which texts, genres and competences are powerful, then, depends upon an analysis of how and to what ends specific clienteles use literacy in identifiable contexts, institutions and social relations. So we could reframe the questions of 'powerful literacy' to inspect those practices, texts and genres featured in the curriculum: Powerful for what purposes? In what institutional sites? In whose interests? Affiliated with what kinds of cultural capital in the social system?

The point here is simple: different educational institutions (e.g. technical colleges, universities) and different 'streams' within the same institutions (e.g. 'remedial', 'academic', reading ability groups) dispense and require differing kinds of practice and cultural capital. It is crucial to reappraise the different configurations of power, the different institutional sites and the different kinds of knowledges and cultural capital school programs generate. Such a reappraisal, I suspect, would confirm that a lot of what is done in school-based literacy programs purports to lead to valuable, universal and transferable competence and knowledge for out-of-school contexts, but in fact does not.

The construction and distribution of literacy has less to do with student 'individual difference', 'natural development' and teacher 'personal preference' and more to do with stratifying a student population into different kinds and levels of achievement, occupational futures, and hence, social classes. In this way, educational systems are geared for the *social reproduction* of class, power and identity across generations. Schools and other educational institutions construct differing kinds of 'literates', parcelling out and credentialling differing kinds of cultural capital, and hence, social and economic power. To return to my initial point, all texts, genres and practices are not equal, either in terms of the cultural capital they yield in an occupation and social marketplace, or in terms of the kinds of knowledge about the world they enable and encourage. The official, educational production of unequal outcomes is not something which is solely a concern of Higher School Certificate and Scholastic

Aptitude Testing and secondary school (academic and vocational) streaming. It begins in the primary school (Sharp and Green 1975; Anyon 1981). It begins when children's varying cultural, linguistic and background knowledges and competences are picked up by teachers, tests and systems and transformed into differential patterns of success and failure.

Since World War II, all Western nations have set as their aim the achievement of equality of educational opportunity. None the less, different literacies continue to be distributed unequally through schooling. School students from minority groups, lower socioeconomic groups and demographically isolated areas do not gain access as readily to, or mastery of, the same kinds of literacies as those from economically privileged groups within Australian society. Literacy achievement in this country — and with it access to tertiary education, better-paying and high-status jobs — continues to fall along distinctive fault lines of urban/rural location, ethnicity and class. Further, recent research has begun to specify the patterns of differential access to kinds of texts, and social power, by gender.

There is an ongoing debate over the causes of children's differential achievement and access. It is popularly attributed to mass media and popular culture, purported decay in morality and family structure, and deficit socialisation among client groups. As we will see in further examples here, children come to schools with different world-views and values, beliefs and practices — among which are schemata for and about literacy. For now, suffice to say that there is a century-long history across English-speaking countries of trying to defer 'blame' for differing educational access and outcomes to 'fault' in children and parents. Who gets what kinds of literacy, and thereby who is positioned to be able to demonstrate competence with texts in which contexts, is in part the product of schooling. Further, problems children encounter with primary school literacy are linked closely to failure in other aspects of schooling and to unequal credential outcomes.

To return to our starting point, literacy refers to a range of possible reading and writing practices. Some such practices have evolved for criticism, others not; some for the conserving of extant cultural values and knowledges, others for the critique and transformation of those same values and knowledges; some are active, some passive; some, rightly or wrongly, are seen as signs of virtue and power in the society, others not. All literate practices are not of equivalent power in terms of the socioeconomic benefits and cultural knowledges they yield. Nor do schools successfully impart to all socially powerful or critical literacies. This should not come as news to teachers, policy makers, or teacher educators. But what the definition offered here suggests is that the question is not one of 'more or less' literacy, but of 'what kinds of literate practices' are and should be disbursed to children.

Selecting and Constructing Literate Traditions

Literature is a representation of values, perspectives and beliefs of and about cultures. How, then, are the knowledges, skills and values in language arts, reading, children's literature, social studies curricula selected and framed for children in schools? Each educational system and era constructs a 'selective tradition', a version of 'the' culture that is 'powerfully operative in the process of social and cultural definition and identification' (Williams 1977, p. 115). In textbooks and lessons, a selective tradition is embodied in particular versions of cultural knowledges and beliefs, identities and characterisations which become authorised school versions of what 'we' allegedly know and value. What this means is that children in schools are socialised into someone's version of a 'shaping past and pre-shaped present', represented to them as *their* culture, as a 'natural', given social and cultural order, as 'the way things are and should be'.

Because it is so commonly used as a justification of curricular decisions about textbooks, literature and literacy teaching, I have highlighted the pronoun 'we' here. (Does this include 'you', 'me', 'teachers'?). Like the terms '*our* culture' or '*our* society', 'we' is a pronoun of solidarity, often used to refer to an imaginary, singular social and cultural entity which is assigned an almost mythical power (e.g. '*society* makes stereotypes', '*culture* sets norms', '*we* all believe that . . . is a classic'). The fact that I — an Asian migrant from Canada — and many of the readers of this book are not necessarily part of that version of a collective cultural 'we' is not incidental. Often 'Australianness' and an almost cartoon version of '*the* culture' is used to perpetrate myths and stereotypes (Hodge, Fiske and Turner 1987). Such ideologies are used to sell products — from roast chickens and beer to family sedans — and to win mass loyalty and votes. I am not suggesting that there isn't something which might be represented and construed as Australian 'culture' or 'identity'. But it is important to recognise that cultures and identities are dynamic, complex and multifaceted entities — entities negotiated, constructed and contested in everyday life, not reducible to clichés or oversimplifications. Further, public, mass representations of culture and cultural identity — which literature curriculum is — tend to be (silently) exclusionary. They bear reappraisal for what and whom they exclude as for what and whom they include.

Selective traditions of literature and literacy are ideological. That is, they act covertly in the interests of dominant groups precisely because they take on the appearance of being univocal (one-voiced), 'natural' or based on an alleged consensus of interests (e.g. 'what every Australian believes', 'the greats of Australian literature'). Cultures, nation states and communities consist of diversities of texts, interests and group identities. This is increasingly so in contemporary Australia, where a growing percentage of the school-aged populace is from diverse ethnic and linguistic backgrounds (cf. Kalantzis, Cope and Slade 1989). In urban areas across Australia and in many outback areas, schools now feature a majority of students with non-English-speaking backgrounds. These range from children who speak Aboriginal languages, Creoles and non-standard dialects to those children who speak the languages of community ethnic groups which have migrated to Australia. Further, with the century-long rise in retention rates in schooling, increasingly more working class and rural Australian children — who in previous eras might have left school to enter a resource- and agriculture-based workforce — are completing senior secondary school. In terms of simple demographic change, then, the clientele of Australian schools is drawn from a diversity of ethnic, community and social class cultures. In this historical and cultural context, it seems all the more imperative that the 'we' of the selective traditions of school curriculum be re-examined.

Textbooks, lessons and programs influence how students and teachers see and construct aspirations and possibilities for themselves and their communities, the nation and the many cultures and subcultures which comprise it. Taken together, the texts and skills to be taught and learned in classrooms form a cultural 'archive' to be passed on to each successive version of students. This archive, a school-based literate tradition, risks representing a narrow set of interests and excluding the experiences, voices and perspectives of women, ethnic minorities and aboriginal peoples (Taxel 1989; Singh 1989). This is especially the case in recent calls for a common, core 'cultural literacy', which when translated by media and academic commentators into practice looks more like a game-show list of great books, men and isolated facts embodying a narrow, elite version of Anglo-European culture (Cope and Kalantzis 1992).

Of course, all curriculum and instruction consists of inclusions and exclusions of voices and writings, images and symbols, ideas and values, identities and discourses. Consider, for an illustration, the varied secondary school history textbook explanations of the 'causes' and consequences of World War I which one might encounter in Australian, British or US textbooks. No doubt various textual representations ('re-presentations') of the historical 'truth' (what 'we' all know and/or believe) would be brought into play. To take up another example, consider the portrayals of gendered domestic work and childhood which one might encounter in Saudi or Thai school books compared with those featured in Western commercial children's literature.

All written and spoken texts express cultural *discourses* — statements of beliefs and values which recur across various texts. All curriculum and instruction embodies 'points of view' or 'standpoints' on the world (i.e. *epistemologies*) tied to cultural and political interests. In this regard, whether we select a textbook or piece of literature which constructs the landing at Botany Bay as the 'colonisation' and 'coming of European civilisation' to Australia or one which stresses the 'invasion' of indigenous peoples' homeland is a curriculum and, ultimately, a political decision. Whether we select *Possum Magic*, *Blubber*, or books from the series the *Babysitter's Club* forms and structures a selective portrayal of gender identity and relations in school literacy and literature study. Whether we select any literary portrayals of Torres Strait Islanders and

Aborigines at all, and whether these are by mainstream Australians or by members of those communities, together are decisions in a selective portrayal of indigenous peoples.

Once immersed in a dominant selective tradition of schooling, teachers and students tend to take it for granted as an unquestioned system of authority. Curriculum texts, even literary selections, are seen as imparting or fixing 'truth'. Precisely because we are so steeped in dominant cultural traditions, because we have been 'successful' at learning and assimilating these traditions, it is difficult to see what discourses and versions of culture, whose voices, whose experiences and images are not included. Hence, most of us would be hard pressed to cite any background knowledge of, for example: the significant postwar role of women scientists in the development of digital computer systems; the literary work of migrant writers in Australia; the complex trading and language systems developed by Aborigines and Islanders prior to European arrival. These aspects of social history have been omitted, silenced or placed at the margins of curriculum. 'Tokenism' is common. For example, courses in 'migrant' and 'women's' literature, Aboriginal languages and history are unlikely to appear in secondary curriculum. While they might appear in university curriculum, typically they would be elective courses — while a dominant version of the selective tradition (e.g. Elizabethan, Romantic and Victorian poetry) would be required. Where they have been successfully included in many curriculum documents in countries like the USA, conservative critics have criticised such inclusions as signs of 'bias' and 'political correctness', as if the longstanding requirement that all people study, say, Victorian poetry or 19th century British colonial history has been 'unbiased'.

It is not my purpose to suggest that classroom teachers can solve or resolve these issues in any formulaic way; or that by simply changing the overt ideological *content* of textbooks and children's literature, the exclusionary character of much mainstream literacy teaching will be changed. That, as we will see, would require a rethinking of 'talk about texts' in classrooms as well. For now, my aim here is to reframe a central question for primary school literacy teaching: on what grounds is literature chosen?

The 19th century Victorian poet and school inspector Matthew Arnold and current 'cultural literacy' advocates argue that the process of cultural and curriculum selection should be a straightforward application of literary and aesthetic criteria. They would argue that the 'best' of literature surfaces because it has intrinsic worth, value and 'timelessness'. This would explain, traditionally oriented educators would argue, the retention of Shakespeare and the Anglo-European literary canon and the exclusion of popular cultural texts in school and university-based literary studies. It would explain why, for example, 20th century Asian migrant and women writers were not part of my schooling and later university literature studies. At the time I was told: there just weren't any such writers of substance, few had been published, and besides, it was more important to study those British and North American (male) writers of substance. I recall being told by one professor of Renaissance literature that if 'you didn't like Herbert Spenser's poetry, there is nothing wrong with Spenser but something wrong with you'.

The claims of cultural literacy advocates are often circular, tying together quality and longevity to form a closed argument: 'Why has it lasted? Because it is great. Why is it 'great'? Because it has lasted'. As Cope and Kalantzis (1992) argue, the defence of the Western canon of literature is often made on similar grounds, reading something like: 'it is included in the canon of Western culture because it defends our version of the canon'. Note that the criteria for judging quality of literature are themselves shifting, reflecting dominant cultural interests and ideologies. In the 18th century, for instance, drama by Ben Jonson, John Dryden and others was considered 'classic' because it followed all the generic rules for tragedy articulated in Aristotle's *Poetics*. Shakespeare's work was considered by many to be disunified, clouded by pedestrian themes and topics and unworthy of serious study. Similarly, prior to the 19th century, the very virtues which we now associate with 'literary quality' — powerful emotional expression, personal 'voice' and style — were considered signs of low quality.

What is included and excluded, valued and denigrated in literacy and literature is not arbitrary, random or a 'natural' expression of quality or taste (Bourdieu 1986). It is tied up with questions about the power and status of particular representations of culture. This applies to all inclusions and exclusions in school knowledge: particular versions of 'landmark' scientific discoverers and discoveries, versions of gender relations, the 'greats' of literary classics, games and rules for physical education, 'skills' of literacy or the techniques of drawing. These curricular decisions are almost always justified on what we might call 'universalist' grounds (e.g. 'all children need to learn about Christopher Columbus'). In fact they represent not only changing social conventions and material contexts for the use of written language, but also the values, beliefs and interests of dominant groups (Said 1984).

Put simply, in primary classrooms, some stories, some characters, some plots, some genres and some skills are included, others not. In classrooms, some procedures for 'doing' cultural activities with texts are valued, others are literally disallowed — considered uneducational and unnecessary, psychologically inappropriate, in bad 'taste', gratuitous or even subversive. Unsworth (1991) points out that the virtual exclusion of scientific texts and non-literary genres in early primary training has been justified on the grounds that such texts and their affiliated disciplinary and technical discourses are developmentally inappropriate. Such decisions — whether to teach book X, whether to stress genre or skill Y — may appear to have been decided in a 'top-down' manner by editors, textbook authors, publishers, administrators, school officials and those civil servants who make curricula in capital cities. But across all Australian states, primary teachers retain a good deal of discretionary power on which texts, contexts and competences to teach, when and how.

There are no universal 'basics' of reading and writing, no essential, 'organic' sequences governing which texts children should read, when, and how. Literacy is selected, shaped and constructed in schools and in other institutional sites like workplaces, churches, ethnic community organisations and homes. Obviously, the literature, values, ideologies, skills and competences teachers select are influenced by political, administrative and industrial forces (Connell 1985; McNeil 1986). What state and regional jurisdictions, teacher educators, publishers and consultants make available, what principals and key consultants encourage, enable and preclude influence classroom teaching and learning. None the less, teachers are the final arbiters of what will count as literacy in the classroom. Daily life in primary and secondary classrooms entails a series of inclusions and exclusions, of decisions about what to teach and what not to teach, about what can be said and done with written language and what cannot, about what kinds of texts and competences are appropriate and valuable for differing groups of children. All teachers — highly competent and less so, experienced and beginning — are engaged in such choices, whether consciously or not.

Contemporary educational commonsense about literacy dictates that programs need to begin from 'where the child is at' and meet her or his individual 'needs', that teachers need to be 'sensitive' to developmental stages, cultural difference and community life. However well intentioned, in and of themselves these are empty claims. For any 'reading' of the child, her or his background and how this might influence development and achievement is contingent upon one's (theoretical) positions regarding, for example, the influence of 'environment' on school achievement, the structures and consequences of cultural and linguistic difference on the acquisition of English-language literacy, and on one's prescriptive position regarding what *should* be taught and cultivated. I have argued here that these choices are the key *political* decisions in the construction of a selective tradition of literacy in the primary classroom. The challenge has considerably less to do with any 'return to the basics' — whether construed as phonics, handwriting, literary classics or 'skill and drill' — or with a return to 'natural' approaches to literacy. The task at hand is to take up these central choices for inquiry, debate and direct action.

Before Schooling: Language Socialisation

Human speech is a species behaviour. All children, given normal neurological and physiological functioning and participation in a speech community, will develop *communicative competence* with oral language. That is, they will learn to use spoken language appropriately according to the cultural routines and 'speech genres' (Bakhtin 1986) of typical situations. In the day to day experience of participation in a family and community life, children develop 'language functions' (Halliday 1975), mastery of conventional ways of achieving social goals and ends. Hence, in early childhood, language is very much a means of labour, offering tools for shaping, controlling and interacting with one's social and physical environment (Vygotsky 1978) — and indeed tools for the shaping and constructing of identity.

Speech, then, is not developed in isolation. It entails learning, negotiating and contesting ways of conducting social relations with elders, siblings and other community members. Language use occurs in boundaried *speech events* (Hymes 1972). These events are not random or arbitrary, but are rule governed and structured. Although they may seem spontaneous, events such as mealtime conversations, ordering in a restaurant, the rituals of preparing for bedtime and telephone conversations follow identifiable protocols and patterns: some topics and kinds of language are acceptable, particular social roles and relationships are called into play. Hence, for a child, learning how to participate in a mealtime conversation requires apprenticing at a set of rules that govern who can nominate which topics, how to get the floor, what kinds of gestures can and can't be made, when and who can interrupt whom, who has the final 'word', where slang or profanity might be appropriate, even volume levels. The rules and conventions mark out what the philosopher Wittgenstein called 'language games', the structures of which vary across cultures and subcultures, communities and families.

To reiterate my earlier point, these everyday events are sites where relations of authority and power, gender and age are shaped and constructed. Much recent research has focused on the ways in which gendered power is established in everyday talk (Graddol and Swann 1989), specifically on male domination of conversation and other forms of public talk. Consider, for instance, how the rules of order at your household's mealtime — as much as any debate in the Houses of Parliament — evidence the patriarchal and age-related power relations and social status of its members.

Patterns of language use and social identity are learned and established together in early childhood. In some instances, how to participate in an event may be the subject of formal, conscious instruction. For example, in some communities, parents or older siblings might provide younger children with direct instruction on what to say when they answer the phone, or give instructions when a child has neglected a politeness protocol, like 'please' or 'thank you'. In other instances and communities, there is considerably less direct instruction. Knowledge of when, how and where to 'do' a school yard play song, of how to do a rap or 'insult', or of how to participate in a mealtime conversation might be acquired through years of observation and participation. Consider, for example, this passage of simple argument between pre-schoolers (Genishi and DiPaolo 1982, p. 64):[1]

1. Billy: Mine!
2. John: This is yours.
3. Billy: No, it's not. This is mine. This is mine.
4. John: No it's, not.

Even this apparently straightforward and 'natural' speech event has a structured pattern: truth claims (turns 1, 3) are countered by contradictions and denials (turns 3, 4). The structures and contents of events such as children's argumentation vary from speech community to community, and are practised and acquired in play situations. Bear in mind, though, that it is unlikely that anyone sat these two children down and 'taught' them how to argue. In this sense, the knowledge of the rules of interaction and of the attendant power relations for some speech situations are tacit. That is, they are known and acquired, tested and negotiated in everyday face to face exchanges but not consciously taught.

In other instances, children receive explicit instruction on how to 'name', and speak about the world. Here a middle-class Australian mother is talking with her two-year-old child while standing in line in a restaurant:[2]

> We're in a long line, Jason. Aren't we? There are lots of people lined up here, waiting for a drink. Look [pointing] they're carrying a Christmas tree with lots of things on it. They're moving it. Do we have a Christmas tree like that?

Here the parent is providing a running commentary on the world for the child, framing up an imaginary or 'possible world' as if it is a story. Notice that the collective pronoun 'we' is used to position the child in solidarity with the mother's narration. The child did not answer during the 20–30 second monologue by his mother. The mother here is positioning the child through talk — anticipating, modelling hypothetical answers and what he (Jason) might (is supposed to) be thinking. In effect, she is constituting an identity for him. The naming of salient objects ('Christmas tree'), the highlighting of reasons, norms and ethics for actions (e.g. why 'we' line up; how to move things; what 'we' have) come into play here. The child is being situated within a world-view, to 'read' the world from a particular epistemological vantage point. His 'identity papers' are being assembled and put in order through talk. Within this world-view criteria for 'rational' thought, action and analysis are being assembled through talk (Luke 1992; Hasan 1991).

This socialisation into a universe of relations, objects and values occurs as part of daily conversation between pre-school aged children and their caregivers:

> C: Is Pop home?
> M: No . . . They're all out. They're all at work.
> C: Bob and Mark are working.
> M: Yes, Bob's at work. Mark's at work. Everybody's at work.
> C: I not at work.
> M: No, you're only little.
> C: Youse at work?
> M: I don't work. I look after you . . .
> C: Who's playing with Pammie?
> M: Nobody. Who'd look after you if Mummy went to work...eh?
> (Hasan 1986, pp. 133–134)

In conversations with caregivers and peers, children learn how to take 'turns' — how to get the floor, how to ask questions, issue commands and give answers and so forth (Wells 1981). But caregivers and children also are spelling out values, ideologies, identities. What Hasan (1989) calls differential 'semantic resources' are being developed: in this case, schemata for what counts as work (*not* domestic work and child-rearing), how work is broken down and distributed on a gendered basis (*men* work, women raise children), and about who works (Bob, Mark, 'everybody' ⇒ work; Mummy ≠ work). So in this event we find both an enacting of social roles and relations of female caregiver/child ('tenor') and the discussion of namings and ideological contents ('field'), in this instance about gender and labour.

This pattern of 'turn taking', however, is very different from Heath's (1986b, p. 114) description of early childhood language socialisation in a working-class Black American community:

Mother:	[talking to neighbor on porch while Lem plays with a truck on the porch nearby]: But they won't call back, won't happen =
Lem:	= call back
Neighbor:	Sam's going over there Saturday, he'll pick up a form =
Lem:	= pick up on, pick up on [Lem here appears to have heard 'form' as 'on']

Unlike the mothers in the first two transcripts, adults in this community initially 'pay no attention' to children's talk. They rarely address the child directly and often speak about her or him using third person pronouns (as 'she' or 'he'). As shown in this passage, Lem's initial experimentation of language consists of 'repetition' of key words, phrases and rhymes from adult and sibling talk. This leads on to 'repetition with variation' around ages two to three, and then on to the child taking her or his place in the family and community which values dramatic, innovative 'performance' (p. 114). To hear the results of this kind of language socialisation, listen to Lem again, aged between two and three years old. Here he is responding to a prompt from adults — picking up a 'tag phrase', repeating it and turning it into a rhyming 'performance' for family and friends (Heath 1983, p. 110):

> Railroad track
> Train all big 'n black
> On dat traack, on dat track, on dat track
> Ain't no way I can't get back
> Back from dat track
> Back from dat train
> Big 'n black, I be back

There are universal, cross-cultural elements to early language learning (Snow and Ferguson 1977; Halliday 1975), but I have here tried to provide the gist of the cultural and social class variety and structure entailed in learning and using oral language. I want to highlight three broad patterns. First, all children come to school knowing how to participate in identifiable speech genres, having developed 'verbal repertoires' for who can do and say what 'when' with oral language in their communities (Cazden, Johns and Hymes 1972). Second, these events embody and mark out conventional social relations and identities. In the case of early childhood, gender, age and familial authority relations are established (Baker and Freebody 1989). What will count as 'pleasure' and 'desire', 'truth' and 'knowledge' are played out in face to face interaction (Davies 1987). Children have begun to establish who has the right and power to speak, when, about what. Third, and relatedly, all children come to school with semantic resources, that is, with systematic but not necessarily shared sets of 'namings' and 'classification schemes' about the social and natural world (Mey 1985; Fairclough 1989). Language learning is not an individual, idiosyncratic or spontaneous process. It is tied up with class and culture-based learning about and enacting the politics of everyday social relations.

Literacy Events in Homes and Communities

Written language is a social technology, one which entails a set of historically evolving techniques for inscription. As Hammond's (1990) analysis of children's early speech and writing indicates, the lexicogrammatical structures of written language are different from those of speech. Further, recall that the functions and uses of literacy vary greatly across literate cultures and historical epochs. In this sense, literacy is not 'natural'. Many extant tribal cultures operate without writing systems and — left to their own devices — developing children will not necessarily organically or spontaneously develop or 'invent' reading and writing. However, growing up in literate cultures, children encounter, observe and imitate functions and uses of literacy in everyday life (Schieffelin and Ochs 1986). These may vary from ritual reading of children's stories, fables and literature to daily use of functional print like bank slips, signs, labels, advertisements; from initial encounters with informational texts like newspapers to reading character-generated print on television programs and computers.

Members of literate communities introduce children to text through *literacy events*, instances of interaction around and use of text (Heath 1986b). I will outline three literacy events where 'what counts' as reading, and how to 'do' literacy with elders is socially constructed. My aims here are to describe the diversity of 'what counts as literacy' *before* children reach school, and to reconsider popular conceptions about what parents actually do with children and books.

Heath (1986b) describes the 'bedtime story' rituals of children from three communities. In a white, working-class community, Wendy, aged two, is growing up in an environment of simplified Bible stories, nursery and 'real life' stories. Her parents frequently buy Sesame Street, alphabet and number books; the latter feature 'fill in the blank' type activities which Wendy and other children in her community frequently busy themselves with. Here is a transcript of Wendy's bedtime story event with Aunt Sue (Heath 1986b, pp. 106–107):

Social Construction of Literacy

[Aunt Sue (AS) picks up book, while Wendy crawls about the floor, ostensibly looking for something]
W: Uh uh
AS: Wendy, we're gonna read, uh, read this story, come on hop up here on this bed [Wendy climbs up on the bed, sits on top of the pillow, and picks up her teddy bear. Aunt Sue opens book, points to puppy]
AS: Do you remember what this book is about? See the puppy? What does the puppy do?
[Wendy plays with the bear, glancing occasionally at pages of the book, as Aunt Sue turns. Wendy seems to be waiting for something in the book]
AS: See the puppy?
[Aunt Sue points to the puppy in the book and looks at Wendy to see if she is watching]
W: Uh huh, yea, yes ma'am.
AS: Puppy sees the ant, he's a li'l [Wendy drops the bear and turns to book] fellow. Can you see that ant? Puppy has a little ball.
W: Ant bite puppy [Wendy points to ant, pushing hard on the book] . . .

Obviously, the choice of literary content is one factor at work here in the shaping of a selective tradition. Animals are marked out as an appropriate portrayal for the literary 'canon'. What parents (and publishers, teachers and others) deem appropriate literary contents for boys and girls is a key aspect in the formation of gendered identity (Davies 1987). In such early stories, then, values and ideologies are marked as appropriate for 'reading' events, whether they be about Disney and cartoon characters, Sesame Street figures or sports heroes, Dr Seuss and Noddy, or are traditional European fairy tales.

In Wendy's case, the selection of materials and the staging of what one does with the book — 'naming' objects and words — reflects a strong element of the community value system. Because of the strong fundamentalist Christian roots of her community, storying — the construction of tall tales — is shunned. The concern that children stick with 'factual' approaches to texts and knowledge is tied closely to a *moral epistemology* of literacy. In this instance, literacy as a means for knowing about the world is not linked to imagination and fantasy of literature. Rather it is tied directly to naming, an objective cataloguing of events, people, things and, as part of literacy, letters, words and pictures. Hence, even the broad generalisation that all children 'naturally' come to school with facilities at storying depends upon the children, community and culture in question. If asked to make up a 'yarn' or 'tall tale' in Grade 1 'news' or sharing time, for instance, children like Wendy might lack prior experience with 'yarning' and also might run into a moral dilemma about whether such 'storying' is a legitimate activity in the first place.

An aside: like many children brought up in a migrant home culture, I did not receive much exposure to Anglo-European folk tales, rhymes or parables. I, and many of the Asian and Hispanic kids I started school with, had not even heard of 'Humpty Dumpty' or the 'Three Bears' before formal schooling. Much of my early reading experience was of comic books: Disney, superheroes and so forth. I point this out to underline the diversity of literary traditions engaged in early childhood, and to stress the constitutive role of popular culture (Disney, Sesame

Street, the Simpsons, Ninja Turtles) in the formation of print traditions. Children's literature is the site for what Raymond Williams (1977) calls 'residual' and 'emergent' cultural traditions; for both those longstanding, dominant versions of culture (e.g. Enid Blyton, traditional fairy tales) and for emergent alternative versions, which may run both counter and complementary to dominant interests. Included in the latter would be those texts which Lurie (1990) has called 'subversive children's literature' critical of structures of social and adult authority. There are increasing interconnections between the print resources available for children and the characterisations, portrayals and, indeed, commodities from other media (e.g. toys, comics, and cartoons) (Luke 1991). Together with the actual commodities that they speak about and, indeed, endorse, many print texts create a pattern of mutually reinforcing *intertextual references*: the TV cartoon character reappears in the comic book, the cereal package, the music video and in the *Golden Book* primer-level literature available at the grocery checkout.

But literary selection is but one factor at play here. In Wendy and Aunt Sue's bedtime story, what counts as literacy is being shaped by the social relations and patterns of the event. Wendy here is learning that reading is about sitting still, paying attention and answering an elder's questions about pictures in a book, about 'naming' the phenomenal world. She is learning a set of bodily postures and disciplines for 'reading' (Luke, in press) as well as a series of practices with the text. Members of different communities tend to configure bedtime stories differently, shaping community literate traditions. This entails selecting texts, asking differing kinds of questions (where questions are asked at all) and expecting and encouraging different kinds of practices with texts. For instance, the middle-class black and white parents Heath studied tended to ask questions in turn-taking sequences very similar to classroom talk, asking children to draw analogies between textual characters, events and actions and those people they have observed in everyday life. Other parents constructed literacy events with the goal of getting children to learn the physical discipline they affiliated with reading. Yet others stressed letter recognition and the sounding out of words.

Participation in these events entails development of a schema or model for literacy. There children are acquiring different 'theories' of literacy, different senses that this is what books and writing are all about (Cole and Griffin 1986); that one can say particular things about the texts, that elders, authority figures (or perhaps older sisters and brothers) have special roles in literacy events. Again, these events reflect the ideologies and epistemologies (ways of seeing the world, getting and classifying knowledge) of these communities. To illustrate, I draw from a more formal community literacy event, a Sunday school class (Zinsser 1986, p. 58):

Teacher: Anna? Do you have your Bible with you? (Anna holds up her Bible)
Teacher: There it is. What can we call our Bibles? Who knows what another name for our Bible is? Charlie? What do you have with you?
Charlie: SSword.

> Teacher: Your Sword. That's right. What do you do with your sword? James?
> James: Stab the devil.

Here the book is a prop with a very specific religious value and function. The focus of this event is the building of a classification scheme for 'literacy' and 'books' as vehicles of religious belief and action. These children, Zinsser argues, will arrive at school with a very different set of values and practices counting as 'literacy'. Events such as this are, in many ways, yet another more public variation on the 'bedtime story', stressing in this case recall and 'proper', literal interpretations of the Bible. Note here what is included and excluded in this selective tradition: the Bible means what it says, hence figurative, speculative and personal interpretations are not encouraged through question/answer sequences, even at this early stage of community literacy training. Heath and Zinsser both observe that children whose pre-school socialisation has introduced them to (epistemological) practices which treat texts as literal 'facts' tend to have problems in middle primary school grades when classroom activities begin to stress 'comprehension' practices that require displays of knowledge about figurative and non-literal aspects of texts. Further, Zinsser adds, such Sunday school literacy events accustom children to what Bernstein (1990) would term 'strongly framed' institutional literacy events that centre on teachers' providing highly directive, explicit instruction. She queries what will happen if and when these children encounter the cadences and patterns of child-centred, progressive instruction.

Yet not all pre-school home and community literacy events are based on narrative, literary genres. Nor are they all about children answering adults' questions — whether literal or analogical — about texts. Talk with elders and siblings about signs, print displayed on TV and even reading the clock are literacy events. Likewise, signs, labels, cartoons and advertising flyers may be the text around which oral interaction occurs. On the basis of cumulative cross-cultural data on literacy in daily life, we could generalise that 'functional' texts are probably more common in the fabric of everyday life than literary texts. In the following event, an urban Torres Strait Islander pre-school child, Elsey, and her grandmother read. During the event they switch readily from English to Torres Strait Creole, Elsey's first language (Kale and Luke 1991, p. 9).

> Grandma: Shower curtain, plastic curtain
> Yumi gede diswan [we'll get this one]
> Ai lai dis wan [I like this one]
> E, tri dola [Eh, three dollars]
> Elsey: Just onli tri dola? [Just only three dollars?]
> Grandma: O, brokli your favrit [Oh, broccoli's your favourite]
> Elsey: En karit mai favrit [And carrot is my favourite]
> Grandma: Celery, not brokli
> Elsey: Which one?
> Grandma: That wan celery
> Elsey: You think brokli
> Grandma: Mmm...This basket good fo Astro (the family dog) for slip [for sleep]
> Elsey: Which basket?

Child and grandparent take turns commenting on pictures in the text, reading the text when they want additional information about prices and products. Typically for urban bilingual English/Creole speakers, Elsey shifts back and forth between her first language and English while her grandmother speaks predominantly in Creole. But note that the power relations between elder and child are quite different than those of the foregoing events. Here the two are co-participants in the event: grandma does not 'lead' Elsey through the text using questions and staging the interaction. This might be attributable to the fact that Elsey's command of English language literacy is almost as proficient as her grandmother's. But at the same time her status as co-participant rather than subordinate speaker is also characteristic of much day to day bilingual conversation between the two. In this instance, literacy is focused on informational function, it is being shaped in this event as a means for getting information about the world. And it is a means for decision making about, in this case, what to buy.

These speech and literacy events between female caregivers and children in home and community sites give us some sense of the ways in which literate traditions are constructed for many children *before* they reach school. I note here the gender of the caregivers for descriptive, not prescriptive, purposes, and to make the point that in spite of public claims about the increased participation of males in child-rearing, early language and literacy socialisation in many communities continues to be constructed as women's work (Walkerdine 1986). Just as early childhood teaching remains a feminised occupation, in many communities the matrix of home and community literacy work with children (e.g. story reading and bedtime rituals, Sunday school teaching and the doing of children's homework) is not work shared equitably by caregivers regardless of gender. This is neither a 'natural' nor inevitable phenomenon but part of complex political economies of child-rearing and domestic work (Phoenix, Woollett and Lloyd 1991). This seems doubly important precisely because early literacy events enact and represent for children models for age/authority/gender relations. Put quite simply, the messages which emerge from early literacy events suggest that reading to and with children is women's responsibility and work. This pattern extends into children's homework patterns when they reach upper primary and secondary grades (Chandler *et al.* 1986) and it dovetails with the gendered distribution of textual work in patriarchal culture at large (cf. Walton 1992).

A current axiom which has a great deal of currency among many educators and parents reads as follows: the more children are read stories to, the better prepared they are for school. This message is at the heart of numerous parental intervention programs in Australia and the USA, various 'how to' books on child-rearing, and commercial pitches from bookshops, publishers and parent–teacher associations. Yet as Teale (1984) observes, studies of 'the correlations between pre-school experience in being read to and achievement in literacy have generally paid little attention to defining or describing *what constitutes a book-reading*' (p. 111, emphasis added). Research, parent and teacher literature alike has tended to treat increased home story reading *per se* as a panacea for school literacy problems, without adequately attending to the diversity of literate traditions in homes and communities (cf. Williams 1991).

Diverse communities and subcultures socialise their children into variable selective traditions: into different canons of spoken and written stories, into different ways of working with, talking about, using and interacting with text. I have provided examples here which indicate the variance in language and literacy socialisation from the middle class, mainstream 'norm' portrayed in the parents' and teachers' literature as the ideal prerequisite for school achievement. What is crucial here is that children in literate cultures learn competence with spoken language, *and* learn how to conduct themselves according to rule-governed literacy events. These events are tied up intimately with the learning of community values, ideologies and 'namings' of the social and natural world. They are also a means for establishing identity and playing out age, gender and authority relations with caregivers. *Even in its earliest configurations literacy learning is tied up with knowledge and power.*

As noted, children bring these competences to the linguistic 'marketplace' of the school with differing consequences. Several studies have shown that the school acts to select children on the basis of who brings the most mainstream, school-like approaches to speech and literacy events. In Heath's (1983) study, those middle class, 'Maintown' parents prepared their children for schooling long before their formal education began. Home talk shaped a hidden curriculum characterised by many of the features of classroom questioning, procedures for talking and acting around texts, and the genres and styles of literature the children would encounter in schools. Many of these parents were teachers — who began speaking to children in similar turn-taking patterns as those of the classroom as early as infancy, positioning and constructing the children much as the parent portrayed earlier narrating in the restaurant. These same teachers had great difficulty recognising, much less 'using' in effective ways, the difference and diversity of the patterns children brought to school. So, for instance, Lem's facility with performance rhyme might not only have been ignored, but also quite possibly construed as a behavioural problem. Heath (p. 271) comments: 'The seemingly "natural" sequences of habits from them as mainstreams were "unnatural" for many of their students'.

Children, then, do not enter school *tabula rasa*, as blank slates. Nor can the diversity of the competence they bring to school be defined in terms of simple skill 'strengths' and 'deficits', or phonological variation. Just as children bring to the classroom 'verbal repertoires' for speech events, so many bring differing (or, in some cases, altogether absent) repertoires for participation in literacy events. These may or may not complement the structures, ideologies and power relations of school speech and literacy events. The extensive literature on cross-cultural miscommunication signals some of the rudimentary classroom difficulties which arise frequently for Aboriginal and Islander, migrant and working-class children (Christie 1985). For instance, teachers may misconstrue ethnic and minority groups children's language and dialect features and community communication patterns as evidence of behavioural problems, insolence, physical disability or even mental deficiency.

To take another instance, urban Afro-American primary school students repeatedly 'misheard' the intonation patterns of teachers' talk and had difficulty recognising what counted as a question in the classroom (e.g. Cook-Gumperz 1986). In other instances, teachers failed to recognise children's verbal stories and recounts because these lacked the surface linguistic features of conventional textual children's stories (cf. Gee 1990). As Bourdieu (1990) argues, schools and teachers systematically tend to value and valorise those kinds of cultural capital/linguistic competence which fit the values of dominant classes and cultures, and in effect 'punish' children for not having *a priori* what schools are charged with delivering, that is, competence with school-style texts and literacy events.

A responsible primary program which is committed to equal access to critical social literacy would begin from a practical recognition and understanding of the complex play of linguistic and ethnic, cultural and ideological differences at work in modern nation-states. At the same time such a program would need to be wary of trivialising these differences and their very real social and economic concomitants and consequences: unequal accesses to work and wealth, cultural power and knowledge available to particular social classes, cultural groups and genders. It would plot a course to capitalise upon those competences and knowledges of speech and literacy events that children have, and to move them systematically towards facility with those critical and functional practices of reading and writing which are requisite for community life, academic achievement and occupational access. With these home and community variables in mind, we can now reconsider how classroom text and talk together 'construct' dominant selective traditions.

Literacy as Curriculum

Schools and study programs set out for children selections and rules for what is worth reading and writing, how and when. They further shape literacy events, procedures for how to do things with and around text. In classrooms, what 'counts' as literacy and what one can do with the technology of written language is scripted and rehearsed by teachers and students. The consequences, as I have argued, are stratified levels of school achievement, literate competence and, ultimately, inequitable formations of knowledge and power.

But classroom texts, programs and tests do not simply determine students' literacy in any fixed way. According to various cognitive and semiotic theories of reading (e.g. van Dijk 1977; Eco 1978; Spiro, Bruce and Brewer 1981), readers' background knowledge — the sum of knowledge resources gleaned from previous experiences and texts — influences how, where and to what ends they read and interpret texts. As noted, the knowledge and competence brought to schools by children is articulated through their experiences of family, community and social-class cultures,

Social Construction of Literacy

their participation in the language and literacy events of everyday life. Children's world knowledge, which cognitive psychologists metaphorically term 'schema', would include 'frames' or 'scripts' for how language and text works, how the social and natural worlds work, their own identities and families and so forth. We might also call these resources that children bring to texts *intertextual resources*: readers' and writers' stocks of knowledges and experiences with spoken, written, visual and social texts. I define texts to refer not only to books, periodicals and television programs read and viewed, but also to those spoken texts of conversations, and those scripts and scenes of social relations played out in everyday life.

Children use their intertextual resources to read, talk and write about the portrayals and values of literature. At the same time, these resources are elaborated and reshaped through children's participation in school-based programs. In what follows, I will look in more detail at two elements of the social construction of literacy in the primary classroom: children's texts and the patterns of talk in reading and writing lessons.

At its most basic level, school curriculum is made up of the children's literature and textbooks made available by teachers, librarians and others for reading in school and as 'homework'. What is selected as worth reading is the product of complex economic and political relationships involving authors and editors, consultants and administrators, teachers and librarians. Structural curriculum decisions reflect in part the economic imperatives of a transnational publishing industry, and in part political directives and imperatives of state, regional and district school systems. Such forces are at work in 1990s attempts by Australian, Canadian and UK state educational authorities to assemble national curriculum guidelines in literacy. The resultant documents must be acceptable to dominant regional, class and economic constituencies. At the same time, the publishing market has made a rapid transition from a longstanding emphasis on the production and sales of basal reader-style reading series to 'literature-based' reading programs, partly in response to the early and mid 1980s progressive emphasis on literature as a focal point of early childhood curriculum.

Governments and school systems speak of the need for freedom of the press and freedom of access to a range of print materials for children. This of course doesn't preclude ongoing battles over the censorship of material. To give you an idea of the range of social movements and interests which come into play, books banned from some Canadian and US school libraries and classrooms include: *Alice in Wonderland, To Kill a Mockingbird, 1984, Huckleberry Finn, Go Ask Alice, The Outsiders* and works by Roald Dahl, Judy Blume, Dr Seuss and others. Across English-speaking countries, books ranging from textbook descriptions of evolution to versions of human sexuality and religion have been the focus of dispute among educators, parents, politicians and others. Yet controversies over curricular materials as much centre on what is omitted from schoolbooks as on what is included. As noted, the absence of women's, ethnic and migrant literature, labour and ethnic history, even the barring of community languages, have been rallying points among those committed to curriculum that better represents the diversity of interests and histories which make up national cultures (Singh 1989; Apple and Christian-Smith 1990).

The transnational production of children's literature has grown into a multi-billion dollar enterprise for authors and publishers. Yet for school children it is far from a literary 'free market'. No educational system allows children full freedom of choice of texts and books, whether fiction or non-fiction. This occurs for a range of practical reasons, from the sheer physical and financial constraints of making an affordable and varied corpus of books available, to overt state and local conflict over political, moral and religious content. Even in those literacy programs where children are encouraged to select books for sustained silent reading, independent study and leisure reading, these choices are made from books purchased and available in the classroom and library and, in some cases, from commercial book clubs which use classrooms as marketing outlets (Cooper 1992). These books in turn have been selected from the stock of books developed and marketed for children by editorial and sales staff of publishing houses.

In recent years, publishers and authors have begun to respond to the concerns of parents and educators regarding the narrow band of children's life experiences and community contexts featured in children's literature. Hence, more books are available which portray, for instance, single-parent family configurations, migrant communities and children, Aboriginal cultures and history and non-traditional representations of girls and women. Other books deliberately attempt to break out of the Noddy, Dick and Dora portrayals of gender and community. As demand for an alternative body of children's books expands, a market for independent publishers of feminist, Aboriginal and other literatures has become more viable.

Two recent survey studies give us a picture of how an exclusionary tradition quite readily works through local teacher 'choice'. A study where 54 Australian student teachers were given 'free choice' to choose a piece of children's literature that they 'liked' and thought 'primary school children would like and benefit from', reported that 59 per cent of the selections were by male authors and 74 per cent featured males as primary characters (Luke, Cooke and Luke 1986, pp. 212–213). Only two of the 54 selections featured racial minorities, one a 'little Black Sambo' figure, and the other an Arab prince from a folk tale; one of these selections was made by the only black student enrolled in the course, a West Indian migrant. This study was replicated by Jipson and Paley (1991, p. 151) with a sample of 55 American teachers from three states, with an average classroom experience of 12$\frac{1}{2}$ years. Of the 155 books selected, 59 per cent of the selections were by male authors; 99 per cent of the authors were of 'Euro-American heritage'. Furthermore, of the 123 'books with identifiable main characters', 65 per cent centred on males. Only eight books (6 per cent) included main characters from non-white, non-'mainstream' cultures.

These studies provide only a snapshot of local situations and did not undertake any detailed analysis of the literature. Gender and ethnicity of author and protagonist are limited indicators of the substance of the texts in question. But both beginning and experienced teachers' commonsense assumptions about what is 'good literature' and 'what is appropriate for kids to read' may *represent* and *reproduce* an exclusionary version of the literary canon, and relatedly, of contemporary children's culture. These teachers' literature selections stressed boys' experience, downplayed a diversity of social models for girls and women, and virtually excluded ethnic and working class experience and community culture.

The increased publication and availability of diverse children's literature needs to be supplemented with critical debate over the social and literary criteria for the selection of children's literature. Unfortunately, such debate is omitted in those teacher education and in-service programs which expound the glories of 'quality' children's literature without mentioning, must less exploring, how children's literature constructs versions of cultural contexts and social possibilities. To that task we now turn.

What's in a Story?

Texts build up 'possible worlds' (Olson 1986), versions of the social and natural world, by deploying lexicogrammatical resources, that is, by 'wording' the world in particular ways. In an attempt to theorise about how texts influence children's identities, Willinsky and Hunniford (1992) draw from psychoanalytic theory to describe how romance literature acts as a 'mirror' for developing identity. Children construct their identities and life trajectories in relation to the cultural texts that they encounter. Ethnographic studies of readers have begun to show how the characters and contexts portrayed in literature (and, for that matter, on TV, by toys, comics and other social texts) provide templates that readers use to interpret and explain their identities, life situations and possibilities (e.g. Christian-Smith 1992).

We can track this construction of values and identities in a children's literature selection for beginning readers. The primary textbook and literature passages given below have been gathered from research projects in several urban classrooms. They are not meant to be exemplars of children's literature for adoption. All remain in current use; none are award winners. Perhaps what is significant about these texts is their lack of obvious significance: several appeared in more than one classroom we were studying; none were considered problematic by the teachers who used them[3]. The first is a short excerpt of a version of 'Goldilocks and the Three Bears' used in some Grade 1 programs:

> Here are the three bears. This one is the Daddy bear. This one is the Mummy bear. And this one is the baby bear. They go for a walk. Here is Goldilocks. No one is home, says Goldilocks. I can go in. Goldilocks wants some porridge. Here is Daddy bear's porridge. It is too salty for Goldilocks. This is Mummy bear's porridge. It is too sweet for Goldilocks. Here is baby bear's porridge. I like this porridge, says Goldilocks. Look. Baby bear has no porridge . . .

Like many reading series texts designed for beginning instruction, this 'story' has been edited for vocabulary level and sentence length. Hence, there is an extremely high degree of repetition of selected 'sight' or 'key words' (e.g. 'one', 'bear', 'baby') and of sentence structures (e.g. the intransitive 'Here is . . .', 'It is . . .'). Ostensibly, this kind of linguistic simplification and repetition makes the text more 'readable', but only if we define 'readability' in terms of a rudimentary decoding of graphemes into phonemes and recognition of commonly occurring words (e.g. 'Dolch list' words). Readability formulae are used by publishers, editors and textbook developers. They have enjoyed a recent revival because of their use in grammar-checking and word processing computer software. But such scales fail to consider the background knowledge of the reader, contexts and purposes of the reading event, the relevance of semantic and ideological content, and text structure as important variables in whether a text is comprehensible to students (e.g. Kintsch 1986). 'Readability' is certainly not reducible to word and sentence length. Nor is readability solely a property of the text, independent of those intertextual and contextual resources which the child calls into play to do a 'reading'.

But even this simplified text constructs a possible world of gendered action and desire. This begins with the designation of attributes and traits by association (e.g. male preferences and characteristics = 'salty', 'hard'; female = 'sweet', 'soft'). Similar patterns emerge in analyses of children's school books used in New South Wales primary classrooms. Baker and Freebody (1989) analysed 83 000 words of children's beginning reading books, and described several patterns for the wording of gender. The adjective 'little' was associated with boys in 42 instances and girls in 25 instances. However, those adjectives described as 'not little' were linked to boys in 99 instances and girls in 43. In these ways, texts build up lexical resources to 'name' and populate a possible world. In narrative this often entails the setting up of binary oppositions (or dual and opposing relationships between, for instance, good/bad; male/female; truth/lies; black/white) and the presentation of such oppositions as self-evident, truthful and 'natural' in the world.

These versions of community and interpersonal work and relations are built into the *story grammars* of children's literature. Like all written texts, stories themselves can be divided into propositional units, segments of meaning which together make up a generic or 'top-level' structure (Meyer and Rice 1984). Put simply, texts have beginnings, middles and ends, identifiable 'chunks' of texts which act together as parts. Below I have shown how the excerpt of the Goldilocks story can be parsed using a story grammar template (Luke 1988). Each propositional part is named in the brackets:

> Three bears at home (setting/main characters) ⇒ Bears leave home; Goldilocks arrives (initiating event/main character) ⇒ Goldilocks is hungry (Problem #1) ⇒ Father Bear's porridge (Attempt #1) ⇒ Too Salty (Outcome #1) ⇒ Mother Bear's porridge (Attempt #2) ⇒ Too Sweet (Outcome #2) ⇒ Baby Bear's porridge (Attempt #3) ⇒ . . .

Various psychologists, linguists and discourse analysts have different systems for parsing or segmenting the text into key units of meaning or 'macropropositions' (e.g. Toolan 1988). The activity is valuable because it enables teachers to highlight for children the generic structure of stories, video and cinematic texts. Knowing how to segment, identify and predict the semantic parts of any text can be a powerful tool in making sense of that text, and in reproducing and/or revising its structure and contents.

But my focal concern here is with how the social characterisations of the story segments act together to construct a *syntax of actions* (Luke 1988). How segments are chained together represents binary relationships between cause/effect, protagonist/antagonist, problem/solution, attempt/try. The key questions here are: What are the patterns of agency presented? Who is doing what to whom? Who is causing and solving problems? Specific identities (both animal and human), social relations and social and organic consequences of human action are 'naturalised' by their enshrinement in stories (Hodge and Kress 1989). In the Goldilocks story and across a range of traditional European folk tales, specific cultural types and patterns are presented as 'typical', commonsense and logical. Females and children cause problems (in this instance, Goldilocks' desires for food and sleep), which are solved by older males, often authority figures (i.e. Father Bear). Here female characters and, more generally, children are not portrayed as cognate, thinking individuals. Furthermore, in a great deal of children's literature, animal characters act as 'ideological decoys' (Stibbs 1990, p. 128). That is, the 'animals-as-humans' portrayals of the bears normalise the social interactions and family configurations portrayed. Masked as part of a natural and animal domain, societal configurations and ethical issues become invisible and self-evident to children.

Having grown up within these literary traditions, you might respond that this is all pretty innocent stuff. But a steady diet of these possible worlds comprises a dictionary of meanings, constructing one's commonsense about, in this case, gender, family and childhood. Consider, for instance, how the story grammars of archetypal Western movies string together a set of propositions about the relationships between cowboys, the military and Native Americans. Who causes the problems for, say, John Wayne and colleagues? Who resolves them? How? The repetition of characteristic syntaxes of action across cultural texts constructs, reiterates and builds stereotypes. In another analysis of the popular *Storybox* reading materials, Gilbert and Rowe (1989) describe a consistent pattern of gender portrayal. There, males are more frequently portrayed as protagonists, operating in a diverse range of occupations; while women typically are portrayed in traditional, 'helping' and domestic roles. Ethnicity is virtually invisible and silent throughout. While the surface features of many such reading series change over time, partly to take on board new approaches to the teaching and learning of reading, in many cases the actual models of society and action have changed little since postwar basal reading texts like *Fun with Dick and Jane*. Children and women are portrayed as the catalysts for what I have described here as the 'initiating event' and 'problem' segments of stories, the solution of which tends to rest with older males. This is a picture of patriarchal authority in action.

These possible worlds of children's literature complement and reiterate, for instance, caregivers' talk about gender described in the previous section, and the kinds of narrative encountered in cartoons and children's television. Consider, for instance, who creates and who solves problems in most situation comedies; or the patterns of agency in the story grammars of *Bugs Bunny* and *Roadrunner* cartoons. Subtly, at multiple levels and sites, spoken, written and visual texts comprise a *cultural hegemony*: a dominant 'complex of experiences, relationships and activities' which serve particular economic interests and are realised in a range of cultural texts, in effect, appearing and reappearing as part of one's everyday commonsense about the world (Williams 1989, p. 59). In this way, a dominant cultural tradition of values and ideas is established *intertextually*. That is, the child's identity, world-view and semantic resources are built up in relation to a range of spoken, written and visual texts which recirculate and reiterate complementary discourses and statements, themes and portrayals.

As noted in the Goldilocks story, many children's books are purpose-built; that is, they are designed to teach letter and sound blends (phonics) and 'sight words' (word recognition), often at the expense of the story having any substantive content or portrayal at all. Consider, for example, the following beginning reading text:

Mother and the children are going to look at the ducks.
'Where are the ducks?' said David.
'Here they come,' said Ann.
'Quack, quack,' said the ducks. 'We are hungry.'
'Here is the bread,' said Martin.
'Quack, quack,' said the ducks.
'Thank you for the bread. Quack, quack, quack.'
Martin looked at the bread.
'I am hungry,' he said.
Ann shouted, 'Martin is a duck. Martin is a du-uck.'
'Quack quack quack,' said Martin the duck. 'I am a hungry duck.'
'I am a hungry duck too,' said David.
'Quack, quack, quack,' said Ann.
Mother said, 'Come on, Martin Duck, and David Duck, and Ann Duck. Come on, children.'
Ann said to the ducks, 'We are going away. We are going home.'
'Quack, quack,' said the ducks.

This text has several design features, including a deliberate emphasis on the presentation of quoted speech. There is a high degree of lexical repetition in this text of the key words 'ducks' (13), 'quack' (15), 'hungry' (4), the names of the children and so forth. It also is structured to repeat grammatical structures in succession (e.g. 'Martin is a duck. Martin is a du-uck.' ... 'I am a hungry duck ... I am a hungry duck too'). The intention here is to, quite literally, repetitively 'teach' the recognition and recitation of these key words and sentence patterns, and thereby make the text accessible. At the same time, the representation of direct speech in early childhood texts is often justified as a way of easing children's movement from the lexicogrammatical structures of speech to those of written text. Unfortunately, the children's talk here bears little resemblance to any child's talk (Baker and Freebody 1989).

Whatever the instructional purpose for this text, there is little attempt by the authors to pick up any themes or portrayals which might be of relevance or interest to children. Even an apparently 'meaningless' basal reading series text normalises and naturalises representations of social identity, relations and actions. The mirror that children gaze into is a universe where authority and agency, identity and action, cause and effect, male and female are defined and exemplified. Here we 'see' and 'hear' the Anglo-Australian nuclear family on an outing, replete with striped frocks and T-shirts. The ideological version of 'childhood' portrayed here further reinforces the images of child rearing as women's work and of children as unthinking, inarticulate and silly: their approach to 'play' consists of imitating animal noises.

In so far as the worlds mirrored in children's literature diverge from children's background knowledge and experience, they risk positioning the child reader as 'other', as alien to the possible world of the text. Certainly, for purposes of generating children's interest in early reading there are decided advantages to presenting texts which represent everyday family and community lives. And there are well-grounded arguments for the significance of textual representation in the formation of children's cultural and gendered identities (e.g. Davies 1987; Christian-Smith 1992). For those historical 'outsiders' of early literacy instruction — urban working class, migrant, Aboriginal and Islander children — sympathetic and realistic portrayals of their life experiences need to be incorporated into children's textbooks and literature.

But I am not arguing here for a naive reconstruction of a children's literary canon which features only those texts which directly and literally represent local experience. What can be lost in calls for 'relevance' is a recognition of capacity of written language to build and depict contexts specifically 'other' to those of everyday life, whether fantasy texts or texts about historically or geographically inaccessible cultures and places. As a technology of representation, writing enables the construction of imaginary and distant possible worlds. In this sense, while an effective jumping off point for early literacy teaching, a narrow focus on texts which describe and recontextualise children's community patterns and experiences might have a constraining effect. For many children, mass media and school texts will be their primary means for learning about the non-local, for access to information about diverse cultural events, patterns, identities and spaces.

I have argued here that children's literature and reading series textbooks represent and construct versions of human action and social structure. But the same texts also construct and position the reader to see and 'read' the world and the text from particular vantage points. Through a range of textual devices, texts 'hail' readers, that is, they mark out how and by whom they are to be read, a 'reading position' (Kress 1985). The following passage is from William Saroyan's short story 'The Great Leapfrog Contest' (in Mellor, O'Neill and Patterson 1987, p. 41):

It looked pretty bad for the boy from Texas. We couldn't understand how he could take so much punishment. We all felt that Rex was getting what he had coming to him, but at the same time everybody seemed to feel badly about Rosie, a girl, doing the job instead of one of us. Of course, that was where we were wrong. Nobody but Rosie could have figured out that smart way of humiliating a very powerful and superior boy.

In this passage, various literary devices are brought into play to construct a standpoint on gender relations. Central to the establishment of that point of view is the role and position of the narrator. Throughout the narrator never uses 'I' in self-reference, a device that would signal participant-narration. Rather, the pronoun 'we' here constructs the narrator, the group of boys (of which the narrator is a member), and the readers as a single entity. The reader is thus positioned to 'look', 'understand' and 'feel' from a generalised perspective: 'everybody' felt badly about 'a girl, doing the job instead of one of us'.

In these ways, the reader is invited to see the world through the eyes of the author/narrator, accepting his perception of Rosie Mahoney, the ethnically mixed community that 'we' share and his script or framework for interpreting the events described. Claims, like 'it looked pretty bad for the boy from Texas', become shared perceptions of narrators and readers. The narrator's judgements of the gender identities and relationships portrayed ('Rosie . . . a tough little Irish kid . . . didn't fight girl-style, or cry . . .') become the reader's as well. Hence, by unifying the narrator's and readers' perspectives, a singular vantage point on events as described is forwarded. The narrator concludes that, despite being a 'tomboy' and 'unfeminine', Rosie later allowed the 'woman in her' to surface 'to such an extent that she became one of the most beautiful girls in town...and married one of the wealthiest young men'. Solidarity with the narrator/author enables and encourages the reader to 'see' the world as he would. A similar phenomenon can even be achieved in an early primary school picture book like *Rosie's Walk*. There the visual layout of the page invites the reader/child to take on the epistemic point of view of the character: to see the community as Rosie would.

To summarise: children's literary texts operate in two distinct yet complementary ways. First, they construct possible worlds of childhood and identity, history and social relations. Constructions such as those in the 'Goldilocks' and 'Ducks' texts present an extremely limited and potentially disabling version of what children (and adults) are capable of doing and thinking. Second, through the deploying of various textual techniques and resources, children's literary texts influence their own 'reading' and interpretation, positioning an 'ideal reader' (Eco 1978) to take up a particular way of seeing that text and world. In other words, these school books socially construct a version of knowledge, and socially construct relations of power between texts and readers.

Yet the values, characters and possible worlds presented in children's literature do not *determine* their readers' values and world-views. Whatever authors' (ultimately unrecoverable) intentions are, even pre-school children come up with divergent readings of stories. Davies (1992) documents children's diverse readings of the popular Canadian children's book, *The Paperbag Princess*. In interviews, pre-school children talked about the gender values of the text in oppositional and at times idiosyncratic ways. In the primary school literacy program, the actual uptake of children's literature depends greatly on what is said and done in classroom talk.

Constructing Literacy in Classroom Talk

The pieces of a selective tradition of literacy are assembled in classroom practice at 'how to do' reading and writing. Some possible practices and texts are included, others omitted. As in home and community events, the child reader's taste is influenced and shaped by the values and criteria for literature expressed in talk with elders. At the same time, instructional events build activity structures which guide student readers and writers through sequenced procedures and positions for doing literacy (Tharp and Gallimore 1988). These social contexts and relations with expert literates organise and reorganise those cognitive processes and procedures affiliated with how to use the technology of writing (Cole 1988; Newman, Griffin and Cole 1989).

In classroom talk, children learn how and on what grounds to select texts, how they are to talk about and treat texts, what the teacher and school value as significant signs of a 'good' reading or writing. In what follows, I want to query what exactly is being socially constructed as 'literacy' in much classroom talk, and use this as a springboard for discussion of how we can question and reconstruct selective literate traditions in classrooms. Note that the lessons in the following transcripts are not presented as exemplars of 'good' or 'bad' teaching. Rather I want to show how patterns of talk (often unintentionally) generate particular rehearsals of literate practice. Then I will move on to suggest how we can re-evaluate these patterns in our own classrooms.

Classroom talk sets out unequal 'speaking rights' (Cazden 1988) for participants in the classroom, situating students and teachers in relations of power (Kress 1985). Teachers' uses of questions and commands, for instance, are ways in which authority and control are asserted. Patterns of classroom talk thus construct a message system not only for how one 'does' subject/disciplinary knowledges (e.g. chemistry or history), but also for the social relations for 'talking science' (Lemke 1989) and, I would add, 'talking reading', 'talking writing' and so forth. In this way, seminal connections between cultural knowledge, social power, and literacy are constructed face to face in primary school classrooms.

Like home literacy and speech events, the patterns of interaction in the classroom consist of conventions and protocols, procedures done but frequently invisible to participants. Speech and literacy events can be tracked variously in terms of 'acts', 'turns' and 'moves' taken by students

Literacy Learning and Teaching

and teachers (Edwards and Westgate 1987). The teacher initiation ⇒ student response ⇒ teacher evaluation (IRE) sequence is a typical pattern of classroom talk (Mehan 1979). The following brief exchange from a discussion of the 'Ducks' story shows the IRE at work:

T: What happened in the story? [Initiate]
S: David and Ann was acting like a duck and they said they were hungry and ate some bread. [Response]
T: That's right. [Evaluate]

In much Western schooling, this model acts as a 'default mode' (Cazden 1988). While it is functionally suited to evaluating recall of facts and data, it may deter alternative and varied patterns of classroom interaction and knowledge construction. This is the case in the following primary school small-group reading discussion (Baker and Freebody 1989, p. 176):

T What else has he got on to keep him wet, uh dry.
Ss hh wet
T Robert.
S Boots?
T Yes bit, boots what do we call those big boots?
S Gumboots!
T Two names that I know of, don't call out hands up, Nicholas did you have one? Yes Nicholas?
N Gumboots.
S Call them gumboots and there's another name too . . .

Here 'what counts as reading' is being constructed according to very straightforward rules governing classroom talk. The 'response' turn requires that students come up with a single word ('Boots', 'Gumboots') which names an object in a picture in the text. As Baker and Freebody suggest, this repeated pattern begins to define and shape reading as a guessing game. The IRE exchange is repeated until the teacher 'hears' the naming that indicates that the students have read the text according to her criteria. That naming, as the teacher notes, has to be done after you've properly secured the floor by putting 'hands up'.

As in Aunt Sue and Wendy's bedtime story, the following classroom event has the added focus on the choreographing and disciplining of children's bodies. Here 15 Grade 1 children are arrayed around the teacher on the floor. The teacher sits before them on a chair, turning pages of an enlarged print book about 'Billy Goats' which is mounted on an easel (Luke, in press):

S1: I've gotta pair of socks like that.
T: David, will you just sit up straight. Michael, just sit up straight and face the front. When we first look at this, I was looking at this book and there's something different about the goats. But around here [points to picture] . . . what were all the goats wearing? [turns page]
S2: Go . . . gooo
S3: Ah beard, . . . a little beard, and they all gotta little beard.

42

T: [loudly] A beard. What do they all got on the first page? What do they all got around their necks?
S1: Ah bells, a one has//
S3: //Bells
T: [loudly] Bells. Well actually I was wrong. I thought that no one has bells, but I got it straight anyway. So . . . has the little billy goat gotta bell? Michael, if you can't sit down you can practise sitting up straight at recess. OK? Sit down. But . . . ssshhh . . . What's the big billy goat got?

As in the 'Gumboots' passage, this lesson highlights for the children what objects in the pictures are worth attending to and naming. This is done through a combination of talk ('what we see') and physical pointing by the teacher. The signs of accurate reading here are elicited through an IRE pattern, in which the child provides brief single word statements in response to the teacher's 'what' questions. The teacher's evaluation of the child's 'reading' consists of a paraphrase ('a beard', 'Bells'), marked by an increase in volume. There right and wrong 'namings' are confirmed by the teacher.

Much of the teachers' talk here is devoted to what we might term 'control' issues. Specifically, the bodily postures and procedures of reading are being shaped here. In many primary classrooms, reading is a physical and moral discipline that entails, among other things: 'sit[ting] up straight', 'fac[ing] the front', 'sit[ting] down', focusing one's 'look' at text pictures and particular salient objects and features on the pictures, and, in instances, even shaping one's mouth in visible ways (Luke, in press). All teachers rely on and interpret how children hold their bodies as evidence that the children are successfully participating in the lesson.

But classroom talk may structure literacy to involve far more than the production of single word namings. The following passage is from a secondary school discussion of a novel. Here what will count as 'literary criticism' is built (Hammond, cited in Freebody, Luke and Gilbert 1991):[4]

S. Well, she's very independent . . she's kind, and caring . . . I guess she's creative in a way, able to . . . um . . . you know, cooking and that.
T. OK, Amy, can you add something?
S. She's got a lot of courage and//
T. //a lot of courage . . . how do we see that?
S. Um . . . like she keeps herself alive, and she thinks there's no-one else around on the earth.
T. She keeps herself alive when there's no-one else around. Good. Yes, Shirley, can you add to that?
S. Um, she's very soft-hearted, she . . . like, she thought Mr. Loomis was bad but she, when he got sick she still looked after him.
T. Yes.

The teacher here uses more open-ended questions (e.g. 'Can you add something?', 'how do we see that?') to prompt more extended comments about characters. The repeated pattern is as follows: students affiliate a series of adjectives ('independent', 'kind', 'caring', etc.) with a nominated character. The teacher's evaluation is to repeat back tag phrases (e.g. 'a lot of courage . . .'), and then to append requests for textual evidence or examples ('how do we see that?'). In response, the student provides relevant recount of story grammar/plot information. What is at issue here is not whether the student's response or the teacher's method is right or wrong. My point here is that the criteria and procedures for doing literary criticism in a particular way are being socially constructed through talk. Signs that the student has 'experienced' the novel, of an appropriate 'reader response', consist of labelling characters and then justifying the labels by reference to textual details and evidence. Successful signs of 'having read the novel' here entail describing characters and affiliating those descriptions with sequences of events or plot.

Similar kinds of shaping of the text form and content take place in those lessons which aim to 'integrate' reading and writing. The following Grade 1 classroom lesson is taken from an urban classroom of 20 children, several of whom are of Aboriginal or Torres Strait Islander background. Here the teacher is working through a 'modelled writing' session, in which children make suggestions as the class collaborates in the construction of a story (Luke 1992).

T: ... OK, there's a name, what comes next.
S1: ...
T: Yes Nadia.
S2: A story starter.
T: A story starter. What do you figure will be the best story starter for a story about a princess and a dragon? Kim?
S3: Once upon a time.
T: Once upon a time is a pretty good one, yes?
S4: A long time ago?
T: I like that one. Yes, Daniel.
S5: A long long time ago?
T: Oh, That's very good. Know your story starters don't you? That was lovely. What about, last night.
S3: Yesss ... Noo ...
S5: Yea, Last night there was a dragon comin' to get me.
T: I like stories about dragons and princesses a long time ago. So I'm gonna have Daniel's story starter, with ... what do I have to start with ...
Ss: 'A' ... [confusion]
T: What do I have to start with?
Ss: [Unison] ... Big A.
T: Good, 'a long, long time a ...'
Ss: a
T: 'ago, there lived a princess'. . . .

This lesson focuses on naming and filling in the parts of the story: first the 'name' or title, then the 'story starter'. In their responses, children submit possible wordings for that part, including 'once upon a time', 'a long time ago' and so forth. However, there is more to this than simply learning the structure of the story. Models of literary 'taste' and convention are being established. Specifically, the appropriate ideological contents for the possible world of the story are being formed. Here the lesson identifies not only the stylistic conventions of 'story starters', but also appropriate ideological contents. In this case, the designated title and 'starter' marks out an historical or mythological story ('a long, long time a . . .'). For the teacher, this modelling of what authors do invokes 'what I like': a possible world of dragons, Anglo-European princesses and, as the story is filled out over the course of the lesson, 'handsome' princes who rescue blonde princesses.

A selective tradition is in action here, one in which the identification of textual form and contents, stylistic and ideological choice and how one goes about talking about texts are established in classroom interaction. Simply put, children's literacy is being 'done' and 'made' through classroom work, that work is talk. In these lessons, classroom talk remains focused on anticipating the 'naming' that the teacher is looking for — whether that naming consists of pictographic features, key words, plot information or the generic parts of the story. The social construction of literacy through classroom talk signals to students that this is what one does as part of 'reading', 'writing', 'authoring' and literature study.

As noted, these transcripts are not presented as models to emulate. I do not want to discount or debate the intents of the lesson plans here, or to query the value of the specific skill orientation of each lesson. In each case, no doubt, the teacher has conscious intents; these might range from the teaching of vocabulary and word recognition, to aspects of comprehension and composition, character analysis or literary appreciation. But if we 'bracket' or 'suspend' our assumptions about whether what is intended in these lessons indeed is educationally worthwhile, we can begin to see how literacy events form a powerful hidden curriculum, one which signals and establishes what counts as a valued display of literacy by a student. Such displays, however intended or unintended, carry powerful messages about what can and should be done when reading and writing, in school and out.

At the onset of this chapter, I argued that literacy was a malleable social technology, and that schooling was responsible for constructing and shaping for students the potential functions and uses of literacy, for laying out the horizons for what mature literacy might be used for. The foregoing examples of the social construction of literacy are not exemplars, but they mark out areas of concern. In much classroom talk, the emphasis is on teachers interrogating students about texts, not about students learning to question and analyse, appraise or argue with or about texts. In all of the foregoing classroom events the student's primary responsibility is to reproduce and comply with a teacher's 'preferred reading' or 'writing'. These events are as much about establishing the authority and procedures for classroom order as they are about reading and writing (Baker 1991). Here what counts as literacy apparently has less to do with learning how texts work, to what ends, possible applications and alternatives, and more to do with an uncritical reproducing of these preferred readings and writings.

Critical Social Literacy in the Classroom: A Beginning

What kinds of social power and cultural knowledge should be constructed in literacy education? More specifically, which texts, genres and competences should be selected and taught? How should they be shaped in classroom lessons? I have argued here that these questions can only be addressed in the context of broader sociological and historical understandings of literacy. To conclude, I want to revisit key questions about the social construction of literacy in the primary school.

I began this chapter by trying to cut across debates over the 'basics', stressing the need for all to achieve critical social literacy: flexible and wide-ranging social competences with a range of texts; the capacity to use text for educational and occupational purposes; and the capacity to analyse and criticise the texts and ideologies of contemporary work and culture. Tracing the links between literacy and equity, I reviewed the historical and contemporary role of mass schooling in the reproduction of unequal levels of social access and cultural capital. I showed how schools and communities construct selective traditions of literacy, noting how difficult it is for us, as products of these traditions, to assess their consequences. Whether we like it or not, literacy is tied up with the distribution and division of knowledge and power. For teachers, the matter at hand is who gets what kinds of literacy from schooling.

Beginning from this appraisal of the social consequences and possibilities of literacy, I described how children develop complex intertextual resources in community and family socialisation. For their part, schools shape and select: (1) a corpus of texts; (2) specific genres; and (3) preferred practices to be rehearsed in classroom events. School texts portray the world and position readers. School lessons shape and regulate the acts of reading and writing in unintentional, and often disenfranchising ways.

But in current educational debates, the way forward frequently is confused by contending claims about literacy and equity. Describing a 'postprogressivist' approach to literacy, Cope and Kalantzis (1992, p. 113) clarify the challenge for schools, curriculum and teachers:

> A postprogressivist pedagogy ... would build on the insights of progressivism by using differential pedagogies, starting with students' differential experiences. But at the same time, its objective would be a commonality which did not exclude difference by its inclination to force homogenisation around singular cultural principles such as nationalism. Nevertheless, ... schooling cannot provide social access with a fragmented curriculum which leaves difference as difference. There are common linguistic, cognitive and cultural conditions for access to social goods, and, albeit by means of differential, specialised pedagogies, these should be the singular objectives of curriculum. An acceptance of enduring difference ... is an essential pedagogical precondition to achieving these singular ends.

This is a timely and important description of the strategic and practical variables in teaching for critical social literacy. We have seen here how unequal 'access to social goods' begins at the earliest stages of schooling, where many programs are unable to recognise and capitalise on those 'differential experiences', competences and resources which children bring to classrooms, particularly those children from Islander and Aboriginal, migrant and working-class communities. A recognition of cultural, class and gender differences should lead to a more inclusive literature and literacy curriculum, one which represents and offers far more diverse and challenging identities and voices, histories and experiences instead of the 'homogenisation' of much children's literature and reading materials.

But while the foregoing may be *necessary* to redress longstanding exclusions, it may not be *sufficient* to guarantee equal access to critical literacy. If equality of access to cultural and economic resources requires identifiable 'linguistic, cognitive and cultural conditions', then indeed literacy programs must go beyond the recognition of difference towards direct introduction to those knowledges, discourses, texts and genres necessary for academic success and sociocultural power. As I have shown here, learning to read and write necessarily entails learning an epistemological and political standpoint on the world. In this light, a critical social literacy that values critique and analysis, innovation and appraisals for action may be of social, economic and political benefit for communities, for individuals and for cultures.

If our aim is to reassess selective traditions in order to remake them in the interests of diverse groups of learners, we can begin by questioning those choices implicit in every lesson we teach. To do so, I return to the Grade 1 'Princess and the Dragon' lesson in progress (Luke 1992):

T: ... Now, when you write a story Alison, there's something very important you gotta do. You gotta keep reading your story as you write it because you might miss out a really important word. So I'm gonna read mine again [points to story script on paper]: 'A long, long time ago there lived a princess'. I think I can make it a bit better than that.
S1: A dragon too.
T: No, no. No. What. How bout: when you think about a princess, what'do you think about?
S2: A prince ...
T: No.
S2: A prince ...
T: No, what do you think she'd look like?
S3: A ...
T: With long hair? What colour?
S3: Yellow, black ... [chorus laughter]
T: What about long, long golden hair.

Of this and other lessons, we can ask:

1. What kind of literary canon is being constructed here? Whose identities, voices, histories and experiences are included and omitted?
2. Which genres are being selected here? What kinds of social and economic power do these yield? For whom? In which institutional sites?

3. What practices are being shaped and valued in the literacy event? What kinds of competences are counting as displays of 'reading' and 'writing' in this literacy event? Are children developing strategies and competences to question, analyse and critique texts and ideologies?

To answer simply: first, the content selected and shaped here omits identities and possible worlds of cultural significance or educational value for the children. Second, in this lesson and across the program in this classroom, students study 'stories' almost exclusively, rarely reading and writing any other genres. Third, the lesson encourages compliance and reproduction of what the teacher deems appropriate style and content.

One of the Islander girls comments, laughingly, that the princess could have black hair. This is a critique and rewriting of the 'fairy tale' genre. Here is an opportunity for these children to talk about and write the genre differently and innovatively, in their interests. Here is an opportunity for the teacher to highlight how the text works, and to introduce a language for talking about textual and cultural variables, possibilities and alternatives. Yet that opportunity is not taken up by the teacher, who simply ignores the comment. The politics of literacy are at work in each choice we make about what to include and what to omit. This lesson is about the shaping of identity, knowledge and power.

Acknowledgements

The author thanks Len Unsworth for his editorial encouragement, advice and patience. Early drafts of the sections 'Literacy as a Social Semiotic Technology' and 'Literacy and Power: Regulating the Word' were developed as part of Christie, Devlin, Freebody, Luke, Martin, Threadgold and Walton (1992). The members of that research team offered valuable advice on those sections. An earlier version of the analysis of the Saroyan passage in 'What's in a Story?' appears in Freebody, Luke and Gilbert (1991).

Notes

1. All transcripts quoted here from other sources retain their original features and marking.
2. This excerpt was recorded on 26 December 1991 in Townsville by the author.
3. The 'Goldilocks' and 'Ducks' texts were collected in a 1991 Australian Research Council study of 'The Literacy and Numeracy Learning of Urban Aborigines and Islanders in Early Childhood Education'.

4. This transcript was collected by Jennifer Hammond of the University of Wollongong and is from her work in progress. An earlier analysis of it appears in Freebody, Luke and Gilbert (1991). The author thanks her for access to the data.

References

Anyon, J. (1981) 'Elementary schooling and the distinctions of social class', *Interchange*, 12: 118–132.
Apple, M.W. and Christian-Smith, L.C. (eds) (1990) *The Politics of the Textbook*, Routledge, New York.
Arnove, R. and Graff, H.J. (eds) (1987) *National Literacy Campaigns*, Plenum, New York.
Baker, C.D. (1991) 'Literacy practices and social relations in classroom reading events', in *Towards a Critical Sociology of Reading Pedagogy*, eds C.D. Baker and A. Luke, John Benjamins, Amsterdam.
Baker, C.D. and Freebody, P. (1989) *Children's First School Books*, Basil Blackwell, Oxford.
Bakhtin, M. (1986) *Speech Genres and Other Late Essays*, trans. V. McGee, eds C. Emerson and M. Holquist, University of Texas Press, Austin.
Bernstein, B. (1990) *The Structuring of Pedagogic Discourse: Class, Codes and Control*, Vol. 4, Routledge, London.
Bourdieu, P. (1986) *Distinction: A Social Critique of the Judgement of Taste*, trans. R. Nice, Routledge and Kegan Paul, London.
Bourdieu, P. (1990) *Language and Symbolic Power*, ed. J. Thompson, Polity Press, Cambridge.
Bourdieu, P. and Passeron, J.C. (1990) *Reproduction: In Education, Society and Culture*, 2nd edn, trans. R. Nice, Sage, London.
Bruner, J. (1991) 'The narrative construction of reality', *Critical Inquiry* 18: 1–21.
Carter, R. (ed.) (1990) *Knowledge about Language and the Curriculum*, Hodder and Stoughton, London.
Cazden, C. (1988) *Classroom Discourse*, Heinemann, Portsmouth, New Jersey.
Cazden, C., Johns, V.P. and Hymes, D. (eds) (1972) *Functions of Language in the Classroom*, Teachers College Press, New York.
Chandler, J., Argyris, D., Barnes, W.S., Goodman, I.F. and Snow, C.E. (1986) 'Parents as teachers: Observations of low-income parents and children in a homework-like task', in *The Acquisition of Literacy: Ethnographic Perspectives*, eds B.B. Schieffelin and P. Gilmore, Ablex, Norwood, New Jersey.
Christian-Smith, L.C. (ed.) (1992) *Texts of Desire*, Falmer Press, London.
Christie, F., Devlin, B., Freebody, P., Luke, A., Martin, J.R., Threadgold, T. and Walton, C. (1992) *Teaching English Literacy: A Project of National Significance on the Preservice Preparation of Teachers for Teaching English Literacy*, Vol. 1. Department of Employment, Education and Training/Northern Territory University, Canberra/Darwin.
Christie, M. (1985) *Aboriginal Perspectives on Experience and Learning: The Role of Language in Aboriginal Learning*, Deakin University Press, Geelong, Victoria.
Cole, M. (1988) 'Cultural psychology: A once and future discipline', in *Nebraska*

Symposium on Motivation: Cross-Cultural Perspectives, ed. J.J. Berman, University of Nebraska Press, Lincoln.

Cole, M. and Griffin, P. (1986) 'A sociohistorical approach to remediation', in *Literacy, Society and Schooling*, eds S. deCastell, A. Luke and K. Egan, Cambridge University Press, Cambridge.

Connell, R.W. (1985) *Teachers' Work*, Allen and Unwin, Sydney.

Cook, J., Homer, D. and Nixon, H. (1991) *Access Gained, Agency Lost: The Politics of English Teaching in the 1990s*, School of Arts, University of South Australia, Adelaide.

Cook-Gumperz, J. (ed.) (1986) *The Social Construction of Literacy*, Cambridge University Press, Cambridge.

Cooper, D. (1992) 'Retailing gender: Adolescent book clubs in Australian schools', in *Texts of Desire*, ed. L.C. Christian-Smith, Falmer Press, London.

Cope, B. (1990) 'Facing the challenge of 'back to basics': An historical perspective', *Curriculum Perspectives* 10(2): 20–33.

Cope, B. and Kalantzis, M. (1992) 'Contradictions in the canon: Nationalism and the cultural literacy debate', in *Literacy in Social and Cultural Contexts*, eds A. Luke and P. Gilbert, Allen and Unwin, Sydney.

Davies, B. (1987)*Frogs and Snails and Feminist Tales*, Allen and Unwin, Sydney.

Davies, B. (1992) 'Beyond dualism and towards multiple subjectivities', in *Texts of Desire*, ed. L.C. Christian-Smith, Falmer Press, London.

Davis, N.Z. (1987) *Society and Culture in Early Modern France*. 2nd edn, Polity Press, Cambridge.

deCastell, S.C., Luke, A. and MacLennan, D. (1986) 'On defining literacy', in *Literacy, Society and Schooling*, eds S. deCastell, A. Luke, and K. Egan, Cambridge University Press, Cambridge.

Delgado-Gaitan, C. (1990) *Literacy for Empowerment*, Falmer Press, London.

Delpit, L. (1988) 'The silenced dialogue: Power and pedagogy in educating other people's children', *Harvard Educational Review* 58: 280–298.

Diehl, W.C. and Mikulecky, L. (1988) 'The nature of reading at work', in *Perspectives on Literacy*, eds E.R. Kintgen, B.R. Kroll and M. Rose, Southern Illinois University Press, Carbondale.

Eco, U. (1978) *The Role of the Reader*, Indiana University Press, Bloomington.

Edelsky, C. (1991) *With Literacy and Justice for All: Rethinking the Social in Language and Education*, Falmer Press, London.

Edwards, A.D. and Westgate, D.P.G. (1987) *Investigating Classroom Talk*, Falmer Press, London.

Fairclough, N. (1989) *Language and Power*, Longman, London.

Fish, S. (1980) *Is There a Text in this Class? The Authority of Interpretive Communities*, Harvard University Press, Cambridge, Massachusetts.

Foucault, M. (1972) 'The discourse on language', in *The Archaeology of Knowledge and the Discourse on Language*, trans. A.M. Sheridan-Smith, Harper and Row, New York.

Fowler, R. (1991) *Language in the News: Discourse and Ideology in the Press*, Routledge, London.

Freebody, P., Luke, A. and Gilbert, P. (1991) 'Reading positions and practices in the classroom', *Curriculum Inquiry* 21: 435–457.

Freebody, P. and Welch, A. (eds) (1992) *Knowledge, Culture, and Power: International Perspectives on Literacy as Policy and Practice*, Falmer Press, London.

Freire, P. (1968) *Pedagogy of the Oppressed*, Herder and Herder, New York.

Freire, P. and Macedo, D. (1987) *Literacy: Reading the World and the Word*, Bergin and Garvey, South Hadley, Massachusetts.

Gee, J.P. (1990) *Social Linguistics and Literacies: Ideology in Discourses*, Falmer Press, London.

Genishi, C. and DiPaolo, M. (1982) 'Learning through argument in the preschool', in *Communicating in the Classroom*, ed. L.C. Wilkinson, Academic Press, New York.
Gilbert, P. (1990) 'Personal growth or critical resistance? Self-esteem in the English curriculum', in *Hearts and Minds: Self Esteem and the Schooling of Girls*, eds J. Kenway and S. Willis, Falmer Press, London.
Gilbert, P. and Rowe, K. (1989) *Gender, Literacy and the Classroom*, Australian Reading Association, Adelaide.
Gore, J. (1992) 'What can we do for you! What can 'we' do for 'you'? Struggling for empowerment in critical and feminist pedagogy', in *Feminisms and Radical Pedagogy*, eds C. Luke and J. Gore, Routledge, London.
Graddol, D. and Swann, J. (1989) *Gender Voices*, Basil Blackwell, Oxford.
Graff, H.J. (1987) *The Legacies of Literacy*, Indiana University Press, Bloomington.
Habermas, J. (1976) *Legitimation Crisis*, trans. T. McCarthy, Heinemann, London.
Halliday, M.A.K. (1975) *Learning How to Mean*, Edward Arnold, London.
Halliday, M.A.K. (1978) *Language as Social Semiotic*, Edward Arnold, London.
Hammond, J. (1990) 'Is learning to read and write the same as learning to speak?', in *Literacy for a Changing World*, ed. F. Christie, Australian Council for Educational Research, Melbourne.
Harvey, D. (1987) *The Condition of Postmodernity*, Polity Press, Cambridge.
Hasan, R. (1986) 'The ontogenesis of ideology: An interpretation of mother child talk', in *Language, Semiotics, Ideology*, eds T. Threadgold, E.A. Grosz, G. Kress, M.A.K. Halliday, Sydney Association for Studies in Society and Culture, Sydney.
Hasan, R. (1989) 'Semantic variation and sociolinguistics', *Australian Journal of Linguistics* 9: 221–275.
Hasan, R. (1991) 'Rationality in everyday talk: From process to system', Paper presented at the Nobel Symposium on Corpus Linguistics, Stockholm.
Heath, S.B. (1983) *Ways with Words: Language, Life and Work in Communities and Classrooms*, Cambridge University Press, Cambridge.
Heath, S.B. (1986a) 'The functions and uses of literacy', in *Literacy, Society and Schooling*, eds S. DeCastell, A. Luke and K. Egan, Cambridge University Press, Cambridge.
Heath, S.B. (1986b) 'What no bedtime story means: Narrative skills at home and school', in *Language Socialization Across Cultures*, eds B.B. Schieffelin and E. Ochs, Cambridge University Press, Cambridge.
Hodge, R., Fiske, J. and Turner, G. (1987) *Myths of Oz: Readings in Australian Popular Culture*, Unwin Hyman, Sydney.
Hodge, R. and Kress, G. (1989) *Social Semiotics*, Polity Press, Cambridge.
Hymes, D. (1972) 'Models of interactions of language and social life', in *Directions in Sociolinguistics: The Ethnography of Communication*, eds J.J. Gumperz and D. Hymes, Holt-Rinehart, New York.
Jipson, J. and Paley, N. (1991) 'The selective tradition in teachers' choice of children's literature: Does it exist in the elementary classroom?', *English Education* 23: 148–159.
Kalantzis, M., Cope, B. and Slade, D. (1989) *Minority Languages and Dominant Culture*, Falmer Press, London.
Kale, J. and Luke, A. (1991) 'Doing things with words: Early childhood language socialization', in *The Literacy Agenda*, eds E. Furniss and P. Green, Heinemann, Portsmouth, New Jersey.
Kintsch, W. (1986) 'On modeling comprehension', in *Literacy, Society and Schooling*, eds S. deCastell, A. Luke and K. Egan, Cambridge University Press, Cambridge.

Kress, G. (1985) *Linguistic Processes in Sociocultural Practice*, Deakin University Press, Geelong, Victoria.
Lemke, J. (1989) *Talking Science*, Ablex, Norwood, New Jersey.
Luke, A. (1988) *Literacy, Textbooks and Ideology*, Falmer Press, London.
Luke, A. (in press) 'The body literate: Discourse and inscription in early childhood literacy training', *Linguistics and Education*.
Luke, A. (1992) 'Stories of social regulation: The micropolitics of narrative in the primary classroom', in *The Insistence of the Letter: Literacy and Curriculum Theory*, ed. B. Green, Falmer Press, London.
Luke, A., Cooke, J. and Luke, C. (1986) 'The selective tradition in action: Gender bias in student teachers' selections of children's literature', *English Education* 18: 209–218.
Luke, C. (1989) *Pedagogy, Printing, Protestantism: The Discourse on Childhood*, State University of New York Press, Albany.
Luke, C. (1991) 'On reading the child: A feminist poststructuralist perspective', *Australian Journal of Reading* 14: 109–116.
Lurie, A. (1990) *Don't Tell the Grown-ups: Subversive Children's Literature*, Little Brown, Boston.
Martin, J.R. (1992) 'Technology, Bureaucracy and Schooling: Discursive Resources and Control', Unpublished paper, University of Sydney.
McNeil, L. (1986) *Contradictions of Control*, Routledge and Kegan Paul, London.
Mehan, H. (1979) *Learning Lessons*, Harvard University Press, Cambridge, Massachusetts.
Mellor, B. O'Neill, M. and Patterson, A. (eds) (1987) *Reading Stories*, Chalkface Press, Scarborough, WA.
Mey, J.L. (1985) *Whose Language? A Study in Linguistic Pragmatics*, John Benjamins, Amsterdam.
Meyer, B.J. and Rice, G.E. (1984) 'The structure of text', in *The Handbook of Reading Research*, ed. P.D. Pearson, Longman, New York.
Newman, D., Griffin, P. and Cole, M. (1989) *The Construction Zone: Working for Cognitive Change in School*, Cambridge University Press, Cambridge.
Olson, D.R. (1986) 'Learning to mean what you say: Toward a psychology of literacy', in *Literacy, Society and Schooling*, eds S. deCastell, A. Luke and K. Egan, Cambridge University Press, Cambridge.
Oxenham, J. (1980) *Literacy: Writing, Reading and Social Organization*, Routledge and Kegan Paul, London.
Phoenix, A., Woollett, A. and Lloyd, E. (eds) 1991, *Motherhood: Meanings, Practices and Ideologies*, Sage, London.
Porter, P., Lingard, R., Knight, J. and Chant, D. (eds) (1992) *Educational Reform in Hard Times*, Falmer Press, London.
Poster, M. (1990) *The Mode of Information*, University of Chicago Press, Chicago.
Said, E. (1984) *The World, the Text and the Critic*, Vintage, New York.
Schieffelin, B.B. and Ochs, E. (eds) (1986) *Language Socialization Across Cultures*, Cambridge University Press, Cambridge.
Scribner, S. and Cole, M. (1981) *The Psychology of Literacy*, Harvard University Press, Cambridge, Massachusetts.
Sharp, R. and Green, A. (1975) *Education and Social Control*, Routledge and Kegan Paul, London.
Shotter, J. and Gergen, K. (eds) (1989) *Texts of Identity*, Sage, London.
Singh, M. (1989) 'A counter-hegemonic orientation to literacy in Australia', *Journal of Education* 171: 34–56.
Snow, C. and Ferguson, C. (eds) (1977) *Talking to Children: Language Input and Acquisition*, Cambridge University Press, Cambridge.

Spiro, R.J., Bruce, B.C. and Brewer, W.F. (eds) (1981) *Theoretical Issues in Reading Comprehension*, Lawrence Erlbaum, Hillsdale, New Jersey.

Stibbs, A. (1990) *Reading Narrative as Literature: Signs of Life*, Open University Press, Milton Keynes.

Taxel, J. (1989) 'Children's literature: A research proposal from the perspective of the sociology of school knowledge', in *Language, Authority and Criticism*, eds S. deCastell, A. Luke and C. Luke, Falmer Press, London.

Teale, W. (1984) 'Reading to young children: Its significance for literacy development', in *Awakening to Literacy*, eds H. Goelman, A. Oberg and F. Smith, Heinemann, Exeter.

Tharp, R.G. and Gallimore, R. (1988) *Rousing Minds to Life: Teaching, Learning and Schooling in Social Context*, Cambridge University Press, Cambridge.

Threadgold, T. (1989) 'Talkin' about genres: Ideologies and incompatible discourses', *Cultural Studies* 3: 121–127.

Toolan, M.J. (1988) *Narrative*, Routledge and Kegan Paul, London.

Unsworth, L. (1991) 'Linguistic form and the construction of knowledge in the factual texts for primary school children', *Educational Review* 43: 201–212.

van Dijk, T.A. (1977) *Text in Context*, Longman, London.

Vetter, R. (1992) 'Discourses across literacies: Personal letter writing in a Tuvuluan context', *Language and Education* 5: 125–148.

Vygotsky, L. (1978) *Mind in Society*, eds M. Cole, V. John-Steiner, S. Scribner and E. Souberman, Harvard University Press, Cambridge, Massachusetts.

Walkerdine, V. (1986) *Surveillance, Subjectivity and Struggle: Lessons from Pedagogic and Domestic Practices*, University of Minnesota Press, Minneapolis.

Walton, C. (1992) 'Gender and Ethnicity: Constructions of Difference', Paper of the Australian Applied Linguistics Association Conference, Sydney.

Wells, G. (ed.) (1981) *Learning Through Interaction*, Cambridge University Press, Cambridge.

Wickert, R. (1990) *No Single Measure*, Sydney Institute of Advanced Education, Sydney.

Wilden, A. (1982) *System and Structure: Essays in Communication and Exchange*, 2nd edn, Tavistock, London.

Williams, G. (1991) 'The origins of literacy: Reconsidering home-school language relationships in reading', *Australian Journal of Reading* 14: 161–167.

Williams, R. (1977) *Marxism and Literature*, Oxford University Press, Oxford.

Williams, R. (1989) 'Hegemony', in *Language, Authority and Criticism*, eds S. deCastell, A. Luke and C. Luke, Falmer Press, London.

Willinsky, J. and Hunniford, R.M. (1992) 'Reading the romance younger: The mirrors and fears of a preparatory literature', in *Texts of Desire*, ed. L.C. Christian-Smith, Falmer Press, London.

Zinsser, C. (1986) 'For the Bible tells me so: Teaching children in a fundamentalist church', in *The Acquisition of Literacy: Ethnographic Perspectives*, eds B.B. Schieffelin and P. Gilmore, Ablex, Norwood, New Jersey.

2
Children's Literature: What to Look for in a Primary Reading Program

Maurice Saxby

Contents

Literature, Life and Learning   57

Literature and the Reader   60

What do Children Look for in their Reading?   62
    Plot
    Character
    Multiculturalism
    Time and Place
    Theme
    Humour

Techniques Authors Employ   69
    Irony
    Satire
    Point of View: Narrative Stance
    Person
    Stream of Consciousness
    Journals, Letters, Diaries
    Tone
    Style
    The Implied Reader
    Tell-tale Gaps

The Range of Literature   75
    Poetry and Verse
    Traditional Literature
    Fantasy

Turning Children on to Books: Teaching Children's Literature   81
    Wide versus Close Reading
    Literature-based Reading

References
References to Children's Books
Appendix: Teaching Resources Material

A Primary Reading Program

Literature, Life and Learning

In today's climate of 'literature-based reading' the early catchcry of 'children learn to read by reading books' has become almost a cliché. As early as 1946 the American author Clifton Fadiman wrote, 'Those to whom reading is fated to become important generally shake hands with books early' (Fadiman 1946, p. xiv). Another American, Strickland Gillilian, in 'The Reading Mother', puts the case another way:

> You may have tangible wealth untold:
> Caskets of jewels and coffers of gold.
> Richer than I you can never be —
> I had a Mother who read to me.

The most important factor in developing literary skills is early access to literature: in the first place to the oral literature of nursery rhymes and folk and fairy tales and then to books which will immediately capture interest, stir the imagination and absorb the listener into the world of story. The four year old who is so familiar with Beatrix Potter's *The Tale of Peter Rabbit* that the brow furrows and the body language becomes urgent when voicing the advice of the friendly sparrows who flew to Peter 'in great excitement, and implored him to exert himself' is already well on the way to decoding print. More importantly, print is associated with life as it is known to be.

The raw material of all true literature is experience. Potter's Peter Rabbit is every child — curious, explorative, risk-taking. Her Squirrel Nutkin is every show-off, every cheeky imp who takes on the adult world. Allan Baillie's prize-winning picture story *Drac and the Gremlin* came from observing his own children at play and from the universal experience of 'let's pretend'. Margaret Wild's *The Very Best of Friends* derives from the suffering and stages of grief endured by adults and children alike who have lost a loved one. *Sadako and the Thousand Paper Cranes* by Eleanor Coerr is the moving story of a child who was two years old when an atom bomb was dropped on Hiroshima and who ten years later developed leukaemia as a result of radiation. Roger Vaughan Carr's *Firestorm!* is not just about the holocaust which on Ash Wednesday in 1983 claimed the lives of victims in both Victoria and South Australia, it is about the aftermath of the survival and the ensuing psychological damage to human lives. *The Inner Circle* by Gary Crew explores, among other things, two problems frequently faced in today's fractured society: an insecure white youth, a loner, who is trying to come to terms with his parents' break-up and their trying to buy his affection; and the predicament of an Aboriginal youth from a warm, accepting extended family adrift and misunderstood in a white person's city.

Experience, the starting point for all stories, whether it be part of an author's own life happenings or the observed and vicariously felt experience of others, is then shaped by language. The vocabulary and language patterns of true literature are harmonious with and attuned to the initiating experience, and are expertly and cunningly crafted by the author's skill and aesthetic sense.

The vocabulary of *Peter Rabbit*, for example 'implored him to exert himself'. 'It was a blue jacket with brass buttons, quite new', is neither emasculated nor trivialised. It is fullblooded and it flows rhythmically to catch a child's ear with sound patterns and so familiarises the listener/reader with the ways language can be best used to convey meaning. So with *Sadako, Firestorm!, The Inner Circle* and other works of literature. The author selects experience, then uses language to order and craft it into an appropriate and satisfying form.

Back in 1963 Rumer Godden, who has been writing successfully for children since 1946, supplied the *Horn Book Magazine* with an imaginary correspondence between Beatrix Potter and Mr V. Andal, editor for the De Base Publishing Company Inc. and who wanted Miss Potter to rewrite her books to a vocabulary limited to 450 words 'prepared by a trio of philologists' for a series of 'reissues, in a modern production, of famous books that have become classics for children'. The inducements extended over several weeks with Mr V. Andal explaining that his philologists 'are often able to help an author put his, or her, delightful thoughts into plain words — simple enough for a child to understand' (Godden 1973, pp. 133–139).

This satirical correspondence actually puts forward the crux of the argument that has been used to promote basal readers and reading schemes with their highly controlled (and therefore stilted and distorted) vocabulary and strictly structured sentence and language patterns. Worst of all, the subject matter of such reading materials is cosy, safe and highly artificial — because it comes not from the writer's immediate or felt experience of life but from what the writer imagines childhood experience to be, or, even worse, what the writer feels children *should* experience: safe, conservative family and social situations.

The basal reader mentality was and is far worse than the wide range of juvenile fiction which dominated the children's book market until the 1950s — epitomised by Enid Blyton, Laura Lee Hope (*The Bobbsey Twins*), Capt. W.E. Johns and Georgette Heyer — and which still abounds in cheap romance and adventure series. At least the above writers tell swiftly paced yarns which hook potential readers and provide them with the necessary bulk for their literary diet — 'roughage' as Peter Dickinson puts it, arguing that sometimes all children need to read or reread something 'which makes absolutely no intellectual or emotional demands on them' (Dickinson 1973, pp. 101–103). Many postgraduate students in my own literature classes admit that they went through a phase of reading indiscriminately, including a great deal of trash. As one put it, she came to *Pride and Prejudice* via The Famous Five.

Formula fiction, for this is what it is, may well be the bait that lures some children to books and helps establish the reading habit; but it is not literature. And a diet wholly of literary candy floss is hardly likely to encourage linguistic growth or literary maturity.

True literature nourishes the mind, promotes sensory awareness, develops emotional sensitivity and provides a rich linguistic environment.

Well-written fiction, along with good non-fiction, nourishes the mind with facts, as well as with ideas — what could be called 'hard knowledge'. At the age of nine I learned what a coracle was when I first discovered *Treasure Island* and read about Ben Gunn's clumsy homemade boat. Decades later I recalled the incident when visiting the British Museum and seeing a real coracle. My first visit to England became the following of a familiar map: Sherlock Holmes's Baker Street and Wordsworth's Westminster Bridge were familiar territory. Scores of Australian children who have never visited Sydney are, through reading Ruth Park's *Playing Beatie Bow*, familiar with The Rocks area as it is today and also with the sanitation and living conditions of life there in 1873.

Ideas also — or 'soft' knowledge — come from good fiction. Nadia Wheatley's picture book, *My Place*, illustrated by Donna Rawlins, helps develop the concept of time and social change just as her *The House that was Eureka* makes the point that history repeats itself, but in a slightly different guise.

In *Playing Beatie Bow*, Abigail, the protagonist, ponders the concept of time and comes to the conclusion that it is 'a great river, always moving, always changing, but with the same water flowing between its banks from source to sea' (Park 1980, p. 195). The characters in Sophie Masson's ideas-packed fantasy *Fire in the Sky* also speculate about the nature of time. A girl who lives in medieval France says 'There are other worlds besides the ones we live in, that's all. What is time after all? If it is a road, we can travel back and forth on it can we not?' To which the philosophising Tad, an Australian boy from the present, replies 'It's like the supernova . . . It happened long before your time, yet it's still happening, it's not finished. You can't see it here, now, but where we come from, it's there bright' (Masson 1990, pp. 49–50).

Abigail in *Beatie Bow* returns in time to the crowded, jostling, smelly, raucous life of The Rocks. The reader's senses are assailed — and sharpened — by what Abigail experiences there: 'the smell of rotting seaweed, ships, wood smoke, human ordure, and horses and harness'. Sprigs of dried lavender burnt on the coals camouflage the odour from the chamber pot. Through Abigail's senses the reader experiences ugliness as well as beauty:

> She was in a dark, evil-smelling room, and before her stood a mountainous woman holding a blood-spattered fist to her hairy chin. She must have weighed nearly a hundred kilos; there seemed no end to her full skirts and vast blouse of gaudy striped silk. Out of the sleeves poked sausagey hands covered in rings. Ferret eyes gleamed at Abigail; the sausage hands filled themselves with her hair and jerked brutally (Park 1980, p. 87).

Not only does Abigail — thus the reader — extend her sensory perceptions through her return to a Victorian Sydney slum, but through her association with the Tallisker family and especially the boy, Judah, her emotional susceptibility is enlarged and refined. Because her emotions are aroused she can begin to understand her parents' strained then healed relationship and her own ambivalent attitude to her father.

Literature, from the old folk and fairy tales through ancient myth and legend, helps develop sensory and emotional acuity. Perrault's story of Cinderella not only develops a sense of the cinders and grit of the hearth along with the glitter and glamour of the ball but it also gives hope to the lonely, the deposed and the insecure child.

The ancient tale *Diamonds and Toads* is structured on conflicting sensory and emotional images, as well as opening up concepts of moral worth. Beowulf's visit to Hrothgar at Heorot is a brilliant collage of sensations; his epic fight with Grendel arouses feelings of desperation, determination and endurance. Demeter's long search for Penelope speaks of a desolate and deprived earth as well as a mother's pain. When Perseus slays Medusa horror writhes around the victor's feet even as his winged sandals speed him on his way to Andromeda.

Literature, then, opens up the world of ideas, transcends time and place, titillates the senses so that the reader, like Edmund in C.S. Lewis's *The Lion, the Witch and the Wardrobe* yearning for the White Witch's turkish delight, will want more and more. Children who lead only safe, secure and protected lives can vicariously learn something of want, hunger, fear and loathing. The sharp edge of reality may not be present but the reader becomes at least a spectator and learns that life can be cruel, unfair and deeply painful. More importantly, perhaps, the lonely, the mistreated, the outcast, the outsider, the ugly duckling who is 'different' learns not only the comforting fact that there are others who feel equally rejected (and there always have been) but that there can indeed be 'a happy issue out of all our afflictions', provided one perseveres and faces calamity with steadfastness, endurance and some courage. Thus literature gives birth to faith.

At its best, a work of literature, because of its aesthetic qualities of unity, harmony and wholeness, possesses a radiance which lights up the human spirit — the 'soul' — producing what James Joyce terms an epiphany — a revelation. For me, R.L. Stevenson's *Treasure Island* and Lewis Carroll's *Alice's Adventures in Wonderland* brought such an awakening; the experience described by C.S. Lewis as 'surprised by joy'. I have witnessed this spiritual quickening in the lives of children, brought about by books like Colin Thiele's *Storm Boy*, Patricia Wrightson's *The Nargun and the Stars* and Joan Phipson's *Bianca*. One small child said of Madeleine Winch's picture book, *Come By Chance*, 'It made me understand that I need never be truly alone'.

So in literature as in life, thought, emotion, understanding, sensory perceptiveness and language are inextricably related. A reader's experience is constantly being enriched by language, and, at the same time, language is sharpening experience because it is providing the tool by which to recognise and name it.

Literature and the Reader

Literature, then, is a two-way interactive process. The reader brings to the text — both verbal and visual in the case of illustrated books — his or her perceptions of real life experiences then takes from the text what the author and/or illustrator has to offer; but in proportion to the reader's previous experience and literary environment. So enrichment from reading is a spiralling process. Each new book that is assimilated into the reader's experience provides new insights that can be brought to bear on the next book read — provided the book is true literature and has something worthwhile to offer. Disembodied basals and carefully tailored reading schemes are usually exercises merely for the sake of exercise and lead the reader nowhere.

A simple picture book like Eric Carle's *The Very Hungry Caterpillar* develops the concepts of number, size, the days of the week, certain types of food *and* metamorphosis through simple but highly imagistic language. The story opens with the alliterative lines 'In the light of the moon a little egg lay on a leaf'. It then leads the perceptive reader to the understanding — perhaps even the revelation — that we must be true to our own natures if we are to achieve our potential and become all that we are capable of becoming.

Any child saturated with nursery rhymes and folk tales early knows intuitively that the words — the text — mean more than they say. They may not know that 'Mary, Mary Quite Contrary' originally referred to Mary Queen of Scots, but they do pick up messages about defiant contrariness, often puzzling in a fascinated way with what some today call the subtext or the deeper structure of the rhyme. The old tale of 'Rumpelstiltskin' implies that when we name something we gain power over it. Jason's quest for the golden fleece is one of the great archetypal narratives symbolising humanity's ongoing search for honour, fame and riches, whatever the cost. It is a prototype for Michael Ende's *The Neverending Story*. Rose's cat in Jenny Wagner's *John Brown, Rose and the Midnight Cat* can symbolise a threat from the outside, or death, or it can simply remain a domestic pet, according to what the reader brings to the story. If, as it does to some, it overtly represents death, something not to be feared, the reader could be on the way to apprehending the imagery of Ted Hughes's *The Iron Man* and, ultimately, the complex social and emotional symbolism of Russell Hoban's *The Mouse and His Child* or Victor Kelleher's *Baily's Bones*.

Through early exposure to nursery rhyme, story telling, picture book sharing and being read to, children gradually come to discern how books work, the way texts are to be read, that reading between the lines and beyond the lines is far more important than reading the lines themselves. Margaret Meek in *How Texts Teach What Readers Learn* demonstrates that given exposure to sufficient graded multilayered texts, texts which reveal by implication, a young reader moves smoothly from reading for story — what happens next — to interpreting the mythic implications of the text. *Rosie's Walk* by Pat Hutchins, discussed at length by Meek (Meek 1988, pp. 8–13), can lead on to John Burningham's *Mr Gumpy's Outing*, then to his *Come Away from the Water, Shirley* and then to his *Granpa*. Anthony Browne's *Bear Hunt* and Annalena McAfee's *Kirsty Knows Best*, with illustrations by Anthony Browne, are subtle indicators that things aren't always what they seem on the surface, that there is a 'hidden agenda' in most human activity. This understanding is crucial to a full appreciation of junior novels like Florence Parry Heide's

The Shrinking of Treehorn or Christine Nostlinger's *Conrad: The Hilarious Adventures of a Factory-made Child*.

The implication inherent in Maurice Sendak's *Outside Over There* that there are hidden forces, both malign and benign, at work seeking to disrupt our equilibrium, a recurring theme in modern literature, is easily grasped by a child reared on folk tales. This understanding will open up a full enjoyment of Lewis's *The Lion, the Witch and the Wardrobe*, Allan Baillie's *Megan's Star*, Victor Kelleher's novels, especially *The Red King* and *Baily's Bones*, Gillian Rubinstein's *Space Demons*, young adult fiction including Katherine Scholes's *The Blue Chameleon* and Gary Crew's brilliantly crafted *Strange Objects* — or even junior fantasies such as Emily Rodda's *Pigs Might Fly*, *The Best Kept Secret* and *Finders Keepers*.

If fulness in reading — the development of 'the complete reader' — is a steady developmental progress dependent upon the reader being supplied with the necessary literary food for each new insight, it is essential that parents and teachers be familiar with a wide range of texts to meet the growth needs of each individual. For reading is as idiosyncratic as living and growing.

Nevertheless, as in physical development, there are patterns — however irregular — of growth, and basic nutrients of which adults should be aware. The alert teacher knows not only his or her students and what they look for in their reading, but also the books that will satisfy their demands. In matching books to each student's interests, reading ability and level of literary growth the teacher will be ensuring that the individual child is developing linguistically and in literary appreciation. So each class will have a judiciously selected range of literary forms and genres — picture books, novels, realism, fantasy, historical fiction and also books of varying complexity in plot, characterisation, setting and theme. The books will cross stereotyped gender roles with patterns of culture. They will broaden children's perceptions of literary form including humour.

What do Children Look for in their Reading?

Plot

In response to the above question most children reply immediately 'A good story; excitement, adventure, mystery'. E.M. Forster in *Aspects of the Novel* insists that the novel must tell a story; what is termed 'plot'. In the past many children's authors wrote to a formula: becoming lost, trapped by the tide, captured by villains and the inevitable escape or rescue, the chase, a fight. There are still plenty of formula situations in children's novels, even in Australia: the sheltered city child running the gauntlet of rural hazards; the country kid overwhelmed by city sophistication or corrupted by it. Australian children's fiction has a plethora of preoccupied children who get into trouble for being inattentive in class. Hackneyed predictable plots are all very well, but only for the inexperienced or hesitant reader who needs to be able to predict correctly and is developing confidence in reading.

There are, after all, only a small number of basic experiential human predicaments, so the challenge to the writer is to find a new form or expression for familiar situations. Gillian Rubinstein in *Space Demons* and *Skymaze* gives life to a menacing computer game as a variation on age-old themes: the ongoing fight between good and evil, love and hate, and the hero's perpetual growth toward maturity.

An author must always be looking for something original to say and say it with style. Plots can be episodic as in Rutgers Van der Loeff's *Children on the Oregon Trail*, or Esther Hautzig's *The Endless Steppe* or even Emily Rodda's *Finders Keepers*, where the adventure is sustained and developed in a series of self-contained episodes; or they can follow the classic dramatic structure of an introduction, followed by a series of crises leading up to a climax, after which comes the dénouement, the conclusion or rounding off. Gillian Rubinstein's *Answers to Brut*, Allan Baillie's *Little Brother* or Caroline Macdonald's *The Lake at the End of the World* follow the mode of a rising and falling action which can actually be graphed.

Most plots for children involve some form of adventure: adventuring, or going forth on a journey, either through a series of escapades, or merely by moving forward in time, the adventure of growing up as in Simon French's *All We Know* or Libby Gleeson's *I am Susannah*.

Adventuring almost always involves danger and things going wrong (*Treasure Island*; Theodore Taylor's *The Cay*), a state of disequilibrium to which stability needs to be restored. French's Arkie, in *All We Know*, is at a turning point when her life is full of minor conflicts that need to be resolved for her growth to maturity.

Conflict is a major ingredient of all plots: people with the environment; person against person; people with authority; good versus evil; social opposites; youth versus age; the divided self. A see-sawing unresolved conflict develops tension which can also be graphed as the action rises and falls; and often the conflict arises out of a mystery: what is the secret of the cave in Helen Frances's *The Devil's Stone*?

The action and conflict in today's novels are usually as much internal as external. Conflicts within a character's psyche — for example, many of Joan Phipson's young people or the children in Allan Baillie's *Hero* — are brought to the surface and faced, if not resolved, in the course of the physical action. Whether the action is internal or external the plot should never be static. Children need action in their stories.

Character

Danger and trouble come to people, individuals. Frank Richards who wrote the 'Billy Bunter' stories in *The Magnet* created stereotypes: Billy

Bunter, the Fat Owl of the Remove at Greyfriars School, the headstrong lively undisciplined Harry Wharton and his chums Bob Cherry, Frank Nugent, Johnny Bull and Hurree Jamset Ram Singh, all characterised by their names. Stereotypes still abound in today's fiction: Robin Klein's bitchy girls and her brash insecure Erica Yurken of *Hating Alison Ashley*; Max Dann's incorrigible bully, Peter Dusting, worst best friend of the fearful Roger Thesaurus (*Adventures With My Worst Best Friend*); Maureen Stewart's revolting liar Maria Smales of the seemingly endless *Dear Emily* series, or Dianne Bates' Grandma Cadbury who drives a semi-trailer called Tootsie.

As with formula plots, stereotypic characters — caricatures or stock figures — like the thousands seen weekly in television sitcoms and soapies, support the fledgling reader by being recognisable, predictable and reassuring. (Klein's Penny Pollard is a supreme example.) Such characters are usually 'flat' — the reader doesn't see them in the round (although we do see the underbelly of the brash Erica Yurken) — and they tend to be static: more of the same as in the *Dear Emily* books. Complex, fully rounded characters, on the other hand, make far greater demands on the reader's sensory, emotional and intellectual powers. Katherine Paterson's *Bridge to Terabithia* is ultimately so satisfying because the reader is given the opportunity to know Jess Aarons and his friend Leslie so intimately that when Leslie is killed the reader grieves with, rather than for, Jess. Cynthia Voigt's Dicey Tillerman and Jeff Greene are two of the most memorable and poignant characters in contemporary fiction because their lives unfold as do those of each of us, slowly and gradually.

The reader pieces the saga together as it develops over some half dozen related books which are the antithesis of a 'series'. Ivan Southall's Josh Plowman may not please the macho adult reader, but he is convincingly real. We know him from the inside, out.

Clifton Fadiman, writing of Mark Twain, provides the clue to the success of writers like Paterson, Voigt, Southall, French and Gleeson.

> Now when Mark Twain wrote *Tom Sawyer* and *Huckleberry Finn*, he never stopped to figure out whether his 'boy psychology' was correct, or whether his story was properly adapted to a given age level. He wrote because he was passionately interested in himself, and the Mississippi River in himself, and the boy still alive in himself. Children ever since have unconsciously felt this intense reality, and that's what they've loved. (Fadiman 1946, p. xvii)

Simon French confesses that he has personal sympathy with the outsider, the loner, the introvert. Modern children's literature, including Australian, includes a goodly proportion of Snook Pascoes suffering from a sense of inadequacy (*Blue Fin* by Colin Thiele) possibly because writers tend to be introverted and because the majority of children, simply because they *are* children, are questioning their self-sufficiency. Fortunately there are writers who also focus on intelligent, self-assured characters, especially girls — E.L. Konigsburg's *From the Mixed-Up Files of Mrs Basil E. Frankweiler* or Brian Caswell's *Merryll of the Stones*, are both books which exemplify the modern trend toward freeing up gender roles.

Since Gene Kemp's *The Turbulent Term of Tyke Tiler*, children's literature has had its fair share of stalwart, up and doing girls, and, in Robin Klein, for example, not a few wimpish boys.

Multiculturalism

Characters in children's books written in English prior to the 1950s were generally about white, middle-class Anglo-Saxons. The influx of black ex-colonials to Britain instigated a rush of multicultural books (Jan Needle's *My Mate Shofiq*) in Britain and the Negro ground swell in America resulted in a large number of black but universal characters in American fiction, from William Armstrong's powerful *Sounder* to Mildred Taylor's *Roll of Thunder, Hear My Cry*.

After an initial period of casting Aborigines and new Australians as racial stereotypes, then a phase of including somewhere in the book a token Aborigine or migrant family, Australian writers for children now generally reflect the truly multicultural nature of Australian society. Characters in Libby Hathorn's junior novels, for example *Paolo's Secret* or *Jezza Sez*, have names like Paolo Beccochi and Costa Dante who have relatives in Italy or Greece. Nadia Wheatley's *Five Times Dizzy* and *Dancing in the Anzac Deli* broke new ground by showing sympathetically the interaction inside as well as outside a migrant family. More recently Diana Kidd's *Onion Tears* focuses poignantly on the anguish of a boat child separated from her parents as well as her homeland and her pet canary. *Pigs and Honey* by Jeanie Adams realistically represents an Aboriginal extended family out on a pig hunt; and Margaret Sharpe's *The Traegar Kid* is the story of a visit to Brisbane from Alice Springs told through the eyes of a developing Aboriginal girl.

The characters in children's books are now as diverse and as multifaceted as is modern society itself.

Time and Place

There are no bounds on time and place. Indeterminate or generalised settings have given way to real towns, suburbs or country areas. One American sleuth was able to determine, by a close study of Patricia Wrightson's own work, the exact location of Wongadilla, Charlie and Edie's property in *The Nargun and the Stars*. Those who visit Wrightson recognise at once the setting for Mrs Tucker's house in *A Little Fear* and the locale of *Moon-Dark*. The geography of Joan Phipson's *Bianca* can be traced to the Wyangella Dam in New South Wales.

Paradoxically, the more specific the sense of place and time the more universal a book is likely to be in its implications. As a boy in primary school, Capt. Marryat's *The Children of the New Forest* and Harriet

Beecher Stowe's *Uncle Tom's Cabin* gave me a deep sense of belonging to and being part of a particular slice of history, and thus part of the ongoing life of 17th century Britain and 18th century America respectively. As an adult reader of children's books, Gary Crew's *Strange Objects* sharpened and refined images from my reading in history about the wreck of the *Batavia* off the coast of Western Australia in 1629 and the fate of the mutineers among the survivors. Crew, by recreating the landscape which Wouter Loos and his companion, Jan Pelgrom, traverse and by throwing the searchlight of psychological analysis on the two men, explores the timeless and universal theme of human relationships, particularly under stress and hardship. Another book, about the same shipwreck, Deborah Lisson's *The Devil's Own*, on the other hand, because the landscape is stage-crafted and the characters only figures on a screen, becomes merely another time-slip novel. There is little abiding sense of place.

In a helpful pamphlet, 'I Know That Place!', produced for the Primary English Teaching Association, Edel Wignell makes the point that setting has a far-reaching and profound effect on plot, character, mood and atmosphere as any reader of *Wuthering Heights* will attest! Wignell quotes Ruth Park in an interview telling how she attends to historical detail and setting; part of the secret of the success of *Playing Beatie Bow*. Also quoted by Wignell is my own reaction to Jeannie Baker's collage picture book, *Where the Forest Meets the Sea*, set in the Daintree Forest area in Northern Queensland, my belief that Baker's book 'confirms the value to man of elemental things and the enduring pattern of nature itself' (Saxby, in *Magpies*, March 1988, p. 21).

Wignell explains that:

> The quality of universality means that children can respond with 'I know that place!' whether the setting is familiar or unfamiliar in real life. Indeed this 'knowing' may extend to entirely imagined settings, such as C.S. Lewis's Narnia or Tolkien's Middle Earth. (Wignell 1989, p. 3)

Edel Wignell has herself used the inner city of Melbourne for *Escape by Deluge* which, along with Patricia Wrightson's *An Older Kind of Magic*, set in one of the government offices in Sydney's Bridge Street, adjacent to the Botanical Gardens, provides Australian readers with an understanding of what it is like to grow up in the heart of a city.

Earlier, Australian children's books tended to be set in the bush, on pastoral properties or in small country towns. Patricia Wrightson, then Eleanor Spence, then Lilith Norman moved the novel to the city. Lilith Norman in *The Shape of Three* was one of the first to contrast not only the geography but the accompanying social mores of Sydney's affluent harbour-side suburbs with the working-class thrift of its western outreaches. In *A Dream of Seas* she depicts perfectly the ethos of a seedy Bondi, epitomised by flats named Santa Rosa beyond which lie the sea, the surf and the board-riders in wet suits. Apart from the fact that the boy, Seasie, becomes one with the seals which obsess him, the Bondi setting is essential to the development of the plot and the innate theme conveyed in the title.

Setting, then, is an integral part of a novel's structure. Australian novels with local settings help provide a sense of national identity while novels with authentic exotic settings can help develop a sense of internationalism. At the highest level, books like *The Wind in the Willows, Storm Boy* or *A Dream of Seas* help attune the reader to the rhythms of nature and the universe.

Theme

The interaction of plot, setting and character provides the theme in a work of literature: the idea or ideas produced by the experience being explored by the author. Ultimately the worth of a work of fiction depends on the worthwhile nature of the theme and the artistry with which that theme is expressed in terms of plot, character, setting and structure.

Ephemeral pot-boilers and light escapist literature for adults or for children seldom handle enduring themes in anything but the most superficial way. Blytonesque adventures have, at best, the theme of wish fulfilment and self-gratification. Romantic fiction is seldom little more than 'sweet dreams'.

One of the signs of a healthy growth in children's literature is the development of socially relevant and sometimes complex themes. Nineteenth century children's fiction stressed manly fortitude and pious behaviour embedded in unrealistic themes of valour and vain glory. Early 20th century fiction used family solidarity and mutual helpfulness as recurring themes: the 'Little Women', 'Anne of Green Gables' syndrome. Mary Grant Bruce in Australia, through her Billabong series, dramatised the theme of mateship and social obligations, while Ethel Turner in her more serious novels raised questions about social welfare and the plight of the poor.

As early as 1880 in Australia, Louisa Anne Meredith in *Tasmanian Friends and Foes, Feathered, Furred and Finned* made a plea for the conservation of the natural environment in Tasmania. Our first well-known fantasy, Ethel Pedley's *Dot and the Kangaroo* (1899), is also an impassioned argument for the preservation of our wild life. The artistic problem with books such as *Dot and the Kangaroo*, which applies equally to a good many contemporary works, like Ruth Park's *My Sister Sif* or Midas Dekker's *Whale Lake*, is that the conservation theme is tacked onto rather than integrated with the structure. *My Sister Sif* and many other well-meaning books, along with the 19th century religious tracts, are blatantly propagandist, with passages of pure pedantry and didacticism. Children don't necessarily shy away from books that preach at them, but even the best — the most enduring — of books from the Sunday School movement, such as titles by Hesba Stretton, seek to persuade by example rather than by admonition. One of the few highly commendable contemporary Christian books, for example, is Nan Hunt's *Never Tomorrow*, which subtly draws the distinction between true Christian charity — in the full meaning of 1 Corinthians 13 — and the brainwashing domination practised by many 'way-out' sects in the name of religion. A successful series of conservation books is that by S.A. Wakefield beginning with *Bottersnikes and Gumbles* where the strongly imagined but disgusting Bottersnikes represent the forces of pollution and the droll, squashy Gumbles contain something akin to a life force.

Children's books today range widely in theme and dare to tackle previously taboo subjects. From Denmark has come, to my knowledge, the first children's book dealing sympathetically with a homosexual relationship, and the Australian writer Morris Gleitzman in *Two Weeks With the Queen* tackles the theme of approaching death including that of an AIDS victim. Death, the final taboo, is the theme, treated without sentimentality, in not a few fine modern children's novels including Paterson's *Bridge to Terabithia*, Michelle Magorian's *Goodnight Mr. Tom*, Doris Buchanan Smith's *A Taste of Blackberries*, Jean Little's *Mama's Going to Buy You a Mocking Bird* and Libby Hathorn's *Thunderwith*, along with picture books like Barbara Bolton's *Edward Wilkins and His Friend Gwendoline*, Margaret Wild's *The Very Best of Friends* and Mem Fox's *Sophie*.

Humour

Although today's children, in particular, are prepared to contemplate through their literature weighty themes such as war and peace, social justice, conservation, even death and dying, they also look for humour in their reading — funny books.

The source of what children find humorous varies with age and with the individual. While there are stages of humour, these stages can co-exist and quite old children can still respond to the toddler's yukky and lavatory humour, but in a more or less sophisticated form, as instanced by the enormous popularity of Roald Dahl's whizzpopping *BFG* and of Paul Jennings' stories 'Spaghetti Pig Out', 'Skeleton on the Dunny' and his junior novel, *The Paw Thing*, which features a cat called Singanpoo.

The development of a sense of humour parallels intellectual and emotional development. As children perceive the complexities of life so the opportunities for humour increase, the visual giving way to the verbal.

Middle primary children respond to the planning and setting up of practical jokes and to outrageous behaviour — as in Libby Hathorn's *All About Anna* and *Looking Out for Sampson*. Physical clowning and contortion is to them hilariously funny — for example, Ruth Park's *When the Wind Changed*; and this is the peak period for joke books, riddles, puns and Knock Knocks, hence the popularity of Dahl's *Charlie and the Giant Glass Elevator* and other books with inbuilt jokes. Duncan Ball well knows that this age group delights in thinking and talking animals taking a rise out of humans, as happens in his *Selby* series. Anna Fienberg's *Wiggy and Boa* also exploits the absurd and the impossible, always a source of humour.

Upper primary children still enjoy insults and hostile humour, clichéd unoriginal and repulsive jokes (*How to Eat Fried Worms* by Thomas Rockwell), but they are also responsive to tongue-in-cheek ironic humour as in Dick King-Smith's animal books, for example *Harry's Mad*, or Sid Fleischman's folksy send up of the hill-billy farmer, *McBroom's Wonderful One-Acre Farm*, or his spoof on medieval royalty, *The Whipping Boy*.

In general, the sources of humour are universal: exaggeration, incongruity, surprise, ridicule, defiance, the absurd. Slapstick comedy and verbal humour are perennial and are always prone to excessive use; but even vulgarity, as Raymond Briggs has proved, can be handled with style.

Humour helps reduce anxiety, makes psychological pain bearable, expresses subconscious fears and wishes, increases flexibility of thought and stretches verbal acuity.

Techniques Authors Employ

Young readers may well find certain authors and books funny or appealing for other reasons without necessarily being able to say why. Only gradually does an understanding of literary technique develop, and it is the role of the teacher subtly to bring about an awareness of how an author gains a certain effect. Understanding of the technical aspects of any art form — music, painting, dance, drama, literature — increases the audience's enjoyment of the end result.

So books in school and class libraries will range from conventional narratives, adventure and romantic literature to stories with an ironic twist or which are subtly satiric. They will use a variety of narrative techniques, from the conventional third-person approach to variations of first-person narrative such as stream of consciousness, letters, diaries and journals. They will vary in tone, style and what is expected by the author of the reader.

By alerting individuals, groups or, at times, the whole class to the wide range of literary techniques — discussed below — that authors use to give relevance and potency to the experience explored in their books, teachers are truly implementing a reading program which has literature as its base.

Irony

When Peter Rabbit comes across a white cat in Mr McGregor's garden Beatrix Potter describes the scene with light irony, akin to innuendo: 'Peter thought it best to go away without speaking to her; he had heard about cats from his cousin, little Benjamin Bunny'. Pamela Allen's picture book *My Cat Maisie* is based on the central irony that a small boy can be wilder than a stray cat. Through exposure to such early examples of situational and verbal irony — 'The Boy Who Cried Wolf', 'The Fox and the Grapes' and other fables of Aesop — children begin to realise that words and images can imply more than is being said. Indeed the actual intent can be expressed in words which carry the opposite meaning as in the old Epaminondas stories. 'Brer Rabbit and the Tar Baby' is a classic example of irony.

Satire

More biting than irony is satire which ridicules human frailty, institutions or beliefs through humour and wit, 'sending' up what is being ridiculed. There are countless reluctant or kindly dragons in contemporary children's literature satirising the stereotyped dragons of mythology. *Pongwiffy: A Witch of Dirty Habits* by Kaye Umansky belongs to a long line of satirised witches — who are thus rendered impotent. Instead of being horrific they become ridiculous.

Graham Oakley, well known for his *Churchmice* books, has written and illustrated two satirical extended picture books suitable for primary and even secondary school children. *Henry's Quest* is about a latter-day Don Quixote, a bicycle-riding knight on a quest — for petrol. In *Once Upon a Time: A Prince's Fantastic Journey* elements of the fairy tale are treated ironically and with some satire in a mock-heroic style. In the same vein is Ann Weld's *Fractured Fairy Tales and Ruptured Rhymes*. The most sustained witty and cohesive satire for Australian children is undoubtedly Randolph Stow's *Midnite The Story of a Wild Colonial Boy* which pokes fun at the bushranging ethos, along with colonial and British society in the time of Queen Victoria. An enjoyment of these books prepares the way for the appreciation of the great satires of literature such as Swift's *Gulliver's Travels* and is a test of intelligence and sophistication in reading.

Point of View: Narrative Stance

Irony and satire frequently work by inverting a traditional point of view. Anthony Browne does this with the fairytale 'Hansel and Gretel' by illustrating the Brothers Grimm story using modern settings: a working-class family with hard-faced uncaring parents and two bewildered children. Fiona French illustrates her *Snow White in New York* in art deco style and claims that 'Snow White's stepmother was the classiest dame in New York. But no one knew that she was the Queen of the Underworld. She liked to see herself in the New York Mirror.' *The True Story of the 3 Little Pigs* by A. Wolf as told to Jon Scieszka and illustrated by Lane Smith claims that the old version is actually a frame-up which takes place when Wolf walks down the street to ask his neighbour for a cup of sugar to make a birthday cake for his dear old granny.

Person

Most narratives are related in the third person by an omniscient author and move chronologically in time. Ethel Turner's *Seven Little Australians*, among other things, traces Meg's growth into young womanhood through the eyes of a slightly amused onlooker.

Often in children's literature the voice of an implied narrator breaks through. Although Simon French's *Cannily, Cannily* is told in the third person the voice is clearly that of Trevor, the son of itinerant parents: 'they were moving to another town now, further to the north. It was like this all the time and with bemused resignation he guessed that the next place would be much the same as the last.'

The step to first-person narrative is a short one. The age, gender, outlook and temperament of the narrator becomes an indicator of the implied reader. Duncan Ball's Roger who relates *The Ghost and the Goggle Box* series brings a note of incredulous credibility to quite fantastic tales: 'I expected to hear music come out of the speakers but instead there was only a faint rumbling noise'. Thus the extraordinary is authenticated just as it is in Emily Rodda's *Crumbs!* which begins with a part disclaimer: 'Now that I'm a bit older, I can see why my parents didn't believe me.'

Robin Klein in *Hating Alison Ashley* uses Erica's voice to establish her as the put-upon long-suffering hypochondriac. In *Laurie Loved Me Best* Klein alternates the two personas of Julia and Andre to establish two contrasting lifestyles that have sufficient pain in common to draw the two girls together.

Diana Kidd in *The Day Grandma Came to Stay (and Spoilt my Life)* has her narrator include letters to help the reader see more than one side of the story and to flesh out the narrator's personality. In *Onion Tears* Kidd again uses first-person narrative plus letters to provide background information to Nam-Huong's present situation and to underline the inherent pathos of her story.

Stream of Consciousness

Whether the author chooses to tell the story in the third or the first person it happens increasingly that the thoughts, musings, internal monologue of the main character are shared with the reader. Both Simon French and Libby Gleeson, along with other writers, use italic type to indicate the free flow of associative thinking. Jenny Pausaker in *Can You Keep a Secret?* set in Melbourne in the Great Depression of the 1930s, and which aims to show that capitalists and socialists (commos) have human failings and strengths in common, uses a boy from the wealthy suburb of Kew as narrator. At the beginning of each chapter she uses italics to show Graham's ruminations on what is happening and how he is feeling about it. Thus the first-person narrator, rather than the author, becomes the commentator and an arbiter of ideas.

Journals, Letters, Diaries

A character's thoughts and feelings are often best expressed through some intensely personal form of writing. Beverly Cleary in the USA established the letter form in *Dear Mr Henshaw* where a troubled boy pours out his heart to his favourite author whose replies can be gathered from the missing correspondence. Maureen Stewart in her voluminous *Dear Emily* series balances Maria's picture of her brother by having Greg also write to Emily in *Love from Greg*.

Diaries can be facetious and lightly ironical — for example, Margaret Wild's *The Diary of Megan Moon (Soon to be Rich and Famous)* — or used to reveal deep hurt in an intimate if wry way as in Frank Willmott's *Breaking Up*. The most poignant of all fictional journals is that of Marina, the elective mute in John Marsden's 1988 Book of the Year, *So Much to Tell You*.

Increasingly, authors make use of letters, reports and other 'point of view' materials to develop a complex multifaceted view of their characters. Libby Gleeson in *Dodger* combines third-person narrative, stream of consciousness (in italics), personal histories, letters, notes and commentary to develop both external and internal action. Writing for young adults, Nadia Wheatley in *The House that was Eureka* and *The Blooding* intersperses her narrative with newspaper reports which act as a dramatic 'chorus' commenting on the action. Gary Crew, also, uses what art critics would call post-modernist techniques. Aidan Chambers, the English writer, has in public lectures openly acknowledged his debt to the techniques of the modern media — close-up, frozen frames, flashbacks, panning — in his experimental novels, *Breaktime, Dance on My Grave* and *Now I Know*. Even in *The Present Takers*, a novel about bullying among school girls aimed at primary-age readers, Chambers constructs a grid or a network rather than a linear narrative.

The narrative mode or discourse of contemporary children's literature has borrowed not only from movies and the modern media but even from newer forms of fiction games such as Choose Your Own Adventure and Fighting Fantasies. Gillian Rubinstein's *Beyond the Labyrinth* not only features a boy who is a devotee of fighting fantasies but provides alternative endings — 'if you threw over 6' or '6 or under'. The book is digitally arranged in sections which tick forward relentlessly. Children could profitably discuss with their peers and with teachers the contemporary proliferation of experimental forms and narrative techniques. They could even be encouraged to write down their own personal viewpoint of classroom incidents, using as motivation Rachel Flynn's *I Hate Fridays: Stories From Koala Hills Primary School*.

Tone

The point of view and the narrative stance help develop the tone of a book. Robin Klein's Penny Pollard, through her letters, diaries and commentaries, establishes a tone which mocks authority and middle-class conventionality beneath which lies a basic need to be loved and accepted. So it is with *Hating Alison Ashley.*

Robin Klein, like Judy Blume in America and Roald Dahl in Britain, is able to establish a 'chummy' tone, where the author acts as confidante and forms an alliance with the reader against the stuffiness of the establishment. Such authors offer literary bribes to their readers, who should be encouraged to examine carefully the technique at work. Here is Dahl writing of his grandmother in a self-revelatory book called *The Witches*: 'I couldn't believe my grandmother would be lying to me. She went to church every morning of the week and said grace before every meal and somebody who did that would never tell lies. I was beginning to believe every word she spoke.' For using such an approach Dahl has been labelled 'subversive'. Both he and Paul Jennings certainly establish a nudge-nudge, wink-wink tone and capitalise on the irreverence of the young. Jennings in 'Cow Dung Custard' mixes the tone of the tall story — Dad 'once grew a pumpkin that was so big it took four men to lift it' — with the bar room joke, 'the kids at school called me the Cow Dung Kid'.

Margaret Mahy, the New Zealand writer, in her stories and novels for primary school readers also uses an exaggerated mocking tone tossing about language like a light-hearted Dylan Thomas. With titles like *The Great Piratical Rumbustification, The Great White Man-Eating Shark, Raging Robots and Unruly Uncles* or *The Blood-and-Thunder Adventure on Hurricane Peak* she trades on melodrama enriched with literary allusion, scientific speculation and polysyllabic language that rolls off the tongue. Margaret Mahy writes with apparent but deceptive simplicity. Wit, irony and exaggeration abound. Her characters are larger than life yet like Norvin, the pretend great white man-eating shark, they contain the very essence of complex human nature.

Style

So each writer through his or her idiosyncratic view of life, way of thinking, mode of expression adopts an individual and unique style. Margaret Mahy has a perpetual dry but impish grin breaking through her use of language. Norvin has frightened the swimmers of Caramel Cove by pretending to be a great white man-eating shark.

> There, nuzzling up to him, was a great white man-eating shark — a female. Norvin was such a good actor that she did not realize he was merely pretending to be a shark. She gave him a very loving glance.

Gillian Rubinstein in *Space Demons* can write with slow deliberation, creating an atmosphere of threat and menacing evil: 'The darkness stretched away forever, into eternity. The whole universe was blocked out.'

Allan Baillie can move the reader to tears while still seeming to remain laconic. In his short story 'Only Ten' Hussein is an enigma, nicknamed

The Shah. At a swimming carnival he reluctantly strips away his purple T-shirt.

> The main scar, a bloodless seam, ran from his right shoulder to his left hip. The second scar was a second belly-button punched in his side. Marks of shrapnel and a bullet. A soldier's wounds.

Style provides a writer's literary features, as recognisable and as varied as the human face or form. Experienced readers intuitively recognise a writer from the style; inexperienced readers need help and encouragement. But in coming to know a writer's style the reader is welcoming a friend.

The Implied Reader

Just as in life people seek among the like-minded for their friends, so writers, often unconsciously, single out their readership. Tone and style, narrative stance, the interaction of plot and character, the simplicity or complexity of theme, choice of vocabulary and idiom — all imply a readership. Bob Graham's picture book, *Crusher is Coming*, through its cover, endpapers, title page and opening text implies a family-oriented and perceptive early school age listener–reader. 'Peter has just cleared his room. He is giving all his stuffed animals to his sister Claire, because tough Crusher is coming home after school tomorrow.' The implication of the word 'tough' fills in any gaps in the reader's understanding of Peter, provided the reader has some experience of family and peer relationships.

The length of the opening sentence (6½ lines), on the other hand, plus the number of co-ordinated clauses along with the title of the book *The 27th Annual African Hippopotamus Race* by Morris Lurie, implies a lively primary reader with a sense of humour. The dust jacket of Jenny Pausaker's *Can You Keep a Secret?* implies a psychological adventure thriller, but the opening mental monologue, the setting, the subject and the way it is developed implies a reader who is not only politically aware but who can make connections between real life and fiction. (There is frequent reference to Graham's addiction to *Chums* and his self-modelling on heroes of the Empire.)

Aidan Chambers says 'the idea of the implied reader derives from the understanding that it takes two to say a thing. In effect it suggests that in his book an author creates a relationship with a reader in order to discover the meaning of the text.' (Chambers 1980, p. 252). It would not be beyond willing upper-primary readers to examine the ways in which Pausaker or Gleeson, or French or any other writer creates this relationship and what the text means to them.

Tell-tale Gaps

Chambers also uses the term tell-tale gap when an author refuses to spell out all the intended meaning but leaves space for the reader to manoeuvre the meaning for himself. Sometimes the reader is left to close the book off because of an unresolved ending — or to extend the life in the book beyond its pages. The formula adventure story, domestic comedy or yarn leaves no breathing spaces. Chambers discusses crucial gaps in Maurice Sendak's *Where the Wild Things Are*, Alan Garner's *The Stone Book Quartet* and Reiner Zimnik's *The Crane* (1980, p. 265). Bob Graham always refuses total closure even in picture books for beginning readers.

Simon French's Arkie in *All We Know* not only has a life beyond the book, but the significance of the photographs she takes and the one she steals from a cave and then returns is never entirely spelled out. French leaves that for the reader to ponder.

Patricia Wrightson's Mrs Tucker in *A Little Fear* makes a last defiant gesture of burning the fowl house but the reader is left to work out the consequences. The closing poetic pages of Wrightson's *Balyet* carry all the weight of poetic imagery. The reader is free to interrogate the text, as is true of all worthwhile fiction. The gaps can be filled with the reverberations set up by the text.

The Range of Literature

Children's literature, then, is as wide-ranging as the authors who write it and the children who read it. But if children merely master the mechanics of decoding and do not take meaning from and respond to the text they are merely 'barking at print'. And if they do not become committed and enthusiastic habitual readers they are passing up the opportunity for personal enrichment and leaving untouched a literary smorgasbord which can be as nourishing as it is tempting.

Teachers, then, need to sample and know the wide range of children's literature, from wordless books, through concept books for the pre-schooler, picture stories that demonstrate that print has meaning and that 'story' is one way of ordering and making sense of our world, to the various genres of the novel. As children wander around and explore intellectually within the framework of story they can often test hypotheses and relate their own experience to that of the characters in the story. Are single-parent families necessarily deprived, or can there be compensations? Why do certain people establish a special relationship, or bonding? How does environment affect the individual's perception of life and life's values? These are the sorts of questions literature can raise.

Non-fiction can also raise questions, but it also often gives, rather than suggests, answers. Factual books provide information. Some works of non-fiction raise important questions, too, and because of the skill in the writing and the style excite the senses and evoke an emotional response.

Round Buildings, Square Buildings and Buildings That Wiggle Like a Fish by Phillip M. Isaacson combines brilliant photography with verbal imagery that is highly poetic: 'In the moonlight it [The Taj Mahal] becomes the old emperor, asleep and dreaming.' The study of non-fiction is too vast a subject to be included here, but there is no reason why books such as Isaacson's should be excluded from the literature program.

Poetry and Verse

Ideally a child's first introduction to literature should be oral. Stories, often expressed in verse or formulaic patterns of language, existed long before they were written down.

Fragments of old stories, popular catchcries and snippets of linguistic fun belonging to the common people — the folk — survive in the form of nursery rhymes and action songs. Their modern counterparts carry on the tradition as playground chants and rhymes, skipping and counting games, autograph verse and parodies of advertising jingles, political slogans and the like.

Although there are now many excellent illustrated collections of nursery rhymes available they best serve as reference material for parents and teachers. The rhymes, like folk and fairy tales, are best heard and learnt aurally. While the language patterns are being enjoyably and unconsciously absorbed the listener's stimulated imagination is busy forming private images. Later, the words can appear on paper to be seen as the symbolic representation of that which has been internalised with pleasure. Good illustrations can at that point help a child to realise that there are many images of the same reality.

Children have their own currency of playground rhymes, limericks, rude verse, insults and taunts as attested by the Opies in England (Opie 1959), Ian Turner (1969) and June Factor in Australia. Factor's work resulted in the publication of her collections beginning with *Far Out, Brussel Sprout!*, enormously successful with children delighting in adult recognition of their own subculture. This publishing phenomenon led to a spate of childish doggerel, *Putrid Poems*, *Vile Verse* and the like, a little of which goes a long way, and which can be used cautiously in the classroom.

Humorous verse, however, is perennially popular, much of it embodying witty word play, irony and light satire. Ogden Nash and Edward Lear were forerunners of Australia's Doug MacLeod whose *In the Garden of Bad Things* introduced the mode of horror poems and whose *The Fed Up Family Album* takes a satirical look at family life (somewhat less kindly than does Michael Rosen in Britain), and who helped bring poetry back into favour among children.

Humorous narrative verse has never been lacking in Australia, with our riches of early convict and bush ballads. These have been given a new lease of life through the many contemporary picture book versions beginning with Desmond Digby's wonderful illustrations in *Waltzing Matilda* by A.B. Paterson and the Niland twins' comically apt illustrations in *Mulga Bill's Bicycle*. Ballads in all languages represent folk culture, are highly memorable and are invaluable for establishing in young listeners indelible images and patterns of language which will never fade from their lives, but will go on enriching them into old age.

It is important, however, that children not be provided with a diet of only humorous, narrative, satirical or social realist verse. Lyric poetry, that is, poetry with inbuilt verbal melody, attunes the ear to the harmonious sounds and patterns of language and the inner ear — the mind and the senses — to the beauty and the wonder of nature, the world around us and to all that is best in human experience, even the yearning of the human spirit.

If Wordsworth, Keats and Shelley or even Thomas Hardy and D.H. Lawrence seem a little remote for 20th century Australian children there are now plenty of poets and collections of poetry which will not only confirm but stretch their experience and help lift their eyes from the mundane to the quiet hills or even the beauty of the busy streets. Max Fatchen, Colin Thiele, Jenny Boult and Bill Scott have published collections which skilfully mix the serious with the light-hearted, which are accessible but not lightweight. Bill Scott combines bush wisdom with space-age speculation and an enduring perceptiveness about human nature.

There is no dearth of good poetry anthologies which should be at the ready in every classroom for quick reference and for precious minutes of sharing. The teacher who reads — expressively but not in an elocutionary manner — poetry to his or her class is providing access to language in its most precise, concise, economical and rhythmic form — patterns to live with and models for thinking, speaking and writing. Would that every classroom had perpetually available Clare Scott-Mitchell's *When a Goose Meets a Moose* and *Apples from Hurricane Street*, Jill Heylen's and Celia Jellett's *Someone is Flying Balloons* and *Rattling in the Wind*, Jack Prelutsky's *The Walker Book of Poetry for Children* or Alf Mappin's *Sing in Bright Colours*. Further recommendations for poetry collections along with graded and annotated reading lists are available in *First Choice: A Guide to the Best Books For Australian Children* by Maurice Saxby and Glenys Smith.

Traditional Literature

Just as poetry is an oral–aural literary form meant to be experienced through the ear, so is that body of folk literature which has been handed down by word of mouth, sometimes for centuries, before ultimately being transcribed onto clay, papyrus, vellum or paper. Traditional literature includes fables and parables, folk and fairy tales, epics, hero tales, myths and legends. Further discussion of these forms — or genres — is found in *Give Them Wings: The Experience of Children's Literature* by Maurice Saxby and Gordon Winch.

Listening to and later reading the old folk tales like 'The Three Bears', 'The Three Little Pigs', 'The Three Billy Goats Gruff', 'Henny Penny' and

'The Gingerbread Man' introduces children to literary conventions: the way story works. The stories are clearly structured and employ recurring motifs: the threesome family, journeys, challenges, wishes and dreams. Thus they teach prediction and anticipation. The language is repetitive and rhythmic in the best sense — 'Trip-Trap! Trip-Trap! went the bridge. "WHOSE THAT tripping over my bridge?" roared the troll', — provided that an authentic version is used and not an emasculated sanitised, basal reader version. (And beware publishers who reproduce traditional literature without acknowledging the source or the name of the reteller!)

Just as there is now a choice selection of poetry books so there is on the market a wide range of gloriously illustrated folk and fairy tales with art work by consumate artists such as Errol Le Cain, Lisbeth Zwerger, Susan Jeffers, Junko Morimoto, Barbara Cooney, Tomi de Paola and Dick Roughsey who recreate the mood and the cultural flavour of the stories. Folk tales provide a truly multicultural literature in that they are of the many peoples from around the world. They should form an essential part of any literature program and any teaching that aims to arouse international understanding. The modern world must never lose the cultural heritage of, say, the Middle East. The *Arabian Nights* stories are as cross-cultural as the *Brer Rabbit* stories from the Deep South (via Africa) of America or the stories of *King Arthur* and *Robin Hood* from Britain. Rodney MacRae's illustrations for *Aesop's Fables* capitalise on the multicultural nature of the stories.

The value of traditional literature to today's children cannot be overestimated. All modern literature has its origins in ancient traditions. From the folk and fairy tale and from myth is derived modern fantasy, although there is not a little social realism to be found in folk tales such as one from Scandinavia — 'The Farmer Who Looked After the House', retold by Wanda Gag as *Gone is Gone*. From the epic hero tales spring both realistic and romantic adventure as can be seen by studying the chart and following the heroic pattern in Saxby and Ingpen's *The Great Deeds of Superheroes*. Their *The Great Deeds of Heroic Women* indicate the sources of both adventure tales and that body of inspirational literature motivated by exploits in both war and peace and by spiritual charisma.

Bettelheim (1975) in *The Uses of Enchantment* perhaps goes too far in the psychoanalysis of fairy tales but he does alert us as to why and how the stories came into being and their value to humankind. The multitude of youngest sons and seeming simpletons heralds the plethora of modern novels featuring the child who is rejected, clumsy, incompetent, who feels inferior; the 'wait for me, wait for me' syndrome which recurs in the work of authors like Thurley Fowler. Perhaps the Libby Hathorn, Robin Klein pain in the neck heroines are distant relatives of Cinderella's sisters. Searching for such prototypes is a much more fruitful, meaningful and enjoyable intellectual challenge to children than endless book reports and extension activities provided in many teachers' guides.

If lower-primary children derive emotional security from fairy tales as Bettelheim suggests, middle and upper primary find in Beowulf, Perseus, Demeter, Athena and their heroic companions role models for ego growth and the development of the super ego. We all need heroes. Not that the ancient heroes, male or female, were perfect. Hubris, or pride, as Kenneth Grahame demonstrates in *The Wind in the Willows* with Toad, always precedes a fall; and there are terrible lessons to be learned from the behaviour of even Odysseus or Guinevere.

Fantasy

The impulse to explore the unknown, to speculate about origins, to explain the inexplicable which gives rise to myth — creation stories, the dealings of the gods with mortals, the search for eternal life, the exploration of the 'otherworld' — also motivates the writer of fantasy. Fantasy is humankind thinking, pondering, dreaming, seeking to push back the edge of vision; to penetrate the interface of reality.

Emily Rodda in her fantasies postulates the other side, the outside, a secondary world where across the Barrier life is different to what we take for granted and where time is not measured in our time. The mapping of other worlds goes back to mythology and also to the first children's book written purely to entertain, *Alice's Adventures in Wonderland*. Wonderland, Oz, Peter Pan's Never-Never land, Narnia, Middle Earth, Earthsea, Prydain, Camazotz, Terabithia even, are 'other' or secondary worlds which have a territory which can be explored. More importantly they represent magical images of the mind and the imagination. Children and inept authors play games of 'let's pretend' or 'make believe'. The children's book market abounds in fanciful dreams, trips to enchanted faraway lands, toys that come alive, animals that chatter inanely, koalas competing in swimming races and clones of Little Noddy. These are not fantasies. They are coyly whimsical pretence.

Some children, usually in private, but sometimes with a friend (like C.S. Lewis and his brother) conjure up a secondary world, their own Terabithia, where they truly grow in stature, perform marvellous deeds, break barriers of time, place and even mortality and follow their gleam to fulfil their destiny. This is the stuff of fantasy and is to be encouraged and emulated. Children must 'hold fast to dreams'. They need St George to inspire them if they are to become knights in armour even if the armour does not shine brightly forever. They need to commune with Aboriginal Potkooroks, play with Bitarrs, hunt with Turongs, fear the Mahracks, and be wary of the Tutugals if they are to relive that older kind of magic which today is theirs only through the power of their own minds and from folklore and true fantasy.

As technology advances with frightening rapidity human speculation and dreaming inevitably shapes technological images — hence science fiction which began with Jules Verne and H.G. Wells. Many of those writers' fictions have become fact; and today's science fiction may well become tomorrow's established truth. So young readers in a computer age need to flex their imaginative powers through reputable works of science fiction and with writers like Lee Harding who dramatise the psychological implications of science and technology.

Children as well as adults have always been fascinated by the supernatural, the possibilities of life beyond life, the power of the mind and extrasensory perception. Children read surreptitiously Wilde's *The Picture of Dorian Gray* and Stevenson's *Dr Jekyll and Mr Hyde* before there was a children's literature of the supernatural. With the decline of organised worship, the loss of orthodox religious faith and the burgeoning of New Age philosophies has come a tremendous increase in tales of the unexpected, bizarre, spooky stories and explorations of the supernatural in children's literature. Not just harmless, spoofy stories of wizards and witches, but an endless supply of short stories suggesting that the supernatural does exist. Novels such as Mary White's *Mindwave*, Allan Baillie's *Megan's Star* and a good many of Victor Kelleher's novels, such as *The Hunting of Shadroth* and *The Forbidden Paths of Thual*, suggest that extrasensory perception could be a reality and that the power of the mind has as yet been untapped by modern society.

Teachers should be aware that some parents abhor any suggestion of the occult and object to witchcraft even when treated satirically. Yet Kelleher's novels, for instance, or Ruth Park's *Beatie Bow* raise serious questions of 'the gift' of seeing beyond the confines of here and now. Essentially that is what all literature does. It frees the spirit and sets the imagination soaring.

Any literature program, then, should be carefully selected to encompass a wide range. It should seek to introduce children to:

1. Realistic fiction that deals with life as we know it to be, not shirking the painful or ignoring problems.
2. Romantic fiction including adventure that is escapist, what we would like life to be like; larger than life situations which are recognised and accepted for what they are.
3. Fantasy that liberates prosaic imaginations.
4. 'High' Literature with a capital L, regarded by some popularists as elitist and 'beyond the children in my school'. A frequent complaint is that books which win awards from adult juries sit on the library shelves. Why?

The most reluctant, inexperienced and hesitant reader is a potential bookworm. Membership of organisations like the Puffin Bookclub and subscribers to a student-run journal like *Rippa Reading* (Appleton 1990) suggest that there are as high a proportion of committed appreciative readers in our school communities as there ever was. Indeed the tremendous growth of quality children's literature would hardly be sustained were it read only by teachers, librarians and academics. A day spent in a good children's bookshop would convince the sceptic that a good many children are capable of enjoying 'the best' of literature. The adage that children will give you what you expect and demand of them is particularly true of reading.

A Primary Reading Program

Turning Children on to Books: Teaching Children's Literature

To inspire an enthusiasm in children for literature is not difficult but there are certain fundamental factors that must be operative:

1. The child needs to be in contact with a parent, teacher, librarian, an operative 'other' who is enthusiastic and knows the field of children's literature.
2. There should be a plentiful and accessible supply of attractively presented books covering a wide range of types and topics.
3. There should be opportunities for reading even within the school timetable. Sustained silent reading is not a time filler.
4. Reading aloud — possibly the next most important factor after (1) — should be regular, an integral part of the school day; and it should run from pre-school through to late high school. Even competent, enthusiastic readers can benefit from a teacher's sympathetic oral interpretation. Aural comprehension runs in advance of visual comprehension because of the help given by intonation and expression.
5. It helps, too, if children are encouraged to own books, so school bookclubs should be encouraged. The visit of a knowledgeable bookseller is not necessarily a sales pitch. It could be a vital part of the literature program.
6. Parents should be involved. Having parents monitoring and signing a reading list is one thing (and highly authoritarian); holding author talks or topic evenings to do with children's literature is of far greater and more permanent value.
7. A crucial adjunct to (1) is the teacher who knows his children so well and is interested enough to drop a recommendation — even lend a book — at the right time. Books should be matched to the individual. 'Here is a great book, you should read it', gives way to 'You enjoyed *Playing Beatie Bow* so I'm sure you would enjoy *Fire in The Sky*'.

Trevor H. Cairney has written *Other Worlds: The Endless Possibilities of Literature* (1990) in which he makes a passionate plea for building up communities of readers and exploring literature with that community. He then goes on to provide things for teachers to 'do' with certain books. Even primary school teachers are beginning to ask 'But what do I "do" with a book like this?'. Do they have to 'do' anything? If the book is good enough it will 'do' its own work in terms of linguistic and personal development.

Of late there has been published a plethora of literature activity books. Stemming from *Literacy Through Literature* (1985) by Terry D. Johnson and Daphne R. Louis and their *Bringing It All Together* (1987) there have been various literature guides, storylines and literature-based reading programs to help the busy teacher program literature and language activities, possibly without needing to read the books. Instant access! As a result classes all around Australia are being asked to create literary sociograms, draw story webs or maps, retell a novel from the point of view of the villain (the antagonist) or a minor character, or write an alternative ending.

Gillian Rubinstein did the latter herself — deliberately — for *Beyond the Labyrinth*. I suspect that she and any author of integrity labours over their endings. How presumptuous to alter them! Some books leave the ending open — there is no closure — so if a reader feels inclined he or she may well continue the story beyond the life of the book.

I suspect, however, that very few adults indeed, after becoming lost in, say, Keri Hulme's *The Bone People* or having come away spellbound from a film like *Babette's Feast*, would rush off to draw up a literary sociogram or construct a story map. Yet we ask children to do this!

This is not to suggest that literature-based activities should be banned. But they should be used sensitively and sparingly.

Wide versus Close Reading

Rather than reading one particular book, especially in the primary school, teachers should be trying to develop wide reading. The voracious reader can digest pulp along with the nutritious and will eventually become self-selective. So enthusiastic exposure to a wide range of literature should be a primary aim.

Every primary classroom teacher has ample opportunity to make literature part of the fabric of the pupils' lives. Apart from recommending 'the right book to the right child at the right time' there is always the opportunity to slip in a reading or plug a book which has relevance to work across the curriculum. Allan Baillie's *Hero* can be slotted in with a study of flooding and conservation as well as with discussions of personal development and social interaction. Morris Gleitzman's *Two Weeks with the Queen* can become part of a study of travel, major world cities, health care, AIDS education.

There are many long-standing techniques for promoting books for wide reading. Most of them are elementary and require no elaboration.

1. Authors talks. Short of having an author visit the school, publishers supply background information about their writers and there are now available publications, listed in the appendix, containing biographical and bibliographical information.
2. Collect and introduce books on a common theme, for example inner city dwelling, bullying, animal antics.
3. Read regularly key passages that will sell the book. Allow children to predict.
4. Outline the story up to a given point and allow students to fill out the plot by reading for themselves.
5. Do a profile of characters likely to appeal to your group, for example Erica Yurken, Peter Dusting.
6. Discuss the dust jacket and predict the story.
7. Do the same with the title.

A Primary Reading Program

8. Throw up chapter heads on the overhead projector and discuss likely plot complications.
9. Set the scene of the book dramatically, using audio and visual aids where appropriate, for example Tom Roberts's 'Bailed Up' to introduce a bushranging book.
10. Read and discuss the publisher's blurb.
11. Have children make recommendations to the group suggesting why the book should appeal.

Some teachers encourage students to maintain a reading log, others a journal where they write their personal response to a book. (Some successful authors admit to having done this voluntarily when young.) This is encouraging children to read closely and carefully. The activities suggested in Johnson and Louis (1985, 1987) are designed to do just that. But close reading should lead always to more responsive, or appreciative, reading. Occasionally a teacher may well read a short story, a poem, a passage aloud and have the listeners jot down their feelings and reactions during the reading. The ensuing discussion could encourage the listeners to analyse why they reacted as they did.

Discussion is generally less painful than written activity for students; it provides the teacher with instant feedback, and cross-fertilisation of ideas is possible. Ideally there should be opportunity for teacher and pupil to discuss books on a one to one basis; and it does help if the teacher has read the text.

Years ago the poetry appreciation lesson in primary schools provided for a close and detailed examination of a text. Often the 'lesson' degenerated into a teacher-dominated explication of rhyme, rhythm, imagery and poetic structure. Children should be made aware of poetic techniques: for example, how the imagery in both poetry and prose creates a certain effect and carries meaning; how rhythm can be organic to a poem or a piece of prose, adding to its intensity or dramatic effect. The teacher can lead such discussions — not all learning is student-centred discovery learning — but the emphasis should be on shared enjoyment.

Perhaps the worst crime a teacher can commit with a literature program is to rip out passages from novels for 'comprehension' and other language activities — underline the describing words/adjectives, create a spelling list from Chapter 5, etc. Of course all students at times require direct instruction to acquire and consolidate language skills. An unfamiliar tricky word may need syllabification; dictionary use is never taboo; silent letters may have to be explained. At times it is profitable to examine how Patricia Wrightson's prose varies according to her purpose. Even R.L. Stevenson admitted to learning the craft of writing by 'aping Hazlitt' and copying the style of others. That is how writers develop. It is a question of tact and timing. It is also a question of having multiple resources. Literature — real books — is one resource and a powerful one. But in addition atlases, directories, textbooks and other materials can be consulted. There will be worksheets and teacher-produced material to meet the needs of an individual or group. That is what teaching is all about.

Literature-based Reading

When 'literature-based reading' was first becoming recognised a colleague, Glenys Smith, and I compiled a series of 18 anthologies of literature designed for approximately Years 3–9. For the two primary levels Len Unsworth and Vivienne Nicoll prepared teachers' books which spell out in a clear logical form a time-honoured approach (although never articulated in this way before) to developing response: getting ready for the text, getting into the text; coming back to the text; and going beyond the text. In essence they suggest arousing interest in the text, which is the intent of suggestions (1) to (11) in the 'Wide versus Close Reading' section above. Looking closely at the text — for example, dramatising a passage from a novel — requires a close examination of plot, character, tone, meaning. 'Coming back to the text' is using activities selectively to 'provide opportunities for readers to refine their reactions to the behaviours of various characters, or to the story's events and conclusion' (Nicoll and Unsworth 1990, p. 13). This could entail a written activity stimulated by the text, say, headlines and an editorial for the *Zambezi Zephyr* reporting on the 27th Annual African Hippopotamus Race. 'Going beyond the text' relates one particular piece of literature to others — following up the work of an author, reading widely novels exploring death or any other topic.

Suggestions for 're-creative activities', aids to intensive study and ways of stimulating response abound in educational literature: dance and drama activities; puppetry; art presentations, murals, dioramas, models, cut-outs, costume design; musical accompaniment; radio plays; reader's theatre; journalistic and media approaches. An imaginative, creative teacher has ample opportunity for integrating literature across the curriculum without killing the literature. Traditional literature, particularly, the old folk tales, myths and legends, is time weathered and tough. While tender contemporary novels, Patricia MacLachlan's poetic *Sarah, Plain and Tall*, say, could be bruised by undue handling, the old tales don't scar easily. Aesop is good for dramatisation, pictorial representation, discussion. King Arthur can stand up to a comparative study with, say, El Cid or Roland. 'Who is the most reprehensible — Medea or Circe?' could well be debated. The lives of the saints in *Heroic Women* could provide a context for discussing contemporary humanitarians.

All is grist to the mill to a wise and sensitive teacher. But once the joy of literature gives way to literature as fodder for worksheets and limitless cloze exercises a teacher needs to take serious stock of his or her classroom practice. Too much philosophising, claims Keats in *Lamia*,

> ... will clip an Angel's wings,
> Conquer all mysteries by rule and line,
> Empty the haunted air, and gnomed mine
> Unweave a rainbow.

So it is with literature. The rainbow must never be unravelled.

References

Appleton, J. (ed.) (1990) *Rippa Reading*, SCEGS Redlands, Virginia Allman, Sydney.
Bettelheim, B. (1975) *The Uses of Enchantment: The Importance and Meaning of Fairy Tales*, Thames and Hudson, London.
Cairney, T.H. (1990) *Other Worlds: The Endless Possibilities of Literature*, Nelson, Melbourne.
Chambers, A. (1980) 'The Reader in the Book', in *The Signal Approach to Children's Books*, ed. Nancy Chambers, Kestrel, London.
Dickinson, P. (1973) 'A Defense of Rubbish', in *Children and Literature: Views and Reviews*, ed. Virginia Haviland, Scott Foresman, Glenview, Illinois.
Fadiman, C. (1946) *Reading I've Liked*, Hamish Hamilton, London.
Forster, E.M. (1927) *Aspects of the Novel*, Cape, London.
Gillilian, S. (1986) in *The Read-Aloud Handbook*, by Jim Trelease, Australian adaptation by Moira Robinson, Penguin, Melbourne.
Godden, R. (1973) 'An Imaginary Correspondence', in *Children and Literature: Views and Reviews*, ed. Virginia Haviland, Scott Foresman, Glenview, Illinois.
Johnson, T. and Louis, D. (1987) *Bringing It All Together: A Program for Literacy*, Methuen, Sydney.
Johnson, T. and Louis, D. (1988) *Literacy Through Literature*, Methuen, Sydney.
Lewis, C.S. (1955) *Surprised by Joy*, Bles, London.
Masson, S. (1990) *Fire in the Sky*, Angus and Robertson, Sydney.
Meek, M. (1988) *How Texts Teach What Readers Learn*, Thimble Press, Stroud, Gloucestershire.
Nicoll, V. and Unsworth, L. (1989) *Dimensions Teachers' Book Level I*, Nelson, Melbourne.
Nicoll, V. and Unsworth, L. (1990) *Dimensions Teachers' Book Level II*, Nelson, Melbourne.
Opie, I. and P. (1959) *The Lore and Language of School Children*, Oxford University Press, London.
Park, R. (1980) *Playing Beatie Bow*, Nelson, Melbourne.
Saxby, M. (1988) 'Know the Illustrator, Jeannie Baker', in *Magpies* 3 (1), March: 20–21.
Saxby, M. and Smith, G. (1986–89) *Dimensions*, Eighteen Anthologies, Nelson, Melbourne.
Saxby, M. and Smith, G. (1991) *First Choice: A Guide to the Best Books for Australian Children*, Oxford University Press, Melbourne.
Saxby, M. and Winch, G. (1987) *Give Them Wings: The Experience of Children's Literature*, Macmillan, Melbourne.
Turner, I. (1969) *Cinderella Dressed in Yella*, Heinemann, Melbourne.
Wignell, E. (1989) 'I Know That Place!' *PEN.72*, Primary English Teaching Association, Rozelle, NSW.

References to Children's Books

Adams, Jeanie (1989) *Pigs and Honey*, Omnibus, Adelaide.
Aesop's Fables (1990) illus. by Rodney McRae, Margaret Hamilton, Sydney.
Allen, Pamela (1980) *Mr Archimedes' Bath*, Collins, Sydney.
Allen, Pamela (1982) *Who Sank the Boat?*, Nelson, Melbourne.
Allen, Pamela (1990) *My Cat Maisie*, Viking, Melbourne.
Armstrong, William (1969) *Sounder*, Penguin, London.
Baillie, Allan (1985) *Little Brother*, Nelson, Melbourne.
Baillie, Allan (1988) *Drac and the Gremlin*, illus. by Jane Tanner, Viking Kestrel, Melbourne.
Baillie, Allan (1988) *Megan's Star*, Nelson, Melbourne.
Baillie, Allan (1989) *Mates*, Omnibus, Adelaide.
Baillie, Allan (1990) *Hero*, Penguin, Melbourne.
Baker, Jeannie (1987) *Where the Forest Meets the Sea*, Julia MacRae, London.
Ball, Duncan (1984) *The Ghost and the Goggle Box*, Angus and Robertson, Sydney.
Ball, Duncan (1985) *Selby's Secret*, Angus and Robertson, Sydney.
Bates, Dianne (1987) *Grandma Cadbury's Trucking Tales*, Angus and Robertson, Sydney.
Bates, Dianne (1989) *Grandma Cadbury's Safari Tours*, Angus and Robertson, Sydney.
Bolton, Barbara (1985) *Edward Wilkins and His Friend Gwendoline*, illus. by Madeleine Winch, Angus and Robertson, Sydney.
Browne, Anthony (1978) *Bear Hunt*, Hamish Hamilton, London.
Bruce, Mary Grant (1910–42) *The Billabong Series*, Ward, Lock, London.
Burningham, John (1970) *Mr Gumpy's Outing*, Cape, London.
Burningham, John (1977) *Come away From the Water, Shirley*, Cape, London.
Burningham, John (1978) *Would You Rather?*, Cape, London.
Burningham, John (1984) *Granpa*, Cape, London.
Carle, Eric (1970) *The Very Hungry Caterpillar*, Hamish Hamilton, London.
Carr, Roger Vaughan (1985) *Firestorm!*, Nelson, Melbourne.
Carroll, Lewis (1988) *Alice's Adventures in Wonderland*, illus. by Anthony Browne, Julia MacRae, London. (First published 1865.)
Caswell, Brian (1989) *Merryll of the Stones*, University of Queensland Press, Brisbane.
Chambers, Aidan (1978) *Breaktime*, The Bodley Head, London.
Chambers, Aidan (1982) *Dance on My Grave*, The Bodley Head, London.
Chambers, Aidan (1983) *The Present Takers*, The Bodley Head, London.
Chambers, Aidan (1987) *Now I Know*, The Bodley Head, London.
Cleary, Beverly (1983) *Dear Mr Henshaw*, Julia MacRae, London.
Coerr, Eleanor (1977) *Sadako and the Thousand Paper Cranes*, Hodder and Stoughton, Sydney.
Covernton, Jane (1985) *Putrid Poems*, Omnibus, Adelaide.
Covernton, Jane (1988) *Vile Verse*, Omnibus, Adelaide.
Crew, Gary (1986) *The Inner Circle*, Heinemann, Melbourne.
Crew, Gary (1990) *Strange Objects*, Heinemann, Melbourne.
Dahl, Roald (1973) *Charlie and the Giant Glass Elevator*, Allen and Unwin, London.
Dahl Roald (1982) *The BFG*, Cape, London.
Dahl, Roald (1983) *The Witches*, Cape, London.
Dann, Max (1982) *Adventures With My Worst Best Friend*, Oxford University Press, Melbourne.

A Primary Reading Program

Dekkers, Midas (1982) *Whale Lake*, Deutsch, London.
Ende, Michael (1979) *The Neverending Story*, Lane, London.
Factor, June (1983) *Far Out, Brussel Sprout!*, Oxford University Press, Melbourne.
Fienberg, Anna (1988) *Wiggy and Boa*, Dent, Melbourne.
Fleischman, Sid (1972) *McBroom's Wonderful One-Acre Farm*, Penguin, London.
Fleischman, Sid (1986) *The Whipping Boy*, Methuen, London.
Flynn, Rachel (1990) *I Hate Fridays: Stories From Koala Hills Primary School*, Viking, Melbourne.
Fox, Mem (1989) *Sophie*, illus. by Craig Smith, Drakeford, Melbourne.
Frances, Helen (1983) *The Devil's Stone*, Omnibus, Adelaide.
French, Fiona (1986) *Snow White in New York*, Oxford University Press, London.
French, Simon (1981) *Cannily, Cannily*, Angus and Robertson, Sydney.
French, Simon (1986) *All We Know*, Angus and Robertson, Sydney.
Gag, Wanda (1936) *Gone is Gone*, Faber, London.
Garner, Alan (1976) *The Stone Book Quartet*, Collins, London.
Gleeson, Libby (1987) *I am Susannah*, Angus and Robertson, Sydney.
Gleeson, Libby (1990) *Dodger*, Turton and Chambers, Perth.
Gleitzman, Morris (1990) *Two Weeks With the Queen*, Pan, Melbourne.
Graham, Bob (1987) *Crusher is Coming*, Lothian, Melbourne.
Grahame, Kenneth (1908) *The Wind in the Willows*, Kestrel, London.
Grimm, Jacob and Wilhelm (1981) *Hansel and Gretel*, illus. by Anthony Browne, Julia MacRae, London.
Hathorn, Elizabeth (1985) *Paolo's Secret*, Methuen, Sydney.
Hathorn, Elizabeth (1986) *All About Anna*, Methuen, Sydney.
Hathorn, Elizabeth (1987) *Looking Out for Sampson*, Oxford University Press, Melbourne.
Hathorn, Elizabeth (1989) *Thunderwith*, Heinemann, Melbourne.
Hathorn, Elizabeth (1990) *Jezza Sez*, Angus and Robertson, Sydney.
Hautzig, Esther (1968) *The Endless Steppe*, Hamish Hamilton, London.
Heide, Florence Parry (1971) *The Shrinking of Treehorn*, Kestrel, London.
Heylen, Jill and Jellett, Celia (1984) *Someone is Flying Balloons*, Omnibus, Adelaide.
Heylen, Jill and Jellett, Celia (1987) *Rattling in the Wind*, Omnibus, Adelaide.
Hoban, Russell (1967) *The Mouse and His Child*, Faber, London.
Hughes, Ted (1968) *The Iron Man*, Faber, London.
Hulme, Keri (1985) *The Bone People*, Hodder and Stoughton, London.
Hunt, Nan (1989) *Never Tomorrow*, Collins, Sydney.
Hutchins, Pat (1969) *Rosie's Walk*, The Bodley Head, London.
Isaacson, Philip M. (1988) *Round Buildings, Square Buildings and Buildings that Wiggle Like a Fish*, Julia MacRae, London.
Jennings, Paul (1985) *Unreal!*, Puffin, Melbourne.
Jennings, Paul (1986) *Unbelievable!*, Puffin, Melbourne.
Jennings, Paul (1988) *Uncanny!*, Puffin, Melbourne.
Jennings, Paul (1989) *The Paw Thing*, Puffin, Melbourne.
Jennings, Paul (1990) *Round The Twist*, Puffin, Melbourne.
Kelleher, Victor (1979) *The Forbidden Paths of Thual*, Kestrel, London.
Kelleher, Victor (1981) *The Hunting of Shadroth*, Kestrel, London.
Kelleher, Victor (1988) *Baily's Bones*, Kestrel, Melbourne.
Kelleher, Victor (1989) *The Red King*, Kestrel, Melbourne.
Kemp, Gene (1977) *The Turbulent Term of Tyke Tiler*, Faber, London.
Kidd, Diana (1988) *The Day Grandma Came To Stay (and Spoilt my Life)*, Collins, Sydney.

Kidd, Diana (1989) *Onion Tears*, Collins, Sydney.
King-Smith, Dick (1984) *Harry's Mad*, Gollancz, London.
Klein, Robin (1983–1989) *Penny Pollard Series*, Oxford University Press, Melbourne.
Klein, Robin (1984) *Hating Alison Ashley*, Puffin, Melbourne.
Klein, Robin (1988) *Laurie Loved Me Best*, Puffin, Melbourne.
Konigsburg E.L. (1967) *From the Mixed-Up Files of Mrs Basil E. Frankweiler*, Macmillan, London.
Lewis, C.S. (1950) *The Lion, the Witch and the Wardrobe*, Bles, London.
Lisson, Deborah (1990) *The Devil's Own*, Walter McVitty, Sydney.
Little, Jean (1984), *Mama's Going to Buy You a Mocking Bird*, Viking Kestrel, London.
Lurie, Morris (1969) *The 27th Annual African Hippopotamus Race*, Puffin, Melbourne.
MacDonald, Caroline (1988) *The Lake at the End of the World*, Kestrel, London.
MacLachlan, Patricia (1985), *Sarah, Plain and Tall*, Julia MacRae, London.
MacLeod, Doug (1981) *In the Garden of Bad Things*, Puffin, Melbourne.
MacLeod, Doug (1983) *The Fed Up Family Album*, Puffin, Melbourne.
Magorian, Michelle (1981) *Goodnight Mr. Tom*, Kestrel, London.
Mahy, Margaret (1981) *Raging Robots and Unruly Uncles*, Penguin, London.
Mahy, Margaret (1989) *The Blood-and-Thunder Adventure on Hurricane Peak*, Penguin, London.
Mahy, Margaret (1989) *The Great Piratical Rumbustification*, Dent, London.
Mahy, Margaret (1989) *The Great White Man-Eating Shark*, Penguin, London.
Mappin, Alf (1975) *Sing in Bright Colours: Poetry From Australia*, Westbooks, Perth.
Marryat, Capt. Frederick (1985) *The Children of the New Forest*, Penguin, London. (First published 1847.)
Marsden, John (1987) *So Much To Tell You*, Walter McVitty, Sydney.
Masson, Sophie (1990) *Fire in the Sky*, Angus and Robertson, Sydney.
McAfee, Annalena (1987) *Kirsty Knows Best*, illus. by Anthony Browne, Julia MacRae, London.
Meredith, Louisa A. (1880) *Tasmanian Friends and Foes, Feathered, Furred and Finned*, Marcus Ward, London.
Needle, Jan (1978) *My Mate Shofiq*, Fontana Lions, London.
Norman, Lilith (1971) *The Shape of Three*, Collins, Sydney.
Norman, Lilith (1978) *A Dream of Seas*, Collins, Sydney.
Nostlinger, Christine (1976) *Conrad: The Hilarious Adventures of a Factory-made Child*, Andersen, London.
Oakley, Graham (1986) *Henry's Quest*, Macmillan, London.
Oakley, Graham (1990) *Once Upon a Time: A Prince's Fantastic Journey*, Macmillan, London.
Park, Ruth (1980) *Playing Beatie Bow*, Nelson, Melbourne.
Park, Ruth (1980) *When the Wind Changed*, Collins, Sydney.
Park, Ruth (1986) *My Sister Sif*, Viking Kestrel, Melbourne.
Paterson, A.B. (1970) *Waltzing Matilda*, illus. by Desmond Digby, Collins, Sydney.
Paterson, A.B. (1973) *Mulga Bill's Bicycle*, illus. by Kilmeny and Deborah Niland, Collins, Sydney.
Paterson, Katherine (1977) *Bridge to Terabithia*, Penguin, London.
Pausaker, Jenny (1990) *Can You Keep a Secret?*, Angus and Robertson, Sydney.
Pedley, Ethel M. (1899) *Dot and the Kangaroo*, Angus and Robertson, Sydney.
Phipson, Joan (1988) *Bianca*, Viking Kestrel, London.

A Primary Reading Program

Potter, Beatrix (1902) *The Tale of Peter Rabbit*, Warne, London.
Potter, Beatrix (1903) *The Tale of Squirrel Nutkin*, Warne, London.
Prelutsky, Jack (1983) *The Walker Book of Poetry for Children*, illus. by Arnold Lobel, Walker, London.
Rockwell, Thomas (1973) *How to Eat Fried Worms*, Franklin Watts, London.
Rodda, Emily (1986) *Pigs Might Fly*, Angus and Robertson, Sydney.
Rodda, Emily (1988) *The Best Kept Secret*, Angus and Robertson, Sydney.
Rodda, Emily (1990) *Crumbs!*, Omnibus, Adelaide.
Rodda, Emily (1990) *Finders Keepers*, Angus and Robertson, Sydney.
Rubinstein, Gillian (1986) *Space Demons*, Omnibus/Puffin, Adelaide.
Rubinstein, Gillian (1988) *Answers to Brut*, Omnibus/Puffin, Adelaide.
Rubinstein, Gillian (1988) *Beyond the Labyrinth*, Hyland House, Melbourne.
Rubinstein, Gillian (1989) *Skymaze*, Omnibus/Puffin, Adelaide.
Saxby, Maurice and Ingpen, Robert (1989) *The Great Deeds of Superheroes*, Millennium, Sydney.
Saxby, Maurice and Ingpen, Robert (1990) *The Great Deeds of Heroic Women*, Millennium, Sydney.
Scholes, Katherine (1989) *The Blue Chameleon*, Hill of Content, Melbourne.
Scieszka, Jon (1989) *The True Story of the 3 Little Pigs*, illus. by Lane Smith, Viking Kestrel, London.
Scott-Mitchell, Clare (1980) *When a Goose Meets a Moose*, Methuen, Sydney.
Scott-Mitchell, Clare (1985) *Apples from Hurricane Street*, Methuen, Sydney.
Sendak, Maurice (1962) *Where the Wild Things Are*, The Bodley Head, London.
Sendak, Maurice (1981) *Outside Over There*, The Bodley Head, London.
Sharpe, Margaret (1983) *The Traeger Kid*, Alternative Publishing Cooperative, Sydney.
Smith, Doris Buchanan (1975) *A Taste of Blackberries*, Heinemann, London.
Southall, Ivan (1971) *Josh*, Angus and Robertson, Sydney.
Stevenson, Robert Louis (1886) *Dr Jekyll and Mr Hyde*, Penguin, London.
Stevenson, Robert Louis (1946) *Treasure Island*, Harrap, London. (First published 1883.)
Stewart, Maureen (1987) *Dear Emily*, Penguin, Melbourne.
Stewart, Maureen (1987) *Love from Greg*, Penguin, Melbourne.
Stow, Randolph (1967) *Midnite The Story of a Wild Colonial Boy*, The Bodley Head, London.
Stowe, Harriet Beecher (1852) *Uncle Tom's Cabin*, Jewett, Boston.
Swift, Dean (1967) *Gulliver's Travels*, Penguin, London. (First published 1726–1727.)
Taylor, Milred (1976) *Roll of Thunder, Hear My Cry*, Pergamon, London.
Taylor, Theodore (1969) *The Cay*, The Bodley Head, London.
Thiele, Colin (1963) *Storm Boy*, Rigby, Adelaide.
Thiele, Colin (1969) *Blue Fin*, Rigby, Adelaide.
Turner, Ethel (1894) *Seven Little Australians*, Ward Lock, London.
Umansky, Kaye (1988) *Pongwiffy: A Witch of Dirty Habits*, A & C Black, London.
Van der Loeff, Rutgers (1954) *Children on the Oregon Trail*, Penguin, London.
Voigt, Cynthia (1981) *Homecoming*, Collins, London.
Voigt, Cynthia (1983) *A Solitary Blue*, Collins, London.
Voigt, Cynthia (1984) *Dicey's Song*, Collins, London.
Wagner, Jenny (1977) *John Brown, Rose and the Midnight Cat*, illus. by Ron Brooks, Kestrel, Melbourne.
Wakefield, S.A. (1967) *Bottersnikes and Gumbles*, Collins, Sydney.
Weld, Ann (1990) *Fractured Fairy Tales and Ruptured Rhymes*, Omnibus/Puffin, Melbourne.

Wheatley, Nadia (1982) *Five Times Dizzy*, Oxford University Press, Melbourne.
Wheatley, Nadia (1984) *Dancing in the Anzac Deli*, Oxford University Press, Melbourne.
Wheatley, Nadia (1985) *The House that was Eureka*, Viking, Krestel, Melbourne.
Wheatley, Nadia (1987) *My Place*, illus. by Donna Rawlins, Collins Dove, Melbourne.
Wheatley, Nadia (1988) *The Blooding*, Viking Kestrel, Melbourne.
White, Mary (1980) *Mindwave*, Methuen, Sydney.
Wignell, Edel (1989) *Escape by Deluge*, Walter McVitty, Sydney.
Wild, Margaret (1988) *The Diary of Megan Moon (Soon to be Rich and Famous)*, Collins, Sydney.
Wild, Margaret (1989) *The Very Best of Friends*, illus. by Julie Vivas, Margaret Hamilton, Sydney.
Wilde, Oscar (1962) *The Picture of Dorian Gray*, Penguin, London. (First published 1891.)
Willmott, Frank (1983) *Breaking Up*, Collins, London.
Winch, Madeleine (1988) *Come By Chance*, Angus and Robertson, Sydney.
Wrightson, Patricia (1972) *An Older Kind of Magic*, Hutchinson, London.
Wrightson, Patricia (1973) *The Nargun and the Stars*, Hutchinson, London.
Wrightson, Patricia (1983) *A Little Fear*, Hutchinson, London.
Wrightson, Patricia (1987) *Moon-Dark*, Hutchinson, London.
Wrightson, Patricia (1989) *Balyet*, Hutchinson, London.
Zimnik, Reiner (1956) *The Crane*, Penguin, London.

Appendix: Teaching Resources Material

Some Useful Guides to Children's Literature

Alderman, Belle (1989) *Best Books for Children: The Ashton Scholastic Guide*, Ashton Scholastic, Gosford.
Children's Book Council of Australia (1986) *Books For Children*, 9th edn, Children's Book Council, Victorian Branch, Melbourne.
Children's Book Council of Australia (1988) *Books for Children, A Bicentennial Supplement*, ed. Glenda Benness and Eileen Nelson.
Dunkle, Margaret (1988) *Books for Kids: A Guide to the Best in Children's Reading for Australian Parents and Teachers*, Collins, Sydney.
Lipson, Eden Ross (1988) *The New York Times Parent's Guide to the Best Books for Children*, Random House, New York.
Taylor, Bing and Braithwaite, Peter (1986) *The Good Book Guide To Children's Books*, Australian edn, Penguin, London.
McMurtrie, Gai (1990) *Real Books For the (Less) Successful Reader: An Annotated List of Titles*, Macquarie University Special Education Centre, Sydney.
McVitty, Walter (1985) *The PETA Guide to Children's Literature*, Primary English Teaching Association, Sydney.
Noël, Ena (1990) *The New Classics: A Selection of Award Winning Children's Books*, ALIA, Sydney.

Saxby, Maurice (1988) *Collecting Puffins: A Guide for Parents and Teachers*, Penguin, Melbourne.
Saxby, Maurice and Smith, Glenys (1991) *First Choice: A Guide to the Best Books for Australian Children*, Oxford University Press, Melbourne.

Author Information

Chevalier, Tracy (1989) *Twentieth-Century Children's Writers*, 3rd edn, St. James Press, London.
Dunkle, Margaret (1987) *The Story Makers: A Collection of Interviews with Australian and New Zealand Authors and Illustrators for Young People*, Oxford University Press, Melbourne.
Dunkle, Margaret (1989) *The Story Makers II*, Oxford University Press, Melbourne.
McVitty, Walter (1986) *Australian Children's Authors*, Macmillan, Melbourne.
McVitty, Walter (1987) *Australian Childrens' Illustrators*, Macmillan, Melbourne.
McVitty, Walter (1989) *Authors and Illustrators of Australian Children's Books*, Hodder and Stoughton, Sydney.
Nieuvienhuizen, Agnes (1991) *No Kidding: Top Writers for Young People Talk about their Work*, Pan Macmillan, Melbourne.
The Authors and Illustrators Scrap Book: Featuring 24 Creators of Australian Children's Books (1991) Omnibus, Adelaide.

Useful Reviewing and Critical Journals

The Literature Base, edited by Alf Mappin, 10 Armagh Street, Victoria Park, WA 6100. $18.00 for four issues.
Magpies: Talking About Books, edited by Alf Mappin, 10 Armagh Street, Victoria Park, WA 6100. $22.50 for five issues.
Orana: Journal of School and Children's Librarianship, c/- ALIA, 367 Jones St., Ultimo, NSW 2007. $16 annually.
Papers: Explorations Into Children's Literature, edited by Alf Mappin, 10 Armagh Street, Victoria Park, WA 6100. $35.00 for three issues.
Reading Time: The Journal of the Children's Book Council of Australia, edited by John Cohen, PO Box 62, Turvey Park, Wagga Wagga, NSW 2650. $20.00 for four issues.

3
Beginning Reading with Children's Literature

Len Unsworth and Mary O'Toole

Contents

Early Reading Development: Learning How Texts Mean 95
 Texts that Teach
 Scaffolding Young Reader's Interactions with Literary Texts
 Attending to Print — Progressive Approximation
 The Sounds of Language in Contexts of Use
 Reading Development as a Social Process

Planning and Managing Whole Class Programs 113
 An Author Study for Kindergarten!
 Reading Books by Pat Hutchins: The Unit Plan

Further Dimensions to Classroom Work with Children's Literature 133
 Children's Literature in Other Cultures and Other Languages
 Varieties of Literary Forms
 Literary Texts and Technology
 Different Types of Classroom Programs

Conclusion 135

References
References to Children's Books
Appendix: Transcript of a Shared Reading

Early Reading Development: Learning How Texts Mean

> Reading is whole-task learning, right from the start. From first to last the child should be invited to behave like a reader . . . (Meek 1982, p. 24)

We now have a lot of information about how young children, 'right from the start', are invited into and supported in their apprenticeship to the home literacy practices that are valued within their culture (Scribner and Cole 1981; Heath 1983; Teale and Sulzby 1986). We have also known for a long time that being read to aloud at home is a key predictor of effective progress in reading development at school (Durkin 1966; Clark 1976; Wells 1981, 1986). More recently we have learned more of what it is about being read to at home that facilitates reading development at school (Dombey 1983; Wells 1986) and that these aspects of home reading practices vary significantly among different social groups (Williams 1990). What is clear is that success in school reading is not the result of explicit teaching of sound–symbol relationships at home nor is it the result of an emphasis on children's accurate recoding of simplified readers (Wells 1986, p. 156). The importance of shared reading at home lies mainly in the opportunity it provides for young children to begin to learn how the medium of written English makes meaning differently from spoken English. For this to occur, early reading materials must be capable of initiating young children into the culturally relevant ways in which text form constructs meanings as narrative, poetry, factual reports, etc. In this chapter the focus will be on children's fiction and the proposal that children's literature encourages the development of particular reading behaviours which cannot be engendered through many of the stories written for contemporary reading schemes. We are beginning to learn more about 'the teaching role of the text and its writer' (Meek 1982, p. 20); the ways in which adults 'scaffold' young readers' interactions with texts; the successive approximations which characterise young children's oral reading development; and the essential interrelationship of these aspects of learning to read.

Texts that Teach

> . . . what the beginning reader reads makes all the difference to his view of reading . . . (Meek 1982, p. 11)

Certainly children's literature offers a wealth of picture story books, poems, rhymes, etc. that are meaningful, interesting and attractive to young children and are hence likely to encourage positive attitudes to books and reading. Literary texts engage young children because they address the significant issues that children are deeply concerned with in their lives. But more than this, literary texts teach young children to become active, interpretive readers in ways which are not made possible by 'reading books' which are primarily instructionally oriented. Literary texts provide children with experience of a variety of narrator–reader relationships which teaches them how to become simultaneously the teller and the told — and this is crucial if they are 'to learn to read a book, as distinct from simply recognizing the words on the page' (Meek 1988, p. 10). Literary texts afford children the *space to play* so that they are encouraged to construe meanings from the interpretive contexts constructed by the text form. At the same time authors who are sensitive to the needs of inexperienced readers incorporate subtle textual support for the development of these kinds of reading behaviours. This can be appreciated by looking closely at the form of children's picture story books.

One well-known classic to consider is Pat Hutchins' *Rosie's Walk*, which has been discussed on a number of occasions by Margaret Meek (1982, p. 46; 1987, p. 2; 1988, p. 12). As Meek points out, this text of 32 words, with its classical beginning, middle and end structure, seems simple.

> But each double-page spread with its three words of text is full of possibilities. At 'over the haycock' there are terrified mice, a static tethered goat, the fox leaping so near to Rosie. (The reader has to 'read' the scratch marks that indicate jumping.) On the next page the fox is buried in the hay; there's a different expression on the face of the goat, Rosie is walking on. (Meek 1988, p. 12)

How does the very young reader work out the relationship between the words on the page and the story of *Rosie's Walk*? The fox, who is a major protagonist, is never mentioned in the text. The author sets up the game so that the reader learns to look at the bottom right-hand corner of the double-page spread to see what might follow over the page. This pattern of clues is repeated four times. So by the time the reader gets to 'through the fence' he or she knows to look ahead for the next obstacle. No sooner has the reader learned that the game is to look for what happens next than the author changes the pattern by withdrawing the support, so that for the last incident two pages have to be turned.

> The fox and the reader have ignored the empty cart which the jumping fox tips so that it knocks over the beehives; not exactly what we expected, but there as a possibility from the very first picture. (Meek 1988, p. 12)

Rosie's Walk can be read over and over again to satisfy the intrigue of multiple interpretive possibilities.

> ... there is no possibility of a single right reading that suggests whether Rosie knew all the time that the fox was behind her, or that she didn't. And who is the joke about, the hen or the fox? The possibility is easily understood — it can be seen in the pictures — that, within the fiction, by the way form controls content, both readings are not only possible at the same time, but are necessary. (Chambers 1985, p. 127)

The form of the text teaches children how the reader is in league with the author. This is a valuable reading lesson which many children do not learn — not because they cannot read the words but because the texts they have access to do not teach them the significance of attending to what the author is *not saying*. (Meek 1982, p. 47)

The *space to play* metaphor (Williams 1987) is a helpful way of characterising the distinctive quality of literary texts which promotes reading development as active, interpretive behaviour.

> Stories, from the perspective of narrative theory, are like an adventure playground in which the nature of the game played is strongly influenced by, but not wholly determined by, the structures available. We can't play just any game around the structures, but there is also not just one game we are allowed to play. Given the space the playground makes available, we can find many different positions for ourselves and go on playing until we decide to explore new spaces and new structures within them. (Williams 1987, p. 358)

Williams also provides a very useful discussion of Shirley Hughes' *Alfie Gets in First*, which illustrates again how the author scaffolds the inexperienced reader's efforts in negotiating the story via the print.

> *Alfie Gets in First*, Shirley Hughes' amusing story of a little boy's attempt to establish himself as first in the family, provides an illustration of a sensitive balance between ushering young readers towards meaning and telling them directly. Early in the story, as the pattern of interaction between Alfie, his mother and his sister is established, much is told directly: Alfie is drawn running ahead to the house, and the language informs directly: 'Alfie ran on ahead because he wanted to get home first'.
>
> Similarly, he is depicted in language and picture, sitting on the top step in triumph, waiting for his mother and sister to arrive: 'I raced you!' called Alfie. 'I'm back first, so there!'
>
> A subtle shift in narrator–reader relationship occurs at the point where Alfie, inside the house on his own with the shopping basket containing the key to the door, bangs the door closed. In advance of the language, the illustrations suggest the dimensions of the problem: Alfie is inside, his mother is still outside: he clearly can't reach the catch and the letter box is also too high. The simple formulations of how the problem might be solved are immediately but indirectly disconfirmed by the illustration, then directly disconfirmed by the language of the next page. *Young readers are shown first, then told.* (Williams 1987, p. 359–60, italics added)

Williams goes on to discuss this patterning in the rest of the text and points out that this may be a simple story but it is not simply told.

> The text is organized to offer a very rich experience to young readers, an experience through which their thinking and prediction is valued by the author in a way which takes account of *both* their ability and their inexperience. (Williams 1987, p. 360)

Fortunately there are now a great many such literary texts available for beginning readers. They make use of quite small amounts of printed text which combine with illustrations to construct contexts for developing young children's understanding of the conventions of literacy and literary understanding at the same time. Favourites among these are the books of John Burningham (*Mr Gumpy's Outing*; *Come Away from the Water, Shirley*; *Time to Get Out of the Bath, Shirley*; *Granpa*). *Mr Gumpy's Outing* is a cumulative tale which introduces children to traditional storytelling dialogue through a repetitive pattern 'building a story one step, and, in a book, one page-turning, at a time' (Meek 1988, p. 15). The cat, the dog, the pig, the sheep, the chickens, the calf, all, in turn, ask to join Mr Gumpy on his boat. But the repetition encompasses variation in ways of asking permission:

> 'May we come with you?' said the children . . .
> 'Can I come along, Mr Gumpy?' said the rabbit . . .
> 'Have you a place for me?' said the sheep . . . etc.

In a similar way children see variation within the pattern of Mr Gumpy's answers:

> 'Yes,' said Mr Gumpy, 'if you don't squabble.' [children] . . .
> 'Yes, but don't hop about.' [rabbit] . . .
> 'Yes, but don't keep bleating.' [sheep] . . .

But, as Meek points out, the reading lessons about how dialogue appears on a page, the formal ways of making requests, the way sentences appear on the page, are accompanied by a much more important lesson:

> I'd say this is the most important lesson of all . . . When we want to make new meanings we need metaphor. Here the young reader discovers that the admonitions 'don't flap' (chickens) and 'don't muck about' (the pig) are two-sided phrases with bi-lateral meanings. In the context of Mr Gumpy's boat, the words *mean more than they say*. (Meek 1988, p. 16)

Learning to be alert to the many ways in which texts mean more than they say is a key resource which literary texts offer to young readers. Meek goes on to discuss how this is achieved through the text and illustrations in the *Shirley* books and in *Granpa*. Experience with texts of this kind leads children to enjoy reading stories as a game which includes fascination with the 'constructedness' of the text — Meek says 'they watch the reading game as they play it' (Meek 1987, p. 4). Anthony Browne's *Bear Hunt* was the means by which one very inexperienced eight year old reader was alerted to this crucial role of the reader as being both the teller and the told (Williams 1987). In *Bear Hunt* the bear hero is chased by hunters but saved by his creator who gives him a pencil to draw himself out of trouble. The following segment was being read aloud:

> One day bear went for a walk.
> Two hunters were hunting.
> They saw bear.
> Look out! Look out, Bear!

At this point the young boy asked intently, 'Who says that?' The significance of the child's question is summed up by Meek: 'This is the lesson at the heart of the reading business: who says; who sees? Whose voice do we hear when the text says 'I', and whose when it doesn't?' (Meek 1987, p. 4). The question for us as teachers is how do we use texts with beginning readers which make these kinds of reading lessons possible?

Scaffolding Young Reader's Interactions with Literary Texts

> To learn to read, children need the attention of one patient adult, or older child, for long enough to read something that pleases them both. (Meek 1982, p. 9)

We have argued that the text itself is an integral component of the social context of shared reading that children experience at home and that the form of the text greatly influences the kinds of interpretive behaviours that can be developed. The rich, multilayered meanings of the kinds of literary texts referred to above are crucially important not only because they offer distinctive interpretive contexts but also because they encourage recurrent contexts for shared interpretation. Frequently young children like to hear the same story over and over again. In the case of these texts, successive readings can yield progressively more interesting possibilities so that the child's engagement and interpretive facility increases exponentially. This assumes that the pattern of adult–child interaction in sharing the book encourages the child to attempt more and more complex comments and predictions over time. The power of such recurrent contexts was pointed out by Goldfield and Snow (1984). They found that the child made use of previous conversations about the book, spontaneously introducing information that had been previously introduced by the mother to increase greatly the complexity of information dealt with in successive mother–child shared reading interactions with the same book. This kind of revisiting of favourite literary texts throughout the early years of schooling would enhance early reading development more than simply having young children 'progress' to new books as rapidly as possible simply on the basis of their being able to accurately read the text aloud.

Accounts of the processes whereby parents act as mediators for or facilitators of their child's interaction with texts emphasise extensive amounts of interactive talk about the text in which the children are encouraged to initiate comments and questions and in which the parents provide support for the children's negotiation of text meanings. Scaffolding was the term used by Bruner (1978) to describe the parents' strategies, based on shared understandings, for creating a context into which the child's incomplete responses could be accepted and responded to. A later account of aspects of this process were described in terms of contingency maintenance behaviour (Wells 1980), in which the parent follows the child's response with expansions of meaning or extensions of the child's response or uses questions to clarify the child's attempts to represent knowledge about the text. Consistent with these descriptions were Snow's (1983) accountability procedures, where the parent again makes use of shared knowledge of the text to support the child while at the same time demanding a higher level of performance. Of obvious importance in all of these accounts is the extent and quality of the parent's interaction through talk with the children about the texts they are sharing. The significance of this to the reading development of three and a half year old Anna is summarised in a study of shared-reading by Dombey (1983):

> Precisely because her experience of narrative is embedded in a conversation in which she is frequently allowed an initiating role, she is learning the active role in the discourse which she must take if an ideational or an interpersonal meaning is to be constructed which has any significance for her and for the already existing network of meanings she has in her head. She is learning to interrogate the text, learning for a story to be created in her mind, the listener (or the reader) cannot rely on a passive receptivity, but must play an active part in the asking of questions, the drawing of inferences and the constructing and testing of hypotheses. (Dombey 1983, p. 41)

Shared reading at home may centre on picture story books that are more challenging than the stories many children encounter at school. Four year old George enjoyed reading Beatrix Potter's *The Tale of Peter Rabbit* with his mother Sandra (Simpson 1987). He had read it many times during the previous 12 months and currently was able to choose to read the tale from three different published formats — a large hardback, an old paperback and a 'miniature' paperback, the latter a recent gift from his grandmother. During this particular reading there was a lot of talk about the text including many questions asked by both George and his mother (see the appendix for a transcript of this reading).

George's mother asked several different kinds of questions. Some were to encourage his involvement in predicting the evolving story:

> Shall we find out? (line 116)
> I think they have, what's happening? (line 130)
> But, what do you think is going to happen? (line 133)
> Ooh. What's happening? (line 181)
> How is he going to get there? (line 192)

Other questions encouraged reconstruction of the story through the probing of George's recall of the story from previous readings:

> Whose coat is it? (line 206)
> What happened to Peter Rabbit then? (line 219)
> What happened to Flopsy, Mopsy and Cottontail? (line 227)
> And what did they have for supper? (line 229)
> Yes, and what did they pick off the trees? (line 232)

Some of Sandra's questions focused on deriving meaning from the pictures:

> Where are they putting the blackberries when they've picked them? (line 63)
> What else can you see? (line 183)
> Where's he sitting? (line 186)

Beginning Reading

Who can he see over there? (line 188)
And what's on the other side of Mr McGregor? (line 190)
And what's this, dangling underneath the coat? (line 208)

A number of questions solicited George's opinion or judgement:

Do you think so? (line 194)
Do you think that's him? (line 35)
Do they look frightened? (line 211)

Some of George's own questions were concerned with the understanding of what is portrayed in the pictures:

Is that Peter Rabbit? (line 11)
Is Peter Rabbit in this picture? (line 30)
That one there? (line 34)
Who's dat? (line 58)

Some of his questions indicated his knowledge that the print constructed the meaning and his curiosity about how to access this effectively:

Do you have to start here? (line 4)
Or where the picture is? (line 6)

Then on two subsequent occasions during the reading he indicated that he was trying to keep his place in the print as the story progressed:

What's this one about? (line 65)
What's this one about? (line 154)
(referring to passages of text)

George also sought confirmation of the story development:

He won't be captured won't he. (line 45)

He sought new information:

How come that's where they live? (line 38)

and also used questions to clarify unfamiliar language:

Where's 'down the lane'? (line 57)
What means 'alive' (line 174)

Questions of this kind go beyond simply dealing with unfamiliar vocabulary. George is learning how the resources of language are used to construct meanings through language forms that are characteristic of written text. The familiar conversational dialogue in which the sharing of the narrative is embedded enables George to take the initiative in seeking to understand the written form. This can be seen in the sharing of the following segment as Sandra reads:

> Peter gave himself up for lost, and shed big tears; but his sobs were overheard by some friendly sparrows, who flew to him in great excitement, and implored him to exert himself.

It is not just the unfamiliar vocabulary that differentiates this from the conversation with his mother. There is also the metaphorical use of the familiar word 'lost'; nominalisation of the attribute 'in great excitement' (instead of 'they were greatly excited'); and use of the unusual verbal process 'implored' to report the indirect speech in the final clause 'implored him to exert himself'. George was not satisfied when Sandra turned the page and continued reading. He did not fully understand and wanted to do so. His question was quite forceful:

> Did dey help him? (line 129)

Through this kind of intense interaction during many readings over a long period of time George had learned to 'read' some portions of the story. At least he could tell the story and nearly match the words in interpreting the text (see examples of George's reading in the next section, 'Attending to Print') so we could say he was reading.

Other common foci of parent–child interaction during story reading include relating the fictive world of the text to the child's experiential world (Dombey 1983, p. 30; Chapman 1986, p. 12; Williams 1990, p. 20) and expanding the child's world by explaining additional background information to the text (Chapman 1986, pp. 14–16; Williams 1990, p. 19). The most frequently mentioned advantage to children of shared reading at home is their increased facility in negotiating 'decontextualised' or 'self-contextualising' language (Dombey 1983; Sulzby 1985; Wells 1986, p. 156; Gray 1987) so that in listening to stories, children are learning about narrative text *per se*, and the processes or strategies involved in constructing meaning from written language.

Attending to Print — Progressive Approximation

> The children who teach themselves to read do it by turning the pages of books and looking at the pictures long before they tackle the print. (Meek 1982, p. 11)

Children who are encouraged to engage in 'reading-like behaviour' (Doake 1985) from their earliest years learn to construct meaning directly from print as a gradual process of approximation eventually resulting in responses to the print of their favourite books which are not unlike the readings produced by adults. For many children this transition occurs in enjoyable situations over the years of their early childhood in a manner indistinguishable from other aspects of their development. A very clear representation of this is provided in Harper Lee's novel, *To Kill a Mockingbird*, when young Scout experiences her first day at school (pp. 23–24):

> I suppose she chose me because she knew my name; as I read the alphabet a faint line appeared between her eyebrows, and after making me read most of *My First Reader* and the stock-market quotations from *The Mobile Register* aloud, she discovered that I was literate and looked at me with more than faint distaste. Miss Caroline told me to tell my father not to teach me any more, it would interfere with my reading.
>
> 'Teach me?' I said in surprise. 'He hasn't taught me anything, Miss Caroline. Atticus ain't got time to teach me anything,' I added, when Miss Caroline smiled and shook her head. 'Why, he's so tired at night he just sits in the living room and reads.'
>
> 'If he didn't teach you who did?' Miss Caroline asked good-naturedly. 'Somebody did. You weren't born reading *The Mobile Register*.' . . .
>
> I mumbled that I was sorry and retired meditating upon my crime. I never deliberately learned to read, but somehow I had been wallowing illicitly in the daily papers. In the long hours of church — was it then I learned? I could not remember not being able to read hymns. Now that I was compelled to think about it, reading was something that just came to me, as learning to fasten the seat of my union suit without looking around, or achieving two bows from a snarl of shoelaces. I could not remember when the lines above Atticus's moving finger separated into words, but I had stared at them all the evenings in my memory, listening to the news of the day, Bills To Be Enacted into Laws, the diaries of Lorenzo Dow — anything Atticus happened to be reading when I crawled into his lap every night. Until I feared I would lose it, I never loved to read. One does not love breathing.

Detailed accounts of the processes of approximation by which young children gradually come to be able to read printed text aloud with adult-like accuracy are now well documented (Doake 1985; Chapman 1986; Thomas 1987; Mills 1988). The kinds of social contexts which facilitate the emergence of children's increasingly more accurate oral reading behaviour are part of their experience long before children begin to 'tackle the print'.

> During Raja's eleventh month, he started to identify some of his favourite books by name when asked to bring one to a parent. He could be drawn from almost any other activity simply by someone beginning to read one of his favourite stories. He began spending long periods of time (up to 45 minutes on occasions) in independent play with his books, gaining mastery over opening them and turning their pages, laughing at certain pages. His library of familiar stories had grown to 32. (Doake 1986, p. 6)

As young children begin to attend to print, at first together with the adult reader and then gradually more independently, they show a range of oral reading behaviours, which Doake (1985) characterised as: mumble reading; co-operative reading; completion reading and fluent reading. These are not hierarchical stages. In four year old George's reading of *Peter Rabbit* with his mother (Simpson 1987), all four kinds of reading are exhibited. The following extracts from the transcript (see the appendix for the full transcript) show George's reading in italics.

Mumble reading is seen on lines 29 and 102 (see appendix), where George reads along with his mother. He knew the story but was not sufficiently confident to enunciate the words or couldn't remember the exact words.

> He rushed all over the garden. (line 101)
> *(mumble)*   *(mumble . . .)*

George exhibited co-operative reading on eight occasions, where his mother paused to provide the opportunity for him to complete the sentence, for example as shown in lines 67–68:

> But Peter was very . . .
>   *was very naughty*

Completion reading occurred on seven occasions, where George's mother paused to provide the opportunity for him to take up the reading (e.g. lines 74 and 75):

> First   (Yes, he did)
>   *H, He ate some lettuce*

George also engaged in some fluent reading-like behaviour. He maintained the meaning and the pace of the reading, but his reproduction is not word perfect, nor is it likely that he could read those words outside of the context of this story. The original words of the text are given first and George's reading is shown in italics (lines 84–88):

> But round the end of the cucumber frame, whom should he meet but Mr McGregor. (*The Tale of Peter Rabbit*, pp. 24–25)
>
> *But round the cucumber frame who did she . . . who did he meet?*
> *Ahh, let's see what happens.*
> *That's right, but . . .*   Oh No!
>   *Mr McGregor*

George's control of the form of language in this segment of the story is very interesting. It can be partly explained because this is a climactic part of the story and George's excitement and engagement with the story has led him to attend very closely to the language at this point. But it is also interesting that the form of the language here is quite different from the forms of oral language with which George would be more familiar. In ordinary conversation it would be more likely to take the form:

> He saw Mr McGregor just as he got to the end of the cucumber frame.

In the written version, the adversative 'But' carries the anticipation that something is amiss. This is emphasised by the choice of the locative ('round the end of the cucumber frame') to occupy first position in the clause — usually occupied by the subject, in this case Mr McGregor, as in the spoken version above. The effect of this is to keep the 'given' information in theme position (Halliday 1985) and to delay the revelation of the subject, allowing the focus to fall appropriately on Mr McGregor at the end of the clause. The effect is to set the stage and then have the action burst onto it when Mr McGregor is announced. Not only is George negotiating the recoding of the print, at the same time he is learning how linguistic resources are deployed differently in written language to make the meanings that engage us in stories.

It is not surprising that children such as Raja and George occupy themselves in independent play with their books which comes to incorporate approximating reading behaviours — they are simply continuing the process that has begun as they and their parents read stories together. The following examples from Doake (1985) of pre-school children at different ages show how young children approximate reading favourite books which they have had read to them many times (Figures 3.1 and 3.2).

The development of one child's reading through shared reading with a teacher during the first year of school has been documented by Anne Thomas (1987). Thomas exemplifies the progress of Karen's shared reading from her entry to school at age 4 years 10 months until the end of her first year of school. The context of Karen's shared reading experience at school reading, described in detail by Thomas, cannot be reconstructed here. Three partial transcripts are quoted to illustrate Karen's development over the 12 months (Figures 3.3, 3.4 and 3.5; K = Karen and A = Anne Thomas).

The egg jumped. 'Oh, oh!' said the mother bird. 'My baby will be here! He will want to eat.'	Ow ow! A mummy bird baby here. Someping a eat. ('a' used throughout to replace 'to' and 'for')
'I must get something for my baby to eat!' she said. 'I will be back.' So away she went.	'Must baby bird a eated. Dat way went. Fly a gye.
The egg jumped. It jumped and jumped! Out came the baby bird.	Ig jumped and jumped. Out baby bird!
'Where is my mother?' he said. He looked for her.	Whis my mudder? She look a her and look her.
He looked up. He did not see her. He looked down. He did not see her.	Her look up, look down. See her. (Damion cannot yet form a negative, so he uses the affirmative in all such cases, adding a special intonation and a shake of the head.)

Figure 3.1 Damion, 2.0 years, retrieving Are You My Mother? by P.D. Eastman

Literacy Learning and Teaching

> The kitten and the hen were not his mother. The dog and the cow were not his mother. Did he have a mother?
>
> 'I did have a mother,' said the baby bird. 'I know I did. I have to find her. I will. I WILL!'
>
> So the pussy wasn't his mother. The hen wasn't his mother. The dog wasn't his mother. The cow wasn't his mother. And the baby bird said 'Did I have a mother?' And he DID!
> What a sad face. That one says: Did he have a mother? Did he have a mother? HE DID!

Figure 3.2 *Lisa Jane, 4.0 years, retrieving* Are You My Mother? *by P.D. Eastman*

> *Rosie's Walk*
>
> K. Rosie
>
> A. THE HEN
>
> K. WENT FOR A WALK (she pauses to look closely at the picture) and someone's going to trip up on that rake and it's going to flip up in the air, if they tread on that end.
>
> A. Who's going to tread on it? ROSIE THE HEN WENT FOR A WALK ACROSS . . .
>
> K. THE YARD.
> I knew it was going to happen — he's bumped his nose. (She giggles)
>
> K. She's still walking. She . . .
>
> A. What's Rosie doing?
>
> A. ROSIE THE HEN WENT FOR A WALK ACROSS THE YARD, AROUND. . . .
>
> K. THE POND.
> He's taking a drink. Well he's trying to hide from her.
>
> A. I wonder if Rosie knows he's here?
>
> K. I don't think so. The frogs knew!
>
> A. I think so. They got a fright. I don't know if Rosie

Beginning Reading

K. Mmm

K. She'll probably get lifted up (referring to the gadget used for hoisting grain/flour to and from the mill). (Turns the page.) No she hasn't. The flour's tipped out!

K. He's in trouble behind there.

K. And all the bees — they're chasing him. They're zooming off to catch him.

K. FOR TEA . . . BED. (Refers to final picture.) You shut that up first (Rosie's door) and then you put that up there (Rosie's ramp).

K. Mm . . . she'll probably get eaten up!

knows he's there . . . OVER THE HAYCOCK . . . there's a big pile of hay drying in the sun.

A. PAST THE MILL

A. All the flour's tipped out hasn't it . . .
THROUGH THE FENCE . . .

A. UNDER THE BEEHIVES. The fox is looking a little different now.

A. AND GOT BACK IN TIME

A. And then she'll be safe won't she?

Figure 3.3 *An initial sharing of* Rosie's Walk *(4 years 10 months)*

Literacy Learning and Teaching

K. I think I should read: Rosie's Walk again . . . ROSIE'S WALK . . . FOR

A. WENDY.

K. AND STEPHEN. ROSIE THE HEN WENT FOR A WALK. She doesn't even know that he's hiding under there, when she walked down the ramp . . . (turns page).

K. She . . .

A. Where did she go?

A. She went ACROSS

K. THE YARD (looks at picture on the next page). He fiddled there and he flinged up in his nose (turns page). SHE . . . THE . . . Silly me! AROUND THE POND (turns page). He's under the water (she laughs) (turns page). OVER THE HAYSTACK (turns page). He's trying to hide (turns page). PAST THE MILL (turns page). The flour's tipped out on him (turns page). THROUGH THE HOLE IN THE FENCE (turns two pages). PAST . . . UNDER THE BEEHIVES (turns page — indistinct utterance) (turns page) AND GOT IN THE FARM AGAIN.

Figure 3.4 Rosie's Walk *again (5 years 3 months)*

By the time she was 5 years and 3 months old she had read *Rosie's Walk* innumerable times, not necessarily with me, but in class, at home or to herself. Although she had known the text, mostly off by heart a few weeks before, she now was aware that the print carried the message. Her eyes were on the text as she read and she was aware of a mismatch if what she said did not match with the cues on the page, as can be witnessed in the reading of the last page of the book. (Thomas 1987, p. 12)

K. This book, I don't know.

K. (She continues to study the front cover) I know. He's going to try . . . he's going to try to grow into these clothes, I think. I don't know the story but I think it might be.

K. Bom, bom, bom! (Touching other books on the table that are written by that author.)

K. Pat Hutchins! Pat Hutchins!

K. Yes. DON'T FORGET THE BACON.

K. BY Pat Hutchins.

K. CLOCKS AND MORE CLOCKS.

K. DON'T FORGET THE BACON! . . . GOODNIGHT OWL! I know that . . .
K. (She starts to read the text.) TITCH

K. NEW TROUSERS. They are a bit short.

A. Right . . . YOU'LL SOON GROW INTO THEM, TITCH.

A. It's your friend Pat Hutchins again, isn't it?

A. Yes, that's right! I think there may be some others there.

A. ROSIE'S WALK, TITCH . . . I think there may be another one.

A. Yes, Right, let's enjoy this one, shall we? YOU'LL SOON GROW INTO THEM TITCH . . .

A. (Turns page.) Look they've got a list of all her books here! CHANGES, CHANGES. And the next one, you know.

A. And the next one?

A. NEEDED

A. (laughs)

Literacy Learning and Teaching

K. (Turns page.) I bet these are going to be Titch's new trousers.

        A. I wonder . . . HIS BROTHER PETE SAID . . .

K. 'YOU CAN HAVE MY OLD TROUSERS,' (text then reads 'They're too small for me') 'THEY ARE TOO SMALL FOR ME' I bet they're too big!

        A. THEY'RE STILL . . .

K. 'A BIT BIG FOR ME,' SAID TITCH. 'YOU'LL SOON GROW INTO THEM' SAID TITCH. (She laughs.) Poor Titch!

        A. That's what I think.

Figure 3.5 *Reading* You'll Soon Grow into Them, Titch *(5 years 9 months)*

In a more detailed discussion of the transcript of this reading session, Thomas (1987, p. 15) shows how Karen's miscues indicate her ability to construct meaning from textual cues (Figure 3.6). As Thomas points out, 'brand' and 'pair' are unfamiliar to Karen in print. But she achieves a resolution of 'brand-new' by the end of the text segment.

---

                                                          blue
So dad and Titch went shopping. They bought a brand-new

                                                     1 *new picture of*
                   brown   2 *a   new*
pair of trousers, a brand-new sweater and a brand-new
packet
pair of socks. And when mother . . . brought their brand-new

Figure 3.6 *Reading miscues (shown in italics)*

Children like Karen are well on the way to becoming readers, as distinct from just children who can read. There is now growing evidence of this kind of reading experience and development in classroom contexts (McKenzie 1986; Williams and Jack 1986; Dombey 1988a, b; Mills 1988).

The Sounds of Language in Contexts of Use

> Songs, jokes and rhymes are the best way to explore sounds. (Meek, 1982, p. 42)

Early reading development is not primarily focused on recoding the marks on the page to sound. Beginning readers are concerned with how the written text as a whole functions to construct meaning in a particular context or situation. In learning how to behave as readers they learn from whole to part. Shared experience of written texts with a more experienced reader makes children familiar with the generic structure of texts and how these achieve different social purposes. They also learn about the range of real and imagined experience with which written texts are concerned and the ways in which the form of written English varies from the oral language forms with which they are more familiar. At the same time they are learning from many sources, including their own attempts at writing, about the way graphic symbols code information in the form of letters and words.

All of this learning provides the non-visual knowledge which readers bring to texts and use to construct meaning from them (Smith 1985, p. 14). In early reading children draw heavily on non-visual information, their oral renderings approximating the gist of the written text. They gradually integrate their use of visual and non-visual cues until they are able to predict simultaneously the meanings and wordings of what they are reading. Their growing awareness of grapho-phonic relationships derives from their increasingly intensive engagement with the meanings of whole texts. In the case of some texts, such as some poems, rhymes and jingles and jokes, the meanings are primarily concerned with the playful enjoyment of sound–symbol relationships, for example *Drummer Hoff* (Barbara Emberley), *Mr Magnolia* (Quentin Blake) and *The Chicken Book* (Garth Williams). In sharing such texts specific attention to grapho-phonic relationships is functional and enjoyable. However, it is counterproductive to overemphasise the significance of sound–symbol relationships in accessing all texts (Meek 1982, p. 42; Smith 1985).

The ability of readers to make use of predictability and to develop efficiency and fluency in reading is highly dependent on their background knowledge in relation to the text and their familiarity with the generic staging and lexico-grammatical form of the written texts they encounter. When this background knowledge is strong, reading can proceed on the basis of minimal visual cues. When the generic structure and/or aspects of experience or the grammatical form of the language is unfamiliar, the reader is forced to rely increasingly on grapho-phonic cues within the visual information on the page. An over-reliance on sounding out individual letters (or letter combinations) and words often results not only in a lack of fluency and enjoyment but in the loss of purpose and meaning. Effective readers use semantic, syntactic and grapho-phonic cues in an integrative manner, varying their relative emphases as the need arises. Many ineffective readers rely too heavily on grapho-phonic cues. Reading is a complex but unitary process and not a set of discrete skills which can be taught separately and in turn and, ultimately, bolted together.

Reading Development as a Social Process

> A book, a person, and shared enjoyment: these are the conditions of success. The process should begin at an early age and continue as a genuine collaborative activity until the child leaves school. (Meek 1982, p. 9)

What children learn about reading and through reading are completely interconnected and are determined by the texts they have access to and the social contexts in which those texts are encountered. The interpretive contexts for reading are influenced by the characteristics of the texts themselves. Children who are introduced to the multilayered meanings of picture story books and children's literature through interaction with an experienced reader are learning a different form of English and a range of meanings which are not available through oral language or through the linear meanings of texts constructed especially for the purpose of instruction in reading (Graham 1984; Dombey 1983; Meek 1982). They are also learning through such shared readings that their role as a reader is an active, interpretive one. This is because the text form invites such a role and the explicit scaffolding of the adult provides the appropriate interactive base for extending young readers.

From the point of view of teaching, the factors that are significant in the development of children who become early independent readers are the social processes that facilitate such development. Important aspects of these processes include:

- the incorporation of a wide range of appropriate written language in an enjoyable, functional manner into the normal social routines that the child experiences;
- the collaborative exploration of written language with an experienced reader in these routines;
- the provision of recurrent, enjoyable and supportive contexts where the same texts may be 'revisited' over time;
- access to quality children's literature.

The challenge for us is to determine how to construct the kinds of classroom contexts which will take account of these issues. We will first need to consider practical ways of obtaining the quantity and range of quality texts to use with the children. The next consideration will be to facilitate the teacher and small groups of children interacting closely with the texts. This will entail the generation of a range of learning activities consistent with the kind of interactive, meaning-centred activity of the shared reading experience. We also need to make use of classroom organisation and management strategies that allow the teacher to work intensively with some groups of children while other children are working independently and semi-independently. Our experience of contemporary classroom practice indicates that many teachers of young children are addressing these concerns. The suggestions which follow attempt to illustrate and further explore the best of current practice as it reflects the insights gained from recent theory and research.

Beginning Reading

Planning and Managing Whole Class Programs

We have argued that the kinds of readers children become depends largely on the kinds of texts they have access to and the kinds of interactions they experience with those texts. We want children's first encounters with school reading activities to include experiences with literary texts. Right from the start we want young children to be encouraged to behave like readers and, through exploring the 'space to play' in good children's literature, to come to enjoy reading in an active, interpretive way. We know the kinds of books that are productive of this kind of development and we know the kinds of adult interactive behaviours associated with the shared reading of books that are most facilitative. How can we provide in classrooms of 20 to 30 or more young children the recurrent, enjoyable and supportive contexts where engaging children's books are introduced and periodically revisited, where each child reads and talks with the teacher about the texts, where there is close attention to print and sound–symbol relationships and progressive approximation to effective, independent reading behaviour?

Such a goal is difficult but not unrealistic. In our experience many teachers have worked co-operatively to develop exceptional programs which have involved collaboration with parents, teacher-librarians, support teachers, classes of older pupils, the community library and others. The development of a facilitative classroom context involves a good deal of work on many fronts over considerable time — from the detail of developing a dynamic classroom library, a reading corner, listening post facility, a publishing centre, etc. to establishing time for independent silent reading, times for parents or other experienced readers to read aloud to children, liaison with parents, home reading schemes, book clubs, etc. It is not possible, in the space available, for us to take this kind of comprehensive perspective on classroom organisation and programming. What we offer in this section is an example of detailed lesson planning of day to day work in a fairly simple but realistic outline of a two week program for children who are well into their first year of school — or at the beginning of their second year.

An Author Study for Kindergarten!

We have organised this program around a selection of books by Pat Hutchins. We have chosen these books because they are supportive of novice readers, many of whom very quickly learn to read them independently. At the same time many of these books offer the multilayered meanings which invite often complex and contesting interpretations. One longer text (*The Very Worst Monster*) has been included to emphasise that children's reading development can benefit significantly without them necessarily learning to read all of the text in every book which is the focus of reading lessons.

The sessions are planned for about 45 minutes to an hour and comprise a unit of work extending over about two weeks. Of course, it would be quite possible to extend this period or conclude at the end of the first week. The stages within each session are flexible but generally adhere to the following pattern:

- orientation to collaborative reading;
- introduction of new book;
- collaborative reading of the new book;
- exploration of text meanings;
- consolidation of text processing;
- extension reading/writing activities.

Although it is useful to think systematically about the stages in a lesson and the kinds of learning experiences that typify these stages, it is also crucial that these do not degenerate into formulaic rituals. The organisation of these sessions must be responsive to the possibilities afforded by the form of the text and the experiences and needs of the children in being able to benefit from those possibilities. After outlining the purposes of these lesson segments and the kinds of activities that may be involved in them, we will show how they have been used in planning the unit of work based on the selections from Pat Hutchins' books.

ORIENTATION

This stage makes use of material which is familiar and/or easily and confidently dealt with by the children. Initially it might involve making one or two selections from a variety of chants, poems, songs, rhymes, etc. — for example, 'Five little ducks went out one day . . .' (Scales 1981, p. 131) or 'One, two, buckle my shoe . . .' (Davies *et al.* 1987, p. 43). These are sung/read by the teacher and the class as a whole group. When the words are pretty well known by heart, they can be displayed on a chart and the teacher can informally encourage the children to 'read' as they perform, by pointing and rehearsing lines with them. The aim is for maximum participation as a group with familiar, easy material so that the children feel confident in contributing to the activity. As the children gain more experience, the same purpose can be achieved by rereading familiar and favourite picture story books (including those which have been introduced in previous lessons), using group readings with improvised drama, etc. as well as sharing children's own writing and the results of previous class/group work. This stage occupies about the first five minutes of the lessson.

INTRODUCTION OF NEW BOOK

The purpose of this stage is to arouse interest in the book by drawing attention to its external characteristics and noting features such as the cover design, the title, the name of the author and the publisher. This provides the opportunity to discuss the book as a social artefact — some children may have seen the book before, they may have heard of the author or have other 'Picture Puffins', or some other such imprint, at home. Children may use cues from the book cover to suggest what kind of a book it is and what it may be about, etc. There is also the opportunity to attend to children's developing knowledge of sound–symbol relationships in identifying the name of the author and the title. For example, the following questions could be asked. Are there any children in the class whose first name is the same as that of the author? Whose names are different but start the same way as the author's? Similarly, whose surnames and names begin with the same capital letter as words in the title — 'Hunter', for example — or 'where have we seen that word before?' The title and author's name (and perhaps also associated names and words) can be written on the blackboard, further demonstrating and rehearsing the sound–symbol relationships. This stage also occupies about five minutes or so.

COLLABORATIVE READING
There are five steps in this section of the lesson:
1. the teacher's initial reading of the book;
2. initial discussion with the children about the story;
3. a second reading with informal participation by the children as a group;
4. follow-up discussion drawing on further observations about the story to scaffold directed participation in a third reading;
5. a third reading with teacher-directed participation by the children, chorally in small groups or as individuals as appropriate.

The teacher's initial reading provides a model for the children. Ideally, teachers should be seated to the side of the book placed on an easel or stand so that they can look at the book with the children as they read. It is not essential for the book to be a 'big book' for this to work quite satisfactorily if the children are seated on the floor, close to the teacher. Children should be encouraged to comment on what they thought about the story, what they noticed about the text and the illustrations, any patterns they noticed or what puzzled them, etc. Then the teacher can suggest that he or she reads the text again so that they can review their comments and see what else they notice. He or she should suggest to the children that they join in the reading. By using gesture, glance and movement teachers can demonstratively encourage the children to participate at appropriate points. The follow-up discussion should include the planning of systematic participation by the children in the third reading. This might amount to allocating groups of children to read particular parts (three different groups to read the parts of the three little pigs, for example, and the whole class to join in with the Wolf's threat — 'I'll huff and I'll puff . . .'). It might also include allocating some children the task of making sound effects, for example, to accompany the 'Billy goats Gruff' walking over the bridge. These steps might well vary according to the form of the text and the experience of the children, but the object is to engage them in the 'reading' of the story within a supporting and enjoyable context. The section may take about 15 minutes.

EXPLORATION OF MEANINGS

This 'talk around text' is crucial to the development of what it means to be a reader. Children can explore the patterns and puzzles, the deliberate ambiguities of the illustrations and the text and the perspectives from which the story is told. The form of the texts makes it possible for the children to initiate these important questions. Did Rosie the hen (*Rosie's Walk*) know all the time that the fox was following her? Was there really a monster in David McKee's *Not Now Bernard*? If Max just had a dream about the 'Wild Things', how come it is a full moon when he goes to his bedroom and not a full moon when the forest grew and he was with the Wild Things? (Maurice Sendak, *Where the Wild Things Are*). Who said 'That was not a nice thing to say to Grandpa' in John Burningham's *Granpa*? This stage takes about five to ten minutes.

CONSOLIDATION

This is where children interact closely with print to confirm and extend their meaning-making strategies based on their integrative use of cues from the semiotics of illustration, overall text structure, grammatical patternings and grapho-phonic relationships. They need structured opportunities to deal directly with print, to learn and rehearse the grammatical and grapho-phonic knowledge that is essential to the development of their facility with written language. This stage of the lesson will often be undertaken as small-group work and occupies about 15 minutes. There is no suggestion here that children should be grouped according to any crude notions of 'reading ability', which would be quite counter-productive. Rather the groupings should be functionally organised so that some children, even if they are not very experienced readers, can undertake work with a good deal of independence from the teacher so that he or she can systematically allocate time to more intensive interaction with each child in the class. Listening post tasks, re-creations of stories with flannel-board illustrations, text reconstructions or text innovations, labelling of illustrations, etc. can be varied to achieve this. One group of children is targeted for more intensive teacher interaction each day.

EXTENSION

There should always be extending activities available — and not just for those children considered to be more experienced or advanced readers. In some cases extension activities may be started as a whole class activity with a good deal of teacher direction and then children allocated roles in completing the activity when time is available to them. An example would be the construction of a captioned collage of the scene from Pat Hutchins' *The Wind Blew* where all of the objects are mixed up in the sky. The children draw the background and then paste on representations of the articles to form their collage. Some of these might come from advertisements in magazines, etc. and could therefore include a cut out label. In other cases the children may need to bring actual objects from home, such as a balloon, and for other objects models may need to be used, for example cotton balls pasted on to represent the judge's wig.

Captioning of the latter objects would require the children to retrieve the print from the book. Such a task is quite demanding for many young children and could be undertaken initially as a whole class activity which the teacher orchestrates, demonstrating how it is to be done. Children could then be encouraged to bring appropriate materials from home and keep these in a box so that they are available for later independent work on their own or small-group collages. Other similar extensions of work done as a class might involve the construction and insertion of 'speech balloons' into stories, the recording of children's retellings, etc.

Extension activities might also include simply supplying a 'book box' of stories related thematically to the one being dealt with. For example, when dealing with Pat Hutchins' *The Very Worst Monster*, assemble copies of David McKee's *Not Now Bernard*, Hiawyn Oram's *Angry Arthur*, Rosemary Wells' *Noisy Nora* and Franz Brandenberg's *I Don't Feel Well*.

The children should always know that there is an interesting variety of activities they can do when they have finished the particular task at hand.

Reading Books by Pat Hutchins: The Unit Plan

WEEK 1

Session 1

Orientation
Begin with some familiar counting rhymes or chants about animals or hunters. A simple example is the following well-known chant where the teacher or one group of children says one line then the others repeat it:

The Squeedgee Hunt

We're going on a squeedgee hunt ...	Slap slap slap slap
We're going to catch a big one	Slap slap slap slap
I'm not scared	Slap slap slap slap
What's that ahead	Slap slap slap slap
etc.

Alternatively, poems like Charles Causley's 'I saw a Jolly Hunter' could be used with the devising of appropriate actions to accompany it:

I saw a jolly hunter
With a jolly gun
Walking in the country
In the jolly sun

In the jolly meadow
Sat a jolly hare
Saw the jolly hunter
Took jolly care

Hunter jolly eager
Sight of jolly prey
Forgot gun pointing
Wrong jolly way

Jolly hunter jolly head
Over heels gone
Jolly old safety catch
Not jolly on

Bang went the jolly gun
Hunter jolly dead
Jolly hare got clean away
'Jolly good' I said

Introduction
Display a selection of books written by Pat Hutchins along the blackboard ledge or in 'the book corner' and explain to the children that over the next couple of weeks they are going to read some stories written and illustrated by the same person. Try to obtain a photograph of Pat Hutchins and provide some biographical information about the author. This might be summarised on a chart and read to the children.

PAT HUTCHINS
Pat Hutchins was born in England. She wanted to illustrate books. Because nobody would give her a book to illustrate, she decided to write her own books and illustrate them. The first book she wrote was *Rosie's Walk*.

Show the children the displayed books and ask if they have seen any of the books before. If they have invite the children to identify any book which is familiar to them. They may like to share what they know about the book. Show the book cover to the class and ask them to read the title together. Repeat this procedure with any other books which are familiar to the children.

Show the children the book *1 Hunter*. At one level this is a simple counting book, whose form and illustrations provide support for novice readers so that they will experience success in their early readings of the text. But the illustrations also offer considerable possibilities for elaboration of the concern with counting. As indicated above the next steps involve helping the children to identify the title and the author, inviting children to then read these, writing them on the blackboard, identifying children with the same name as the author, etc., writing their names on the board and drawing attention to sound–symbol relationships in the process.

Invite the children to suggest what the book may be about, asking them to indicate what has given them their clues.

Collaborative Reading
Begin by reading the whole book aloud to the children. It is useful to record the teacher's reading of the text so that the tape can become a

Beginning Reading

resource for later class work or can be borrowed by individual children to take home. Proceed with the collaborative reading stage as detailed above.

Exploration
Invite the children to share what they remembered most about the book, to say if anything puzzled them or if they noticed any patterns in the book. Discuss the ways in which the words and the pictures both tell the story and invite children to comment on any other stories which might be told but which are not mentioned in the words.

Consolidation
1 *Hunter* Mural. The children work in pairs and each pair is provided with two copies of the following pictures:

1	Hunter	6	tigers
2	elephants	7	crocodiles
3	giraffes	8	monkeys
4	ostriches	9	snakes
5	antelopes	10	parrots

Each pair is also provided with a large amount of green paper cut out to represent trees and grass. The children are asked to paste each set of two pictures of the various animals side by side on a piece of used computer paper and to paste the green paper representing the grass and trees over one of the pictures so as to hide part of the animals. They then label the pictures by copying from the text or by pasting on labels provided by the teacher.

As the pairs finish their work they come to the front of the room where there are four sets of a jigsaw-like puzzle to work out. The puzzle consists of word cards and pictures of animals and the parts of animals that have been camouflaged in the book *1 Hunter*. Children who have difficulty in recognising the words are aided by the jigsaw aspect, but, of course, it is much quicker to assemble the puzzle by relating the words directly to the picture.

Extension
An extension of the consolidation activity would be for the children to construct or complete a similar puzzle but using different animals. Pictures and names could be stencilled for them or they could simply cut out and label pictures from magazines.

A book box of associated titles could be assembled for the children to read when they have time available. These could include *Anno's Counting Book* by Mitsumasa Anno, *Animal Jigsaws* by Jim Howes, *Who?* by Marcia Pearson and *Who's in the Shed?* by Brenda Parkes.

Session 2

Orientation
Ask the children to look at the display of Pat Hutchins' books again and to locate the book that was read yesterday. Ask the children to identify

the title and author of the book and review what was learned yesterday about related names and words and letter–sound relationships.

Reread the book, inviting the children to join in and to be thinking about which part of the book they would like to read. Have prepared labels for the animals so that there are enough for each child to be allocated to one animal. This means about three labels for each of the nine animals mentioned. Ask the children which animals they want to be and distribute the labels. Read the book again with the children reading their nominated parts. If this proves to be enjoyable, have the children swap their labels and read the text again.

Introduction
Write the title of the book *Rosie's Walk* on the blackboard and help the children to recognise and read the title. Some may know the word 'walk' from encountering the word in their environment and some may be able to work out 'Rosie' if they know people with similar names, for example Rosa. Once again note the letter–sound relationships and list associated class names and familiar words.

Ask the children who they think Rosie might be and then ask them to locate this book among the display of Pat Hutchins' books. Once they see the book cover they may be encouraged to say much more about Rosie and what her walk might entail.

Collaborative Reading
Again it is useful to record the teacher's initial reading of this story. The children will find it very easy to join in the second reading and during the discussion it is often surprising to see how much of the detail of the story they pick up as being told by the illustrations, for example the impending doom for the fox which is foreshadowed as Rosie walks 'past the mill' and her foot becomes entangled in the line attached to the suspended flour bag. The third reading may be extended to include several children reading the text individually if they wish to. It is not uncommon for this to occur and it provides a great deal of satisfaction to have read a 'whole book' by oneself!

Exploration
Explore further with the children the way the story meanings are made — the fact that the fox is never mentioned in the text, the role of other animals. Extend their awareness of foreshadowing and discuss its effect, note the print within the illustrations, etc. What are we to make of Rosie's demeanour? What would it mean if she did know that the fox was there all the time? In this exploration try to build on the children's observations and encourage them to raise issues.

Ask the children to close their eyes and think about the two Pat Hutchins books they have read. What things are the same about them? What things are different?

Consolidation
In this segment the children would work in four groups. Each of the activities is fairly short. They involve substantial prior preparation of

materials by the teacher. One group works directly and intensively with the teacher consolidating the reading of *Rosie's Walk* while the other groups can work on their tasks with occasional teacher oversight but without the need for intensive teacher supervision. It is possible, but not necessary, to have the groups rotate so that each one works on each task.

- Listening Post Activity

The children listen to the tape of *1 Hunter* and follow the text. They then match a set of word cards and picture cards based on the book; for example:

10 parrots — picture of 10 parrots
7 crocodiles — picture of 7 crocodiles

This can be easily checked by the teacher at a glance. When the children have finished this, they listen to the reading of *Rosie's Walk* on the tape.

- Story Reconstruction

Write the text of the story onto large sheets of paper and pin these across the wall of the room. Provide children with cut-outs of the illustrations and have them pin (or blu tack) these to the sheets of paper to remake the story. Once again this can be easily overseen by the teacher without intensive involvement.

- Story Innovation

To do this activity you will need to be prepared to take apart two copies of *Rosie's Walk*. Put the pages onto sheets of cardboard so that you have one complete text of which all the pages can be completely rearranged. Ask the children to see how many ways they can rearrange the pages so that the story would be told in a different order and still make sense.

- Rereading with the Teacher

This is the group with which the teacher interacts most intensively. It is a way of supporting those children who have not been progressing as confidently as their peers. Initially read the book again with the children and then encourage them to read. On completion of this reading and discussion provide each of the children with a stick or glove puppet of Rosie or the fox and work with them on retelling the events of the walk from the point of view of their character.

Extension

Provide the complete text of the book but cut into the segments as they appear on the pages in the book. Ask the children to reconstruct the text of the story. When this is completed provide them with the 32 words of the story each on separate cards and ask them to reconstruct the story again.

Ask the children to read the story again and list all of the animals they can see in the illustrations apart from Rosie and the fox. This could be done by providing the children with cards like the ones used for *1 Hunter*, i.e. 1 goat, 2 frogs, 2 mice, 1 bird, etc.

Assemble a book box of extension reading possibilities such as *Fancy*

That! by Pamela Allen, *Hattie and the Fox* by Mem Fox, *The Chicken Book* by Garth Williams and *The Fox Went Out on a Chilly Night* by Peter Spier.

Session 3

Orientation
This lesson could begin with the chants from Session 1 and then some of the children's displayed reconstructions based on *1 Hunter* and *Rosie's Walk* could be read together. Various individuals might then be encouraged to read their own reconstructions or other children's displayed work which they really like.

Introduction
Tell the children the title of the book (*Goodnight Owl*) which you are going to read and ask them to volunteer to find the book from the display of Pat Hutchins' books. Before they begin to look, encourage the children to be strategic in thinking about the written form of the title, i.e. ask them what the words would start with. Of course the picture on the cover will be a clear cue for many children. Ask the children to suggest what the book may be about.

Look at the title page with the children and discuss the dedication: 'For Morgan's Granpa'. Ask the children who they think Morgan might be. Refer back to *1 Hunter* and *Rosie's Walk* to see if Pat Hutchins dedicated these books to anyone.

Collaborative Reading
The repetition in this book will facilitate the children's participation in the reading. By the third reading it is possible to have children allocated to parts and to be experimenting with sound effects and different voice tones to enhance the dramatic reading of the book. This time it may be fun to tape the children's final reading of the story and to play it back to them.

Exploration
Even though this book is fairly straightforward, it is interesting to see how alert the children will be to the detail of the illustrations and story development. For example, because of the counting associated with *1 Hunter*, some children are likely to comment on the numbers of different kinds of birds — why is there only one woodpecker, but two starlings? Some birds appear in the picture on the page before they are mentioned in the text. Are some of the birds not mentioned in the text? Why was the owl so patient? Was he thinking all the time about how he was going to keep them awake?

Consolidation
- Listening Post Activity

The children listen to their recording of the story and then listen a second time but this time each pair is provided with a copy of the book in which the verb indicating the sound of the bird/animal has been covered. The children are given these verbs printed on 'post it' paper strips or on paper with 'blu tack' and as they hear the story they are to attach the word card to the story text.

- Counting Activity

Prepare cards again in the manner of *1 Hunter* but applied to the illustrations of *Goodnight Owl*, i.e. 1 cuckoo, 2 starlings, 4 sparrows, etc. The children work in two subgroups of three to add these cards to the relevant pages of the book. They position the cards to label the appropriate birds/animals.

- Word and Sound Repetitions

Show the children that the sound the animal makes on every page is repeated. But ask if they have noticed that some other words are repeated and some sounds are the same. Provide the group with numbered plastic sleeves for each page in the book and ask them to put sleeve number one over the first page and draw with coloured texta around the words that are the same or have the same sound. Invite them to continue to do this for the remainder of the book. (Since the pages of *Goodnight Owl* are not numbered, you will need to pencil in page numbers so the children can match them with their numbered 'sleeves').

- Reading with the Teacher

Work with one group of children to produce a choral reading with sound effects and record this on another tape.

Extension

Begin with the children a chart of animals and the sounds they make. Initially start with the information from *Goodnight Owl* and then expand:

cows	moo
dogs	bark
cats	meow
horses	neigh

Children could look in other books to add to the list, for example *Mr Gumpy's Outing* by John Burningham and *Too Much Noise* by Ann McGovern.

Put together a book box of associated titles for the children to read, for example *Animal Noises* by Mary O'Toole, *Trouble in the Ark* by Gerald Rose, *Goodnight, Goodnight* by Eve Rice and *Wind* by Ron Bacon.

Session 4

Orientation

Ask the children to identify the three books in the Pat Hutchins' display which have been shared in class. Ask them to indicate their favourite and then read each of the favourites with the group that nominated them

Literacy Learning and Teaching

joining in. Discuss ways in which reading aloud skills may be improved. Invite children to volunteer to read their favourite book aloud to the class.

Read aloud to the children one or more of the following poems:

'The Wind' by James Reeves, 'Go Wind Go' by Lilian Moore, 'Wind on the Hill' by A.A. Milne and 'Who Has Seen the Wind?' by Christina Rossetti (in De Regniers *et al.* 1988).

Introduction

Ask the children to find the book *The Wind Blew* from the other Pat Hutchins books displayed. Once again encourage the children to be strategic in their reading of the title as was suggested in previous lessons. Discuss with the children some of the personal hazards of windy weather and what kinds of things this book may deal with as suggested by the cover illustration.

Collaborative Reading

Before reading the story, note again the dedication — this time 'For Mark'. Some of the children will now be well aware of the foreshadowing that Pat Hutchins includes in her illustrations so they will be able to say before you read the next page what the wind is going to blow away. Because of this, the repetitive pattern and the rhyme, this book lends itself to a kind of oral cloze which can be incorporated into the second reading to encourage pupil participation — just pause before the end of the second line on each page and the children will be able to complete it.

Exploration

Once again the children will enjoy pointing out how the pictures tell the story ahead of the text and exploring the print within the illustrations (*News*: Gale force winds; *Mail*, etc.). They might well be encouraged to compare the role of the pictures in books like this one and *Goodnight Owl* with the role of the pictures in *Rosie's Walk*.

Consolidation

● Listening Post Activity

The children listen to the story on the listening post, following the book which has the text reproduced on cards pinned over the original texts on some pages to construct a 'rhyming cloze' task; for example:

> And not content, it took a hat,
> and still not satisfied with th— —,
> it whipped a kite into the air
> and kept it spinning round up there.
> It grabbed a shirt left out to dry
> and tossed it upward to the sk—.
> It plucked a hanky from a nose
> and up and up and up it r— — —.

● Labelling 'a'

Provide the group with a photocopy of the third last page of the book with arrows leading from the objects to 'boxes' into which the children can either paste the labels they have been given or go through the book, select the name of the object from the print and write it in the appropriate box.

- Labelling 'b'

Provide this group also with a photocopy of the third last page and similarly ask them to label the characters in the story.

- Captioned Mural

Show the children how to do a captioned mural as described at the beginning of this section on planning and managing whole class programs.

Extension

Provide the children with the text for each page reproduced on a separate card. Invite the children to see how the text could be rearranged to make the story in a different order and still make sense. Why can some sections not be rearranged?

Ask the children to read *Mrs Mopple's Washing Line* by Anita Hewett, and select some of the consolidation activities above to apply to that story.

Session 5

Orientation

Take a class vote to find the most popular book dealt with so far. Read this book again as a class, perhaps allocating groups and/or individuals to read particular parts.

Display an enlarged copy of the third last page of *The Wind Blew* (the same page used for group work activities in the previous session). This can be done by using the enlargement facility on a photocopier or by making an overhead transparency of the page, projecting it onto a large piece of chart paper on the wall and tracing over the picture. Also have available on cards the labels for the objects and the people and work with the children to affix the labels to the picture.

Read *The Wind Blew* again with the children joining in.

Introduction

Play the memory game 'I went to town and I bought . . .'. The children sit in a circle and each must repeat what the last child said and add to the list another item that he or she bought. Tell the children the last Pat Hutchins book for this week is *Don't Forget the Bacon*. Write the title and author on the board and once again have the children locate the book from the display.

Collaborative Reading

Even after the first reading the children will be able to join in on the repetition of 'and don't forget the bacon'. Through the discussion of the story and the pictures the children will be able to make more use of the picture cues to assist them in joining in the second reading of the text. The second part of the book greatly facilitates this shared reading, with picture cues for the distracting items like 'A pile of chairs' on one page and 'A flight of stairs' on the adjacent page. These two pages cue the children to predict what will be on the next page by their remembering the association of the rhyme. When the next page does show 'A pound of pears', the illustration on the adjacent page is there to confirm it. These are the patternings which the children can be encouraged to make explicit in their discussion of the story and hence make explicit to everyone the way to read this story. On the third reading, pages such as 'A pound of pears' and 'A cake for tea' could be the targets for individuals or groups of children to read. The teacher could nominate them before turning the page. The support offered by the form of the text and the explicit discussion of this will facilitate the children's success.

Exploration
Of course there is a great deal to explore in this text — the difference between 'speech balloons' and 'thought clouds', the use of bold-face print and the importance of question marks and exclamation marks in making the meanings of this story. There is also a lot of 'environmental print' incorporated into the illustrations. There is the 'untold' story of the poor old dog being tormented/tantalised by the butterfly throughout the story — and, 'is the easiest way to remember something in fact to say it, over and over again?'

Consolidation
The consolidation is probably best undertaken as group work, allocating tasks such as the following. If further work is required the groups can rotate around the tasks. Alternatively, tasks two and three could be undertaken as whole class activities.

- Listening Post Activity

The teacher prepares the following labels superimposed on a drawing of each item to fit over the 'thought clouds' in the second half of the book.

> A pile of chairs.
> A flight of stairs.
> A pound of pears!
> A rake for leaves.
> A cape for me.
> A cake for tea!
> Six clothes pegs.
> Six fat legs.
> Six farm eggs!

The children first listen to the story on the tape and on the second listening they work in pairs to blu tack the thought clouds made by the teacher over the top of the existing ones in the book. This task can be made more demanding by covering the thought clouds in the book and by preparing new 'clouds' which are not superimposed on picture cues.

Beginning Reading

- Grapho-phonic Cloze

Reproduce the following pages of the book, using 'white out' to construct the following contextualised, grapho-phonic cloze.

>A pile of — —airs
>A flight of — —airs
>A —ound of —ears!
>A —ake for leaves.
>A ca—e for me.
>A ca—e for tea!
>Six clothes —egs.
>Six fat l— — —.
>Six farm e— — —!

The children work in pairs to fill in the missing letters and then read the book to check. Each reproduced page can be placed in a plastic sleeve and the children can write their answers using water-based texta. This facilitates changing their answers and makes the teaching resource reusable. If overhead transparencies of the reproduced pages are made, the activity can become a basis for whole class discussion.

- Text Innovation

Work with the teacher to construct another story, based on shopping at the hardware store:

>'A packet of nails   (snails, sails, bales, rails, tails . . .)
>A 10 cm bolt   (salt, colt, vault . . .)
>New fuse wire   (fire, hire, tyre . . .)
>and don't forget the glue'

Extension

At the end of the week it is useful to have a time for children to be able to complete any extension activities they have started in previous sessions and not finished. Alternatively, children may use this opportunity to undertake extension activities they have not selected during the week. A useful book to extend this session is John Burningham's *The Shopping Basket*. Some children may be able to read it themselves or it could be made available on a cassette tape. Students might try to compose a story like *Don't Forget the Bacon*, using the first page of *The Shopping Basket* as a starting point.

WEEK 2

During week 2 the session format is different. Instead of introducing a new book each day, one longer story, *The Very Worst Monster*, forms the basis of the sessions for the whole week. The children are introduced to reader's theatre and what is meant by 'scripting' and are supported in eventually producing a reader's theatre performance of *The Very Worst Monster*.

The orientation stage of the sessions is very similar to those of the first week. The children now have five stories with which they are fairly confident and they can choose one of these to begin each session with shared reading. There are some variations on this procedure and where appropriate these are indicated within each of the sessions below. It is also useful to include short fun activities such as tongue twisters like the following:

>   Monsters munch much mush
>   Mummies munch much mush
>   Many mummies and many monsters
>   Must munch much mush

The introduction stage for presenting the new text is only relevant for the first session and after the first day the collaborative reading, exploration and consolidation stages take a different form. The extension work involves the provision of thematically related books which children are encouraged to 'read' and discuss even when they cannot independently construct meanings from the print. Examples of such books are *Not Now Bernard* by David McKee and *Angry Arthur* by Hiawyn Oram. Pat Hutchins' books, *Titch* and *You'll Soon Grow into Them Titch*, could also be related.

Instead of detailing the sessions for the second week in stages as was done for the first week, the implementation of the basic procedures, with the modifications noted above, will be assumed and the session descriptions will focus on the new activities for week 2.

Session 6

During the collaborative reading stage the children's attention is drawn particularly to the dialogue and the speech markers in the text. This can be done by focusing more on what Hazel said and encouraging the children to join in with her statements. In the exploration stage the children's understanding of how the text signals actual words spoken can be further elaborated. This can be extended to discuss how we know what Hazel is feeling when the book doesn't tell us directly how she is feeling. Similarly, we know long before the text explicitly informs us that the family is very proud of Billy. Such discussion can form a basis for children's appreciation of the way in which, in some stories, the reader is shown what characters are like rather than simply being told.

When it comes to the consolidating stage, the children can be reminded of the speech bubbles and thought clouds in *Don't Forget the Bacon*. Initially the class can work as a whole group with the teacher as he or she elicits from them what parts of the text could be placed in speech bubbles on each page, writes up the speech bubbles as the children identify the text segments, and places them appropriately (using blu tack) onto the illustrations. The children are then allocated (usually as pairs) to a page of the book which has two people speaking. For example, the first page has Pa and Hazel speaking, so two children would be allocated to that page. The next page has Grandpa and Hazel speaking, so another two children would be allocated to that page and so on. Allocation of all such pages in the book will require 18 children. More experienced readers in the class could form a second group, with these children being allocated parts rather than pages. For example, the most experienced readers would be allocated the parts of Ma and Pa, then another good reader the part of Hazel, and then the other characters with smaller speaking parts are allocated. In this way, all of the children have some dialogue to learn to read which is manageable for them. The children are given the speech bubbles for the pages to which they were allocated. The story is then read again with both 'casts' — the teacher rehearsing the dialogue parts with each child. The children are invited to take their speech bubbles home and to bring a 'paper bag monster mask' (or some other simple monster disguise) to wear when they read the book together the next day. They may get some help in practising reading their speech bubbles at home.

Session 7

This session will begin of course with the teacher first reading *The Very Worst Monster* again with the children encouraged to join in informally. This is followed by a reading when the children read the dialogue on their allocated pages — perhaps adorned by their monster masks/disguises from home.

The consolidation work is undertaken via group work with the class working in their functional groupings derived from their previous allocation to dialogue parts. The purpose of this basis for grouping is to have the children teach their peers how to read the sections of dialogue they were allocated and which they are now fairly confident of reading themselves. The 18 pupils allocated pages of the book are regrouped according to character parts. So all of the 'Hazels' (eight), plus the judge, could form one group. The second group would be the four 'Pas', the three 'Mas', Grandpa and Grandma (nine children again). The third group would be the more experienced readers from yesterday who were allocated parts rather than pages. Each of these groups in turn work with the teacher's supervision to teach fellow group members how to read their individual dialogue sections, so that the children become more confident in attempting to read all of the dialogue for their own character (and some others) in the book.

While one of the groups is working with the teacher as indicated above, a second group is listening to the teacher's reading and the children's readings of *The Very Worst Monster* on the listening post. The third group is undertaking a speech bubble location task, demonstrated by the teacher in yesterday's lesson. The children are divided into two or three subgroups of about three pupils. Each subgroup is given a full set of speech bubbles for the book and the children work together to place the speech bubbles in the appropriate illustrations by finding the corresponding dialogue in the story.

An extension activity is to regroup the children from their original dialogue-learning groups into smaller groups of four so that two of the 'Hazels' are grouped with two of the 'Pas' and so on to enable the children who are 'expert' with all the 'Hazel' dialogue to tutor the pair of 'Pas' in reading this and vice versa. The regrouping can be extended to cover more combinations of characters so that eventually all of the children have learned from each other to read confidently most of the dialogue in the book.

Session 8

In this session read to the children a related book such as David McKee's *Not Now Bernard* and discuss with them how you changed your voice to show how the characters were feeling. Discuss with the children how they can change their voices by varying the volume, tone, pitch and the speed to show clearly what the character meant and what he or she felt when speaking. Invite them to suggest interpretations of some of the dialogue in *The Very Worst Monster*.

Suggest to the children that this work would be very important if the book were made into a television show or a play, as books often are. Indicate that actors work from scripts not books and show them again the first couple of pages of the book as well as an overhead transparency of what a corresponding script might look like. For example:

Pa: My son is going to grow up to be the Worst Monster in the World.
Hazel: No, he's not. I am.
Grandpa: Look at those strong fangs! He can bend bars with his teeth!
Hazel: So can I.

Discuss with the children how the two texts are similar and how they are different. How do we know who says what in a story? How do we know who says what in a play? Discuss the role of the narrator in a story and identify which parts of the text are the narrator's. Ask about the need for a narrator in the play script above. This can also lead to a discussion about stage directions. Modify the above overhead transparency to include these aspects then jointly construct with the children a script for the book up to the point where Billy wins the contest. This involves reading each page with the children and then eliciting from them how the script should be written, modifying their suggestions where necessary and writing the resulting text onto the overhead projector transparencies so the children can see how this type of text is written.

This takes most of the session time but could be extended to include the following group work activities which could also be undertaken on a rotation basis.

- Reading a Reader's Theatre Script

One 'cast' of seven or eight pupils (including a narrator) practises reading the script which has just been jointly composed and tapes their reading for self-evaluation and review.

- Writing a Reader's Theatre Script

This task could only be taken on independently by children who were quite advanced or by a group working with a parent, teacher's aide or older student who could help the children with the task. This group could work in pairs to construct a script for the last three pages of the book. It could be done on overhead projection sheets so that each group's effort could then be displayed and discussed by the class.

- Performance Aspects of Oral Reading

This group works with the teacher to extend their experience of voice variation and gesture in oral reading performance. They could also be introduced to the idea of annotating and coding a script to help signal different ways of reading it aloud.

Session 9

This is the session where the children practise their reader's theatre presentation. The scripts prepared on the overhead projector should be duplicated so that each child now has his/her own copy. Negotiate casting of the characters with the children. It will usually be possible to have three or four 'casts' in a class of about 30 children. While two groups practise their performance with the teacher giving advice and support, the other two groups can be given the opportunity to perhaps indulge in some face painting (preferably with the assistance of parent helpers) or impromptu costuming from a box of old clothes, wigs, long fingernails, etc. collected by the staff for the purpose. The groups then of course rotate so that each cast is helped by the teacher to perfect its performance and each cast also has the fun of dressing up, etc. The teacher should ensure that all the children have their scripts pasted onto manilla folders and that each has highlighted his or her 'part'. Ideally this should be in preparation for performing this piece of reader's theatre on the following day, but additional rehearsal sessions may be needed. When the children are ready the performance can be scheduled and perhaps taken to another class or even performed at a school assembly.

Session 10

This session might well be the occasion of the public reader's theatre performance. If this is the case, it is important to provide the children with the opportunity for a final rehearsal and to establish with them how you as the teacher (or the teacher of the other class) will give cues if necessary to keep the performance going.

This session should also provide opportunities to review and extend both the children's literary and literacy development over the past two weeks. In the first part of the session children could be invited to read, or request to be read to them, books they have read over the period of this unit of work or books which have been displayed but which they have not had a chance to look at. The following are some of Pat Hutchins' books which have not been specifically mentioned and about which the children may now be curious: *The Surprise Party*, *Tom and Sam*, *One-eyed Jake*, *The Doorbell Rang*, *The Tale of Thomas Mead*. Of course the children may well be interested in the books by other authors which have been associated with their work.

The following activities are divided into two main groups. The first provides contexts for the children to explore and express their understanding of literary issues and the second focuses on their developing facility with print in their reading and writing. The children could undertake these activities in small groups and come together as a whole class to share their responses.

Literacy Learning and Teaching

- Expressing Literary Understanding

The children talk together about the books they have used and seen in the display area and sort them into piles or categories and rearrange the display accordingly. They will then be asked to tell the rest of the class why they have grouped certain books together and why they have set up the display in their particular way.

From the other authors they have read or noticed in the display area, the children are asked to discuss which one they would nominate to form the basis of another unit of work such as the one they have just completed. With adult assistance they might locate additional books by this author in the class or school library. Once again they will be asked to set up a display of these books and talk to the class about why they recommend this particular author study.

For the 'twenty questions' exercise the children work in pairs. One child thinks of a book which has been used in class and the partner has to guess what it is. The partner may ask questions about the book to help him but may not ask for the title or the names of any of the characters.

- Confirming Literacy Development through Reading and Writing Activities

Children work in pairs to play 'hangman' based on the titles of books read in class.

In this next activity the children work in pairs. Each child secretly chooses a page from a nominated book which has been read in class and prepares a sheet of paper indicating the dashes for the words and letters in each word on the page; for example:

```
___  _____  _____
_  _____  ___  _____
___  _  _____  __  _____
_____
```

They then take turns in guessing one letter at a time in order to complete the text for the page. If the letter guessed appears anywhere on the page the partner must write it on the appropriate dash. At any time the children can guess the whole text. The first one to identify correctly the page of text wins. They then must complete the dashes for their partner's text to write the page out completely.

Children work in pairs to construct a task for another pair or the whole class to undertake, for example a text reconstruction — copying out the text of a book and cutting it into strips for reassembly. They could also construct a matching task based on the books read. One column would be things encountered in the books and the second column would be descriptions from the book. The task is to match the description to the thing. For example:

fat	legs	(*Don't Forget the Bacon*)
bad	baby	(*The Very Worst Monster*)
striped	flag	(*The Wind Blew*)
etc.		

Finally, it is important to involve the children in a co-operative evaluation of the unit, inviting them to note what tasks they have completed, how they worked and what they have learned as well as inviting them to evaluate the activities — which ones were interesting and they would like to do more of, which were boring, which were easy, which were difficult, etc. As far as possible the children's suggestions through the activities detailed above and their informal and formal feedback should be taken into account (and be seen by them to be taken into account) in the planning of future work.

Further Dimensions to Classroom Work with Children's Literature

Although it is important to be systematic in planning classroom work with children's literature, the organisation needs to be related to the experience of the children, and to the contexts for interpretation constructed by the form of the texts which are being read. Ritualised routines can lead to a situation where what counts as effective participation by children is their compliance in maintaining the well-known sequences of the lesson. We need to avoid simply following the steps in a procedure regardless of the form of the text being used. What is a useful orientation to shared reading for one book may well be irrelevant to another. For example, it is not always productive to ask children to predict what the story may be about from the cover and title of the book. For some books there is just no point in doing this — *Mr Magnolia* by Quentin Blake, for example. In the previous section we tried to show how one could be systematic in organising classroom activities but flexible and responsive to what the book had to offer and what the children needed to learn at the same time. Because we have concentrated on providing the details of lesson planning, the scope of children's literature for infant classes and the range of possible learning experiences and classroom organisational practices could not be addressed in any detail. Below we will outline some of the additional dimensions which can be explored from the perspectives we have discussed.

Children's Literature in Other Cultures and Other Languages

In talking with young children and their caregivers, it is important to talk about the kinds of children's books they are familiar with outside the school. In households which speak a language other than English, there may be a collection of children's books in the child's first language which parents may be prepared to allow children to bring to school. Some parents may be able to come to school to read such books to other speakers of the same language. There are also many English language picture story books which have been translated. Other opportunities include the sharing of traditional stories from the oral culture of people from different ethnic backgrounds.

Varieties of Literary Forms

As well as using a variety of different types of picture story books, there are the rich resources of traditional tales, songs and other forms such as wordless picture books (e.g. Shirley Hughes' *Up and Up*, Raymond Briggs' *The Snowman* and more recently Jeannie Baker's *Window*) and poetry (collections such as Jack Prelutsky's *The Walker Book of Poetry*, Alf Mappin's *Sing in Bright Colours*, June Factor's *Far Out, Brussel Sprout!, All Right, Vegemite!, Unreal, Banana Peel!*) — an invaluable guide to the choice and use of poetry is *Word Magic* (McVitty 1985). Classroom work should provide children with access to the rich range of children's literature.

Literary Texts and Technology

Some children now entering school will come with a good deal of experience of literary texts gained from the electronic media. Some will have had books with read-along tapes at home and some will have viewed story reading programs on television and perhaps seen well-known stories on film. We have described one approach to using audio-cassette tapes in the classroom but this could be extended to make use of film, film strips and video. There is now a lot of children's literature available in audio-visual format. Western Woods, for example, produce a range of films and sound recordings which are faithful adaptations of children's books.

Different Types of Classroom Programs

Our sample program was an author study, but, of course, there are many other bases for developing coherent units of work. A simple variation would be to undertake an illustrator study. But one might also base programs on thematic studies such as 'adjusting to changes in family structures' (*Are We Nearly There?* by Louis Baum), 'bullying' (*Willy the Wimp* and *Willy the Champ* by Anthony Browne) or 'environmental issues' (Jeannie Baker's *Where the Forest Meets the Sea* and *Window*, Michael Foreman's *Dinosaurs and All That Rubbish*). There could also be work based on humorous narrative poems such as Ogden Nash's 'The Tale of Custard the Dragon' or the Nilands' illustrated version of Paterson's *Mulga Bill's Bicycle*. Clearly the teacher's own knowledge of children's literature is an invaluable resource in generating a variety of inviting classroom programs.

Conclusion

The approach taken here is based on the understanding that children's literacy and literary development are fundamentally social processes. Children's ideas about what reading is are built from the literacy practices they observe and participate in as members of a community with a particular position in the social structure of the culture. What counts as reading in school is constructed socially by teachers and pupils as they interact with various books. The choice of books and the kinds of classroom activities that are generated from them are therefore crucially important in influencing the kinds of readers (and writers) that children become. It is the teachers' responsibility to provide access to culturally valued literacy practices that may not be found within the child's own community. This means that the teachers need to have the knowledge and resources to intervene as expert, authoritative (but not authoritarian) leaders. They need to balance explicit teaching based on books that they prescribe for classroom work with opportunities for children to choose independently their own reading material and make responses and undertake tasks which satisfy their own needs. At times teachers will need professional and managerial support from colleagues, advisors, paraprofessionals and parents, but the literacies and learning that are on offer from children's literature cannot be provided by books written specifically for reading schemes and, as we have shown, children's literature can be made accessible to children regardless of their background or reading experience. By refining our professional practice in managing children's literature in the language curriculum, we will notice not that more children can read but that more children are readers!

References

Bruner, J.S. (1978) 'Learning how to do things with words', in *Human Growth and Development*, eds J.S. Bruner and R.A. Garton, Oxford University Press, Oxford.

Chambers, A. (1985) 'Tell me: are children critics?', in *Booktalk: Occasional Writing on Literature and Children*, The Bodley Head, London.

Chapman, D. (1986) 'Let's read another one', in *Roles in Literacy Learning*, International Reading Association, Newark, Delaware.

Clark, M. (1976) *Young Fluent Readers: What They can Teach Us*, Heinemann, London.

Davies, L., Leibe, F. and Matthews, J. (1987) *Bright Ideas Teacher Handbooks: Language Resources*, Scholastic, Marlborough, UK.

Doake, D. (1985) 'Reading-like behaviour: Its role in learning to read', in *Observing the Language Learner*, eds Angela Jaggar and Trika Smith-Burke, International Reading Association, Newark, Delaware.

Doake, D. (1986) 'Learning to read: It starts at home', in *Roles in Literacy Learning*, eds Duane Tovey and James Kerber, International Reading Association, Newark, Delaware.

Dombey, H. (1983) 'Learning the language of books', in *Opening Moves: Work in Progress in the Study of Children's Language Development*, ed. M. Meek, *Bedford Way Papers* 17, Heinemann, London.

Dombey, H. (1988a) 'Partners in the telling', in *Language and Literacy in the Primary School*, eds M. Meek and C. Mills, Falmer Press, London.

Dombey, H. (1988b) 'Stories at home and at school', in *The Word for Teaching is Learning: Essays for James Britton*, eds M. Lightfoot and N. Martin, Heinemann, London.

Durkin, D. (1966) *Children Who Read Early: Two Longitudinal Studies*, Teachers' College Press, New York.

Goldfield, B. and Snow, C. (1984) 'Reading books with children: the mechanics of parental influence on reading achievement', in *Promoting Reading Comprehension*, ed. J. Flood, International Reading Association, Newark, Delaware.

Graham, J. (1984) 'Reading literature with a slow learner', in *Eccentric Propositions*, ed. J. Miller, Routledge and Kegan Paul, London.

Gray, B. (1987) 'How natural is "natural" language teaching — employing wholistic methodology in the classroom?', *Australian Journal of Early Childhood* 12: 3–19.

Halliday, M.A.K. (1985) *Spoken and Written Language*, Deakin University Press, Geelong, Victoria.

Heath, S.B. (1983) *Ways with Words: Language, Life and Work in Communities and Classrooms*, Cambridge University Press, Cambridge.

McKenzie, M. (1986) 'Cultivating teacher power', in *Roles in Literacy Learning*, International Reading Association, Newark, Delaware.

McVitty, W. (ed.) (1985) *Word Magic: Poetry as Shared Adventure*, Primary English Teaching Association, Sydney.

Meek, M. (1982) *Learning to Read*, The Bodley Head, London.

Meek, M. (1987) 'Playing the texts', *Language Matters* 1: 1–4.

Meek, M. (1988) *How Texts Teach What Readers Learn*, Thimble Press, Stroud, Gloucestershire.

Mills, C. (1988) 'Making sense of reading: Key words or Grandma Swagg?', in *Language and Literacy in the Primary School*, eds M. Meek and C. Mills, Falmer Press, London.

Scales, D. (1981) *Rigby Moving into Maths: Teachers' Resource Book*, Rigby, Melbourne.

Scribner, S. and Cole, M. (1981) *The Psychology of Literacy*, Harvard University Press, Cambridge, Massachusetts.

Simpson, S. (1987) 'An analysis of a mother–child shared reading of a picture-story book', paper presented as part of the requirements for a course within the M.Ed. Language in Education program at the University of Sydney.

Smith, F. (1985) *Reading*, 2nd edn, Cambridge University Press, Cambridge.

Snow, C. (1983) 'Literacy and language: Relationships during the preschool years', *Harvard Educational Review* 53: 165–89.

Sulzby, E. (1985) 'Children's emergent reading of favourite story books: A developmental study', *Reading Research Quarterly* 20: 458–81.

Teale, W. and Sulzby, E. (eds) (1986) *Emergent Literacy: Writing and Reading*, Ablex, Norwood, New Jersey.

Thomas, A. (1987) 'Snapshots of a young reader and her books', *Language Matters* 1: 8–17.

Wells, G. (1980) *Some Antecedents of Early Educational Achievement*, British Psychological Society, Edinburgh.

Wells, G. (1981) *Learning Through Interaction: The Study of Language Development*, Cambridge University Press, Cambridge.
Wells, G. (1986) *The Meaning Makers: Children Learning Language and Using Language to Learn*, Hodder and Stoughton, London.
Williams, G. (1987) 'Space to play: The use of analyses of narrative structure in classroom work with children's literature', in *Give Them Wings: The Experience of Children's Literature*, eds M. Saxby and G. Winch, Macmillan, Melbourne.
Williams, G. (1990) 'Variation in home reading contexts', paper read to the Fifteenth Australian Reading Association Conference, Canberra, July 1990.
Williams, G. and Jack, D. (1986) *The Role of Story: Learning to Read in a Special Education Class*, Arizona Centre for Research and Development, University of Arizona.

References to Children's Books

Allen, Pamela (1989) *Fancy That!*, Puffin, Melbourne.
Anno, Mitsumasa (1985) *Anno's Counting Book*, Macmillan, London.
Bacon, Ron (1985) *Wind*, Ashton Scholastic, Gosford, New South Wales.
Brandenberg, Franz (1982) *I Don't Feel Well*, Puffin, Harmondsworth.
Baker, Jeannie (1987) *Where the Forest Meets the Sea*, Julia McRae, London.
Baker, Jeannie (1991) *Window*, Julia McRae, London.
Baum, L. (1986) *Are We Nearly There?*, The Bodley Head, London.
Blake, Quentin (1981) *Mr Magnolia*, Fontana, Picture Lions, London.
Briggs, Raymond (1980) *The Snowman*, Picture Puffin, Harmondsworth.
Browne, Anthony (1978) *Bear Hunt*, Hamish Hamilton, London.
Browne, Anthony (1986) *Willy the Wimp*, Methuen, London.
Browne, Anthony (1987) *Willy the Champ*, Methuen, London.
Burningham, John (1970) *Mr Gumpy's Outing*, Cape, London.
Burningham, John (1977) *Come Away from the Water, Shirley*, Cape, London.
Burningham, John (1978) *Time to Get Out of the Bath, Shirley*, Cape, London.
Burningham, John (1983) *The Shopping Basket*, Fontana, Picture Lions, London.
Burningham, John (1984) *Granpa*, Cape, London.
Causley, Charles (1979) 'I Saw a Jolly Hunter', in *Figgie Hobbin*, Puffin, Harmondsworth.
De Regniers, B., Moore, E., White, M. and Carr, J. (1988) *Sing a Song of Popcorn: Every Child's Book of Poems*, Scholastic, New York.
Emberley, Barbara (1967) *Drummer Hoff*, The Bodley Head, London.
Factor, June (1983) *Far Out, Brussell Sprout!*, Oxford University Press, Melbourne.
Factor, June (1985) *All Right, Vegemite!*, Oxford University Press, Melbourne.
Factor, June (1986) *Unreal, Banana Peel!*, Oxford University Press, Melbourne.
Foreman, Michael (1974) *Dinosaurs and All That Rubbish*, Puffin, Harmondsworth.
Fox, Mem (1986) *Hattie and the Fox*, Ashton Scholastic, Gosford, New South Wales.
Hewett, Anita (1970) *Mrs Mopple's Washing Line*, Puffin, Harmondsworth.
Howes, Jim (1987) *Animal Jigsaws*, Macmillan, Melbourne.
Hughes, Shirley (1981) *Alfie Gets in First*, The Bodley Head, London.
Hughes, Shirley (1981) *Up and Up*, Collins, London.

Hutchins, Pat (1969) *Rosie's Walk*, The Bodley Head, London.
Hutchins, Pat (1969) *Tom and Sam*, The Bodley Head, London.
Hutchins, Pat (1970) *The Surprise Party*, The Bodley Head, London.
Hutchins, Pat (1974) *Titch*, Puffin, Harmondsworth.
Hutchins, Pat (1975) *Goodnight Owl*, Puffin, Harmondsworth.
Hutchins, Pat (1978) *Don't Forget the Bacon*, Puffin, Harmondsworth.
Hutchins, Pat (1978) *The Wind Blew*, Puffin, Harmondsworth.
Hutchins, Pat (1980) *The Tale of Thomas Mead*, The Bodley Head, London.
Hutchins, Pat (1982) *1 Hunter*, The Bodley Head, London.
Hutchins, Pat (1985) *You'll Soon Grow into Them, Titch*, Puffin, Harmondsworth.
Hutchins, Pat (1986) *The Very Worst Monster*, Puffin, Harmondsworth.
Hutchins, Pat (1988) *The Doorbell Rang*, Puffin, Harmondsworth.
Hutchins, Pat (1988) *One-eyed Jake*, Puffin, Harmondsworth.
Lee, H. (1963) *To Kill a Mockingbird*, Penguin, Harmondsworth.
McAfee, Annalena and Browne, Anthony (1984) *The Visitors Who Came to Stay*, Hamish Hamilton, London.
McGovern, Ann (1967) *Too Much Noise*, Scholastic, New York.
McKee, David (1987) *Not Now Bernard*, Arrow, Random Century, London.
Mappin, Alf (1975) *Sing in Bright Colours: Poetry from Australia*, Westbooks, Perth.
Milne, A.A. (1966) 'Wind on the Hill', in *Now We Are Six*, Methuen and Hicks Smith, Sydney.
Moore, Lilian (1967) 'Go Wind Go', in *I Feel the Same Way*, Atheneum.
Nash, Ogden (1981) 'The tale of Custard the Dragon', in *Custard and Company*, Ogden Nash and Quentin Blake, Puffin, Harmondsworth.
O'Toole, Mary (1987) *Animal Noises*, Macmillan, Melbourne.
Oram, Hiawyn (1984) *Angry Arthur*, Picture Puffin, Harmondsworth.
Parkes, Brenda (1986) *Who's in the Shed?*, Methuen, Sydney.
Paterson, A.B. (1973) *Mulga Bill's Bicycle*, illustrated by Kilmeny and Deborah Niland, Collins, Sydney.
Pearson, Marcia (1984) *Who*, photographed by Richard Vaughan, Ashton Scholastic, Gosford, New South Wales.
Potter, Beatrix (1902)*The Tale of Peter Rabbit*, Warne, London.
Prelutsky, Jack, (1983) *The Walker Book of Poetry*, illustrated by Arnold Lobel, Walker, London.
Reeves, James (1987) 'The Wind', in *The Wandering Moon and Other Poems*, Puffin, Harmondsworth.
Rice, Eve (1980) *Goodnight, Goodnight*, Picture Puffin, Harmondsworth.
Rose, Gerald (1977) *Trouble in the Ark*, Ashton Scholastic, Gosford, New South Wales.
Sendak, Maurice (1970) *Where the Wild Things Are*, Puffin, Harmondsworth.
Spier, Peter (1981) *The Fox Went Out on a Chilly Night*, Puffin, Harmondsworth.
Wells, Rosemary (1978) *Noisy Nora*, Fontana, Picture Lions, London.
Williams, Garth (1984) *The Chicken Book*, Fontana, Picture Lions, London.

Appendix: Transcript of a Shared Reading

George (4 years) reading *The Tale of Peter Rabbit* with his mother, Sandra. Sandra's speech is in normal text and George's speech is in italics; (****) = unintelligible speech; ( ) = pauses.

1   Don't worry about the microphone just, you read me the story.
2   *Okay, but when it comes on.*
3   It's going. It, it will be taping us ( )
4   *Do you have to start here?*
5   Well . . .
6   *Or where the picture is?*
7   Well that's the name of the story.
8   What's the story called?
9   *Peter Rabbit.*
10 That's right.
11 *Is that Peter Rabbit?* (pointing to drawing)
12 Yes, that's a picture of Peter Rabbit.
13 Come on, you read me the story.
14 *I'm really looking forward to this.*
15 Come on then. (Pause)
16 *Mm, waiting for it to come on.*
17 Well you see it doesn't come on, what it does is that it will just tape
18 us so we can go ahead and read, there you are, there's the start
19 of the story. ( )
20 *But I don't know what it is.*
21 Well, we're going to read it together, aren't we?
22 *Yeah.*
23 Once upon a time
24   *time*
25 There were ( ) four little ( ). . . ,
26   *little bunnies,*
27 And their names were ( ). . . , what?
28   *were*
29 *Flopsy, Mopsy, (****). Flopsy, C, Cottontail, Peter Rabbit.*
30 *Is Peter Rabbit in this picture?*
31 Yes he is
32 *Where?*
33 He's looking at us isn't he?
34 *That one there?*
35   Do you think that's him? (George nods)
36 They lived in, they lived with their mother in a sandy bank.
37 Under the root of a very big fir tree.
38 *How come that's where they live?*
39 I think rabbits like to live underneath trees in branches or
40 in holes in the ground because they feel safe there.

Literacy Learning and Teaching

41 'Now my dears,' said old Mrs Rabbit ( ) one morning. 'You may go
42 into the fields or down the lane, but don't go into Mr McGregor's
43 garden. Your father had an accident there, he was put in a pie
44 by Mrs McGregor.'
45 *He won't be captured won't he.*
46 I hope not!
47 'Now run along and don't get into any mischief, I'm going out.'
48 Then old Mrs Rabbit took her basket and her umbrella
49 *Hmm*
50 And went through the woods to the baker's
51 *and went down* (****) *down the* (whisper)
52 What's she going to buy at the baker's?
53 *Don't know!*
54 She bought a loaf of bread and five currant
55   *Yes*   *rant buns.*
56 Yes. (laughter) You like currant buns don't you George?
57 Where's 'down the lane'?
58 *Who's dat?*
59 I think that might be . . . Who went picking blackberries?
60 *Them* (pointing to the picture)
61 What are their names?
62 *Flopsy, Mopsy and Cottontail.*
63 Where are they putting the blackberries when they've picked them?
64 (pointing to the picture) *in the basket.*
65 What's this one about?
66 Well you've just read the page (George grins broadly)
67 But Peter was very . . .
68   *was very naughty,*
69 Ran straight away . . .
70   *away to Mr McGregor's*
71 Yes and he squeezed under
72   *under the gate.*
73 That's it, turn the page. (whispered)
74 First   *Yes he did*
75   *H, he ate some lettuce*
76 And then what else did he eat?
77 *Carrot!*
78 Ah, he must have been getting full.
79 What else did he eat? (George shrugs)
80 They're special things called radishes. (Pointing to the picture.)
81 Turn the page.
82 Ohh dear, and then feeling rather sick, he went to look for
83 some parsley.
84 *But round the cucumber frame, who did she* (self corrects) *who did*
85 *he meet?*
86 Ahh, let's see what happens.
87 That's right, but . . .   Oh no!
88   Mr McGregor
89 *He's not going to get catchured!*

90 Oh, look what's happening?
 91 *Because . . .*
 92 *I think he's not going to get catchured.*
 93 *Read this part.*
 94   Mr McGregor was on his hands and knees planting
 95 out his cabbages, but he jumped up and ran after Peter
 96 waving a rake and calling out
 97 'Stop thief!'
 98 Yes. Oh, look at poor Peter Rabbit, he's running isn't
 99 He?
100 Peter was most dreadfully frightened.
101 He rushed all over the garden.
102 (****) (***)
103 And he'd forgotten his way back to the . . .
104   gate.
105 Yes to the gate.
106 He lost one of his shoes amongst the cabbages, and the other shoe
107 amongst the potatoes.
108 Can you see it? (George nods)
109 After losing them, he ran on four legs and went faster. So that
110 I think he might have got away altogether if he hadn't
111 Unfortunately ran into a gooseberry net, and got caught by the
112 large buttons on his jacket. It was a blue jacket with brass
113 buttons, quite new.
114 Ohh no   He might do
115 *He might get away again*
116 Shall we find out?
117 *Yes.*
118 Peter gave himself up for lost,
119 And he shed big tears
120 *I think this one is here* (turning the page)
121 That's where he gets trapped on that page.
122 Let's read this page
123 Look, he's caught, he can't move
124 He shed big tears, but his sobs were overheard from, by some, by
125 some friendly sparrows, who flew in, who flew to him, in great
126 excitement, and implored him, to exert himself.
127 Mr McGregor came up with a sieve
128 which he . . .
129 *Did dey help him?*
130 I think they have, what's happening?
131 *Going to squash him.*
132 Well if Mr McGregor's fast enough.
133 But, what do you think is going to happen?
134 *He's fast.*
135 Let's see what happens.
136 Ahh!
137 *He's really fast.*
138 Yes, and he ran into a toolshed and jumped into a can. It would
139 have been a beautiful thing to hide in if it hadn't, if it had

140 not have had so much water in it.
141 What's happened?
142 Mr McGregor was quite sure that Peter was somewhere in the
143 toolshed,
144 *Mmm Kerchoo!*
145   That's right.
146 Perhaps hidden under a flowerpot. He began to turn them over
147 carefully, looking under each and presently Peter sneezed
148 *Kerchoo!*
149 And Mr McGregor was after him in no time.
150 And tried to put his foot upon Peter who jumped out of the window
151 upsetting three plants. The window was too small for Mr
152 McGregor and he was tired of running after Peter. He went back
153 to his work.
154 *What's this one about?*
155 Well after Peter sat down to rest, he was out of breath and trembling
156 with fright, and he had got not the least idea which way to go.
157 So he was very damp with sitting in that can. After a time he
158 began to wander about going lippity, lippity, not very fast and
159 looking around.
160 Oh!
161 He found a door in the wall. But it was locked, and there was no
162 room for a fat little rabbit to squeeze underneath. An old mouse
163 was running in and out over the stone doors. And she was
164 carrying peas and beans to her family in the woods. Peter asked
165 her the way to the gate, but as she had such a large pea in her
166 mouth that she couldn't answer him, she only shook her head at
167 him. Peter began to cry.
168 Then he tried to find his way straight across the garden he
169 became more and more puzzled. Presently, he came to a pond where
170 Mr McGregor filled his watering cans. A white cat was staring at
171 some gold fish. She sat very still, but now and then the tip
172 of her tail twitched as if it were alive.
173 Peter . . .
174 *What means 'alive'?*
175 Alive means moving and jumping and living.
176 Alive is the opposite of dead.
177 And when you are dead your body doesn't move anymore.
178 Peter thought it was best to go without speaking to her. He had
179 heard about cats from his cousin little Benjamin Bunny.
180 Let's turn the page, let's see what happens.
181 Ooh. What's happening?
182 *There's the gate!*
183 Yes. What else can you see?
184 (George points to the illustration.) No, you tell me.
185 *Peter Rabbit.*

Beginning Reading

186 Where's he sitting?
187 (George pointing) *On the wheelbarrow.*
188 Oh, he's up so nice and high, who can he see over there?
189 *Mr McGregor.*
190 And what's that on the other side of Mr McGregor?
191 *The gate?*
192 Yes. How is he going to get there? ( )
193 *He can just sneak past him.*
194 Do you think so?
195 Shall we try?
196   *okay*
197   Let's have a look.
198 Peter got down very quietly off the wheelbarrow and started
199 running as fast as fast as he could go, along a straight wall behind some
200 blackcurrant bunch, bushes. Mr McGregor caught sight of him at
201 the corner. Peter did not care. He slipped underneath the gate
202 and he was safe at last in the woods outside in the garden.
203 Oh, what's this?
204 *Coat-hanger*
205 It's a coat-hanger is it?
206 Whose coat is it?
207 *Peter Rabbit's.*
208 And what's this, dangling underneath the coat?
209 *shoes.*
210 Yes. Mr McGregor hung up the little jacket and the shoes for a
211 scarecrow to frighten the blackbirds. Do they look frightened?
212 (Shake of George's head.)
213 Peter never stopped running or looked behind him till he got to
214 the big fir tree. He was so tired that he flopped down on the
215 floor of the rabbit hole and shut his eyes. His mother was busy
216 cooking, and she wondered what he had done with his clothes. It
217 was the second little jacket and pair of shoes that Peter had
218 lost in a fortnight!
219 Oh, dear. What happened to Peter Rabbit then?
220 *Let's read it again.*
221 Well let's just finish it off.
222 Let's see what happened to Peter Rabbit.
223 I'm sorry to say that Peter Rabbit was not very well during that
224 evening. His mother put him to bed and made some Camomile tea
225 and she gave a dose of it to Peter. One tablespoon to be
226 taken at bedtime!
227 What happened to Flopsy, Mopsy and Cottontail?
228 *They were good little bunnies.*
229 And what did they have for supper?
230 (George points to the illustration.) What's that?
231 *Milk.*
232 Yes ( ) and what did they pick off the trees?
233 They put them in their little baskets

234 Do you remember?
235 *I want to read this part here, this one* (referring to another
236 book)
237 Well finish this one first.
238 They had blackberries and milk and bread for supper.
239 *Let's read this one now* (holding the next book).
240 Shall we listen?

4
Managing the Language Program: Children's Literature in the Primary Classroom

Len Unsworth

Contents

What Kind of a Resource is Children's Literature?   147
    What Counts as Children's Literature and Literary Understanding
    Balancing Explicit Teaching and Collaborative and Independent
       Learning
    Children's Literature at all Stages of Reading Experience

Providing for the Range of Reading Experience Within a Class   154
    The Teacher as Expert Leader
    Making Complex Texts Accessible through Program Management
    Scaffolding Text Interaction and Response — Designing Learning
       Experiences
    Negotiating Units of Work as Collaborative Classroom Enterprises

Planning Classroom Programs   170
    Persephone's Journey to the Kingdom of the Dead
    Peer Conflict and Confrontation
    Space Demons

Conclusion   192

References
References to Children's Books

Managing the Language Program

What Kind of a Resource is Children's Literature?

The note shown in Figure 4.1 was obtained by a student in the course of his collecting data for an honours thesis (Davis 1990). As Maurice Saxby says 'The appeal of story is irresistible' (Saxby 1987, p. 5).

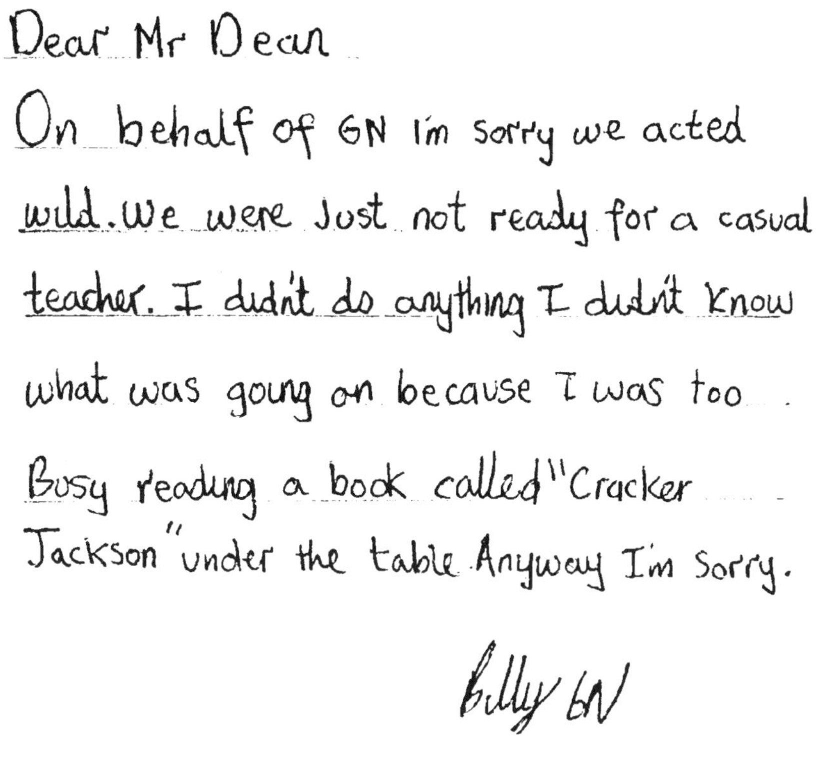

> Dear Mr Dean
>
> On behalf of 6N I'm sorry we acted wild. We were just not ready for a casual teacher. I didn't do anything I didn't know what was going on because I was too busy reading a book called "Cracker Jackson" under the table. Anyway I'm sorry.
>
> Billy 6N

Figure 4.1 *'Dear Mr Dean'*

Children's literature is a rich, inviting and complex resource for learning, however 'real books', 'whole Language' and 'literature-based reading programs' are some of the currently popular aphorisms which mask great diversity in many aspects of classroom work with children's literature. Out of this diversity arise a number of important issues. Two key questions will be considered here:

- What counts as children's literature and as knowledge and understanding of literary texts for primary school children?
- How should the teacher's role accommodate explicit instruction and specific guidance in allocated learning tasks on the one hand, and, on the other hand, facilitation of children's progress in tasks of their own choice from a range of resources and learning experiences?

In this introductory section I will briefly outline the perspective to be developed in relation to these two areas and then develop this with detailed examples of classroom work in the sections which follow.

What Counts as Children's Literature and Literary Understanding

The artificiality and banality of the contrived, vocabulary-controlled readers of traditional reading schemes has been rejected in favour of what some refer to as the 'natural' language of 'real' books and, of course, the much greater interest and appeal to children of much contemporary fiction. But on these simple criteria, it would be difficult to distinguish between much of the recently published fiction that comprises current school reading scheme materials. One difficulty is the inadequacy of such a general and imprecise criterion as 'natural' language. In one sense it is a useful term because it highlights the point that literature uses ordinary language, and that literary use of language is natural to the culture. Literature is not literature through distorting or inflating language or of course through confining itself to 'correct' or 'standard' language. On the other hand, the language of literary texts is frequently 'unnatural' in the sense that it is grammatically quite different from the more familiar forms of oral language.

Children's fiction creates a secondary world textually, in which the writer's use of distinctive patternings of language codes multiple layers and ambiguity of meaning which characterise the possible worlds of good children's literature. Young readers are encouraged to enjoy, via the writer's craft, constructing their own 'readings' of these complex linguistic worlds.

The distinctive multilayering of literary texts allows the reader to take as much or as little as he or she needs or is ready for (Saxby 1987, p. 14). How is this 'multilayering' achieved and what are the means by which the text 'reveals' the possibilities of its meanings? Literary texts use forms and conventions of language and visual images explicitly to introduce ambiguity and contradiction, to make impossible experiences and unlikely connections seem plausible and so challenge the reader to construct new meanings. The kind of reading and interpretive behaviour that literary texts make possible can only be developed through reading and talking about texts which employ the forms and conventions about which young readers need to learn.

A frequent limitation in the use of children's literature in classroom work derives from a preoccupation with the perceived interest of the book to children based on the appeal of the story, the relevance of the experiences portrayed and the opportunities for young readers' 'identification' with characters. Considerations such as these are, of course, important because literature should provide children with pleasure and satisfaction in reading and writing, but literature is verbal art and that pleasure and satisfaction derive both from what is being explored (the themes, the characters and the events) and how the text is constructed (the form of the text). If we are to select books for children that will provide for the development of children's literacy and literary understandings, we need to know what kinds of reading, and hence what kinds of interpretive behaviours, are made possible by the linguistic forms of the texts available to us. Closer attention in classroom work to the language of children's books can extend children's understandings of the ways in which the grammatical resources of language are deployed to construct meanings and hence increase their access to the interpretive possibilities of the texts they encounter. Attention to language form can augment the enjoyment of the story and of learning activities. Approaches to planning learning activities on this basis are discussed in detail in subsequent sections.

Balancing Explicit Teaching and Collaborative and Independent Learning

Reading, as part of language and literacy development, needs to be understood in terms of the complete interconnectedness of linguistic and social processes. Language and literacy development and learning to operate in and learn about the world are one and the same thing. All people put language to certain types of use and in so doing they all learn a linguistic system which has evolved in the contexts of such language use. But which parts of the language system they deploy and emphasise in one type of use or another are significantly determined by the culture — by the systems of social relations in which people are positioned and the roles they learn to recognise and adopt. People do not have access to the whole language system abstractly. They can only know what has been available to them through their experience of social contexts and the ways they have experienced language being used in those contexts. So the knowledge people have of language as a resource for meaning is a function of their access to the range of situation types in which language is used. There will be very significant variation among children in their experience of written language both prior to and during their school years. The range of texts they encounter and the kinds of experiences they have with these texts will influence the kinds of readers and writers they become. So when looking at developing children's language and literacy, it is important to think of children not as asocial, individual beings, but rather as having a position in a network of social relations within an overall societal structure. How children are so positioned determines the range of situations they encounter, how they experience language being used in those situations and what it is possible for them to learn. This applies to the development of children's listening, speaking, reading and writing prior to, within and beyond their experience of schooling.

The teacher's role in teaching through literature and about literature is crucial. He or she is an influential participant in the social construction of children's reading and writing behaviours because he or she can be aware of the variation in cultural influences on children's literacy development and can also monitor literacy development as a social process in the context of the school and classroom.

> The linguistic pattern of a picture book like *Where the Wild Things Are* or *John Brown, Rose and the Midnight Cat* is a feat of selectivity equal to the crafting of a well-made sonnet. The techniques of Southall's *Josh* or Cormier's *I Am the Cheese* and the subtle narrative structure of Chambers' *The Present Takers*, Pearce's *The Way to Sattin Shore* or Cynthia Voigt's *A Solitary Blue* imply and also determine their readership. Some children, sometimes, need help and unobtrusive guidance if they are to match the skills of the reader implied by the author and successfully to fill the 'telling gaps' within the structure. (Saxby 1987, p. 4)

The teacher then, can be the 'trusted book lover in a child's life' who can intervene to provide access to texts which a child would not otherwise have had. This may involve simply the selection and/or allocation of texts but can also profitably extend to sensitive explicit teaching about how meaning is achieved in literary texts. The teacher's own personal knowledge of children's literature is therefore a vital resource as is the ways he or she shares this with the children through reading aloud to them, talking with them about books, designing classroom activities and organising the management of children's literature as a resource for learning.

Children's Literature at all Stages of Reading Experience

A major issue for many teachers in taking into account the wide range of reading experience among children within their classes is the difficulty they see in providing and using with children the range of books necessary to 'match' the various 'levels' of reading ability in the class. The notion of matching a text's 'difficulty level' to a student's 'reading ability' seems to have survived the demise of the graded reading scheme even among some teachers who are committed to the use of children's literature in their language program. Inexperienced readers are thought to need books which are simple but interesting and do not patronise poor readers while more effective readers require texts that will extend their reading. This section will suggest that such dichotomous thinking is not necessary and that a range of texts from picture story books to novels can be used interchangeably with readers at all levels of experience within class groups.

The most ineffective readers in any class should be offered the challenge and engagement of children's literature as a primary resource to develop their reading. The other primary resource they need is an experienced adult reader who will work sympathetically and collaboratively with them to explore the 'invitations' to active involvement in meaning making which such texts extend. Evidence for the benefits of such an approach is well documented (Meek *et al.* 1983; Graham 1984; Williams and Jack 1986).

The work reported by Williams and Jack (1986) was with a special eduation class of 11 children aged from eight years to eleven and a half years who had been categorised 'OA' — 'mildly intellectually disabled'. Their previous experience of reading materials was dominated by graded reading schemes and attention to the development of sight vocabulary from the Dolch list. At the beginning of the project the children's reading behaviours were minimal:

> On resuming school after the summer holiday all the children believed they could not read and several of them appeared from their comments to believe they never would. On our observation two of the children could read single clause sentences using simple vocabulary, one could read only his own name and the other eight could recognize between six and twelve words from the Dolch list. (Williams and Jack 1986, p. 14)

During the year, learning activities were developed around picture books such as *Bear Hunt, There's a Dinosaur in the Park, There's a Nightmare in My Cupboard, John Brown, Rose and the Midnight Cat, The Twits, Hansel and Gretel* and Michael Rosen's poetry. By the end of the year Kylie (who in the middle of the year was still firmly stating 'I can't read') read independently *John Brown, Rose and the Midnight Cat*; Abdullah enjoyed *Bear Hunt* so much that he wrote (with some assistance) a letter to Anthony Browne; Mark H., Mark N. and Scott wrote 'Bear Hunt II'; Raymond, after hearing the teacher and the researcher read Michael Rosen's poem 'If You Don't Put Your Shoes on by the Time I Count Fifteen', called out 'Heah. That's great. I want to read that!' Many other examples of the children's writing and reading testify to the ways in which literature had made literacy events significant achievements in the lives of these children. None of the children could have been called independent readers by the end of the year but they had all made demonstrable progress and more importantly they now wanted to read and believed their reading would develop further.

A shift to the use of a more demanding literary text was the breakthrough for Judith Graham in working with a 12 year old 'remedial reader' — Trevor (Graham 1984). Trevor rejected the readers with simplified language but mature content as 'rubbish', but a coincidental encounter with the Arthurian legend, *Sir Gawain and the Loathly Damsel* (cited in Graham 1984) resulted in sustained, productive engagement with the story. With no more teacher support than was required with the 'reader', Trevor was able to gain satisfaction through his involvement with the story. Graham discusses this in terms of the text providing the kind of contextual support which assisted Trevor in negotiating unfamiliar vocabulary. She also mentions the way in which the literary text changed the social context of the reading lesson. The teacher and student were genuinely collaborating in sharing a text in which the situations and characters mattered to both of them.

It is not productive to think of the 'difficulty level' of a text and the 'reading ability' of a student as two inherently individual qualities or attributes of texts and children that one should try to equate. This seriously underestimates three aspects of the learning situation:

1. the reading and critical capabilities of children;
2. the role of literary texts in cueing interpretive behaviours;
3. the scaffolding of student efforts in a context of shared reading of texts with the teacher.

Underestimating the reading and critical capabilities of children is something that many teachers are particularly susceptible to as a result of the strongly 'individualist' influences of Piagetian psychology in many teacher education courses. Assumptions about stages of cognitive development common to all children of particular ages have had the effect of limiting the kind of work that is undertaken according to received opinion about what is appropriate for children at particular developmental levels (Chambers 1985, p. 152). In contrast to this, the significance of social context in influencing what kind of understandings it is possible for children to achieve is emphasised in the social psychology of Vygotsky (1978, 1986). The importance of this kind of orientation for the education of young children has been well documented (see, for example, Donaldson 1978; Beveridge 1982). It significantly informs the pedagogy of literary and literacy development referred to above in the work of Williams and Jack (1986), Graham (1984) and more recently in accounts of classroom work by Williams (1987), Mills (1988), and Dombey (1988). One crucial principle is Vygotsky's notion of the 'zone of proximal development':

> It is the distance between the actual developmental level as determined by independent problem solving and the level of potential development as determined through problem solving under adult guidance or in collaboration with more capable peers. (Vygotsky 1978, p. 86)

The social context is an active ingredient in the learning process. What children can do depends largely on how the task is to be undertaken. Extending reading development therefore depends on children being helped to read challenging, engaging texts through the scaffolding provided by the teacher and other more experienced readers.

> In any group of children, no matter what their supposed cleverness or lack of cleverness, we find that if they begin by sharing their most obvious observations we very soon accumulate a body of common wisdom that reveals to us the heart of a book and its meaning(s) for us all. Further, even when quite complicated or abstract ideas are approached in this way (through story images and talked-out interpretations) there is little that children cannot grasp. (Chambers 1985, p. 152)

We do not need to think of inexperienced readers in our classes as being limited to particular kinds of texts and not being able to enjoy and benefit from the texts being used by proficient readers in the group. The challenge is to manage the context to make this possible. Suggested strategies to meet this challenge will be progressively detailed below. A preliminary understanding is that children's literature in the form of picture story books, poems, short stories, novels, etc. can all offer intellectual engagement to readers with widely ranging reading experience. Meek (1988) identifies *The Iron Man* by Ted Hughes as an example of a text with which she has demonstrated this principle many times:

> It can be read with pleasure and understanding by children at all stages in school, from the reception class to the sixth form. This is not exaggerated praise but a serious claim, and what happens is not a smooth progression but a series of loopings back to find new awarenesses in oneself as a reader. Some of the youngest readers see as deeply into Hughes' stated intentions for the story as do the oldest. (Meek 1988, p. 30)

Further examples lie in 'The tale of the high school levellers' recounted by Chambers (1985, p. 126). A class of 17 year old students were beginning their two year, A-level course in English literature and were expecting at once to begin study texts such as Shakespeare, the novels of Thomas Hardy and perhaps the poetry of Ted Hughes. Instead their teacher presented them with a range of about 20 children's picture books including Pat Hutchins' *Rosie's Walk* and Raymond Briggs' *Fungus the Bogeyman*. The students were instructed to read the books, talk about them and make notes of anything they might wish to raise in discussion later. Their immediate reaction was one of 'shock-horror' at their teacher's making them attend to baby books. But this quickly changed as the students suggested that these books were so complicated they could not be for young children.

> The ways in which they are complicated are pointed out. Student after student reports subtle interweavings of words and pictures, varieties of meanings suggested but never stated, visual and verbal clues to intricate patterns, structures, ideas. (Chambers 1985, p. 126)

The class quickly became involved in protracted discussions about the possible interpretations of books like Anthony Browne's *Hansel and Gretel* and Maurice Sendak's *Outside Over There*, realising that no matter how simple the books first appeared their form was constructed to invite multiple possible readings.

> Even in *Rosie's Walk*, they realize, there is no possibility of a single right reading that suggests whether Rosie knew all the time that the fox was behind her, or that she didn't. And who is the joke about, the hen or the fox? The possibility is easily understood — it can be seen in the pictures — that, within the fiction, by the way form controls content, both readings are not only possible at the same time, but are necessary. (Chambers 1985, p. 127)

So these advanced English literature students were able to develop their understandings of criticism by using books which in some cases are the ones that best help four and five year olds learn to read.

Providing for the Range of Reading Experience Within a Class

No matter what criteria are used for allocating children to classes or groups, the result will always be a collection of individuals who are more different than they are alike. Approaches to grouping should recognise these differences and emphasise their advantages to all participants in the classroom teaching/learning processes. If groups of children are routinely regarded as identical, or even similar, in terms of their instructional needs, they are less likely to make genuine personal progress, even though they may successfully complete classroom learning tasks (DeStefano *et al*. 1982; Bloome 1983). However, faced with the almost overwhelming demands of attempting to individualise classroom learning, most teachers see the effective grouping of pupils for learning as a valuable way of differentiating learning experiences.

The development of effective grouping, however, requires the abandonment of simplistic procedures based on crude notions of pupils' so-called 'general reading ability', which have been used to establish, within or across grades, (usually three) instructional reading groups thought to be homogenous, or nearly so, in terms of reading ability. The misconceptions about the nature of reading development on which such practice is based, its restriction of the kinds of learning experiences available to children allocated to 'low' groups, the almost complete lack of mobility across groups, the lack of evidence that ability grouping makes any contribution to raising the reading achievement of pupils and other factors, such as negative views about reading and their group among low-ability group members, have been well established in the literature for some time (Hiebert 1983; Collins 1986; Eder 1986).

Detailed guidance for the development of more flexible approaches to small-group work in the classroom is now popularly available (Dalton 1985; Reid *et al*. 1989) but does not specifically address the use of children's literature. Correspondingly, many books dealing with the teaching of children's literature do not deal with the details of classroom management involved in developing effective grouping. Bridging this gap extends beyond a simple application of known management strategies to classroom work with children's literature. The distinctive nature of children's apprenticeship to literary understandings (Meek 1982; Waterland 1985, 1989) and 'how texts teach what readers learn' (Meek 1988) must be coupled with an understanding of cultural variation in children's access to literary texts in order to develop a flexible but functional variety of grouping strategies.

Functional grouping may well incorporate, from time to time, friendship groups, interest groups, spontaneous opportunity groups, groups of experienced readers and groups who experience particular difficulty. But it is not just a matter of ensuring that a variety of group work approaches are used. Rather the selection and variation of the bases for grouping are planned and managed strategically in accordance with fundamental understandings relating teaching and learning and the experience of children's literature. These understandings are based on principles which would include the following:

1. the role of the teacher is that of an expert, authoritative leader;
2. the complexities of literary texts can be made accessible to all children in the class;
3. learning activities can be designed in preparation for the text; for exploring the form of the text; and for reflecting on and extending beyond the text;
4. children's literacy and literary development is facilitated through interaction and collaborative effort on learning activities which have an explicitly negotiated social purpose.

The Teacher as Expert Leader

Functional grouping is designed to increase the amount of time spent by the teacher in direct interaction with the children and also to improve the quality of this interaction. The importance of the supportive adult or experienced reader who shares the young reader's enjoyment of a book is emphasised by Margaret Meek (1982) in her 'conditions of success' in reading. The significance of the adult's initiating role in guiding reading development is not diminished as the child grows older. 'Round about eleven' Meek (1982, p. 149) says, 'the supporting adult's role assumes a new importance'. And in discussing helping young adolescents to choose books, she notes:

> You would think that if a young person and the right book come together the alchemy of literature would produce the indissoluble marriage of true minds. It does happen, and then adults are advised to withdraw from the scene. My experience teaches me, however, that these occasions are not so frequent as we hope, and that most young people need help to find their way to the books that could attract them. (Meek 1982, p. 188)

Teachers certainly do need to provide opportunities for children to read books of their own choice, but I would argue for an extension and further specification of the additional 'help' Meek suggested. It is also the teacher's responsibility to introduce children to new forms of text and to explicitly teach children how these text forms make meaning. From time to time this may mean prescribing one or more texts for attention by particular groups or by the whole class. What is crucial is that the teacher engages in reading these texts with the children and in sharing his/her enthusiasms for the texts. We need to see the role of the teacher in literary discussion as an authoritative but not an authoritarian contributor.

> S/he must remain a leader, usually one with a far greater experience of literature than the others in the group; but s/he must also behave as just another reader — one among others — all of whom have legitimate and valuable interpretations to offer any book. (Chambers 1985, p. 119)

But this valuing of children's responses to the texts does not preclude explicit teaching about how meanings are constructed by text form:

> As leader, the teacher must help each person discover honestly the book s/he has read; then lead on to discover the book which the author, judged by the narrative's rhetoric, can be agreed upon to have written. (Chambers 1985, p. 119)

The flexible nature of this pedagogical relationship between the student and the teacher can be clarified through the concept of *framing*, which refers to

> the degree of control teacher and pupil possess over the selection, organization, pacing and timing of the knowledge transmitted and received in the pedagogical relationship. (Bernstein 1975, pp. 88–89)

Strong framing characterises teacher-directed learning which has been criticised for locating the responsibility for learning with the teacher rather than the student. The student is seen as adopting and regurgitating the teacher's ideas. Weak framing, on the other hand, may place too much responsibility in the hands of the learner who may not have the same access to linguistic and cultural resources as his/her peers. With weak framing the teacher 'relinquishes an expert counselling role in favour of benevolent inertia' (Martin and Rothery 1988, p. 9). The best of both worlds may be achieved by introducing weak and strong framing as a wave-like pattern in teaching practice, with teachers and students taking turns, on principled criteria, in controlling what is transmitted and how (Martin and Rothery 1988, p. 10). Weak framing may be appropriate when inviting and sharing children's responses to their reading at the level of *story*. Stronger framing would be appropriate when the teacher contributes specialised knowledge of 'rhetorical devices' or textual form. This seems to be consistent with Chambers' view of the teacher's role:

> In short, the teacher's skill lies in relating articulated responses to the art, craft, and philosophy of literature, so that the student perceives where s/he stands, where others stand and where the literature is taking her. The teacher raises awareness and is a contributor of specialized knowledge, a guide to further sources, and a synthesizer of disparate and often conflicting comment. (Chambers 1985, p. 119)

The functional approaches to grouping children for learning described below seek to maximise the effectiveness of teacher intervention in personalising learning for all children, including the extending of exceptional learners and supporting the least experienced readers in the class.

Making Complex Texts Accessible through Program Management

Many children genuinely can't 'get into books', not simply because they find the words difficult, they can't 'identify' with the characters or they find the story boring. Perhaps more importantly they do not see the sustained use of the written language of books as functional. It does not match up with their expectations of what language is for (Halliday 1978, p. 57). These children need to be helped to see how the language of books is a functional extension of oral language which relates to their own deep and pressing preoccupations. The suggestions which follow need to be seen from this perspective. The selection and use of materials does need to address the 'decoding' difficulty some children will have, but in the context of their development as 'readers', not simply in helping them to be able to read. The sections on selecting and using texts and the bases for managing groups to scaffold students' work with texts need to be read in conjunction with the subsequent sections dealing with the design of learning activities and the establishment of collaborative, classroom, literary enterprises with explicitly negotiated social purposes.

SELECTING TEXTS

Television, Video and Reading

The security of the 'known text' and the attraction of repeatedly 'revisiting' favourite stories has been shown to provide the recurrent contexts which extend very young children's reading development (Goldfield and Snow 1984; Gray 1986). Television and film viewing are often thought to be in conflict with extending reading but in fact for older children can be 'another manifestation of the security offered by "known text" (Meek 1982, p. 164). Meek goes on to point out that book sales show that whatever books appear as TV serials are widely read, or widely bought. Recent television 'mini-series' of novels like Ruth Park's *The Harp in the South* and Bert Facey's *A Fortunate Life* were utilised by some teachers and resulted in 'reluctant' readers persisting with the text to savour parts of those stories that they found poignant. Of course there are now film versions of many children's literary texts including quite recent releases such as Ruth Park's *Playing Beatie Bow*, *I Own the Racecourse* (Patricia Wrightson), *Let the Balloon Go* (Ivan Southall) and Colin Thiele's novels *Blue Fin* and *Storm Boy*. The availability of videotape versions of such films for hire or purchase now provides an excellent resource for classroom work. The 'video tie-in' can also support access to work on author study and the writer's craft through series such as that produced by Film Australia dealing with authors such as Robin Klein, Percy Tresize and Dick Roughsey. Occasionally there are opportunities to see live theatre productions of adaptations of novels like Robin Klein's *Hating Alison Ashley* or Gillian Rubinstein's *Space Demons*, but video offers the predictability that is helpful in program planning.

Readalong Tapes and Beyond

Children of all ages in the primary school should have stories read to them and this might include the serial reading of a whole novel from time to time. It is a simple matter for the teacher to record his/her own reading on such occasions. The resulting tapes can become a resource for less experienced readers in completing classroom work or in reading at home.

A number of variations on this procedure can help to provide this kind of support for less effective readers:

- the teacher might occasionally prepare a taped reading of a chapter in advance so that less efficient readers can get a 'head start' in preparing for class work;
- very good readers within the class might also undertake to prepare a taped reading of a chapter or two in advance — parents, friends or older students in other classes might also help in this way;
- groups within the class might undertake the preparation of 'readers' theatre' performances (Robertson and Poston-Anderson 1986; Johnson and Louis 1985; Nicoll and Unsworth 1990) in which the less experienced readers would be included in groups working on sections of the novel that had already been dealt with in class and the more proficient readers in groups preparing sections of the novel not yet read by the whole class. The latter readers' theatre performances can be taped and along with the scripts provide an advance organiser for the less experienced readers' efforts to read the original version in the novel;
- the readers' theatre work might be extended to more ambitious dramatisations — perhaps costumed and 'set' — which could then be videotaped and used similarly in support of less experienced readers.

Picture Books, Poems and Novels for All
It is not necessary to insist that less proficient readers be able to read the entire text of a novel individually in order for them to participate productively in work deriving from it. Students might listen and follow a good deal of the story while it is being read aloud by the teacher or they might follow sections of it on tape in class or at home. It is important, however, that such students do come back to interact with some of these sections in print. Such work might be undertaken in interaction with the teacher or as a paired reading with a more proficient reader (additional detailed suggestions for supporting such work are provided in subsequent sections).

There must be some occasions when less proficient readers can work independently in class. One way of facilitating this is to use a range of different types of children's literature in each unit of work. This might include picture story books, poems, extracts and novels. The important thing is that *all* students should deal with all of the selections made so that the less experienced students do not use only the picture books and the more experienced ones the novels (see reference to Chambers (1985) and Meek (1988) above).

The following are the kinds of selections of materials that could form the bases for units of class work on two different themes.

1. Bullying
Picture books: *Willy the Wimp* (Anthony Browne), *Willy the Champ* (Anthony Browne), easier novel: *The Eighteenth Emergency* (Betsy Byars); novel: *The Present Takers* (Aidan Chambers); poem: 'The Bully Asleep' (John Walsh); extracts: 'The Fight', *I Can Jump Puddles* (Alan Marshall), 'Down a hole' *Adventures with my Worst Best Friend* (Max Dann).

2. 'First days at school'
Easier novel: *Ramona the Pest* (Beverley Cleary); novel: *Hating Alison Ashley* (Robin Klein); poem: 'Homework' (Russell Hoban); extracts: (easier) *Pippi Longstocking* (Astrid Lindgren), (more demanding) *To Kill a Mockingbird* (Harper Lee).

Units of work could also be planned around exploring the writer's craft, for example discussing how the narrator roles change to contruct difference in 'point of view'. Once again a range of different types of children's literature could be included in the one unit. These might include picture books like *Bear Hunt* (Anthony Browne) or *Granpa* (John Burningham), short 'chapter books' like *Giant Cold* (Peter Dickinson) and novels like *Josh* (Ivan Southall) or challenging works like *The Stone Book Quartet* (Alan Garner).

FUNCTIONAL GROUPING OF STUDENTS WITHIN CLASSES

While there is a place for some whole class teaching, the emphasis should be on the teacher and children interacting with literature personally within small groups. Whole class participation is useful when the teacher is reading aloud to children, when songs are being sung, for choral reading and for sharing responses to reading.

If students are not used to working collaboratively in small groups, the processes can be introduced gradually, with students first co-operating in pairs to undertake some tasks then combining pairs to share work in progress. Guidelines for introducing small-group learning are detailed in Reid *et al.* (1989) and methods of teaching children how to adopt different roles within groups in Dalton (1985). Successful small-group work is most likely to occur in classrooms where programs are clearly planned in advance and where activities are well organised and controlled. Such an environment is not at odds with warm friendly relations between students and the teacher and the development of independence in learning among the students.

The Teacher's Role and Responsibility for Learning

The importance of the teacher as an authoritative leader and of the wave-like framing of learning experiences was discussed above. To facilitate this, the kind of learning activities occurring in the class at any one time might be considered as fitting into three broad categories:

1. teacher intensive — where most of the time involves fairly intensive teacher–pupil and pupil–pupil interaction;
2. teacher supervised — where pupils progress with occasional guidance and checking by the teacher;
3. teacher independent — where pupils work at a listening post, a learning centre, on collaborative or independent tasks or undertake silent reading or writing such that the teacher is present but not actively involved in their learning activity.

Initially, as teachers introduce small group work, there may be a one to one relationship between these three kinds of learning activities and the three subgroups of approximately the same number of pupils. But gradu-

Literacy Learning and Teaching

ally that one to one relationship changes as more sophisticated permutations and combinations are devised (Unsworth 1986). Nevertheless the distribution of these categories of learning activity is planned strategically to maximise the effectiveness of the teacher's time with pupils.

Principles of Functional Small–Group Organisation

Composition of Groups
- There are no permanently set groups.
- Groups are periodically created, modified or disbanded to reconcile changing student needs and task demands.
- There are times when there is only one group — consisting of all pupils.
- Group size will vary from 2 or 3 to 9 or 10 or more, depending on the group's purpose.

Management
- Pupils should encounter some choices relating to how, when and what work is to be done so that they can exercise some responsibility in organising their own learning.
- Pupil commitment is enhanced if they know how the group work is related to the overall class program.
- There should be a clear, context-sensitive strategy for monitoring and recording students' participation and progress in learning activities.
- There should be a principled distribution of teacher-interactive, teacher-supervised and teacher-independent work among group work activities.

Nature of Group Tasks
- Learning experiences relate to whole texts and genuine communicative experiences rather than fragmented exercises.
- Task structure, level of demand and forms of scaffolding should be differentiated to accommodate the range of experience among children in the class.
- Clear models and demonstrations of work required should be provided.
- Directions for completing tasks and class work routines should be clear and can be referred to if forgotten. This should include options for those who have completed required activities.
- Group tasks should lead to some kind of corporate production, display or exchange involving the whole class and sometimes interaction with other groups within and/or outside the school.

'Priming' and the 'Group-Then-Regroup' Strategy
The objective of this 'group-then-regroup' strategy is to provide planned support for less experienced readers so that they can participate effectively with the children who are more proficient readers in working with literary texts which the less proficient readers would have difficulty dealing with independently. This involves a two-stage learning activity where the first stage is preparatory or prerequisite to the second. In the

first stage children are grouped homogenously into three categories according to their relative dependence/independence on the teacher in being able to carry out the task individually:

DOTs — Dependent on teacher
NIRs — Nearly independent readers
IRs — Independent readers

In some classes there may be more DOTs than NIRs and IRs, while in other classes there may be a large proportion of IRs, so there may well be four or five groups operating in some classes with two or three groups of DOTs and in other classes two or three groups of IRs. During this stage differential support is provided to the groups according to their needs. In the second stage new groups are formed which each contain a mixture of DOTs, NIRs and IRs and all group members are able to contribute due to the 'priming' in stage one. The following section of a unit of work based on C.S. Lewis' *The Lion, the Witch and the Wardrobe* (Nicoll and Unsworth 1989, pp. 79–80) illustrates the strategy.

The teacher reads aloud to the children the first three chapters of *The Lion, the Witch and the Wardrobe* up to the paragraph beginning: 'That day, when it came to the afternoon and there was still no sign of a break in the weather, they decided to play hide and seek.' The object of the task to follow is to stimulate the children to use their cumulating knowledge of the text so they can more effectively understand upcoming episodes and develop a better grasp of the story as a whole. This can be done by encouraging the children to consider what is likely to occur in the next segment of the story up to Edmund's return to the wardrobe — ending with the Queen's reminder: 'Next time! Next time! Don't forget. Come soon.'

The teacher should prepare a reading guide for this section as shown in Figure 4.2. The teacher should also prepare a cassette tape, initially reading the 'guide' and then the extract onto the tape and interpolating the sections of the guide at the appropriate intervals in the text.

For stage one of this activity the groups 'get into the text' in the following manner:

- DOTs work directly with the teacher. He or she works through the 'reading guide', reading the story aloud to the children as they follow the text.
- NIRs may follow the same procedure as the IRs. However, if they have difficulty the audio tape is available for them to check the 'reading guide' and/or read along with the tape.
- IRs follow the printed version of the 'reading guide', reading silently, and discuss their responses.

In stage two of the activity the teacher reconstitutes the groups (which may well now consist of DOTs, NIRs and IRs all in the same group). The groups then consider what is likely to happen after Edmund and Lucy return from Narnia. Within groups, pupils might work in pairs on specific tasks, for example 'Imagine you were Edmund or Lucy and write (or make a recording of) the part of the story where you tell the other children what happened to you'. Even children who have difficulty with

Literacy Learning and Teaching

reading are able to contribute positively to this task because they have been 'primed' through additional teacher support in developing their understanding of the passage.

This 'regrouping' strategy has been applied to a variety of learning experiences in literature programs (Unsworth 1986; Nicoll and Unsworth 1990).

'Through the Wardrobe to Narnia' Reading Guide

1. Read/listen to the extract up to the part where Edmund jumps into the wardrobe and shuts the door.

   'He jumped in and shut the door, forgetting what a very foolish thing this is to do.'

   Now stop!
   Discuss with the other members of your group the possible answers to these questions:
   - (a) What is the first thing Edmund will do now that he is in the wardrobe?
   - (b) What will Edmund begin to feel?
   - (c) What is the first thing Edmund will begin to see?
   - (d) Who is he likely to meet?
   - (e) How do you think Edmund will be feeling?

   Compare your ideas to what really happened in the next section.

2. Read/listen to the next section up to where Edmund hears the sound of bells. STOP.

   Now who do you think Edmund is going to meet?
   How will the meeting occur? Check to see if you were right.

3. Now read/listen up to the part where Edmund thinks something dreadful is going to happen to him.
   'Edmund felt sure that she was going to do something dreadful but he seemed unable to move.' STOP.

   What do you think happened to Edmund? Check to see if you were right.

4. Stop reading/listening at the sentence which begins: 'While he was eating . . .'

   Make a list of the questions you think Edmund is going to have to answer. What do you think might be the reasons for these questions?

   Now read/listen to the last part of the extract and compare your ideas to the text.

5. Tell the teacher you are ready to change groups.

Figure 4.2 *Reading Guide: 'Through the Wardrobe to Narnia'*

Scaffolding Text Interaction and Response — Designing Learning Experiences

Designing learning experiences which scaffold children's text interaction and response requires an understanding of 'the teaching role of the text and its writer' (Meek 1982, p. 20) and the realisation that '. . . Always, *always* the adults who stand between children and books make us the kind of readers we become' (Chambers 1985, p. 132). Teachers have the responsibility for intervening and providing leadership and guidance to children in the development of their literacy and literary understandings. These interventions will sometimes occur spontaneously, at the 'teachable moment', but most frequently will be planned learning experiences. They should include frequent opportunities for 'talk around text', which, although informal, is anything but casual and can frequently take the form of a very systematic and penetrating exploration and analysis of literary experience through 'booktalk' (Chambers 1985, pp. 169–73). Opportunities for dramatic and visual response are also important, but fundamental to intervention in children's literary development is the nature of the opportunities they have for sustained writing: 'If we want to see what lessons have been learned from the texts children read, we have to look for them in what they write' (Meek 1988, p. 38).

Whatever mode the learning experiences take, they should always be derived from, or at least take account of, the distinctive characteristics of the text itself. They should not be part of a repertoire of tasks and activities such as 'preparing a wanted poster of the main character' or 'literary report cards' from which children can choose regardless of the particular book they are reading. Text-specific learning experiences can be designed in preparation for the text; for exploring the form of the text; and for reflecting on and extending beyond the text. They should be enjoyable activities which are implemented differentially according to the nature of the text and the needs and experience of the children and they should be an organic part of a more extended unit of the class program developed around particular literary texts.

The following categorisation of activities should not be seen as an obligatory sequence of learning experiences to be 'applied' to the planning of work on all literary texts to be dealt with in the class program. The relative emphasis given to these categories should be determined primarily by the form of the text itself, the reading experience of the children and the teacher's purposes in planning the work.

PREPARING FOR THE TEXT
Preparatory activities could focus on several ways of generating children's enthusiasm for, and engagement with, books to be introduced in the class program and include:

1. arousing their interest through speculation about the content of the story;
2. building up children's background knowledge about the setting and theme of the book;

3. linking aspects of text form and literary conventions used in the book to children's previous experiences.

Arousing interest
If children are 'reluctant readers' of literary texts, novel ways of introducing books may be crucial. Benton and Fox (1985, p. 115) relate how one of their students, Liz, dealing with a group of inexperienced 11 year old readers, generated enormous excitement about what their new novel was to be about. Several days before introducing the book she provided the children with pieces of paper and invited them to write graffiti which was neatly 'blu-tacked' around the room.

> Windows on her second story classroom were signed EXIT, TEACHERS ONLY, small holes in the skirting board were marked QUIET PLEASE: HILDA AND STAN LIVE HERE and a caption beneath the clock read INSTRUMENT OF TORTURE. (Benton and Fox 1985, p. 115)

The children became intrigued to find out what this had to do with the next book they would be reading and, of course, when Betsy Byars' *The Eighteenth Emergency* was introduced, and the children read about Mouse's dangerous habit in the first chapter, they were already 'in the know', on the inside story.

Prior to introducing Philippa Pearce's *The Battle of Bubble and Squeak*, it might be useful to see if any children have pet mice, rats or guinea pigs at home and to explore the possibility of bringing them to school for a while and even letting other children take them home overnight. This would provide the opportunity to determine which children liked to hold, pet and look after the animals, and children could comment on their own positive and negative feelings. A class survey could be conducted to determine the attitudes of parents and others at home to the idea of having the animals to stay in their house. This investigation of people's attitudes to mouse-like pets would facilitate the children's appreciation of the nature of the struggle in Philippa Pearce's novel. Here the characters' concern for the safety of the gerbils confronts them with the more worrying concern about how much they can trust their mother. In trying to resolve this the characters must weigh up the reliability of their mother's word until now with the intensity of her feelings about the gerbils.

The humour in Lilith Norman's *My Simple Little Brother* depends on the reader being able to share the narrator's amusement at Fieldsy's literal interpretation of Australian idiom. This may not be very familiar to some readers so, before reading, children could be encouraged to collect sayings from their own experience and interview their parents and other adults to find out what sayings they remember. Migrant families may have memories of sayings that were particularly confusing or amusing when taken literally, for example 'He's under her thumb', 'I'm all ears', 'She did it behind his back'.

Building Background Knowledge

Arousing children's interest obviously merges into building background knowledge as indicated in the activities suggested above. In the case of popular novels with historical settings such as Bert Facey's *A Fortunate Life*, preparatory activities which built up the children's understanding of the period would be helpful. These might include interviewing older people who could remember what life was like in rural Australia between the wars and sharing audio tapes of the interviews with the class; inviting such people to visit the class to hold a kind of news conference about their early working lives and so on.

Novels with more contemporary settings may also benefit from some preparatory work if the children do not have relevant background experience. For example some rural children may not be familiar with the dimensions of large city department stores and hence some prior exploration of this would enhance their reading of Joan Phipson's *Hide till Daytime*. Similarly, a reading of Alan Baillie's *Little Brother* would be enhanced if the children had some prior knowledge of Cambodia and some understanding of its recent history.

Foreshadowing Work on Text Form and Literary Conventions

Prior to introducing C.S. Lewis' *The Lion, the Witch and the Wardrobe*, the teacher might discuss with children stories they already know that involve characters who enter into different worlds. The discussion could begin with a popular television series like *Dr Who* — how the Doctor enters different worlds, the fact that he often encounters inhabitants of other worlds who are not human, the representation of good and evil, etc. The discussion could then be extended to books with which the children are already familiar where characters enter different worlds. An excellent example is Maurice Sendak's *Where the Wild Things Are*. If the children do not know this story, it is brief enough to be read aloud to them within the session. This can be the basis for further exploration of the conventions of narrative. For example, when Max returns, his dinner is still hot, indicating that the passage of time in the fantasy world does not correspond with real-world time.

The teacher may want to focus on the forms of narrative which have been used in stories that contain a lesson for the reader. Children might be asked to list stories that fit into this category. Some may know some of *Aesop's Fables*, for example. The teacher could encourage the children to look more closely at this idea of the didactic purpose of stories through considering how vanity is treated didactically in a variety of literary forms for children. He or she might begin by reading/retelling the Narcissus legend. Children might then be asked to indicate other stories they know with this theme. Some might mention *The Emperor's New Clothes*, which could then be reread or retold — perhaps collaboratively. Discussion of this and other stories could focus on *how* the theme was dealt with and on the form of the text. This then would be excellent preparation for considering a more recent story — Morris Lurie's *Arlo the Dandy Lion*.

Preparing by just Reading the Book!
The decision to undertake any preparatory work depends very much on the particular novel and the particular group of children. If they approach literature with enthusiasm, activities to arouse their interest may well be seen as irritating delays. Some books would lose their impact if the teacher planned preparatory work because these books do their own work in enticing the reader. 'They may beckon a reader to settle down inside them and become acquainted even in the opening lines' (Benton and Fox 1985, p. 116):

> In a hole in the ground there lived a hobbit. Not a nasty, dirty, wet hole, filled with the ends of worms and an oozy smell, nor yet a dry, bare, sandy hole with nothing in it to sit down on or to eat: it was a hobbit-hole, and that means comfort. (Tolkien, *The Hobbit*)

There are many novels, of course, which are most effective when introduced directly. Some discussed by Benton and Fox (1985, pp. 116–117) are *The Turbulent Term of Tyke Tiler* (Gene Kemp), *Freaky Friday* (Mary Rodgers) and *The Iron Man* (Ted Hughes).

EXPLORING TEXT FORM

Imaginative involvement in books through the enjoyment of the story is clearly fundamental to reading development. But a concomitant aspect of many children's developing enjoyment of literature is their growing insight into, and fascination with, the novel as a literary construction. There is a tendency to avoid consideration of the 'constructedness' of novels in planning work for children. All too often the story is dealt with as if it were a 'slice of life' and evaluated by teachers and children primarily in terms of its verisimilitude. Sometimes books are chosen because they deal with social issues and are used as an initial focus for a wider investigation of such issues. Such approaches lead to a misunderstanding of what literature is (Chambers 1985, p. 151).

> '"What takes place" in narrative,' Roland Barthes reminds us, 'is, from the referential (reality) point of view, literally nothing; "what happens" is language alone, the adventure of language, the unceasing celebration of its coming.' . . . It is this passionate adventure with language we want for our children. (Chambers 1985, p. 151)

Consequently, in discussing his 'Tell Me' framework, Chambers (1985, p. 169) indicates that some of the questions are 'structural', focusing on 'How the story is told; on form, and not on "what the story is about", on content'. Concentration on content can lead to a non-literary view of the novel as a focus for exploration of social issues or 'the posing of what are little more than comprehension questions about character, plot, theme and meaning . . .'. He argues that a concern with form leads naturally to a consideration of content in such a way that maintains a perspective on the text as a literary construction. Chambers (1985, p. 169) writes: 'Our questions, in short, focus on the reader's experience of the text, and lead the reader to understand and appreciate that experience by considering the way the text was formed by the writing'.

The following brief discussions about episodes from popular children's novels indicate how narrator–reader relationships could be explored through the kinds of questions Chambers recommended. It would be useful to select novels among which there was clear variation in narrative technique and ask children to reflect on selected episodes. The contrasts would help the children to see the variation in text form.

The Clocktower Ghost (Gene Kemp)
Amanda is introduced via the third-person narrator so we are told directly what Amanda is like from the narrator's point of view. Amanda does not speak for herself nor are her thoughts projected. The children could check this by locating the 'thinking', 'feeling' or 'saying' words which show Amanda as the narrator sees her. At the same time that the children are considering what kind of a character Amanda is, they are considering how her character was constructed.

Hating Alison Ashley (Robin Klein)
Alison Ashley is introduced entirely from Erica's perspective. Every detail is given by the first-person narrator — there is almost no dialogue. The children might contrast the explicit expression of Erica's thoughts, feelings and hopes with the portrayal of Alison Ashley entirely in terms of Erica's view of her appearance, possessions and knowledge.

The Present Takers (Aidan Chambers)
A very popular episode in this book is where Lucy is bullied and has her new shoes scuffed by Melanie Prosser and her gang. Here the children can see that the author is not simply telling about the characters, settings and events, but rather through dialogue they are shown what occurs and what the characters are like. The children could be asked to consider how the role of the narrator functions in this kind of text articulating Lucy's point of view; for example:

> 'Other people come in their parents' cars.' She could not help herself. Why should they get away with saying such stupid things? (p. 13)

Children might look for other examples where reality is constructed via the narrator but from Lucy's point of view; for example:

> Tears filled her eyes. Through them, as she bent her head to hide her face, she saw the scuffed and dented surface of her birthday shoes (p. 13).

Cannily Cannily (Simon French)
This novel also provides many examples where the narrator's telling about the characters is balanced by a 'showing' via dialogue; for example:

The group watched him unbelieving . . .
'I reckon you're telling us a lot of crap, Huon.' (p. 36)
'Trevor Huon has decided to grace us with his diminutive presence. How old are you Huon?'
'Eleven.'
'I don't believe you.' The other kids caught the dig at Trevor's lack of height and laughed accordingly (p. 41).

Trevor's point of view is also built into the third-person narration via the projection of his thoughts through the verbs of thinking and feeling:

When he arrived on the playing field to take command of the team's training session, he struck Trevor as looking strangely incongruous (p. 40).

Through discussions of this kind children will begin to see that the reader's alignment with a particular character (as well as shifts in alignment) are not simply due to feelings of identification based on verisimilitude of the story but are rather constructed within the form of the text. Through this kind of orientation in his 'booktalk' with children Chambers found ' . . . at first to our surprise, that children of all school ages not only enjoyed themselves but became, session by session, ever more articulate, ever more perceptive, ever more discriminatingly critical in their talk' (Chambers 1985, p. 169).

Negotiating Units of Work as Collaborative Classroom Enterprises

Here we are concerned with an underlying integrative organisational approach to implementing the guidelines which have so far been discussed in this section.

First I emphasised the teacher's role in providing the academic and managerial leadership which allows children of all ages and reading experience access to a wide range of literary texts. Then I indicated how this can be achieved through the teacher's careful selection and allocation of texts, through the design of 'text-specific' and 'context-sensitive' learning activities and through the functional grouping and 'regrouping' of children for learning. However, the teacher's role is authoritative and not authoritarian. Children are given explicit instruction as well as planned opportunities for collaborative and independent work. A key factor in maintaining coherence in classroom work of this kind is the explicit negotiation of the overall purpose of the work and how the completion of particular learning tasks will contribute to the achievement of this purpose.

The negotiated and 'corporate' quality of a program which maintains the engagement and enthusiasm of the children requires more than interesting stories, relevant topics and tasks which appeal to the children. One contributing feature can be the completion of some tangible product or performance in which the separate efforts of groups and individuals within the class come together. An example of the latter is the production of a slide–tape presentation based on the 'Persephone' story in one of the sample programs in the next section. However, children can also be committed to collaborative effort towards more abstract outcomes if the purposes are explicitly negotiated and the appropriate scaffolding through direct teaching and opportunities for co-operative and independent work are provided. The possibilities of this kind of work were briefly indicated in the section 'Exploring Text Form' above. These are further developed in detailed examples of class programs in the next section.

Programming in this manner does not restrict all children to working on the same materials and tasks and does not imply the same kind of teaching–learning relationship for all children throughout the unit. Even when the whole class is working on the same text there may be considerable variation in the way the work is carried out. This was briefly indicated above with the excerpt from the class program based on *The Lion, the Witch and the Wardrobe* and is elaborated further in the next section with a full class program based on *Space Demons*. Variation in the range of children's literature available for the exploration of themes such as 'first days at school' and 'bullying' has also been mentioned above. A further example is a program (designed by a teacher colleague) exploring 'Families and change', which focused primarily on very different texts — Nadia Wheatley's *My Place* and Libby Gleason's *Eleanor Elizabeth* — and also included work on John Burningham's picture book, *Granpa*, Ruth Park's novel *Playing Beatie Bow* and some of Roger McGough's poetry in *Strictly Private*. But what unifies this kind of work across different texts and different groups of children undertaking different tasks, is not simply similarity of topic or story, but an encompassing attention to the nature of 'storying' — learning how literary texts mean — a perspective on the text as a literary construction. In a class 'author study' of Robin Klein, for example (Roberts and Nicoll 1988), whilst all children might eventually read/listen to the same selection of the author's novels, less experienced readers may focus their work on *The Enemies* while more experienced readers may deal more thoroughly with *Hating Alison Ashley*. Then, through the teacher's orchestration of carefully planned instruction, collaborative group work and sharing, less experienced readers, as well as those more experienced, have the opportunity to contribute as 'experts' to the class exploration of Klein's work. Similar organisation can be applied to other kinds of work with children's literature such as 'genre study'. Different groups of children may work with Alan Baillie's *Megan's Star* and Gillian Rubinstein's *Beyond the Labyrinth* eventually to contribute to a whole class investigation of the ways in which 'science fiction' is made to work in such novels.

Space will not permit an exhaustive exemplification of the suggestions that have been discussed here. However, in order to consolidate some of these suggestions in the form of detailed plans for classroom work, the following section describes three programs for implementation in the middle to upper primary school.

Literacy Learning and Teaching

Planning Classroom Programs

This section contains plans for the following three programs/units of work:

1. Persephone's Journey to the Kingdom of the Dead (1 week);
2. Peer Conflict and Confrontation (2 weeks);
3. Space Demons (3 weeks).

The kind of programming used to initiate this kind of work with children's literature will depend on the past experience of the children and the teacher. So it is not suggested that the following programs can simply be adopted in any classroom. However, it is hoped that the examples of the kind of detailed considerations upon which such classwork might be based will help teachers to generate and/or refine their own designs for class programs appropriate to the contexts in which they are working.

'Persephone' is a short program designed to encourage close attention to the language of the text and to introduce functional grouping and regrouping of pupils in working toward a common goal. 'Peer Conflict' extends this by making use of multiple texts, building in more specific strategies for dealing with the range of pupils' reading experience, and by dealing more directly with the ways in which linguistic form constructs meanings in narrative. 'Space Demons' is designed to provide access to a complex text for children of varying reading experience. It shows the compatibility of simultaneously dealing with story and narrative technique in a range of enjoyable learning activities.

Persephone's Journey to the Kingdom of the Dead

This story, entitled 'Demeter: Goddess of the Grain', can be found in *The Great Deeds of Heroic Women* (Saxby 1990, pp. 25–29). By coming back to this text children can savour the rich visual appeal and sensuous images of the story. One way to do this would be to produce a slide–tape presentation of the story.

Session 1
- After reading and discussing the story, negotiate the allocation of the following parts to the children: Persephone 1; Persephone 2 (pale and wan in the underground); Demeter; Hades; Hecate; Helios; Iris; Hermes; Ascalaphus.
- In most classes three 'casts' will be allocated and possibly an additional group member or two to act as directors and production managers for the photography and tape recording.
- The children who are allocated the same parts (e.g. the three Persephones) revisit the text noting the aspects of costume and make-up they will require.

Session 2
- Children regroup so that all characters can share their ideas about their own make-up and costume with other members of their cast, seeking feedback on their proposals.
- Whole class planning meeting to obtain materials for costumes and make-up.

Session 3
- Class reads the text again to list the additional slides that will need to be taken to provide the background for the presentation, e.g. 'golden fields', the fire of a volcano, dead plants and trees, etc.
- One way to provide this background is to photograph illustrations from books. The responsibility for finding appropriate pictures is divided among the class members. The teacher-librarian may be prepared to assist in conducting a library research workshop to obtain such pictures.

Session 4
- Children don costumes and make-up for the photography session. Take photographs of the children fairly close up against a plain background, e.g. a light colour for Persephone, black for Hades and dark blue for Demeter.
- Arrange to have slides taken of illustrations from the books.

Session 5
- Each cast arranges its slides in order and cues them to the text of the story. Practise reading and projecting the slides on cue.
- Tape record each cast's reading and 'pulse' the tape to project the slides on cue.
- The casts can then share and discuss their productions.

Peer Conflict and Confrontation

This program of work extends over a two week period with about an hour of allocated class time each day. It can work with only a small number of copies of each of the novels used, provided about five copies of a few pages extracted from each novel can be made available. Below (Figure 4.3) is an overview of the program, which is followed by outline notes for implementation.

OUTLINE NOTES FOR IMPLEMENTATION

Session 1: The Present Takers (Aidan Chambers)
Read aloud to the children the second half of Chapter 1 where Lucy is bullied by Melanie and her friends (beginning with 'We only want to *talk* to you' and continuing to the end of the chapter).

Literacy Learning and Teaching

Session	Activity	
1	Peer conflict and confrontation and its 'construction' in stories.	

Whole Class: Teacher reads extract from *The Present Takers*; Teacher-led discussion of story and how it is made — role of narrator and concept of 'point of view'. — Teacher intensive

Small group: Writers' mini-workshop — trying different narrative techniques.

2   Group work: Reading/listening to allocated extracts.

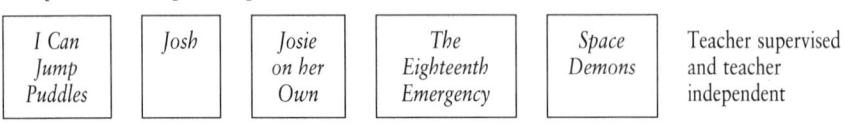

I Can Jump Puddles	Josh	Josie on her Own	The Eighteenth Emergency	Space Demons	Teacher supervised and teacher independent

3–7   Group work: Groups rotate around learning tasks after each lesson.

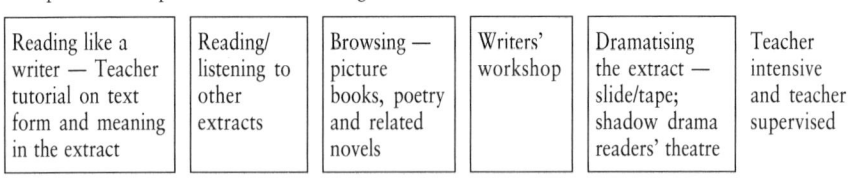

Reading like a writer — Teacher tutorial on text form and meaning in the extract	Reading/ listening to other extracts	Browsing — picture books, poetry and related novels	Writers' workshop	Dramatising the extract — slide/tape; shadow drama readers' theatre	Teacher intensive and teacher supervised

8   Regrouping: New groups in which each member has specialised on different extract.

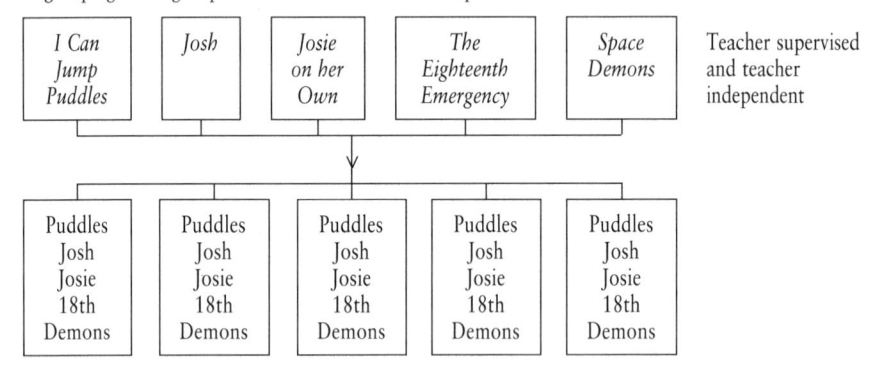

I Can Jump Puddles	Josh	Josie on her Own	The Eighteenth Emergency	Space Demons	Teacher supervised and teacher independent

Puddles Josh Josie 18th Demons	Puddles Josh Josie 18th Demons	Puddles Josh Josie 18th Demons	Puddles Josh Josie 18th Demons	Puddles Josh Josie 18th Demons

9   Preparing for publishing and sharing.

Informal small groupings of pupils:		
Rehearsal of dramatisation	Development of writing	Teacher/ pupil(s) conference

10   Performance of dramatisations.

Figure 4.3 *Overview of 'Peer conflict and confrontation' program*

Managing the Language Program

In talking with the children about the extract, deal with both the content of the story and the way the story is constructed. Ask the children if anything like this has ever happened to them? Did they feel the same as the characters in the story? Then ask if the children felt that the story was happening as they heard it or whether it had happened in the past and was being remembered? Ask if they can say anything about the way it was written that made them feel like that? Some children may notice that the text is heavily dialogic and that the extract is therefore more of a 'showing' of what the characters and events are like, rather than a direct 'telling'.

When we are told directly, how does the role of the narrator function to articulate Lucy's point of view? The children could be helped to see this by showing them the following segment on the overhead projector screen and asking them Who speaks? and Who sees?

'Other people come in their parents' cars.' She could not help herself. Why should they get away with saying such stupid things?

The children might be given a copy of this page of the text and invited to look for other examples of how the reality is constructed via the narrator but from Lucy's perspective; for example:

Tears filled her eyes. Through them, as she bent her head to hide her face, she saw the scuffed and dented surface of her birthday shoes.

Help the children to see that although we are largely 'shown' the events of this incident, the role of the narrator and the reader's access to Lucy's thoughts have the effect of aligning the reader with Lucy's point of view. Divide the class into working groups of three and ask them to consider how this section of the story could be written differently. For example, how would the writing change if Lucy or Melanie were telling the story. Try writing an alternative version of the page distributed (p. 10). Invite the groups to share their versions. What is different? How does this affect your reading of the incident?

Indicate to the children that over the next two weeks they will be able to explore extracts from several books in which young people of about their age have to deal with conflict and confrontation. Display the books from which the extracts are to be taken and invite the children to browse among these when they have spare time. The books are:

I Can Jump Puddles (Alan Marshall)
Josh (Ivan Southall)
Josie on her Own (Gunilla Norris)
The Eighteenth Emergency (Betsy Byars)
Space Demons (Gillian Rubinstein)

Session 2: Reading the Extracts

Negotiate with the children their allocation to one of five groups so that each group reads one of the extracts listed below. (It would be advisable for the teacher to have prerecorded each of the five extracts onto audio-

Literacy Learning and Teaching

cassette as a resource for any child who may experience difficulty with an initial reading of the text.) Allow the entire session for children to read/listen to the extract, discuss it among themselves and, if they wish, to begin reading the book in any time that may remain.

1. *I Can Jump Puddles* (Chapter 16).
2. *Josh* (Chapter 29 — from the beginning of the chapter, p. 156, to p. 159: 'Not an unkind voice but a firm one, accustomed to authority.').
3. *Josie on her Own* (p. 31: 'Noisily the girls tumbled out of the cabin . . .' to p. 34: 'Josie looked down at the floor . . .').
4. *The Eighteenth Emergency* (p. 88: 'The sunlight seemed blinding now' to p. 94: 'You are most certainly welcome. Come around anytime.').
5. *Space Demons* (Chapter 10, p. 94: 'Andrew never had very much to do with Mario Ferrone' to p. 96: 'Moreover things definitely had not been settled with Mario.').

Sessions 3 to 7: Group Work
After each session the groups will rotate until all have undertaken each of the group work tasks outlined below.

Reading like a Writer
In this task the children will be working with the teacher to explore the relationship between story and text form. This work would be similar to that conducted with the whole class dealing with the extract from *The Present Takers*. The purpose of this close interactive work with the teacher is to consolidate the understandings from Session 1 and to give the pupils the confidence to lead discussion of this extract as 'experts' in their new groups formed by regrouping of pupils in Session 8.

Reading Other Extracts
Children should read/listen to the four extracts to which they were not specifically allocated. If there is not time for all children in the group to read all four extracts in the session time, some may need to borrow copies of some of the extracts to complete reading/listening at home. Some children may want to read/listen to extracts again at home even if they have read them in class.

Picture Books, Poetry and Related Novels
This is an opportunity for children to read uninterrupted a range of children's literature related to the topic. Some examples of this kind of material are listed below:

> Picture books:
> *Willy the Wimp* (Anthony Browne)
> *Willy the Champ* (Anthony Browne)
> Poetry:
> 'The Bully Asleep' (John Walsh)

Related novels:
The Enemies (Robin Klein)
The Short Voyage of the Albert Ross (Jan Mark)

Writers' Workshop
Children could work together to generate ideas for writing deriving from the current unit of work and could then begin to draft their work. The teacher could offer some ideas such as the following and then encourage the children to develop these or work on alternatives.

Write about a fight or bullying episode you have witnessed or have been involved in. Consider writing as a participant or as a detached observer.

Create an 'innovation' on a poem such as 'The Bully Asleep'. The children could work collaboratively or individually. The following is an example of innovating on the first two verses of 'The Bully Asleep':

> Original
> One afternoon, when grassy
> Scents through the classroom crept,
> Bill Craddock laid his head
> Down on his desk and slept.
>
> The children came round him:
> Jimmy, Roger and Jane;
> They lifted his head timidly
> and let it sink again.
>
> Innovation
> One afternoon during reading
> With the whole class sat on the floor,
> Shane Murdock up in the back corner
> Gently started to snore.
>
> The children crept up near him:
> Angelo, Kim and Paul;
> Timidly lifted his head from his chest
> and rested it back on the wall.

The children may want to continue with this innovation, construct a different one or write some poetry of their own.

Construct a 'pick-a-path' (choose your own adventure) completion to the 'present takers' or another conflict.

Imagine you, as a teacher, have 'sprung' Melanie and her friends in the bullying episode. Write the next segment of the story, giving an account of the action you take and the girls' response.

What do children of your age fight about? What could be done to resolve the causes of these conflicts?

Dramatising the Extract
Slide–tape presentation. Children take photographs of themselves in costume and make-up, staging particular scenes from the extract. They

then rehearse and tape a dramatic reading of the extract synchronising this reading with the projection of the series of slides.

Shadow drama. Once again this involves a dramatised reading of the extract illustrated by a silhouetted view of the encounter behind an illuminated area using a sheet as a screen to produce a shadow play. Again the children need to synchronise their reading with the actions of the drama.

Readers' theatre. The children rewrite the extract in the form of a script to be performed. If this kind of work is not familiar, a model will need to be provided and discussed (see Session 4 in *Space Demons* program below for an example). Readers' theatre is traditionally performed with minimal props, costumes, etc. and the children read the scripts. However, it could be extended to include the learning of lines, costuming and setting and could then also be videotaped.

Session 8: Regrouping

Regroup the class so that each new working group will contain at least one child from each of the original groups (i.e. *I Can Jump Puddles*, *Josh*, *Josie on her Own*, *The Eighteenth Emergency*, *Space Demons*). Then each new group will consist of children who are each 'expert' on one of the extracts dealt with. However, all children will have read all extracts. Within the new groups each 'expert' child will, in turn, lead discussion about the extract which he or she dealt with in detail. The children will now have had some experience in this kind of booktalk through Session 1 dealing with *The Present Takers* and the intensive small group work with the teacher discussing allocated extracts. However, if children are not used to this kind of work, it may be useful to provide them with cards containing some 'discussion starters' based on Chambers' booktalk framework (1985, pp. 170–173):

- What do you think happened earlier in the story to cause this fight? What clues are there in the extract to these kinds of reasons for the fight?
- Who was telling this story?
- When you were reading the story, did you feel it was happening now? Or did you feel it was happening in the past and being remembered? Was there anything in the writing that made you feel like that?
- Did you feel as if everything were happening to you, as if you were one of the characters in the story? Or did you feel as if you were an observer, watching what was happening but not part of the action?
- Did we get to know what the characters were thinking about?
- Do you think we should read the whole book from which this extract came?
- What other questions should we ask or comments should we make about this book?

Managing the Language Program

Session 9: Preparing for Publishing and Sharing
In the next and final session the original working groups will present their dramatisation of the extract they worked closely with. In this session therefore some groups may need time for rehearsal. This may not always be necessary, especially if children have prepared a slide–tape presentation. Some children may wish to continue with their writing and others may want to conference with the teacher. This session may also afford some children time to extend group work tasks (e.g. videotaping of readers' theatre) or simply to read more of the books they have encountered peripherally in the program.

Session 10: Performance of Dramatisations
To conclude this program time should also be taken to obtain feedback from the children on the books encountered and activities undertaken and to negotiate suggestions for further reading.

Space Demons

Figure 4.4 provides an overview of a program of work based on the novel *Space Demons* by Gillian Rubinstein which extends over a three week period. The time allocation for each day ranges from 30–40 minutes to 60–80 minutes as indicated. A more detailed explanation of the activities and organisation follows.

OUTLINE NOTES FOR IMPLEMENTATION

Session 1
In introducing the book to the whole class, discuss with the children what the book may be about, using the cover and the title as clues. Read Chapter 1 aloud. If there are children who may experience difficulty in reading the book, tape record your reading to the class. The cassettes may then be used with a listening post (or 'walkman') as a resource to support less experienced readers when they want to 'revisit' the text.

After reading, invite the children's comments about the game. How is it similar to or different from the games they already know? How does the author get us into the game — and into the book?

Invite the children's observations on the representations of conflict among the characters introduced in this first chapter.

Session 2
Briefly review Chapter 1 with the children. Read aloud the following extract from the final paragraph:

> He sat and gazed at the screen, amazed. He had a feeling that this was still only the beginning of the game. Now that he had seen the space demons he could not wait to see them again, and to find out what happened next (p. 9).

Literacy Learning and Teaching

Week 1

Session	Time	Activity	
1	30–40 min	*Whole class*: Teacher-led discussion of b/ground knowledge; prediction from title, cover; teacher read Ch. 1; discussion of characters, emerging story and theme of conflict.	Getting ready for the text!
2	30–40 min	*Whole class*: Recap Ch. 1; Teacher read aloud Chs 2 & 3; discuss what story is about, who characters are and how they are constructed (introduce role of narrator and access to characters' thinking — reader as told/shown story).	Experiencing the story and exploring the writer's craft
3	30–40 min	*Whole class*: Teacher read aloud Ch. 4. In context of emerging story and characterisation, further discussion of narrative technique — point of view	Getting into the text!
4	30–40 min	*Whole class*: Teacher (+ experienced readers) demonstration of readers' theatre; teacher reads Ch. 5; extend exploration of point of view.	
5	30–40 min	*Whole class*: Teacher reads aloud Ch. 6.	
	30–40 min	*Group work*: Groups rotate around tasks below after each 30–40 min module for this and the next two sessions.	

Readers' theatre	Speech bubbles & thought clouds	Collage, computer graphics, modelling	Time-lines	Reading/listening post: Chs 7–10

Managing the Language Program

Week 2

Session	Time	Activity	
6, 7	60–80 min	Group work → Rotation	Reading like a writer
8	60–80 min	*Whole Class*: Sharing readers' theatre performance and display of group work tasks.	Getting further into the text!
9	30–40 min	*Regrouping*: All children change from original 'Speech bubbles, etc.' groups to form new groups; e.g.:	

Original groups:
| 12345 a | 12345 b | 12345 c | 12345 d | 12345 e |

New groups:
| 1a2b3c 4d5e | 1e2a3b 4c5d | 1d2e3a 4b5c | 1c2d3e 4a5b | 1b2c3d 4e5a |

	30–40 min	*Whole class*: Teacher reads aloud Chs 11–13.	
10	30–40 min	*Whole class*: Teacher reads aloud Chs 14–16.	
	30–40 min	*Whole class*: Teacher demonstrates and plans with class the new group work tasks below.	

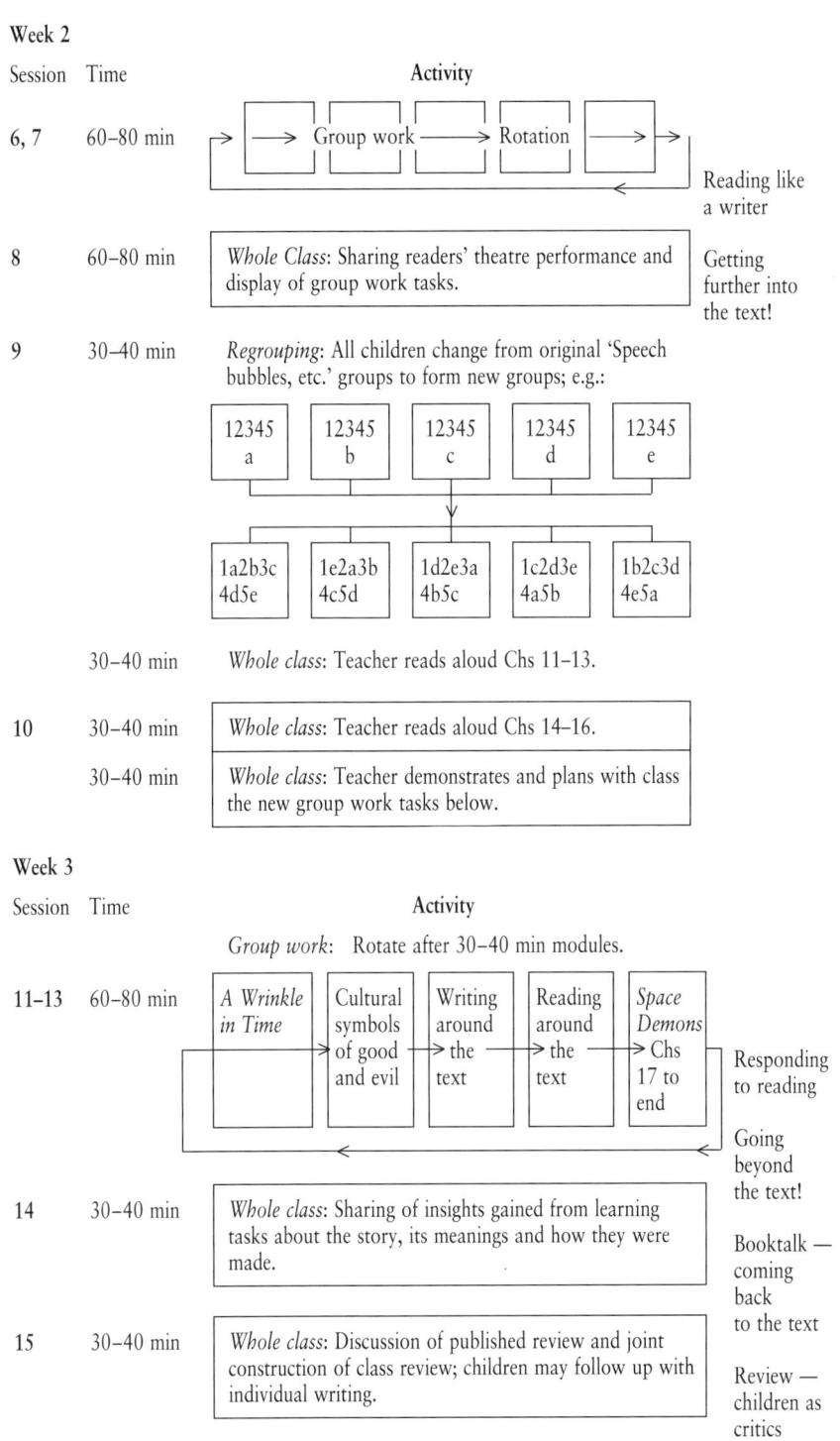

Week 3

Session	Time	Activity	
		Group work: Rotate after 30–40 min modules.	
11–13	60–80 min	*A Wrinkle in Time* → Cultural symbols of good and evil → Writing around the text → Reading around the text → *Space Demons* Chs 17 to end	Responding to reading
			Going beyond the text!
14	30–40 min	*Whole class*: Sharing of insights gained from learning tasks about the story, its meanings and how they were made.	Booktalk — coming back to the text
15	30–40 min	*Whole class*: Discussion of published review and joint construction of class review; children may follow up with individual writing.	Review — children as critics

Figure 4.4 *Overview of* Space Demons *program*

List on the blackboard the children's suggestions as to what might happen next in the game.

Read Chapters 2 and 3 aloud to the class. After reading Chapter 2 ask the children how we know about the conflict between Elaine and Linda? Note that we first hear of this from the narrator. Display the following text segment on the overhead projector screen:

> Neither was very impressed by what she saw. They could hardly have been more different. Elaine, skinny and pale in her jeans and jumper, looked untidy and almost wild, her dark red hair already escaping from her not very efficient plait. Linda's blonde hair was cut in a fashionable style, and she had a certain air of being very well looked after. Her clothes were neat and new and her shoes were polished. All of her looked polished, in fact: polished and cherished. Both girls felt vaguely threatened, and their reaction to each other was guarded and hostile (pp. 17–18).

As well as noting *how* we find out about the conflict, the children may also comment on the writer's construction of social difference as a *basis* for the conflict.

Ask the children to comment on *what* and *how* we know of the relationship between Elaine and John Ferrone. Note with the children that the author provides us with access to what Elaine is thinking during her first encounter with John. Display the following segment on the overhead projector screen to illustrate this:

> 'What's your name?' the boy asked, unsnubbed.
> Elaine realized that he would be hard to shake off. He was about as sensitive as a jackhammer. 'Elaine Taylor,' she said, with a slight upward inflection, meaning, 'You want to make something of it?'
> 'Mine's John,' he said. 'John Ferrone. We live next door to you. That was my brother Mario. He's supposed to wait for me but he never does. He's at high school, Year 8. I'm in Year 7. What are you in?'
> 'Year 7,' she said. This time the inflection meant 'Mind your own business'. She started walking quickly up the road.
> John Ferrone walked along next to her, wheeling his bicycle. 'Did you really pay a hundred thousand for the house?' he said, 'My dad says you were taken for a ride'.
> 'We didn't pay anything for it,' Elaine said. 'It doesn't belong to us. We're just staying in it for a while.'
> 'I didn't think your dad could've afforded it. He's a chippy, isn't he? I saw the ute with all his gear.'
> 'Snoopy little fellow,' Elaine thought angrily.

Children may comment further here on the authors' construction of social difference.

Suggest to the children that as Chapter 3 is read, they might think about what they are finding out about the characters and how the author is providing that information.

Allow time for discussion of this after reading. The children may note the comments by the narrator — especially those at the end of the chapter

Managing the Language Program

about Andrew's feelings toward Ben — and the quoting of characters' thoughts.

Session 3
Read Chapter 4. Stop reading at the bottom of the first page: '. . . even from a distance she could see the woman's eyes starting to glaze over'. Confirm with the children that these are the words of the narrator but notice that the point of view is Elaine's.

> When Elaine came out of the classroom after school, she immediately caught sight of her father across the oval . . .

This should be only a brief introduction to the distinction in narrative between who sees and who speaks. Further brief pauses in reading Chapter 4 can be used to provide further examples so that the children begin to develop an initial understanding of the construction of point of view. The following is one possible example:

> She could never understand how he could deliberate for ages over a little problem like whether or not to get a school uniform, and yet act so impulsively over the major choices of life like jobs and friends . . .
> . . . she felt herself reduced to despair. Her father was so powerful, so stubborn, so much larger than life. Once again he was bulldozing her into a place where she did not want to be (pp. 28–29).

It may be useful to pause once more after reading the following paragraph:

> It was beginning to rain; the bars were damp and slippery and no good for exercising on. Elaine stood by the wooden logs . . . have tea made for her cosy and nice (p. 31).

As the reading of the story progresses, the children may be encouraged to consider whose point of view the narrator conveys and whether the narrator more frequently conveys the point of view of some characters as opposed to others.

Session 4: Introduction to Readers' Theatre
This session requires prior preparation with two children who are good readers (or other experienced readers who may be available to help, such as teacher-aides, student teachers and parents. The first two pages of chapter 5 (ending with 'There's a lot more to come.') should be prepared as a readers' theatre script similar to that shown below:

> *Andrew*: Go on, then, it's all yours!
> *Narrator*: Ben sat down at the console and took the joystick.
> *Ben*: Pretty! No clues?
> *Andrew*: No clues.
> *Ben*: I don't get it. What are you supposed to do?
> *Andrew*: Do you give up?

Ben:	No way! Just give me a hint!
Andrew:	We'll have to call the bet off if I give you a hint.
Ben:	Wait a minute! I just thought of something. Let me try it.
Narrator:	Ben took off his watch and put it in front of him, the seconds flashing.
Andrew:	You got it.
Ben:	Yeah? How many seconds?
Andrew:	Find out for yourself! Did you guess or have you played something like this before?
Ben:	Darren programmed a game with a time control once, but I'd have guessed anyway — there's nothing else it could be.
Narrator:	The second screen came up.
Ben:	Whee! Talk about purple rain!
Narrator:	The silver module collided with an amethyst asteroid and exploded.
Ben:	Tricky!
Andrew:	They follow a pattern. It's not hard once you know it. Let me have a shot, I'll show you.
Ben:	Did I win the bet or not?
Andrew:	You haven't won yet. There's a lot more to come.

For further guidance on preparing readers' theatre scripts see Robertson and Poston-Anderson (1986), Johnson and Louis (1987) and Nicoll and Unsworth (1990).

Rehearse the script with the two readers outside of class time prior to Session 4. Begin the lesson with the readers' theatre performance. After the performance provide all children with a copy of the script. Put the corresponding section from the beginning of Chapter 5 onto an overhead projector slide and read this with the help of the two reading assistants — the teacher reading the narrative sections and those text segments not included in the readers' theatre script such as Andrew's thought: 'And I thought I was being so clever!'.

Discuss differences and similarities between the two texts. What is important to include in the script? Do you need the narrator? Why? Link this to earlier work on how we come to know the characters. Whose voice tells us about them? Is a character's voice as powerful as a narrator's voice?

Read the remainder of Chapter 5. Pause at the bottom of p. 38 to consider switch in point of view when Ben returns from the game. The narrator first describes Ben's reaction from Andrew's point of view:

> Andrew stared at him, not knowing what to say. Ben's face was white, and he was flexing his right hand as though he had been holding something in it . . .

There is then a shift of point of view as Ben speaks and tells of his reaction.

Another useful place to pause would be on p. 45 where the narrator describes the scene of conflict between Andrew's father and mother from Andrew's point of view:

> . . . when he opened the door into the family room even he had to be aware that there was some kind of row going on. His mother

walked abruptly into the kitchen and switched on the dishwasher. He could not see her face, but he could see his father's. Rob looked tired and depressed. His lips . . .

After reading Chapter 5 discuss with the children their feelings about the characters and the ways in which the characters are constructed by the author. Is the reader aligned with characters by the ways in which the author builds those characters in the text?

Session 5: Group Work

Inform the children that after reading Chapter 6 in this session, they will be working together in small groups to carry out some of their own work on the novel including readers' theatre, craft work, timelines, etc.

Read Chapter 6. Next, display to the children the phase 1 group work activities as shown in Figure 4.5. All children will eventually participate in all group activities. Explain to the children that they should work in boy/girl pairs if possible to facilitate the allocation of characters in the book.

The pairs will then be allocated to five fairly even groups. The groups will begin work in this session for about 30–40 minutes. Then for the next two days the language session will be divided into two 30–40 minute modules and groups will rotate around the activities at the end of each session.

Readers' theatre	Speech bubbles & thought clouds	Collage, computer graphics, modelling	Time-lines	Reading/ listening post: Chs 7–10

Figure 4.5 *Phase 1 group work activities for* Space Demons

Readers' Theatre
Each pair should select a short segment of Chapter 6 from which to make a readers' theatre script. They should then write up the script and practise a dramatised reading.

Speech Bubbles and Thought Clouds
The purpose of this activity is to provide a means for the children to further explore the ways in which characters in the book are constructed by the author. The children collaboratively produce a 'wall story' or cartoon version of the novel. Each child takes responsibility for one chapter in the book up to Chapter 6. For each scene the children draw the characters, write their dialogue in speech bubbles, their quoted thoughts in 'clouds' and, as text underneath the frames, the narrator's representation of the characters' thoughts. The children should be provided with an example of part of one chapter such as that shown in Figure 4.6.

Literacy Learning and Teaching

Panel 1:
— Hey, did you just move in?
— Yeah

Panel 2:
— You going to Kingsgate School? I'll walk along with you, show you the way.
— I can find it myself.

She had started new schools so often that she had grown canny. It didn't pay to be too friendly with anyone to start with. Usually the kids who went out of their way to be friendly were the ones nobody else liked. They cornered you and then nobody else wanted to know you.

Panel 3:
— What's your name?
(thinks) You want to make something of it?
— Elaine Taylor

Panel 4:
— Mine's John. John Ferrone. We live next door to you. That was my brother Mario. He's supposed to wait for me, but he never does. He's at High School, Yr 8. I'm in Year 7. What are you in?
— Year 7
(thinks) Mind your own business

Managing the Language Program

Figure 4.6 *Example of speech bubbles and thought clouds*

When the children have finished they should compare their chapters and then look at the ways in which different characters are represented across the six chapters read to date. How do we, as readers, come to know the characters?

Collage, Computer Graphics, Modelling
The children in each group could work individually or in their pairs to complete one or more of the tasks given below.

Construction of a computer cartridge box based on the description in *Space Demons* on p. 4:

> He tore the wrapping off eagerly. Inside was a box containing a computer cartridge. On the box there was an exciting looking picture of a spaceman in a shining white suit, back to back with a rather sinister individual dressed entirely in black, and with black spiky hair. From the side of the picture facing the spaceman another figure advanced, similar to the first, except that its hair was cut in a purple style mohawk. All three characters held cylindrical black weapons from which fiery orange chasers were flashing. Across the picture, in black and purple letters, blazed the words 'Space Demons'. Down the side and along the bottom were a lot of Japanese characters neither Andrew nor his parents could understand.

Construction of mural of the Space Demons' computer screen at various points in the game according to the descriptions on pp. 6–7, 8, 36; for example:

> As the boosters fell away, the game gave a high-pitched shriek, the screen changed to violet, and asteroids of deep purple, amethyst and mauve began to bombard the silver space module (p. 8).

The task could be undertaken as a craft activity or if the school has colour graphics packages for computers the children might construct a facsimile of the Space Demons' screen, using the graphics package.

Carving of a soap, wax or polystyrene model of the gun from *Space Demons*.

Timelines
Review with the children the events of Chapters 4 and 5. Show the children a partial timeline for these chapters similar to that shown in Figure 4.7.

Observe with the children that many of the events in these consecutive chapters are actually occurring simultaneously. Note also the selectivity of events to construct the story. We are not told for example, what happens in Elaine's house on the night of day two. Nor are we told what happens between Andrew and Ben when Andrew calls Ben away from Elaine and John before school (in Chapter 6).

The children in each group should work in pairs to construct a completed timeline for the chapters read to date. Children should then discuss observations such as those noted above and the way in which the actual story time relates to the amount of time taken to construct events

Managing the Language Program

in the novel (discourse time). Sometimes events that would actually occur in only a minute or two extend over several pages in a novel and sometimes events that would be spread over several days are dealt with in a paragraph or two.

Day	Time	Ch	Character	Ch	Character
			Elaine		Andrew
	AM/Home				
	Trvl/Sch				
	AM/Sch				
	AM/Sch/Cl				
	Lunch				
	PM/Sch/Cl				
2	After School	4	At School — E meets D; E & D talk with Mrs F — D/cleaner, E/uniform; E talk with J; M orders J to Lib; E meets L going home after music lesson.	5	A's house — A plays SD with B; B goes into SD and returns; B goes home.
	Night			5	Dinner, M upset; B plays SD alone; R home; R & M row; A goes to bed thinking of SD.

A few days later

	AM/Home				
	Trvl/Sch				
5?	AM/Sch	6	E shows J & B Agadoo dance; L comments to E *re* cartwheels and 2nd hand uniform.	6	A calls B away from E.
	AM/Sch/Cl		E intercepts L's note.		
	Lunch				

Figure 4.7 *Partial timeline for* Space Demons

Literacy Learning and Teaching

Reading/Listening Post: Chapters 7–10
This is an opportunity for the children in each group to continue their reading of the story uninterrupted. To cater for children who may have difficulty in reading the text independently, the teacher should prepare a taped reading of those chapters to be available via a listening post as a resource for inexperienced readers.

Sessions 6 and 7
Rotation of group work activities.

Session 8: Readers' Theatre Performance and Display of Work
Provide some time for final rehearsal. Then each group presents its readers' theatre performance.

In the second part of the session, groups are given time to arrange wall displays of their collage work, timelines and speech bubbles and thought cloud work. Children who need assistance or additional time to complete their work could be accommodated in this time.

Session 9: Regrouping!
All children in the 'Speech bubbles and thought clouds' group were asked to deal with one chapter of the book. New groups should now be formed so that once again they contain one child who dealt with each of the chapters. But the combination of children in each of the new groups will not be the same as for the original group. Within each group the children should be encouraged to share their understandings of the story and the characters and their insights into how these understandings are being influenced by the writer's crafting of the narrative.

Read Chapters 11–13 aloud to the whole class.

Session 10: Responding to Reading — Beyond the Text
Read aloud Chapters 14–16.

In the second part of this session outline to the children the group work activities to be undertaken next week in sessions 11–13. In these sessions the children work in 'friendship' groups to undertake the activities shown in Figure 4.8 on a rotational basis spending about half the session (30–40 minutes) on each of the activities so that by the end of session 13 all children would have undertaken all the activities.

A *Wrinkle in Time*	Cultural symbols of good and evil	Writing around the text	Reading around the text	*Space Demons* Chs 17 to end

Figure 4.8 *Phase 2 group work activities for* Space Demons

188

A Wrinkle in Time (Madeline L'Engle)
Extract 1: Ch. 4, p. 68: 'Mrs Whatsit's wings strained against the thinness of the atmosphere . . .' p. 70: '. . .so that they were incapable of speech'. Extract 2: Ch. 5, p. 82: 'Meg looked into the crystal ball . . .' Ch. 6, p. 86: 'It can be overcome! It is being overcome all the time.'

Discuss with the children how hate, jealousy and envy have been present in *Space Demons* to date. What has this meant for our perceptions of the characters? Explain the context of the extracts from *A Wrinkle in Time* to the children. In the task the children will read the extracts (or follow a teacher-prepared reading of them on a cassette tape). They should then discuss in pairs how evil is represented in the extract. What characterises evil? They could form a definition of evil and then look up the word in a number of dictionaries. How do the discussions in this session relate to notions of evil and how evil is represented in *Space Demons*?

Cultural Symbols of Good and Evil
Brainstorm with the children: how is evil represented/symbolised in our culture? Compile a list of the children's suggestions on the blackboard. Where are most of the symbols from?

In their group work task, the children could extend this, listing symbols of good and evil from movies, picture books, games, paintings, etc. They could explore catalogues and advertising brochures about currently available computer games from this point of view. The children could choose a symbol of evil and try to find the antithesis of that symbol. They could then draw or model their symbols of good and evil, writing a commentary to accompany these representations, indicating why these symbols embody ideas of good/evil.

Writing Around the Text
The following are suggestions for writing which the children may wish to pursue. Alternatively they may wish to propose their own topic.

- *Space Demons* is a prototype of a computer game designed by Japanese Professor Ito. Write a paper which Professor Ito might have produced to explain the game and his purpose in designing it.
- Make a list of questions you would like to ask Gillian Rubinstein about *Space Demons*.
- If *Space Demons* were to be adapted as a 'mini-series' for television, which Australian television actors would you cast as the characters? Make a cast list, justifying your choice for each character. Make this into a wall chart at home including pictures of the actors you select.
- If a *Space Demons* mini-series were to be made, how would each of the actors be dressed? Make a wardrobe list for each character. How would the characters' clothes be important to the meaning of the story?
- *Space Demons II* !!! Design the next game in the series.

Reading Around the Text
A selection of other books by Gillian Rubinstein (and perhaps also some other books which could be related to *Space Demons*) should be displayed in the classroom.

> *Skymaze* (Gillian Rubinstein)
> *Beyond the Labryrinth* (Gillian Rubinstein)
> *Megan's Star* (Alan Baillie)
> *The Pinballs* (Betsy Byars)
> *Answers to Brut* (Gillian Rubinstein)

Try to display at least two copies of each book.

The children in each group work individually or in pairs. They could be given task cards such as the following:

- Look at the title and cover of each book. For each book:
  — make a list of what characters might be involved;
  — briefly jot down what you think the story might be about;
  — what issues do you think the author might be exploring?
- For each book, read the 'blurb' on the back cover and/or on the title page. How close were your predictions?
- Choose the book that you think might interest you the most and read the first chapter: Do you now want to make any adjustments to your original predictions?
- Suggest other books that could be added to this list.

Reading Space Demons *to its Conclusion*
Once again it would be useful to have an audiotape version available if there are children in the class who might experience some difficulty in reading the text independently.

In the second part of Session 13 the children regroup informally to share/conclude their work from the group work tasks. Some may want more time to finish reading *Space Demons*, to display their work on cultural symbols of good and evil or to continue with their writing. Others could pursue their choice of book from the 'reading around' task. Some may wish to read more of *A Wrinkle in Time*. The teacher could make use of this segment of Session 10 to talk with children who may need assistance.

Sessions 11 to 13
Rotation of group work tasks.

Session 14: Coming Back to the Text
This is a time for a teacher-led whole class discussion about the novel drawing on Aidan Chambers' (1985, pp. 170–173) 'Tell Me' framework. Because of the scaffolding provided in undertaking earlier tasks, even inexperienced readers will be well prepared to participate in this 'booktalk'.

Only a few questions from Chambers' framework are shown below to indicate the kind of direction which might be given to the booktalk. As

Chambers points out, the questions are always adapted and rephrased to suit the children with whom one is working.

- Tell me about the parts you liked.
- Tell me about the parts you didn't like.
- Was there anything that puzzled you? Was there anything you thought strange?
- Was there anything that took you by surprise?
- Which character interested you the most? Is that character the most important person in the story? Or is it really about someone else? Which characters didn't you like? Did any of the characters remind you of people you know?
- Who was telling the story?
- Did you notice things in the story that made a pattern?
- How long did it take for the story to happen?
- If the author asked you what could be improved in the story, what would you say?
- We have listened to each others' thoughts about the story and heard all sorts of things about what we have each noticed. Are you surprised by anything someone else has said?
- When you think of this story now, after all the work we have done on it and all we have said today, what is the most important thing about it for you?
Adapted from Chambers (1985, pp. 171–172).

Provide the children with copies of a published review of *Space Demons*. Examples of reviews of *Space Demons* can be found in the following publications:

Reading Time Vol. 31, No. 3, 1987;
The Horn Book Magazine, October 1988;
Books for Keeps, No. 58, September 1989.

If there is time ask the children to read the review in class and then again at home that night, so that it can be the basis of work for the final session on *Space Demons* the next day.

Session 15: Review
Invite the children to share their responses to the review. Summarise points they make on the blackboard. Read the review aloud, stopping to discuss sections relevant to points raised by the children.

Help the children to identify the rhetorical organisation of the review. Invite them to indicate sections of which the review is made up. Discuss the appropriateness and effectiveness of this organisation.

Ask the children to suggest how they might change the review if they were publishing it. Jointly construct (for details of classroom procedure for 'joint construction of texts' see Macken *et al.* 1989; Derewianka 1990) a draft class review of *Space Demons*. This could be done by glueing a copy of the review to the centre of a piece of chart paper and writing modifications with texta on the chart paper indicating where these modifications should be made to the original text.

Invite the children to write their own version of this review for submission for publication to the school magazine, or the journals and newsletters of professional associations such as English teaching associations, etc. Alternatively the children may aim to produce a version for forwarding to the author, reviewer and/or publisher.

Conclusion

What counts as reading, understanding and enjoying children's literature is socially constructed, largely through the kinds of interactions with texts which children experience in classrooms. The sorts of texts that are selected build and sanction particular kinds of reading practices. However, although similar texts might be found within the range of contexts enveloped in terms like 'whole language' or 'literature-based' classrooms, different pedagogies are capable of yielding radically different reading positions and practices. Classroom programs which address the significance of narrative form in children's books in a critical, analytical manner are not very common. The rarity of such discourse analytic approaches, which explicitly address the 'constructedness' of literary texts, means that many children's experience of 'literature-based' programs leaves them with an extremely limited sense of how texts work. Such knowledge is not available to them to enhance their understanding, enjoyment and their capacity to see the story as other than a 'natural' unfolding of events and hence to read in such a way that reads the 'portrayal' against the techniques of construction. The approaches to managing the language program that I have suggested here attempt to provide all children with access to this knowledge. Explicit attention to the ways in which textual form constructs meaning is an important step toward providing children with access to critical literacy and an understanding of how texts position them and their readings. The examples of programs, teaching strategies and texts which have been discussed here indicate how these concerns can be addressed in a context of enjoyable and engaging classroom work with children's literature.

Note

1. I am grateful to Geoff Williams for allowing me to draw on his published and unpublished papers in preparing this work.

References

Benton, M. and Fox, G. (1985) *Teaching Literature Nine to Fourteen*, Oxford University Press, Oxford.
Bernstein, B. (1975) 'Class and pedagogies: Visible and invisible', in *Class, Codes and Control*, vol. 3: *Towards a Theory of Educational Transmissions*, Routledge and Kegan Paul, London.
Beveridge, M. (1982) *Children Thinking Through Language*, Edward Arnold, London.
Bloome, D. (1983) 'Classroom reading instruction: A sociocommunicative analysis of time on task', in *32nd Yearbook of the National Reading Conference*, ed. J. Niles, National Reading Conference, Rochester, New York.
Chambers, A. (1985) *Booktalk: Occasional Writing on Literature and Children*, The Bodley Head, London.
Collins, J. (1986) 'Differential instruction in reading groups', in *The social Construction of Literacy*, ed. J. Cook-Gumperz, Cambridge University Press, Cambridge.
Dalton, J. (1985) *Adventures in Thinking: Creative Thinking and Co-operative Talk in Small Groups*, Nelson, Melbourne.
Davis, J. (1990) 'Literature-based reading in the classroom'. A long essay submitted to the University of Sydney in partial fulfilment of the requirements for the honours degree of Bachelor of Education, University of Sydney.
Derewianka, B. (1990) *Exploring How Texts Work*, Primary English Teaching Association, Sydney.
DeStephano, J., Pepinsky, H. and Sanders, T. (1982) 'Discourse rules for literacy learning in a first grade classroom', in *Communicating in the Classroom*, ed. L.C. Wilkinson, Academic Press, New York.
Dombey, H. (1988) 'Partners in the telling', in *Language and Literacy in the Primary School*, eds M. Meek and C. Mills, Falmer Press, London.
Donaldson, M. (1978) *Children's Minds*, Fontana, London.
Eder, D. (1986) 'Organizational constraints on reading group mobility', in *The Social Construction of Literacy*, ed. J. Cook-Gumperz, Cambridge University Press, Cambridge.
Goldfield, B. and Snow, C. (1984) 'Reading books with children: The mechanics of parental influence on reading achievement', in *Promoting Reading Comprehension*, ed. J. Flood, International Reading Association, Newark, Delaware.
Graham, J. (1984) 'Reading literature with a slow learner', in *Eccentric Propositions: Essays on Literature and the Curriculum*, ed. J. Miller, Routledge and Kegan Paul, London.
Gray, B. (1986) *Creating a Context for the Negotiation of Written Text*, Twelfth Australian Reading Conference, Perth.
Halliday, M.A.K. (1978) *Language as Social Semiotic*, Edward Arnold, London.
Hiebert, E. (1983) 'An examination of ability grouping for reading instruction', *Reading Research Quarterly* XVIII (2): 231–255.
Johnson, T. and Louis, D. (1985) *Literacy Through Literature*, Methuen, Sydney.
Johnson, T. and Louis, D. (1987) *Bringing It All Together: A Program for Literacy*, Methuen, Sydney.
Macken, M., Martin, J., Kress, G., Kalantzis, M., Rothery, J. and Cope, W. (1989) *An Approach to Writing K–12*, Sydney: Literacy and Education Research Network and Directorate of Studies, NSW Department of Education, Sydney.

Martin, J.R. and Rothery, J. (1988) 'Classification and framing: Double dealing in pedagogic discourse'. Paper presented to Post Congress Symposium of the World Congress of the International Reading Association, University of Queensland, Brisbane.

Meek, M. (1982) *Learning to Read*, The Bodley Head, London.

Meek, M. (1988) *How Texts Teach What Readers Learn*, Thimble Press, Stroud, Gloucestershire.

Meek, M. et al. (1983) *Achieving Literacy: Longitudinal Studies of Adolescents Learning to Read*, Routledge and Kegan Paul, London.

Mills, C. (1988) 'Making sense of reading: Keywords or Grandma Swagg?', in *Language and Literacy in the Primary School*, eds M. Meek and C. Mills, Falmer Press, London.

Nicoll, V. and Unsworth, L. (1989) *Dimensions Teachers' Book Level I*, Nelson, Melbourne.

Nicoll, V. and Unsworth, L. (1990) *Dimensions Teachers' Book Level II*, Nelson, Melbourne.

Reid, J., Forrestal, P. and Cook, J. (1989) *Small Group Learning in the Classroom*, Primary English Teaching Association/Chalkface Press, Scarborough, WA.

Roberts, V. and Nicoll, V. (1988) 'Conducting an author study', in *Australian Literature in the Primary Classroom*, Curriculum Development Centre, Canberra.

Robertson, M. and Poston-Anderson, B. (1986) *Readers' Theatre: A Practical Guide*, Hodder and Stoughton, Sydney.

Saxby, M. (1987) 'The gift of wings: The value of children's literature', in *Give Them Wings: The Experience of Children's Literature*, eds M. Saxby and G. Winch, Macmillan, Melbourne.

Saxby, M. (1990) *The Great Deeds of Heroic Women*, Millennium, Sydney.

Unsworth, L. (1986) 'Grouping for personalized classroom learning', in *Getting It Together: Organizing the Reading–Writing Classroom*, ed. W. McVitty, Primary English Teaching Association, Sydney.

Vygotsky, L. (1978) *Mind and Society: The Development of Higher Psychological Processes*, Harvard University Press, Cambridge, Massachusetts.

Vygotsky, L. (1986) *Thought and Language*, MIT Press, Cambridge, Massachusetts.

Waterland, L. (1985) *Read With Me*, Thimble Press, Stroud, Gloucestershire.

Waterland, L. (1989) *Apprenticeship in Action: Teachers Write about Read With Me*, Thimble Press, Stroud, Gloucestershire.

Williams, G. (1987) 'Rumpelstiltskin's secret'. Plenary address to the Annual Conference of the Victorian Reading Association, September, Ballarat, Victoria.

Williams, G. and Jack, D. (1986) 'The role of story: Learning to read in a special education class', in *Revaluing Troubled Readers*, Occasional Papers No. 15, Program in language and literacy, College of Education, University of Arizona.

References to Children's Books

Aesop's Fables (1990) illus. by Rodney McRae, Margaret Hamilton, Sydney.
Baille, Allan (1985) *Little Brother*, Nelson, Melbourne.
Baille, Allan (1988) *Megan's Star*, Nelson, Melbourne.
Briggs, Raymond (1977) *Fungus the Bogeyman*, Hamilton, London.
Browne, Anthony (1979) *Bear Hunt*, Hamish Hamilton, London.
Browne, Anthony (1984) *Willy the Wimp*, Julia McRae, London.
Browne, Anthony (1985)*Willy the Champ*, Julia McRae, London.
Burningham, John (1984) *Granpa*, Jonathon Cape, London.
Byars, Betsy (1974)*The Eighteenth Emergency*, The Bodley Head, London.
Byars, Betsy (1990) *The Pinballs*, Puffin, Harmondsworth.
Chambers, Aidan (1985)*The Present Takers*, Methuen Magnet, London.
Cleary, Beverly (1980) *Ramona the Pest*, Puffin, Harmondsworth.
Dahl, Roald (1980) *The Twits*, Pickwick International, London.
Dann, Max (1983) *Adventures with my Worst Best Friend*, Oxford University Press, Melbourne.
Dickinson, Peter (1984) *Giant Cold*, Victor Gollancz, London.
Facey, Albert (1981) *A Fortunate Life*, Fremantle Arts Centre, Fremantle, WA.
French, Simon (1981) *Cannily, Cannily*, Angus and Robertson, Sydney.
Garner, Alan (1976) *The Stone Book Quartet*, Collins, London.
Gleason, Libby (1986) *Eleanor Elizabeth*, Puffin, Harmondsworth.
Hoban, Russell (1986) 'Homework', in *Challenges*, M. Saxby and G. Smith (Comp.), Methuen, Sydney.
Hughes, Ted (1968) *The Iron Man*, Faber, London.
Hutchins, Pat (1969) *Rosie's Walk*, The Bodley Head, London.
Ireson, Barbara (ed.) (1989) *Fighting in the Break and Other Stories*, Penguin, London.
Kemp, Gene (1977) *The Turbulent Term of Tyke Tiler*, Faber, London.
Kemp, Gene (1981) *The Clocktower Ghost*, Faber, London.
Klein, Robin (1984) *Hating Alison Ashley*, Penguin, Ringwood, Victoria.
Klein, Robin (1985) *The Enemies*, Angus and Robertson, Sydney.
L'Engle, Madeline (1962) A *Wrinkle in Time*, Dell, New York.
Lee, Harper (1963) *To Kill a Mockingbird*, Penguin, Harmondsworth.
Lewis, C.S. (1950) *The Lion, the Witch and the Wardrobe*, Fontana Lions, London.
Lindgren, Astrid (1978) *Pippi Longstocking*, Puffin, Harmondsworth.
Lurie, Morris (1971) *Arlo the Dandy Lion*, Collins, London.
McGough, Roger (1981) *Strictly Private*, Kestrel, Harmondsworth.
Mark, Jan (1980) *The Short Voyage of the Albert Ross*, Granada, London.
Marshall, Alan (1972) *I Can Jump Puddles*, Lloyd O'Neil, Hawthorn.
Martin, R.D. (1981) *There's a Dinosaur in the Park*, ERA Publications, Flinders Park, South Australia.
Mayer, Mercer (1968) *There's a Nightmare in my Closet*, The Dial Press, New York.
Norman, Lilith (1979) *My Simple Little Brother*, Collins, Sydney.
Norris, Gunilla (1969) *Josie on her Own*, Scholastic, New York.
Park, Ruth (1985) *Playing Beatie Bow*, Puffin, Harmondsworth.
Park, Ruth (1988) *The Harp in the South*, Puffin, Melbourne.
Pearce, Philippa (1983) *The Battle of Bubble and Squeak*, Macmillan, London.
Phipson, Joan (1979) *Hide till Daytime*, Penguin, Harmondsworth.
Rodgers, Mary (1983) *Freaky Friday*, Collins Educational, London.

Rubinstein, Gillian (1986) *Space Demons*, Penguin, Melbourne.
Rubinstein, Gillian (1988) *Beyond the Labyrinth*, Hyland House, Melbourne.
Rubinstein, Gillian (1988) *Answers to Brut*, Omnibus/Puffin, Adelaide.
Rubinstein, Gillian (1989) *Skymaze*, Omnibus/Puffin, Adelaide.
Sendak, Maurice (1962) *Where the Wild Things Are*, The Bodley Head, London.
Sendak, Maurice (1987) *Outside Over There*, Harper and Row, New York.
Southall, Ivan (1978) *Let the Balloon Go*, Puffin, Harmondsworth.
Southall, Ivan (1982) *Josh*, Puffin, Harmondsworth.
Thiele, Colin (1963) *Storm Boy*, Rigby, Adelaide.
Thiele, Colin (1969) *Blue Fin*, Rigby, Adelaide.
Tolkien, J.R.R. (1984) *The Hobbit*, Allen and Unwin, London.
Wagner, Jenny (1977) *John Brown, Rose and the Midnight Cat*, Kestrel, Melbourne.
Walsh, John (1986) 'The Bully Asleep', in *Dangers and Disasters*, M. Saxby and G. Smith (Comp.), Methuen, Sydney.
Wheatley, Nadia (1987) *My Place*, illus. by Donna Rawlins, Collins Dove, Melbourne.
Wrightson, Patricia (1971) *I Own the Racehorse*, Penguin, Harmondsworth.

5
Using Systemic Grammar in Teaching Young Learners: An Introduction

Geoff Williams

Contents

Introduction   199

Differences between Traditional School Grammar and Functional Grammar   201

Clauses in English   203
   Clauses and Clause Complexes
   Embedded Clauses
   Finite and Non-finite Clauses

Organising Clauses as Messages   208
   The Structure of Theme in the Clause in English
   Thematic Development in a Simple Recount

Structuring Experience through Grammatical Choices   218
   The Elements of the Experiential Metafunction
   Examples of Different Process Types in *Fantastic Mr Fox*
   Processes and Participants: An Elaboration

Structure within Clauses: The Nominal Group   236
   Variation in the Complexity of Nominal Groups
   Building the Nominal Group Experientially
   'Stacking Things': The Nominal Group Complex
   Verbs as Things

Clause as 'Interact': Interpersonal Grammar   244

Elements of Mood   245
   Subject and Finite
   Selection of Mood and Speech Function

Other Aspects of the Interpersonal Metafunction   250
   Residue
   Vocative

Conclusion   251

References
References to Children's Books

Introduction

Is knowledge of English grammar of practical use for teaching and learning? Not long ago the answer amongst many teachers was an unequivocal 'no'. Looking back over the primary and junior secondary English textbooks of the 1960s one sees page after page of 'drills and skills' work in grammar, remote from actual uses of language in the living of life. School grammar became merely a formalism, and often very confusing for young learners because of the arbitrariness of its systems of rules.

Research evidence on the effects of grammar teaching in the early 1970s suggested, on face value, that traditional school grammar made no important contribution to literacy development. And within linguistics itself the dominant form of grammar, transformational grammar, was proving unproductive for educational purposes. There seemed to be no good reason to continue to teach it.

However, much has changed in the last 10 years. Grammars which are of practical use in teaching have become available. They offer ways of describing real uses of language for genuine social purposes. From a teacher's viewpoint perhaps the most important change has been in the development of functional grammars, which are organised to describe how *meanings* are made in texts, rather than merely describing language structure apart from meaning.

Of these grammars the one which has attracted most interest from teachers themselves is systemic functional grammar. It was initially devised by Michael Halliday, himself a teacher as well as a linguist, and continues to be developed by Halliday and by linguists such as Ruqaiya Hasan (1987), Jim Martin (1992a) and Christian Matthiessen (1992). Part of its particular appeal is that it enables us to relate grammatical structure to ways in which people mean when they use language in context. It is also one part of a comprehensive theory of language, in which descriptions of grammatical structure can be related to social structure through descriptions of types of situation in a culture.

In this discussion I have attempted to provide an introductory description of systemic functional grammar in sufficient detail to enable teachers to begin analysing linguistic patterns for themselves and to begin to explore the potential of grammatical description for assisting young learners. The description is accompanied by brief illustrations of some practical uses of the grammar, though because of the relative complexity of grammatical issues it has been necessary to give more space to the description than the illustrations. On the one hand, it is not possible to illustrate uses of the grammar fully until the system is reasonably well known. On the other hand, learning the grammar takes a considerable effort so at least some indication of the potential of the description is important. The chapter attempts to form some compromise between these two horns of the dilemma, hopefully to provide a way into the more detailed descriptions in Halliday (1985a). I have assumed a knowledge of basic working concepts in systemic linguistics, particularly the concepts of context of situation, register, genre and metafunction. If these ideas are unfamiliar to you there are some texts which would be particularly useful: Halliday and Hasan (1985), *Language, Context and Text*, Christie (1989), *Writing in Schools: Study Guide*, and Halliday (1976), *Language as Social Semiotic*.

In thinking about the teaching of grammar it is useful to distinguish between, on the one hand, teaching of grammar to pupils and, on the other, teachers learning a grammar in order to better understand practical education issues such as language development, literacy learning, learning difficulties and evaluation. Positions on these two issues can be quite different.

In relation to the first issue, political conservatives frequently propose the teaching of grammar as a way of 'returning' to the assumed standards of the past. They are, in fact, wanting to prescribe how language *should* be used, with little reference to how it is actually used in a variety of contexts. Teachers rightly see this proposal as a reductive solution to complex issues of cultural and social change. What is remarkable in this proposal is the ignorance it displays of contemporary developments in the disciplined study of language. So it is important to be careful about investigating what grammar is taught when, and in what contexts of purpose. The fact that no research funding has yet been allocated to explore teaching a functional grammar in schools is a major limitation on educational development. So the question of whether or not aspects of this new grammatical knowledge could be learnt by children remains an open one, still to be addressed by teachers and educational linguists.

On the other hand, teachers have to use language about language every day, so principled knowledge of language structure is very important to them. Currently, much of teachers' metalanguage is concerned with the visual structure of the system of writing — obvious terms like paragraph, full stop, letter, title and so on. Less explicitly, judgements about grammar also have to be made, for example in conferences about draft writing, in interpreting the outcomes of reading tests or miscue analyses and so on. The most ordinary of these questions involve grammatical concepts: is this a full sentence or not? Is this paragraph effectively organised? Is this miscue grammatically equivalent to the original text?

At an even more implicit level, the significance of grammatical structures can be overlooked even when they are directly relevant to learning, as with children's problems in learning many mathematical concepts, particularly when learners are from minority cultural groups. The usual educational diagnosis is that the problems are ones of 'conceptual' learning, as though grammatical structure was irrelevant.

This last point will be developed subsequently because it is potentially the most important reason of all for building up some professional understanding of grammatical structure. In fact it becomes possible to use knowledge of functional grammar to intervene on behalf of young learners, for example to 'unpack' texts explicitly for them to make meanings more accessible, to show why some structure is required in a specific type of text, or to demonstrate to administrators why a learner's difficulties are linguistic (and therefore social) rather than cognitive (and individual).

Knowledge of functional grammar complements and extends thinking about other aspects of language structure. Recent language education work has been particularly focused on the level of *discourse structure*, particularly the schematic structure of genres. Christie and Rothery (1989) and Derewianka (1990) provide helpful overviews of written genres commonly used in schools.

However, notions of discourse structure can usefully be supplemented by descriptions of the structure of clauses, which is what 'grammar' means. In fact the account of generic stages depends on differences in grammatical patterning at clause level, as does the effectiveness of educational texts. Conversely, the dysfunctional aspects of educational texts can often be better understood by examining the grammatical structures closely. Grammatical analysis can therefore make a practical difference with such seemingly unrelated issues as learning difficulties for various minority groups of learners and the assessment of validity of educational tests. Before beginning the discussion of systemic functional grammar itself, it may be useful to outline some of the major differences from traditional school grammars in order to sharpen the claims that this new grammar is qualitatively different from what has previously been available.

Differences between Traditional School Grammar and Functional Grammar

Traditional school grammar is a prescriptive grammar, and prescriptive grammars are based on Latin grammatical forms. Since knowledge of Latin was restricted to certain social class groups in England, the prescriptions of what counted as 'good grammar' became associated with their practices. Thus the concept of 'grammatical correctness' in school grammar comes not from features internal to language itself, but from the social practices of a particular class group.

In fact many texts of school grammar became little more than sets of rules based on these social practices, unrelated to the way people actually used a variety of language. Prescription shifted, as Martin (1992b) points out, from the *grammar of etiquette* to the *grammar of prejudice*. He provides some examples of prescriptive rules, each of which is readily comprehensible and each of which breaks the rule it encodes.

- A preposition is something you should never end a sentence with.
- It is quite wrong to carelessly split infinitives.
- And you should never begin a sentence with a conjunction.

Traditional grammar is also a classificatory grammar, forming words into classes such as noun, verb, adjective, preposition. The particular curriculum practice associated with this aspect was *parsing*, in which 'parts of speech' were allocated to class groups. An example of parsing using traditional grammar is:

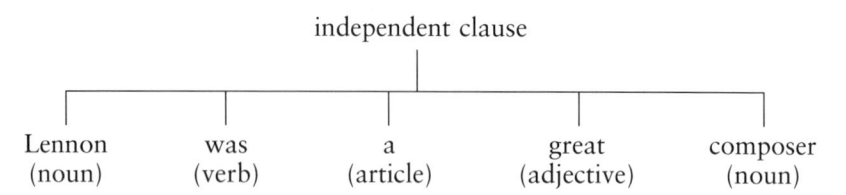

```
                    independent clause
        ┌───────┬───────┬───────┬───────┐
      Lennon   was      a     great   composer
      (noun)  (verb) (article) (adjective) (noun)
```

The problem with this practice from a teacher's viewpoint is that it is difficult to do much with the results of parsing. This kind of grammar is not well oriented to understanding how meaning is built up in a text. In fact it is not really able to deal with texts at all, but rather only with individual sentences, clauses and, mostly, individual words. The sentence was the great focus of attention for the devisers of skills worksheets in the past.

In contrast, systemic functional grammar is a semantically oriented grammar, designed to investigate how *meanings* are made through grammatical relationships in different social contexts. It is also designed to be comprehensive enough to account for grammatical forms in speech as well as writing. It has been developed for different social and educational purposes. In many ways the relationship between traditional and functional grammar is like the relationship between Newtonian physics and theoretical physics after Einstein. In fact the metaphor of relativity is also widely used in functional grammars, and provides useful ways of understanding different perspectives on structure.

One key assumption in functional grammar, as the name itself suggests, is that to understand linguistic meaning the *function* of items in a structure has to be appreciated. The items don't necessarily function in a straightforward additive way, with one word adding to the meaning of the others in the sentence. Rather, their function will be organised through the *system* of relationships which comprises an area of the grammar. The term 'systemic' in systemic functional grammar derives from this assumption.

The one word does not always mean the same thing in different structures. It is often a matter of looking at the function to determine the meaning of the individual word. In the following examples 'disturbing' has somewhat different meanings because the function in each clause is different.

1. The rate of population growth is disturbing.
2. They are disturbing the sacred sites.
3. Disturbing news has been received about their fate.

In (1) 'disturbing' functions as a description of the rate of population growth. In (2) it functions as a process of actually doing something to the sacred sites. In (3) it functions to modify the meaning of news by introducing an interpersonal perspective to the meaning, giving information about the attitude of the speaker to the news. The one word can make quite different semantic contributions to a text.

Perhaps the most important difference between traditional school grammar and systemic functional grammar is the metaphor of choice. Whereas school grammars have prescribed *the* correct form, functional grammar views language as a resource — one which makes semantic choices available to speakers and writers. What it describes is the semantic effect of using one form rather than another, and the systematic relationships between different choices in different regions of the grammar. That is one of the reasons why many of its advocates working in educational linguistics often refer to explicit knowledge of language structure as 'empowering' for learners, since they become able to make choices which are effective within a specific context of language use.

On this issue, relationships between discourse structure and grammatical structure are very important. Recent educational discussion has highlighted the significance of schematic structure of texts, but the appropriateness of these resources depends in turn on the selection of appropriately patterned grammatical resources. The close relationship between discourse structure and grammatical structure is at the centre of the systemic description of language in use. The very idea of a change in the stage of the text in fact means that grammatical resources have been differently deployed.

In thinking about grammatical structure the crucial first unit for description is the clause. I'll first outline some of the major features of clause, then move to discuss some features of grammatical structure within three regions of meaning. The first will be the textual, concerned with the organisation of the text as a 'message'; the second, the experiential, focused on the 'representative' role of language; and the third, the interpersonal, concerned with messages as 'interacts'.

Clauses in English

We can begin by saying that a clause has 'verb' in it. One way to informally begin understanding the concept of 'verb' is to think in terms of some process going on. The process might be one of material action, as in 'He cooked the meal superbly', where the verb is *cooked*. The process might also be one of mental activity such as thinking, feeling or believing, as in 'She *does believe* the story'. Sometimes the process can be one of forming a relationship between things or concepts, typically through some form of 'is' or 'has': 'Her name *is* Michaela', 'He *has* many questions'.

Notice that forms of 'is', 'do' and 'has' can themselves form the verb or be part of a group of words which form a verbal group, as in (1) to (6) below. The term 'verb' tends to suggest a single word but in fact in many clauses the process will involve a group of words, some of which will signal orientation in time (past, present or future) and the phasing of the process over time.

In each of the following lines there is one clause, structured around the verbal group, which is italicised.

1. He *is going* to the show.
2. The child *is* a genius.
3. It *has* four feet with large claws.
4. She *has gone* to Japan.
5. They *do* the house every week.
6. They *do like* the Daintree area.
7. The computer *considered* the problem.
8. She *ate* the dinner.
9. They *had been talking* about the test result.
10. The thunderstorm *broke*.

Sometimes a verbal group can become a larger structure, as in:

1. They *had been going to go* to the movies.
2. She *is beginning to consider* the applications.

In texts, the actual verb may be omitted in the wording of a clause but it is implied by the surrounding structure. The phenomenon is called ellipsis. It is particularly common in dialogue:

Dialogue Excerpt   (Ellipsed elements recovered)

'Where'*s* the salt?' 'On the shelf.' 'Where?' '*Look* closer.' 'What?'	'It *is* on the shelf.' 'Where *is* it?' 'What *did* you *say*?'

Even though verbs are not explicitly included in the structures on the left, each line is a clause because the utterance either explicitly includes a verbal group or the structure implies a verbal group. (Each verbal group is italicised, either in the original dialogue or in the recovered elements.)

Clauses and Clause Complexes

In texts, clauses are often linked together, for example by simply adding one to another, as in (1), or by building an adversative relationship, as in (2), or by specifying a causal relationship, as in (3).

1. ||| Tom, Tom the piper's son *stole* a pig ||and away *did run*. |||
2. ||| She *likes* Joan Armatrading|| but he *likes* Midnight Oil.|||
3. ||| *Don't boil* the egg in the microwave ||because it*'ll explode*.|||

Clauses which are linked to form a sentence comprise a clause complex. However, 'clause complex' and 'sentence' are not quite synonymous terms because 'sentence' is a unit of written language, whereas clause

Using Systemic Grammar

complexes describe both spoken and written language. In speech the boundaries of the clause complex are indicated by the tone contours of the voice: there is nothing like a full stop and capital letter to signal the end of a clause complex. In fact, of course, one complex task for young children learning to write is exactly this, to learn to map the rhythm and tone of spoken language into units of writing at the level of sentence.

When young children first dictate language for adults to write down, typically the clauses will be linked by adding them together to form clause complexes, usually with 'and' or 'and then', with occasional contrasts of various kinds, usually with 'but'. In Text 1, for example, is a kindergarten child's text, dictated to his teacher early in the school year to accompany a painting he'd just completed.

Text 1
That's a ship and that's a duck and that's some bombs and that's a shop and that's a plane.

Text 1a shows Text 1 analysed into clauses, with verbal groups again italicised.

Text 1a
|||That's a ship ||and that's a duck ||and that's some bombs ||and that's a shop ||and that's a plane.|||

The relationship here is simply one of addition. Each new clause is added to the preceding one to form a single clause complex.

Text 2, also dictated by a kindergarten child, Julie, is slightly different in that she uses more variable relationships between clauses and 'punctuates' the clause complexes into structures which are more sentence-like. It is one aspect of a change towards the use of written forms of language.

Text 2
I went to the park, then the rainbow came. I went inside it and I looked colourful. It was at the park and then my Dad came to get me.

Text 2a
||| I *went* to the park, ||then the rainbow *came*. ||||I *went* inside it ||and I *looked* colourful. ||||It *was* at the park ||and then my Dad *came* ||to *get* me.|||

Similarly, the author of Text 3, Angharad, uses some variety in relationships between clauses, as when he explicitly indicates a causal relationship, ''cause that's white sky'.

Text 3

This is the Harbour Bridge and I didn't paint the rest there 'cause that's white sky. And this is the water down here. This is my aunt's flats and that's the big sun and guns come out of here and shoot the baddies on the Harbour Bridge. And then comes a baddie on the Harbour Bridge, but he's too small and the special gun's underneath him, but he doesn't realize they're underneath him.

Text 3a

|||This *is* the Harbour Bridge ||and I *didn't paint* the rest there ||'cause that*'s* white sky. |||And this *is* the water down here. |||This *is* my aunt's flats ||and that*'s* the big sun ||and guns *come* out of here ||and *shoot* the baddies on the Harbour Bridge. |||And then *comes* a baddie on the Harbour Bridge, ||but he*'s* too small ||and the special gun*'s* underneath him, ||but he *doesn't realize* ||they*'re* underneath him.|||

Texts 2 and 3 are still very much in spoken mode, but obviously they are not just strings of clauses added together. As children gain more experience with writing, and as they learn to write across a range of genres and registers they tend to use more complex relationships between clauses.

This is not to suggest, of course, that a more complex pattern of clause relationships is an end in itself. The crucial concept is the appropriateness of the form to the context, including the purpose of the text. Unfortunately it is not uncommon to find children in the upper primary school who produce written texts which, whatever the context, use only additive forms of relationships between clauses.

Embedded Clauses

So far we have considered clauses which occur in text at the same rank or, more informally, have the same 'status'. Sometimes, however, a clause may be 'down-ranked' or embedded inside another clause. When this happens the embedded clause very often functions to define something. It is a device widely used in factual texts, to enable writers to define complex entities, but it also occurs in more everyday examples of conversation.

Here is an example, taken from a Year 3 child's text about a visit to a quarantine station: 'The diseases that the patients *had are* the flu, smallpox, bubonic plague and typhoid fever.' There are two verbal groups here, 'had' and 'are'. (Notice that they are separate verbal groups even though they happen to be adjacent.) The clause 'that the patients *had*' functions to define 'diseases', that is, to specify which diseases are being referred to. It does not have the full status of a clause but is embedded in the clause which is structured around *are*.

||The diseases [[that the patients *had*]] *are* the flu, smallpox, bubonic plague and typhoid fever.||

Here is a further example, taken from children's factual writing.

1. Lions are mammals that are found in Africa.

The analysis into clauses is:

1a. Lions *are* mammals [[that *are* found in Africa.]]

Subsequently some other aspects of this type of embedding will be discussed because it is both a very important resource in writing development and also a source of difficulty in reading for some children.

Finite and Non-finite Clauses

It is useful to notice, again informally, one further important difference between clauses which commonly occurs in texts. The examples we have used so far have involved finite clauses, which means that they have a specific location in time with respect to the 'speaking'. Not all clauses are like this. Consider the sentences:

1. *Opening* the box, they *discovered* jewels of every description.
2. They *did* very well, *considering* the difficulty.

Both sentences comprise two clauses, structured around two verbal groups.

1a. |||*Opening* the box, ||they *discovered* jewels of every description.|||
2a. |||They *did* very well, ||*considering* the difficulty.|||

Obviously there are differences between the clauses within each of the clause complexes. The clauses with the 'ing' form actually depend on the finite clauses for location in time. You can readily see this by changing the tense of the finite clause, as with

|||*Opening* the box, ||they *will discover* jewels of every description.|||

Another very common form of non-finite clause, apart from those with an 'ing' structure, is the type that uses the 'to + lexical verb' pattern, as in 'to sing', 'to laugh', 'to build'. This form is commonly called the infinitive form of the verb. For example,

1. They *will save* hard *to travel* overseas.
2. *To cook* this well you *must have* a very hot oven.

When these are analysed into clauses, the pattern is:

1a. |||They *will save* hard ||*to travel* overseas.|||
2a. |||*To cook* this well ||you *must have* a very hot oven.|||

Commonly both types of non-finite clause will be found in text together with a finite one. Here is an example, followed by the analysis into clauses.

1. *Remembering* the prediction later, they *climbed* into the cave *to shelter* from the worst of the night.
2. |||*Remembering* the prediction later, ||they *climbed* into the cave ||*to shelter* from the worst of the night.|||

Even just an awareness of various types of clauses helps both in editing children's writing and in modelling various patterns during joint construction of texts. However, it is possible to look more closely at the patterning of meaning within clauses, and therefore very specifically at how meanings are built within texts. One aspect of the grammatical system which makes a particular contribution to the coherence of texts is the system of grammatical Theme.

Organising Clauses as Messages

Different aspects of meaning are coded into a clause, relevant to its function and purpose in the text. One of these aspects is the clause as a message, those features of the ordering of the wording which build meaning as the text unfolds. The crucial concepts here are Theme and Rheme. It's perhaps important to stress that the term Theme is being used here as a technical description for an aspect of clause grammar, not in its more general educational or literary sense of the most important, or most general, meaning. Here Theme and the complementary term Rheme have a technical status, just as verbal group had in the previous section.

I will first outline some of the major features of Theme in declarative clauses, those clauses usually used to make statements, then consider thematic development in two contrasting genres, and finally suggest some uses of Theme analysis in editing student writing.

The Structure of Theme in the Clause in English

Theme functions as the 'starting point for the message' (Halliday 1985a, p. 39), the element which the clause is going to be 'about' and it thus has a crucial effect in orienting listeners and readers. Theme is the starting point of the clause, realised by whatever element comes first, and Rheme is the rest of the message, which provides the additional information added to the starting point and which is available for subsequent development in the text.

English uses first position in the clause to signal Theme. Other languages indicate Theme in other ways. Some, for example, add a specific morpheme or other grammatical form. Just as English usually signals plural by attaching 's' or 'es', and other languages use other grammatical resources to signal this meaning, some languages signal Theme through a particular morpheme attached to the thematic element. English does not do this, but rather uses first clausal position as a signal. Because of this organisational difference from their first language, learners of non-English-speaking backgrounds (NESB) often have to learn how to organise an English text's thematic development appropriately, especially for written texts. When a text appears incoherent it is often because this 'message-organising' aspect is inappropriately used, or the organising principles around which it is structured are left implicit, making it difficult for a reader to understand the writer's or speaker's 'topic'.

GENERAL PRINCIPLES OF THEME DESCRIPTION IN ENGLISH

Text 4 was written by a Year 3 child, James, when he was asked by his teacher to write a story early in the school year. To illustrate principles of Theme description I will use some individual clause examples from this text. Later, an analysis of the Theme structure of the whole of his text will be provided, to illustrate the patterning of Theme in a particular genre.

Text 4 *My Holiday in Coffs Harbour*

On the first day we drove to Coffs. We got to Coffs at 3.30 12 seconds. That afternoon we went swimming on the beach. My brother was shocked when I walked deep and I was only up to my ankles in water. the next day we went for a swim in the water. In the afternoon we went shopping went to the Big Banna and I got a boomerang and a icecream. The we went on a bushwalk in a rainforest. The next day we went on a bushwalk that took almost all day but then we went for a walk behind this water-fall. The next day we went on a barbecue with some friends. And I found a natural swing made from a thick vine. On Thursday we went to the beach in the morning and flew kites in the afternoon. On Friday we went to the Mutton Bird Hill Nature Reserve and lots of nest in the ground. Then we brought some prawns. And then my dad bought my a double passionfruit twist icecream. Then the next day we went home.

If we first take just a simple clause such as 'My brother was shocked', we can see that the 'point of departure' is the element 'my brother'. It is the Theme, since it is the element in first position.

Typically in English the Theme is conflated with (or realised by the same element as) the grammatical Subject. This is the case for the first clause. 'My brother' is both Theme and Subject. (The concept of Subject will be discussed in more detail under 'Elements of Mood' below.) If Subject is entirely new to you, you can use a simple procedure to identify it in a declarative clause: add the Mood Tag ', wasn't he?' to the clause. Thus for the above clause we get 'My brother was shocked, wasn't he?'

The Subject is the element referred to by the pronoun in the Mood Tag. 'He' refers to 'my brother'. A further example would be 'That's his room, isn't it?' 'That' is both Theme and Subject.

Marked Theme

Speakers and writers have a *choice* as to what they use as Theme: they are not bound to using Subject as Theme. The unmarked or 'default' option is to use the element which is Subject; the marked option is to use another element. For example, James could write either (1) or (2):

1. WE |drove to Coffs on the first day
2. ON THE FIRST DAY | we drove to Coffs.

In both cases the Theme is the element in first position. In the first case, the option he didn't choose, the Theme is the Subject but in the second it is not. Instead it is an element to do with time. Later we will see how this relates to a systematic patterning of Theme in his text.

Some further examples of Marked Theme in James' text are:

THAT AFTERNOON |we went swimming on the beach.
THE NEXT DAY |we went for a swim in the water.

Notice that these, too, are elements which indicate the chronological movement of the experience he is recounting.

Textual Theme

So far the Themes we have examined have been constructed out of one element, a nominal group or a phrase. However, as speakers develop a text they give it texture by weaving meanings together in a coherent form. One of the major resources available for this purpose is the system of Conjunction. Since conjunctions particularly work to signal relationships between clauses or other longer stretches of text, they occur at the beginning of clauses. When they do so, a multiple Theme structure is formed.

The function of conjunctions is to code features of the logical meaning of texts. Frequently, as we saw in the kindergarten children's texts, they add clause meanings together (often through 'and' or 'and then') or express an adversative relationship (for which 'but' is generally used). They can also work to subordinate one clause to another, expressing causal or conditional relationships through items such as 'because' and 'if'. Halliday (1985a, pp. 50–1) provides a list of English conjunctions together with the closely related class of conjunctive adjuncts, which are items such as 'however', 'therefore', 'in that case'.

This is an important area of the grammar because students often take some time to learn to control conjunctive relations in written texts effectively. Often the specific causal or conditional relationship may be left implicit or shown as an additive relationship. Explicit discussion during joint construction activities can be very useful as a way of demonstrating the effects of conjunctions. (See Halliday (1985b) for a discussion of differences between the structures of speech and writing relevant to this issue.)

In the following sentence the conjunctions are displayed in bold: 'My brother was shocked **when** I walked deep **and** I was only up to my ankles in water.' Both these conjunctions occur at clause boundaries.

|||My brother was shocked || **when** I walked deep|| **and** I was only up to my ankles in water.|||

The Theme of the second and third clauses therefore comprises two elements, the conjunction and the next element.

|||MY BROTHER | was shocked || WHEN I| walked deep || AND I | was only up to my ankles in water.|||

The conjunctive element forms the *Textual Theme* and the following element in these examples forms the *Topical Theme*.

The convention for formally displaying the analysis within systemic linguistics is:

when	I	walked deep
Tx	Top	
Theme		Rheme

Notice now that Marked Themes are elements other than Subject in *Topical* Theme position. (This is a slight refinement on the wording used when Marked Theme was first introduced above.) For example, in the clauses 'She went out but after a short time she returned' the Theme description is:

She	went out
Theme	Rheme

but	after a short time	she returned
Tx	Topical: mkd	
Theme		Rheme

Thematic Development in a Simple Recount

These concepts can be used to analyse the means through which speakers and writers develop texts, and to assist them to refine the method of development in joint text construction and conferencing work. For example, James' teacher commented on the end of his text: Good story! Watch 'and then'! Why James used 'and then' as he did is a question which a Theme description can address. When this is done we can see that 'and then', which actually occurs only once, and similar structures are consistent with the method of development he uses.

Literacy Learning and Teaching

Text 4a is James' text analysed for Theme. Themes are displayed in small capitals.

Text 4a *My Holiday in Coffs Harbour*

ON THE FIRST DAY we drove to Coffs.
WE got to Coffs at 3.30 12 seconds.
THAT AFTERNOON we went swimming on the beach.
MY BROTHER was shocked
WHEN I walked deep
AND I was only up to my ankles in water.
THE NEXT DAY we went for a swim in the water.
IN THE AFTERNOON we went shopping
( ) went to the Big Banna
AND I got a boomerang and a icecream.
THEN WE went on a bushwalk in a rainforest.
THE NEXT DAY we went on a bushwalk that took almost all day
BUT THEN WE went for a walk behind this water-fall.
THE NEXT DAY we went on a barbecue with some friends.
AND I found a natural swing made from a thick vine.
ON THURSDAY we went to the beach in the morning
AND ( ) flew kites in the afternoon.
ON FRIDAY we went to the Mutton Bird Hill Nature Reserve
AND ( ) lots of nest in the ground.
THEN WE brought some prawns.
AND THEN MY DAD bought my a double passionfruit twist icecream
THEN THE NEXT DAY we went home.

From the Theme structure we can see that the reason James uses 'and then' is because he organises the text by the movement of time. The use of 'and then' is also consistent with the use of Marked Themes to do with time, such as 'in the afternoon' and 'then the next day'. Even if he took the teacher's advice and varied the text by changing the 'and then' to 'later' or 'subsequently', etc., this would not make a substantial difference to the *pattern* of thematic orientation in the text.

In fact the Themes he has used are entirely appropriate for this type of text. In a recount the development is usually indicated by conjunctive elements to do with time. It can also be indicated by Marked Themes such as 'On Thursday', 'On Friday' and 'Then the next day'. Otherwise the topical thematic preoccupation of the recount is usually with personal human participants such as 'I', 'we', 'My Dad'.

THEMATIC DEVELOPMENT IN A SIMPLE REPORT
Theme structure in other genres is very different and therefore children often have to be engaged in experiences which help them to learn *how* to

structure their writing in ways appropriate to the genre. The general advice to 'use more interesting sentence beginnings' is not very productive, since what counts as either 'interesting' or appropriate will be a function of the genre in which a writer is working. Explicitness in teaching about the thematic structure of writing in various genres is crucial for NESB children and for some subgroups of speakers of non-standard dialects of English.

To illustrate variation in thematic patterning between genres, Text 5 is a simple text using a report genre written by Anousack when he was in Year 3. (The original was accompanied by a careful drawing of a cricket.)

Text 5   *A Cricket*

A cricket is an insect. It has six legs.
A cricket has three parts to its body: the thorax,
   abdomen, and head.
A cricket has one pair of antennae. Crickets live in dark places although some live in grass. Crickets can camouflage themselves.

It can be seen that even with such a simple report the Themes of the clauses (shown in Text 5a) are quite different from those of a recount or other related forms of narrative.

Text 5a   *A Cricket*

A CRICKET |is an insect.
IT |has six legs.
A CRICKET |has three parts to its body: the thorax,
   abdomen, and head.
A CRICKET |has one pair of antennae.
CRICKETS |live in dark places
ALTHOUGH SOME |live in grass.
CRICKETS |can camouflage themselves.

This seems quite a successful early attempt at independent writing in a genre which was new to Anousack. As he gained confidence and was able to extend his written texts, it would be useful to help him group information thematically in reports, perhaps by distinguishing paragraphs related to physical structure, habitat, defence strategies and so on. Thus the Themes of the opening clauses of successive paragraphs might be: The body of a cricket . . .; Places where crickets live . . .; The cricket's best way of defending itself . . . Obviously there are also a lot of other possibilities, which Anousack himself might explore as he understood more about how thematic patterning works.

Text 6 raises some interesting issues about how children learn to control the development of Theme. It was written by Kylie when she was in Year 5.

Literacy Learning and Teaching

> **Text 6** *Whales*
>
> Whales are facing extinction. The few whales which are left travel along the coastlines of many countries. The whales travel in large groups. Whales are large mammals. They have a layer of skin, blubber, meat, then their bones.
>
> Japan kills around 600 whales per year. When the Japanese hunters arrived in boats to kill some whales Greenpeace went into action. Greenpeace went in inflatable boats close towards the Japanese boat to prevent the killing. Greenpeace managed to save 60 whales, but unfortunately the Japanese did kill 24. The Japanese claim that whale meat is a part of their culture.
>
> I think that there should be a law against the killing of whales but if scientists must do some research they can kill one a year, but the scientists need a permit.

The Themes in Text 6 are displayed below in small capitals. Finite clauses are aligned on the left margin. Non-finite clauses, which generally don't select for Theme, are indented.

> **Text 6a** *Whales*
>
> WHALES are facing extinction.
> THE FEW WHALES [[WHICH ARE LEFT]] travel along the coastlines of many countries.
> THE WHALES travel in large groups.
> WHALES are large mammals.
> THEY have a layer of skin, blubber, meat, then their bones.
> JAPAN kills around 600 whales per year.
> WHEN THE JAPANESE HUNTERS arrived in boats
>   to kill some whales
> GREENPEACE went into action.
> GREENPEACE went in inflatable boats close towards the Japanese boat
>   to prevent the killing.
> GREENPEACE managed
>   to save 60 whales,
> BUT UNFORTUNATELY THE JAPANESE did kill 24.
> THE JAPANESE claim
>   THAT WHALE MEAT is a part of their culture.

> I think
> THAT THERE should be a law against the killing of whales
> BUT IF SCIENTISTS must do some research
> THEY can kill one a year,
> BUT THE SCIENTISTS need a permit.

Looking at the distribution of Themes we can see that the text shows some control of paragraphing, in that each paragraph is organised around related Topical Themes. Speaking generally these are 'whales' in the first paragraph; 'Japan' and 'Greenpeace' in the second; and 'scientists' in the third. Textual Themes also clearly realise logical relationships between the clauses within each paragraph.

The difficulty is, of course, in the relationships between paragraphs, which probably results from uncertainty about the purpose and audience for the writing and therefore uncertainty about appropriateness of generic form. A consequence for the teacher may be not so much in editing the text together with Kylie — there may be little point in going back over such a piece if Kylie herself thinks it is complete — but in planning further input to demonstrate how texts and paragraphs can be thematically organised in relation to the purpose for writing. Looking closely at children's ability to control thematic development of texts in various genres can be very useful for organising discussion and joint construction activities to help learners make choices about various modes of text development.

There is a Theme structure in Kylie's text which introduces a further element in the potential thematic pattern:

BUT UNFORTUNATELY THE JAPANESE did kill 24.

In this clause 'but' is the Textual Theme and 'the Japanese' is the Topical Theme. What, though, of 'unfortunately'? This element is an example of an *Interpersonal* Theme, often used to indicate a writer's or speaker's personal judgement on the meaning. Another element which very commonly occurs as Interpersonal Theme is the use of a person's name in direct address, called the Vocative. An example is: 'Subsequently, John, they went to the restaurant.' The analysis of Theme in this clause is:

Subsequently, John, they went to the restaurant

Tx	Interp	Top	
Theme			Rheme

Expressions of interpersonal meanings such as tentativeness or certainty, elements such as 'possibly', 'perhaps', 'certainly' also commonly occur as Interpersonal Themes.

How far then does a description of Theme extend into the clause, remembering that Theme is the speaker's or writer's 'point of departure'? The short answer is — to the first element which operates as Topical Theme which, as we shall see in the following discussion, is the first element which is involved in building experiential meanings. Halliday (1985a, p. 53 ff.) provides a discussion of the principles on which this convention is based.

In summary, there are three potential elements in the thematic structure of declarative clauses, which is the type of clause through which statements are usually coded. These elements are:

1. *Textual*, functioning to relate the meanings of the particular clause to other parts of the text;
2. *Interpersonal*, often functioning to code the speaker's or writer's personal judgement on the meaning; and
3. *Topical*, functioning as the point of orientation for the experiential meanings of the clause.

Variation in Topical Themes across genres is, as we have seen, an important aspect of writing development. This variation is not, though, only a matter of differences in categories of participants, such as the human participants which are typical in a recount, or participants such as whales or crickets in reports. The level of abstraction in the element operating as Topical Theme is also of importance. In explanations and arguments, for example, writers frequently have to orient readers to complex, general meanings which are well beyond commonsense observations. Using language in this way is basic to Western scientific, business and bureaucratic life.

One resource for building abstract meaning as a point of departure in a clause is embedding, because it enables a writer to build abstract, complex meaning into a 'thing-like' structure. Once an element has been built in this way, new attributes and identities can be associated with it. In the following clause the Theme is not just 'the dolphins' but a longer structure which includes an embedded clause defining which particular dolphins are 'point of departure': 'The dolphins [[which live in the southern oceans]] are threatened by dragnet fishing.' The Theme actually is 'The dolphins which live in the southern oceans' and the Rheme is 'are threatened by dragnet fishing'.

In expository writing such resources are crucial for the abstract packaging of information. (For an extended discussion, see Halliday 1990; Martin 1989.) Here, for example, is the first line from a well-known article by James Wertsch on Vygotsky's theory of human development: 'One of the twentieth century's most imaginative accounts of how human mental activity derives from social activity was outlined by the Soviet psychologist Lev Semenovich Vygotsky (1896–1934).' (Wertsch 1985, p. 1). In this sentence (which is just one ranking clause in length) the Theme is 'One of the twentieth century's most imaginative accounts [[of how human mental activity derives from social activity]]'. Notice that the orientation of the reader to the argument would have been rather different, especially as it was further developed by subsequent clauses, if Wertsch had begun: 'Lev Semenovich Vygotsky outlined one of the twentieth century's most imaginative accounts of how human mental activity derives from social activity.' The Theme here would be 'Lev Semenovich Vygotsky'.

Thinking about how Theme works therefore can often assist in the writing of academic essays, reports and other forms of abstract material. For example, often when people begin to write academic essays at tertiary level they structure Themes around the name of the writer or theorist whom they have been reading in preparation. The name of the writer is the 'point of departure', perhaps because they are oriented to working through a list of authors whose work forms the reference list. However, when an essay is structured in this way the effect for the reader is to meet a catalogue of ideas which seems to be assembled implicitly around the reading list. For example:

> Piaget proposed a cognitive stage theory of child development. He stated that there are four stages of development. His theory affected a lot of maths teaching for a long time . . .
> Freud also proposed a psycho-sexual stage theory of child development. He said that the stages were the oral, the anal, the oedipal, the latent . . .
> Vygotsky didn't think that there were specific stages, but he thought that people developed higher mental processes through social interaction, so the level of development was the product of social interaction and the child's access to semiotic practices . . .

Imagine that the main focus of the essay was required to be 'stage theory in child development'. If the text were reorganised so that Themes indicated stage theory as the 'point of departure', the reader's orientation to the meanings would be very different.

> |||THEORIES OF STAGES IN CHILD DEVELOPMENT have been used by many writers ||to explain the development of mature thinking. |||SUCH THEORIES attempt ||to explain both cognitive and emotional development. |||THE WORK OF PIAGET represents one example, WHICH has been very influential on maths education.|||

When the text is thematised in some such way the 'principle of development' can be made much clearer, with the result that the writing will appear more relevant to the question. The text is also likely to be seen as more successful, other things being equal, because it will appear that 'the writer has good control over her material', to use a frequent comment by examiners.

The concept of grammatical Theme is relevant to types of clauses other than declaratives, for example the imperative type which are very common in procedural texts ('HEAT the garlic in the oil'), and interrogatives, which typically realise questions ('WHY were they dancing in the streets?'). For further information on these aspects see Halliday (1985a, Chapter 3).

What we have been considering here is an aspect of the *textual* grammatical system of the language. In the next section we will begin to look at the grammatical resources for building representations of experience, the *experiential* system, and some of the choices this system makes possible. It is important to keep in mind that the wording of *each* clause can be viewed as realisations of different systems, and that to build a useful account for educational purposes it is important to analyse the structure from at least three different perspectives.

Structuring Experience through Grammatical Choices

The focus here is the question: how does language 'represent' the world of experience? At first it seems such an obvious question — at a commonsense level language appears to work by directly 'naming' and thus 'describing' experience. In fact the idea has a long history in western European culture; for example, in many children's stories to know the name of something is to have power over it, as with Rumpelstiltskin in the traditional tale or with the character Ged in Le Guin's *A Wizard of Earthsea*. In this view names of things may be more or less obscure or opaque, but knowledge is a matter of gaining access to the secret names.

There is some truth in this view, of course, but as we examine different types of text it becomes clear that representations of experience are built not just from vocabulary but from *both* lexis (vocabulary) and grammar. The grammatical resources code relationships between entities, thereby constructing representations of how the world works. There is, for example, a lot of difference in understanding how the world 'works' between a claim that 'birds evolved wings in order to fly' and 'birds' wings evolved, which enabled them to fly'. If only one clause in a whole text is involved it may not be very significant, but as a patterning of grammatical meaning across a text, or even a number of different texts which children read, it becomes very significant.

The grammar of the experiential metafunction is one important resource for understanding how language contributes to learning across the curriculum. Conversely, misunderstanding in many areas of the curriculum can be shown to result from linguistic rather than personal factors. As with the consideration of Theme, using the experiential grammar we can often better understand what counts as development in children's writing and reading, and we can also intervene more effectively through discussion and practical activities.

In this section I will focus on the grammar of transitivity as a way into this aspect of the structure of English. There are actually two sets of descriptions of the experiential metafunction, each with distinct advantages for particular purposes. One is a description of transitivity, the other a description of ergativity. Here I will concentrate on the first one, but you will find an accessible description of ergativity in Halliday (1985a, Section 5.8).

The Elements of the Experiential Metafunction

We saw earlier that clauses are patterned around verbal groups. These form, as it were, the 'nucleus' of the clause. As well, they determine what other elements can be incorporated into the clause once the selection of verbal group or, as we shall now call it, the *Process*, has been made.

Within the experiential metafunction the whole verbal group can be taken as the one element, Process. In some other analyses, particularly in considering the interpersonal metafunction, it is important to analyse within the structure of the verbal group, as we will discuss later in considering interpersonal meaning in the clause.

Together with the Process the clause will include one or more *Participants*. These are the elements which act or are acted on by other elements in the Process. Thus in a clause such as 'He cooked the prawns', the Process is 'cooked' and the two Participants are 'he' and 'the prawns'. Obviously they are not involved in the Process in the same way! In factual texts what is actually acting on what can become quite a complex matter, as in a structure such as 'Dinosaurs' bones were hollowed out to make them lighter', where there is only one Participant, which is acted on: what acts on the bones is left out, forming a kind of covert Participant. Compare this structure with one such as 'Dinosaur bones are hollow, which makes them lighter'.

Additional to the elements of Process and Participants there is the option of adding a *Circumstance*. This is an element which provides further information about meanings such as location in space or time ('she went *yesterday*', 'she went *to the beach house*'), extent of space and time ('she ran *for a long distance*', 'she ran *for a long time*') and manner ('she ran *very quickly*').

Processes are the key to the experiential structure because they establish the grammatical potential of the clause. As language has evolved within different regions of human experience, and has been used for different functions, the structure of the clause has evolved to meet the requirements of these different functions. There are different types of Process, each with a somewhat different grammatical potential available for the selection of Participants and Circumstances. Another way to say this is that each category of Process makes available different potentialities for experiential meanings within the clause. There is a symbiotic relationship here between grammar and semantics, so that the criteria for distinguishing between Process types are both semantic and grammatical.

To illustrate this principle operating in a very simple way, notice that only some types of Process enable a speaker to build representations of other people's thoughts and beliefs. One can say 'She made that bookshelf' but not 'She made that she had left the hospital'. The reason is that 'made' belongs to the category Material Process which does not have the potential to project 'metarepresentations' of experience. An example of a Process that does is the Process 'thought', in 'She thought that she had left the hospital'. These differences in turn reactively affect what can be coded as Participants, and how the attributes of Participants are ascribed.

There are three broad types of Process. One is concerned with 'doings' and 'happenings' such as building, eating, extinguishing, lighting, planting, eroding and so on. These are the Material Processes. Another is concerned with categorising of experience, forming relationships between entities or concepts. Two frequently selected Processes here are 'is' and 'have', and related forms such as 'becomes', 'will be', 'is called' and 'owns'. These are Relational Processes. The third group is concerned

Literacy Learning and Teaching

with the second-order representation of experience: the world of thinking, feeling and perception; and the world of saying. Here there are two related types of Process, similar in their grammatical potential, the Mental and Verbal Processes.

If we were to sketch these into a first, very simple network of options, it would be:

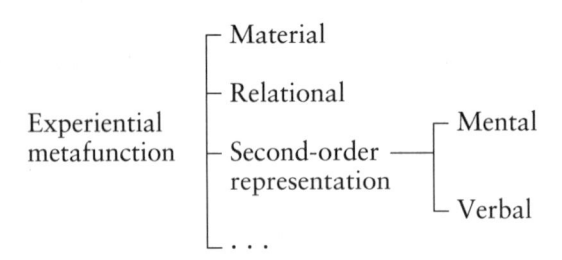

Experiential metafunction
- Material
- Relational
- Second-order representation
  - Mental
  - Verbal
- ...

In order to build up familiarity with the various 'regions' of the process types, here is a lengthy quote (Text 7) from the first pages of Roald Dahl's novel for children, *Fantastic Mr Fox*, selected because it exemplifies a range of different types of Process contributing to meaning. Following Text 7 a selection of Processes within each category is set out. Subsequently each type of Process will be examined in greater detail.

The focus here is on gaining familiarity with Process types; some actual uses of the grammar of transitivity will be illustrated more fully later in the chapter. Following the quote from *Fantastic Mr Fox*, there is a list of clauses for each of the major Process types, which is followed in turn by a discussion of the Processes and their associated Participants.

Text 7 *Excerpt from Roald Dahl's* Fantastic Mr Fox

The Three Farmers

Down in the valley there were three farms. The owners of these farms had done well. They were rich men. They were also nasty men. All three of them were about as nasty and mean as any men you could meet. Their names were Farmer Boggis, Farmer Bunce and Farmer Bean.

Boggis was a chicken farmer. He kept thousands of chickens. He was enormously fat. This was because he ate three boiled chickens smothered with dumplings every day for breakfast, lunch and supper.

Bunce was a duck-and-goose farmer. He kept thousands of ducks and geese. He was a kind of pot-bellied dwarf. He was so short his chin would have been under water in the shallow end of any swimming-pool in the world. His food was doughnuts and goose livers. He mashed the livers into a disgusting paste and then stuffed the paste into the doughnuts. This diet gave him a tummy-ache and a beastly temper.

Bean was a turkey-and-apple farmer. He kept thousands of turkeys in an orchard full of apple trees. He never ate any food at all. Instead, he drank gallons of strong cider which he made from the apples in his orchard. He was as thin as a pencil and the cleverest of them all.

> Boggis and Bunce and Bean
> One fat, one short, one lean.
> These horrible crooks
> So different in looks
> Were nonetheless equally mean.

That is what the children round about used to sing when they saw them.

Mr Fox

On a hill above the valley there was a wood.
In the wood there was a huge tree.
Under the tree there was a hole.
In the hole lived Mr Fox and Mrs Fox and their four Small Foxes.

Every evening as soon as it got dark, Mr Fox would say to Mrs Fox, 'Well, my darling, what shall it be this time? A plump chicken from Boggis? A duck or a goose from Bunce? Or a nice turkey from Bean?' And when Mrs Fox had told him what she wanted, Mr Fox would creep down into the valley in the darkness of the night and help himself.

Boggis and Bunce and Bean knew very well what was going on, and it made them wild with rage. They were not men who liked to give anything away. Less still did they like anything to be stolen from them. So every night each of them would take his shotgun and hide in a dark place somewhere on his own farm, hoping to catch the robber.

But Mr Fox was too clever for them. He always approached a farm with the wind blowing in his face, and this meant that if any man were lurking in the shadows ahead, the wind would carry the smell of that man to Mr Fox's nose from far away. Thus, if Mr Boggis was hiding behind his Chicken House Number One, Mr Fox would smell him out from fifty yards off and quickly change direction, heading for Chicken House Number Four at the other end of the farm.

'Dang and blast that lousy beast!' cried Boggis.
'I'd like to rip his guts out!' said Bunce.
'He must be killed!' cried Bean.
'But how?' said Boggis. 'How on earth can we catch the blighter?'
Bean picked his nose delicately with a long finger. 'I have a plan,' he said.
'You've never had a decent plan yet,' said Bunce.
'Shut up and listen,' said Bean. 'Tomorrow night we will all hide

Literacy Learning and Teaching

> just outside the hole where the fox lives. We will wait there until he comes out. Then . . . *Bang! Bang-bang-bang.*'
> 'Very clever,' said Bunce. 'But first we shall have to find the hole.'
> 'My dear Bunce, I've already found it,' said the crafty Bean. 'It's up in the wood on the hill. It's under a huge tree . . .'

Looking through the passage we can see that various broad types of experiential meaning are built up. Some are to do with the *actions* of characters and what happens to them; some with their *attributes, identity* and *possessions*; and others with what they *think* and *say*.

Examples of Different Process Types in *Fantastic Mr Fox*

MATERIAL PROCESSES: PROCESSES OF 'DOING' AND 'HAPPENING'

In a narrative one would expect that characters would be involved in a range of physical actions, acting on the material world and other characters, and in turn sometimes being acted on by others. Who acts on whom, and on what, is always interesting — the very stuff, in fact, of which narratives are made, since the distribution of actions by characters, and across characters, is central to narrative meaning.

Here are some examples of Material Processes in Text 7:

He *kept* thousands of chickens.
He *mashed* the livers into a disgusting paste and then *stuffed* the paste into the doughnuts.
he *drank* gallons of strong cider
This diet *gave* him a tummy-ache and a beastly temper.
He never *ate* any food at all.
if Mr Boggis *was hiding* behind his Chicken House Number One
So every night each of them *would take* his shotgun
the wind *would carry* the smell of that man to Mr Fox's nose from far away.
'He *must be killed*!'
'How on earth *can* we *catch* the blighter?'
Bean *picked* his nose delicately with a long finger.
Tomorrow night we *will* all *hide* just outside the hole where the fox lives.
until he *comes* out.
Mr Fox *would creep* down into the valley in the darkness of the night

RELATIONAL PROCESSES: PROCESSES OF 'BEING', OF CATEGORISATION AND ATTRIBUTION

As well as acting on things, characters 'are' members of various categories of things such as 'rich men' and 'nasty men'. Characters can also be evaluated by the narrator, who attributes qualities to them, such as being

Using Systemic Grammar

'enormously fat'. Characters may also become known by what they possess, such as here, plans to do damage to other characters. In factual texts, likewise, entities are allocated to classes of things, or are said to possess attributes: dolphins are mammals, the octopus has long tentacles and suction pads.

Relational Processes are a major grammatical resource for developing these kinds of meanings. In this passage Dahl heavily evaluates the characters through the use of Relational Processes, so that a young reader is left in little doubt about what to think of Boggis, Bunce and Bean, on the one hand, or the Fox family, on the other. In other texts, using a more critical perspective, we might be concerned to resist the attributions introduced by a narrator, to develop alternative evaluations of characters. The grammar is, again, a powerful tool for the purpose of critically investigating texts.

Some examples of Relational Processes in Text 7 are:

They *were* rich men.
They *were* also nasty men.
Boggis *was* a chicken farmer.
He *was* enormously fat.
Bunce *was* a duck-and-goose farmer.
He *was* a kind of pot-bellied dwarf.
Bean *was* a turkey-and-apple farmer.
'I *have* a plan'
'You'*ve* never *had* a decent plan yet'
'It'*s* up in the wood on the hill.'
But Mr Fox *was* too clever for them.
Their names *were* Farmer Boggis, Farmer Bunce and Farmer Bean.
His food *was* doughnuts and goose livers.

MENTAL PROCESSES: PROCESSES OF PERCEPTION, THOUGHT AND FEELING

Mental Processes allow speakers and writers to build up characters' internal beliefs and ideas, feelings, reactions and perceptions. What is perhaps most obvious about the 'Mr Fox' passage is that there are comparatively few of this process type — in fact the examples listed below are an exhaustive set for the ranking clauses. The fictive world of this passage is not one of reflection and analysis, but of action and being.

The Mental Processes which occur in Text 7 are:

Boggis and Bunce and Bean *knew* very well
Less still *did* they *like*
Mr Fox *would smell* him *out* from fifty yards off
when they *saw* them.

VERBAL PROCESSES: PROCESSES OF 'SIGNIFYING', INCLUDING 'SAYING'

These processes are in many respects very similar to Mental Processes, in that they enable speakers and writers to represent other people's representations of experience, here through what they say. However, 'say' has

Literacy Learning and Teaching

to be broadly interpreted to mean 'signify', as in 'meant' or 'indicated' or 'showed'.

In Text 7 the major Verbal Process is 'said', acting usually as a dialogue tag to help young readers track the identity of speakers. However, there are just a few other examples of Verbal Processes. These are:

cried Boggis.
Mr Fox *would say* to Mrs Fox
And when Mrs Fox *had told* him
said Bunce.

Processes and Participants: An Elaboration

The intention in the preceding section was to broadly illustrate the major different types of Process within the context of a single narrative text. I will now discuss each process type and associated Participants in more detail.

MATERIAL PROCESSES: POSSIBLE STRUCTURES

For Material Processes, the Participants are Actor and Goal. The Actor is the element which does the action. The Goal is the element to whom the action is done. A clause may include both Participants, or just one, either Actor or Goal.

The grammatical probe through which Material Processes can be identified is 'do', and the test is largely whether the substitution of 'do' makes sense in a given context, as for the clause 'He drank gallons of strong cider'. The probe can then be extended to decide who did the action (Actor role) and to whom or what the action is done (Goal role). Thus for the example, 'what did he do to the gallons of strong cider? — He drank it' makes good sense and is clearly a Material Process.

The order Actor ^ Process ^ Goal gives the *active* form of the clause. The order Goal ^ Process ^ Actor gives the *passive* form.

Analyses for some of the earlier examples of Material Process are given below.

Actor ^ Process ^ Goal

he	drank	gallons of strong cider
Actor	Process	Goal

He	mashed	the livers	into a disgusting paste
Actor	Process	Goal	Circumstance

He	never	ate	any food at all
Actor		Process	Goal

Bean	picked	his nose	delicately	with a long finger
Actor	Process	Goal	Circumst	Circumstance

Goal ^ Process ^ Actor
In this passage, because the Participants doing the action are thematised, clauses tend to be in the active form. (That is, the starting point tends to be a character, not what the action is done to.) Some examples of passive structures, rewritten from the active form but using the same Participants as earlier, are:

Gallons of strong cider	were drunk	by him
Goal	Process	Actor

The livers	were mashed	into a disgusting paste	by him
Goal	Process	Circumstance	Actor

One Participant Only: Actor ^ Process
Neither Actor nor Goal are required in a clause — commonly only one of them is included. For Actor only, the sense is of something doing something, not necessarily to something else. Some examples are:

until	he	comes	out
	Actor	Process	Circ

Mr Fox	would creep	down into the valley	in the darkness of the night
Actor	Process	Circumstance	Circumstance

One Participant Only: Goal ^ Process
Here the sense is of something 'done to', but where the doer of the action is not included.

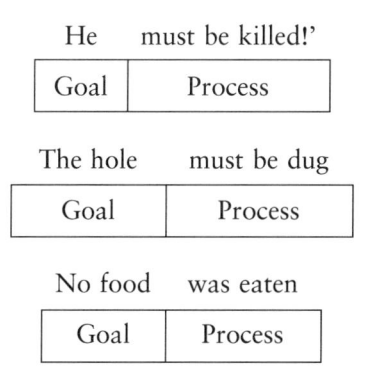

He	must be killed!'
Goal	Process

The hole	must be dug
Goal	Process

No food	was eaten
Goal	Process

These examples are relatively simple semantically, as one would expect in a children's narrative written for inexperienced readers. But consider the following examples, taken from a recent text for children.

1. Today, over 8,500 species of birds populate the skies.

'Populate' is the Process. The Actor is 'over 8,500 species of birds' and the Goal is 'the skies'. This is a metaphorical construction. Because it involves a shift in the grammar of lexical items it is referred to by Halliday, Martin and others as 'grammatical metaphor' (Halliday 1985a). 'Populate' has shifted from the noun form ('today there is a population of over 8,500 species of birds') to the verb form, which may make the interpretation of the meaning of the *action* quite difficult for many young learners. The meaning here may need to be explicitly discussed in joint reading of the text, depending always of course on the linguistic background of the learners.

2. Flight makes enormous demands on a bird's body.

In this example the Participants are abstract representations of physical processes. The Actor is 'flight'. The Goal is 'enormous demands on a bird's body'. 'Demand' is a further example of grammatical metaphor, shifting from the verb form 'to demand', which of course usually has a somewhat different semantic value, to a nominalisation. It packages complex meanings about stress and resistance to natural forces such as gravity and air pressure.

3. Birds are helped in this by a very special metabolic rate.

The Material Process is 'are helped by'. The Goal is 'birds'. The Actor is 'a very special metabolic rate', which is again a complex packaging of abstract meaning, especially because of 'rate', the speed of a category of physical change which is here arrested in time as an entity.

To illustrate from a different perspective the use of a consciousness of the grammar in analysing learning, Text 8 is an example taken from classroom discourse. The general issue here is to attempt to understand why very young children sometimes have difficulty with metalanguage, even with such simple terms as 'word' in the early years of schooling.

The group is a kindergarten class, the children are in their second month of school and the teacher has been reading from a big book called *Toilet Tales*. For a good deal of the lesson the teacher asked the children to specify events that the various characters had participated in, questions such as 'what's the elephant done to the toilet?' and 'what happened in this picture?'

Towards the end of the lesson, one of the children commented, 'That's how you spell pig'. The teacher responded as shown in Text 8.

Using Systemic Grammar

Text 8

Tr: Yes, big and pig are the same, aren't they? That's very good, Christopher. I think I'll have to give you a stamp. You remember that? You see that — big and pig.

Then she asked:

Tr: And what else about big and pig? What else do they do? Gavin?
Cd: Um
Tr: Bobby? . . . Leanne?
Cd: They
Tr: No, what about the words big and pig? Big and pig? Daniel?
Cd: Umm because pigs go oink.
Tr: No, the words big and pig. Fabrice?
Cd: Mm kig.
Tr: Yeah
Cd: Kig.
Tr: Kig's another one.

After many further attempts to get the children to articulate the desired answer the teacher is obliged to provide it.

Cd: Um pig and big.
Tr: Yes. They . . . sound the same.
Cdn: Same.
Cd: *I know one.
Tr: *They're rhyming words.

The point is not, of course, to criticise teachers' language but rather to illustrate how the grammar of a question can implicitly require children to use unfamiliar, register-specific *ways of meaning*. The problem here is mainly with the grammar of the question 'What else do they do?' Here 'do' is a Material Process, and the nominal group which forms the Actor is 'they'. So the children have to, within their limited experience of English grammar, work out what 'action' or 'happening' the *words* 'big and pig' are involved in. Notice Daniel's comment, 'Umm because pigs go oink'. Pigs themselves obviously do a lot of things, but what do words 'do', especially printed words, whatever these may be for children of this age and experience?

Imagine if, developing the first child's observation, the teacher had written the two words on the chalkboard and had drawn the children's attention to the visual and auditory similarity of 'ig'; 'they have the same sound at the end' and therefore 'they are rhyming words'.

LINKING THEME AND TRANSITIVITY STRUCTURES

Whether an active form (Actor ^ Process ^ Goal) or alternatively the passive form (Goal ^ Process ^ Actor) is chosen will depend on what the 'point of departure' is for the development of the text. It is not the case that active forms of the clause are always easier to read than passive forms, a piece of folk wisdom often quoted in educational discussions.

The choice between, on the one hand, 'Honeydew is made by insects called aphids' and, on the other, 'Insects called aphids make honeydew' depends on whether the intention is to develop meanings around 'honeydew' or 'insects called aphids'. Thus:

|||Honeydew is made by insects called aphids, ||and is a source of food for ants.|||

or

|||Insects called aphids make honeydew ||and they are regarded as a major garden pest.|||

We move, then, from Material Processes to the second type introduced through the small initial network, Relational Processes.

RELATIONAL PROCESSES

This type of Process categorises experience into classes of things, and attributes qualities to classes of things. The two verbs which are most often involved, especially in spoken language, are 'is' and 'have'. Other tenses of these same verbs such as 'was', 'had been', or 'was having', 'had been having' and so on can be used.

Other verbs can also be used as Relational Processes; for example: 'call', as in 'she was called Micky', 'represents', as in 'this represents the best writing so far', 'include', as in 'Its prey included insects, frogs, snails, and small lizards', or 'plays', as in 'She played Alison Ashley'. Halliday (1985a, p. 115) gives a list of common examples of Relational Processes.

To illustrate the functioning of this type of process we'll return to some of the examples selected from *Fantastic Mr Fox*, and also include some further examples from a factual text called *Dinosaur* (Norman and Milner 1989).

Dinosaurs *were* reptiles.
They *had* scaly skins.
Some *were* peaceful.
Others *were* fierce, sharp-toothed flesh eaters.
The biggest creatures ever to walk the Earth *were* the sauropod group of dinosaurs.
Tails *can have* a surprising number of uses.

Relational Processes can be subcategorised in various ways to enable us to interpret their functioning more clearly. One important distinction is between the *Relational: intensive* ('is') and the *Relational: possessive* ('has') types. Categorised in this way the examples from *Fantastic Mr Fox* and *Dinosaurs* can be grouped as:

Relational: intensive:
They *were* rich men.
They *were* also nasty men.
Boggis *was* a chicken farmer.
He *was* enormously fat.
Bean *was* a turkey-and-apple farmer.
'It*'s* up in the wood on the hill.'
But Mr Fox *was* too clever for them.
Dinosaurs *were* reptiles.
Some *were* peaceful.
Others *were* fierce sharp-toothed flesh eaters.
The biggest creatures ever to walk the Earth *were* the sauropod group of dinosaurs.

Relational: possessive:
'I *have* a plan'
'You*'ve* never *had* a decent plan yet'
They *had* scaly skins.
Tails *can have* a surprising number of uses.

These two types of Relational Processes are the ones most commonly used in scientific report writing in primary and junior secondary schools. An example of their distribution is given in Text 9, written by a ten-year-old.

Text 9 *Herons*

A heron is a tall waterbird. Its colours are white, black and grey. The heron is longbilled and longlegged. They have large wings and can measure about 65cm from tip of beak to tip of tail. Herons have long, curving necks and legs are held straight behind the body when they are flying.

Herons and egrets are found in swamps and wetlands. Some herons are seen with other waterbirds, others are always alone, hunting. They eat fish, snails, frogs, lizards and mice. They have excellent sight and have few enemies.

Herons fly slowly, sharp eyes ready for prey. From September to January three or four blue-green eggs are laid in a rough nest of sticks. Chicks are covered in down until covered in feathers.

Notice that the writer builds information about herons largely by attributing them to broad classes of things (one member of the set of tall water birds), and by describing the physical attributes they 'possess'.

The categorisation of the Relational Processes in this text is:

A heron is a tall waterbird. (*Relational: intensive*)
Its colours are white, black and grey. (*Relational: intensive*)
The heron is longbilled and longlegged. (*Relational: intensive*)
They have large wings (*Relational: possessive*)

Herons have long, curving necks (*Relational: possessive*)
others are always alone (*Relational: intensive*)
They have excellent sight (*Relational: possessive*)
and (they) have few enemies. (*Relational: possessive*)

As is very typical of scientific reports, the other type of process the writer generally employs is the Material: 'They *eat* fish, snails, frogs, lizards and mice.', 'Herons *fly* slowly', and 'From September to January three or four blue-green eggs *are laid* in a rough nest of sticks.'.

There is a crucial further distinction to be made, which will be considered here only for the 'intensive' type though it also applies to the other subtypes of Relational Processes. Expressed very informally it is the distinction between 'one amongst several' and 'the only one(s)'; that is, the distinction between linguistically adding something to a class ('He was a chicken farmer' or 'He was enormously fat') and, on the other hand, linguistically defining a co-extensive class ('whales are *the* largest sea mammals'). The distinction helps in understanding how definitions and classes of meaning are formed in texts, and therefore how taxonomies in a particular field are built.

The distinction drawn here is between the Attributive, those structures which allocate an element to a class of things which has more members than the element itself ('Gillian is a teacher', 'Gillian is very talented'), and the Identifying, those structures which allocate an element to a class of which it is the only member in that specific context ('Gillian is the teacher', 'Gillian is the outstanding one').

One test of the difference between these two categories is that the elements in the Identifying are reversible ('The teacher is Gillian', 'Gillian is the teacher') and in the Attributive they are not, except in very marked forms, perhaps in poetry, for example (*'A teacher is Gillian').

For some of the examples with which we began, the analysis into Attributive and Identifying categories is:

Relational: intensive: attributive
They *were* rich men.
They *were* also nasty men.
Boggis *was* a chicken farmer.
He *was* enormously fat.
Bean *was* a turkey-and-apple farmer.
But Mr Fox *was* too clever for them.
Dinosaurs *were* reptiles.
Some *were* peaceful.
Others *were* fierce sharp-toothed flesh eaters.

Relational: intensive: identifying
The biggest creatures ever to walk the Earth *were* the sauropod group of dinosaurs.

Notice that the last example can readily be reversed but that none in the first group can. In fact, of course, if we were to attempt such reversals and were to say 'Reptiles were dinosaurs' or 'Fierce sharp-toothed flesh eaters were others (dinosaurs)', considerable violence would be done to the text's taxonomy. The meanings here are certainly not equivalent to the original clauses.

Using Systemic Grammar

Labelling Participants in Relational: Intensive Processes

In order to be able to use these distinctions it's important to have a distinct technical vocabulary to label the different Participants. Whereas for Material Processes we distinguished on the basis of 'the doer' (Actor) and 'the done to' (Goal), for Relational Processes the nature of class relationships has to be indicated through the Participant labels.

For the *Attributive*, this is done on the basis of *Carrier* (the element allocated to the class) and *Attribute* (the class, which can be either a group such as 'chicken farmers' or an adjective such as in: 'He was enormously fat.').

The description therefore is:

They	were	rich men
Carrier	Pro: rel: int: attr	Attribute

But	Mr Fox	was	too clever for them
	Carrier	Pro: rel: int: attr	Attribute

There was one further type of the Intensive: Attributive in the original list. In this type the second element is a Circumstance rather than a nominal group or an adjective. The example was: It's up in the wood on the hill.' The analysis here is quite straightforward, with 'It' forming the Carrier and 'in the wood on the hill' forming the Attribute. It can be useful to label the Attribute as Attribute/Circumstance, to distinguish it from the nominal group type.

'It	's	up in the wood [on the hill].'
Carrier	Pro: rel: int: attr	Attribute/Circumstance

But what of the *Identifying* type of Relational: Intensive processes? Here, by definition, the class of things referred to by the first Participant is the same as the class of things referred to by the second Participant. They are identical in some way. That is the function of this grammatical relationship. So how can they be distinguished?

The most important distinction for our purposes is between 'label' and 'meaning'. (Halliday 1985a, pp. 115–118 gives some further distinctions.) One element will have the function of labelling the entity: it is called Token. The other will have the function of designating the 'meaning': it is called Value. Thus in a clause such as 'Gillian is the outstanding one', the Token is 'Gillian' and the Value is 'the outstanding one'. Since the identifying form can be reversed they can come in either order, either Value or Token first.

One useful way to distinguish between these two roles is to substitute the verb 'represents' for 'is' and test whether in this form the clause is active or passive. Where it is active, the Token will be Subject. Where it is passive the Value will be Subject. Thus:

Gillian   represents   the outstanding one

Token	Pro: rel: inten: id	Value

The outstanding one   is represented by   Gillian

Value	Pro: rel: inten: id	Token

In the example from *Dinosaur* we can see this feature working in a scientific context: 'The biggest creatures ever to walk the Earth *were* the sauropod group of dinosaurs.' Which is Token and which is Value?

'The sauropod group of dinosaurs' is the Token, the name being given to the Value, 'the biggest creatures ever to walk the Earth'. So the analysis is:

The biggest creatures ever to walk the Earth   were (were represented by)   the sauropod group of dinosaurs

Value	Pro: rel: inten: id	Token

Familiarity with this aspect of the grammar can help enormously in understanding how to clarify relationships between categories in some field. Take, as a simple example, another clause from *Dinosaur*: 'The sauropod group of dinosaurs were all plant eaters.' Is this an Identifying or Attributive type? That is, were sauropods the only plant eaters (assuming the reference is only to dinosaurs) or were they only part of the class of plant eaters? The structure of the clause is ambiguous here, and there is nothing in the intratextual context which would clarify the issue for a young reader. Ambiguity of this kind is very common in factual material.

If the wording were to be changed so that it read 'All dinosaurs in the sauropod group were plant eaters', the actual relationship is clearer.

OVERVIEW OF CATEGORIES OF RELATIONAL PROCESSES
Here is a network representation of categories of Relational Processes, together with the other types which have been mentioned so far. (In

working through this rather complex area of the grammar I have not attempted to describe all of the distinctions made in Halliday (1985a), but have attempted to highlight some which are immediately important for understanding children's learning.)

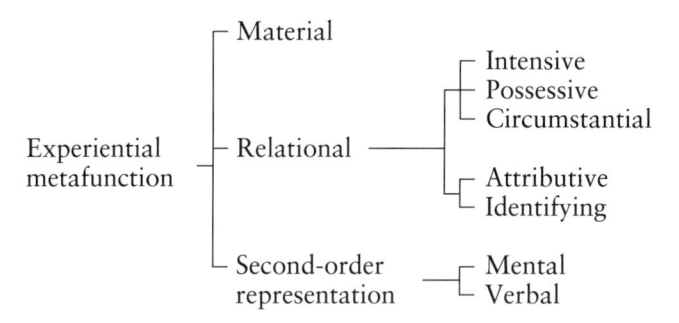

```
                           ┌─ Material
                           │
                           │                      ┌─ Intensive
                           │                   ┌──┼─ Possessive
                           │                   │  └─ Circumstantial
Experiential  ──┼─ Relational ──┤
metafunction               │                   │  ┌─ Attributive
                           │                   └──┴─ Identifying
                           │
                           └─ Second-order  ──── ┌─ Mental
                              representation    └─ Verbal
```

When children have difficulty in understanding a concept, very often it is a matter of not knowing relationships between terms within the grammar of Relational Processes. Sometimes it is also because terms introduced in different relational clauses are not brought into explicit relationship with each other within the specific text. These processes are not, of course, the only means used to categorise experience but they tend to be the ones used to form the more abstract categories, typical of scientific and explanatory writing.

MENTAL PROCESSES
In this type are included Processes of thinking, feeling and perceiving. They are distinguished semantically from Material and Relational Processes, but as well they can be distinguished on grammatical grounds. One of the most important distinguishing characteristics of the grammar is that Mental Processes can 'project' ideas through linked clauses. Material Processes do not do so. In each of the following examples, the first clause involves a Mental Process (which is italicised). The second clause is the projected clause.

		She *remembered*		that she should go.		
		They *believed*		that he would repay them.		
		They *perceived*		that this would be a problem.		
		He *saw*		that this was a way through the maze.		
		They *felt*		the ship was listing.		

The significance of this feature is that Mental Processes enable a writer to develop 'second-order' representations of experience — to record projections of facts, not only facts as determined by the writer/speaker.

Another significant feature is that Mental Processes involve a Participant who is human, or at least which is human-like. This is the role of the Senser, similar to that of Actor in Material Processes in that he or she is the active element in the Process. In the following examples the Senser is shown in small capitals. The first two are the active form; the second two are the passive form.

233

Jenny knew the facts.
The child sensed the disagreement.
The facts were known by Jenny.
The disagreement was sensed by the child.

The tendency to construct a human Participant as Senser is so strong in English grammar that when a non-human Participant is placed in that role, the reader may attribute human-like properties to the non-human entity. This is, of course, culturally very strange to many non-Western peoples.

	the computer sensed the approaching aircraft.	
	|the animals thought ||that this place was good for nests.|	
	|birds decided ||that they should migrate to the south.|	
		all dogs like Pal.		

When there is a second Participant within the clause, apart from the Senser, it forms the Phenomenon. Using the examples above, the Phenomenon is italicised.

Jenny knew *the facts*.
The child sensed *the disagreement*.
The facts were known by Jenny.
The disagreement was sensed by the child.
The computer sensed *the approaching aircraft*.
All dogs like *Pal*.

Another important feature, again in contrast with Material Processes, is the usual form of the present tense. Mental Processes usually take the simple present tense ('thinks'), while Material Processes usually take the 'present-in-present' tense ('is building'). Thus 'She believes that this is for the best' rather than 'She is believing this is for the best'. In contrast, for Material Processes we have 'They are making a new program' rather than 'They make a new program'. This variation of tense with the grammatical category is an aspect which is often difficult for NESB speakers to control because they are not aware of the underlying grammatical and semantic category which is responsible for the variation. It is often useful to provide the reason explicitly.

Other tests for differences between Material and Mental Processes can be found in Halliday 1985a, pp. 106–12).

VERBAL PROCESSES

Verbal Processes are similar to Mental Processes, most importantly in the way that they can 'project' second-order representations of experience. They are most obviously processes of 'saying', as in:

|||They *say* ||that this is only the beginning.|||
|||They *stated* ||that this was the preferred model.|||

They can, however, be concerned with other aspects of signification apart from production of oral language, such as:

Using Systemic Grammar

|||The clock *indicated* ||that it was time to stop.||
|||The sign *showed* them ||that they had gone too far.||

The 'active' role in these clauses is labelled the Sayer. If there is a metarepresentation within the clause, somewhat analogous to the Phenomenon in Mental Processes, it is labelled as Verbiage. The analysis is thus:

You	said	it
Sayer	Pro:verbal	Verbiage

Verbal Process clauses can include two types of Participants which are not analogous to those in Mental Processes, and these are very easily identified. One is the Receiver, the figure addressed, as with 'to me' in 'You said it to me'. The Receiver can be indicated by a single word instead of a phrase, for example 'her' in 'They told her the truth'. The other distinctive form of Participant is the Target, which is a potential of a subcategory of Verbal Processes such as 'blame', 'praise', 'accuse' and so on, where the performance of the process is actually done to the Participant. An example is 'him' in 'They accused him'.

This completes the broad overview of the grammar of the experiential metafunction. Figure 5.1 gives a summary of the Process types and the associated Participants which have been discussed here.

Process	Participants
Material	Actor, Goal
Relational: intensive: attributive	Carrier, Attribute
Relational: intensive: identifying	Token, Value
Mental	Senser, Phenomenon
Verbal	Sayer, Verbiage, Receiver, Target

Figure 5.1 *Summary of selected Process types and Participant roles*

We have now considered aspects of two of the three metafunctions: the textual and the experiential. However, before moving to the third, the interpersonal, it is important to take account of experiential structure at another rank in the grammar, that of group.

So far we have considered structure at the rank of clause. The question to be discussed now is: how are entities built up within a clause? Put slightly differently, this means what sort of *linguistic* element can become an Actor, Goal, Carrier, Theme and so on? The commonsense answer appears to be entities like 'whales' or 'Farmer Bunce'. That is true for the

Literacy Learning and Teaching

texts which have been used as examples so far but if we are to assist children to read and write more complex texts the account must be extended.

Structure within Clauses: the Nominal Group

If we were to analyse only the direct contribution of individual words to the structure of the clause, we would have to divide the clause in this way:

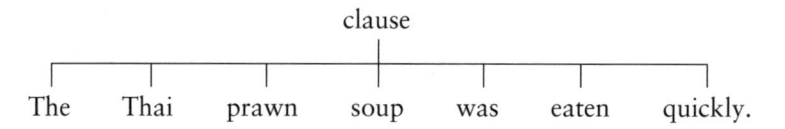

```
                        clause
    ┌──────┬──────┬──────┬──────┬──────┬──────┐
   The    Thai   prawn   soup   was   eaten  quickly.
```

That is to say, each word relates to each other word in the 'same' way. But this form of description loses a lot of valuable information. There are, for example, specific meaning relationships between some words which distinguish them from others. The relationship between the words in 'the Thai prawn soup', for example, obviously is different from the relationship between 'the' and 'quickly'. And in some way 'was eaten' links in a way that 'prawn' and 'eaten' do not. So instead of dividing the clause just into individual words, we can use an intermediate rank, that of group.

When the clause above is divided into groups, the structure is:

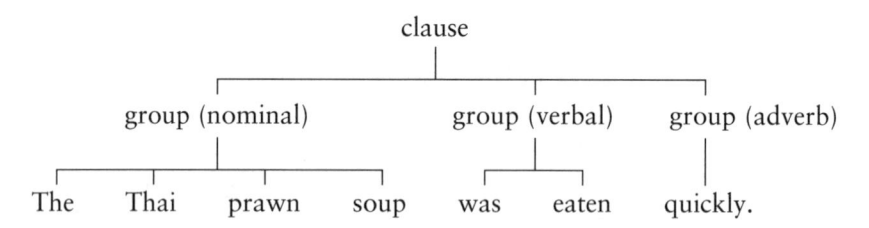

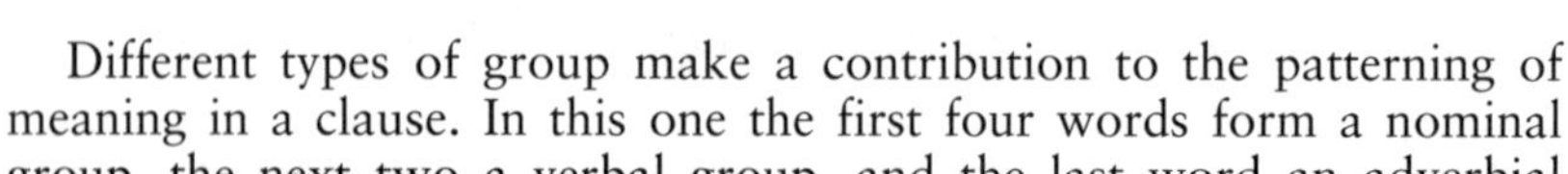

```
                         clause
         ┌─────────────────┼─────────────────┐
    group (nominal)    group (verbal)    group (adverb)
    ┌────┬─────┬────┐    ┌────┬────┐          │
   The  Thai prawn soup  was eaten         quickly.
```

Different types of group make a contribution to the patterning of meaning in a clause. In this one the first four words form a nominal group, the next two a verbal group, and the last word an adverbial group. Notice that it is possible for an individual word to realise a structure at the higher rank, as with 'quickly' in this example. A further example would occur if we were to substitute 'It' for 'The Thai prawn soup': 'It was eaten quickly.'

Within systemic functional theory, the analysis proceeds from the rank of morpheme, to word, to group or phrase, and to clause. Ignoring for now the rank of morpheme, the above example would build up in this way:

clause: The Thai prawn soup was eaten quickly.
group: The Thai prawn soup (nominal group)
was eaten (verbal group)
quickly (adverbial group)
word: The, Thai, prawn, soup, was, eaten, quickly

There are, again, immediate practical educational implications arising from these analyses. One of the most obvious is in the assessment of the so-called 'readability' of texts for children. Most readability formulae give only a very crude indication of textual difficulty and one reason for this is that they are not generally designed to take account of structure at the rank of group. They often work directly from word to clause level, or sometimes even from words to sentences, as is the case if they depend on counting the number of words per sentence.

Whilst it is obviously true that very long sentences are difficult to read, it is possible to have sentences (or clauses) with the same number of words which are likely to be quite different in degree of difficulty. For example, in each of these clauses there are 14 words (and almost the same number of syllables):

Kylie, Linda, Olivia, Jason and their mum were living in Cairns, near Trinity Bay.
Preservation of the unique plants of the Daintree Forest is crucial to Australia's future.

For most young readers the second sentence would be much more difficult to read than the first. So it is not just the number of words, or the number of syllables, but the internal structure of the groups that can also make a difference to accessibility. This is quite an issue in thinking about educational tests, children's access to texts and appropriateness of writing in various registers. The packaging of meaning at the group level is just one source of variation in text complexity but it is a significant one.

It is therefore often worth looking closely at the structure of groups, as well as the structure of clauses.

Variation in the Complexity of Nominal Groups

In English the packaging of information into nominal group structures is a major source of difference between different types of texts, and between the modes of speech and writing (for example, see Ong 1982). In fact there even appears to have been considerable change in the patterning of English scientific writing, as views of the universe and the nature of scientific method evolved over the last five centuries, as Halliday (1988) has shown.

To illustrate the principle of nominal group variation in different types of text, here are three excerpts of text. I have deliberately selected starkly differing texts as a starting point. The first, Text 10, is from a popular short story by Paul Jennings; the second, Text 11, is an expository text to accompany a major museum exhibition; and the third, Text 12, is a brief

Literacy Learning and Teaching

excerpt from a recent discussion of postmodernist theory. Later we will look at texts where the differences are more subtle.

Text 10 *Excerpt from Paul Jennings' 'One Shot Toothpaste'*

'I'm afraid this tooth will have to be filled,' said Mr Bin. 'It's badly decayed.'

Antonio's knees started to knock as he looked at the dentist's arm. He knew that Mr Bin was hiding a needle behind his back. 'Not an injection. Not that,' spluttered Antonio. But it was too late. Before he could say another word the numbing needle was doing its work.

Antonio could feel tears springing into his eyes. He stared helplessly out of the window at the huge, white tooth that was swinging in the breeze . . .

In Text 10 the nominal groups are relatively simple because for the most part they construct specific Participants in the narrative, simply characters such as 'I' and 'Mr Bin', or physical aspects of the setting such as 'Antonio's knees', 'an injection' or 'the dentist's arm'. The level of abstraction in the nominal groups is relatively low because the reference is to specific physical entities; that is partly what makes the story so accessible for inexperienced readers.

Text 11 *Excerpt from* Dreamtime to Dust: Australia's Fragile Environment, *a booklet produced by the Australian Museum (1988).*

ICE AGES AND SEA LEVEL CHANGES

The last 200,000 years have been a period of global climate change. Twice during this time the earth's climate cooled significantly and glaciers covered much of the northern hemisphere.

During these periods of cooling, called Ice Ages, water evaporating from the oceans became locked up in continental ice sheets, rather than returning to the sea in rivers and streams. As a result sea levels around the world dropped significantly, exposing continental shelves and drastically altering the outline of the landmasses.

Text 11 is from a booklet accompanying the exhibition *Dreamtime to Dust* at the Australian Museum, Sydney. Here the nominal groups are much more variable. Though some are still quite simple, such as 'the oceans' and 'the earth's climate', there are others which involve considerable complexity, as, for example, in structures such as 'water evaporating from the oceans', 'these periods of cooling' and even 'a period of global climate change'.

Text 12 is from a text which discusses ideological change in the late twentieth century, which necessarily involves a high level of abstraction. The example is included to illustrate the point that complexity in the nominal group is not necessarily dysfunctional, as is often suggested by the more naive forms of the Plain English movement, but that it can be important for the development of argument. The appropriateness of complexity depends on the social purposes of the text.

Text 12   *Excerpt from D. Harvey (1989),* The Condition of Postmodernity

The symbolic initiation date of Fordism must, surely, be 1914, when Henry Ford introduced his five-dollar, eight-hour day as recommended for workers manning the automated car-assembly line he had established the year before at Dearborn, Michigan. But the manner of general implantation of Fordism was very much more complicated than that.

There are, again, some straightforward groups such as 'Henry Ford' and 'he', but other nominal group structures such as 'the manner of general implantation of Fordism' obviously build a complex idea. So, however, do less obvious examples without such abstract terms such as 'workers manning the automated car-assembly line he had established the year before at Dearborn, Michigan'.

Subsequently we shall see that this latter form of complexity, in which abstract and technical terms are minimal but in which the nominal group is a long, complicated structure, is a major source of difficulty for some children in crucial aspects of schooling. But to understand how this happens a more detailed discussion of the internal structure of the nominal group is needed.

Building the Nominal Group Experientially

English allows writers to form an elaborate structure of qualification of the central 'thing', and this is in marked contrast with the grammatical structure of many other languages. Even a common noun such as 'band' can be the centre of a complex nominal group.

One way to modify the noun is to distinguish a subclass, say 'rock band'. Some information of a more explicitly attitudinal kind, as in 'spunky', can be included. Then information about quantity can be added, as in a specific number, 'two' or through a non-specific expression of quantity, 'several spunky rock bands'. And then, information which points linguistically to an entity can be built in, such as 'these two spunky rock bands'. Sometimes the 'pointing' might be through a possessive form such as 'Australia's' in 'Australia's two spunky rock bands'.

Each of these moves has added a specific kind of variable to the experiential structure of the nominal group. These are set out below.

bands	Thing
rock	Classifier
spunky	Epithet
two	Numerative
these	Deictic (demonstrative)
or	
Australia's	Deictic (possessive)

The function of these elements is as follows. The *Thing* is the base on which the group is built, referring to some class of things, usually realised through a noun.

The *Classifier* distinguishes some subclass of the Thing being referred to.

The *Epithet* 'indicates some quality of the subset', either of an obviously interpersonal kind such as 'spunky' or of a more objective kind such as 'loud'. A major difference from Classifiers is that Epithets can be intensified but Classifiers cannot *in the specific use within the clause*. It is not possible to have a 'very rock band', where the Intensifier 'very' is modifying the Classifier.

The *Numerative* gives either quantitative (one, two . . .) or ordinative (first, second . . .) information. This can be in definite or indefinite form (a few, many, period of, or, following, later).

The *Deictic* 'points' linguistically to the entity. The most common deictics are 'the' for something definite, or 'a' for something indefinite. Deictics are either demonstrative (this, that . . .) or possessive (my, your . . .). When a demonstrative element is included, it can indicate something which is near (this, these) or distant (that, those). Both demonstrative and possessive Deictics can take the form of an interrogative element (which, what . . .; whose, which person's . . .).

Another variable which can be added to the nominal group is the Qualifier. It serves to further define the Thing. It will be either a clause or a phrase embedded in the nominal group, after the Thing. To continue with the example above, if we added an embedded clause as Qualifier we could have a structure such as 'Those two spunky rock bands that are performing in the Domain'.

The convention for showing an embedded clause is [[ ]]. Thus the first example would be written as 'Those two spunky rock bands [[that are performing in the Domain]]'. For an embedded phrase such as 'Those two spunky rock bands on the record cover' the analysis would be 'Those two spunky rock bands [on the record cover]'.

In fact the structure of the Qualifier can become very complicated because it can be realised through a clause complex rather than an individual clause. It is often then difficult for a reader to process what is being established as the concept. Such long embeddings are frequently found in bureaucratic prose, but unfortunately they are also found in basic skills tests, where their use is plainly difficult for many children.

An example of a Qualifier realised through an embedded clause complex occurs in this sentence: 'Colour in the calculator button you would use to find out the distance separating first place and second place.' The nominal group is 'the calculator button you would use to find out the distance separating first place and second place'.

The structure of the nominal group up to the Thing is:

The	Deictic
calculator	Classifier
button	Thing

The rest of the structure is the Qualifier, comprising two clauses forming an embedded clause complex: '[[you would use ||to find out the distance separating first place and second place]]'.

It is possible, of course, to analyse further the structure of the nominal groups within the embedded clauses. If we were to do so we would find another embedding of a clause acting as a Qualifier: 'the distance [[separating first place and second place]]'.

The definition of the precise button involved is linguistically complex. In fact the example is taken from the New South Wales Basic Skills Test in Numeracy for Year 6, 1990. The item is unlikely to give a valid indication of the mathematical understanding of a large percentage of NESB children.

To further illustrate the function of the Qualifier here are analyses of the structures of some of the earlier examples:

1. 'water evaporating from the oceans':

    | Water | Thing |
    | evaporating from the oceans | Qualifier |

2. 'The symbolic initiation date of Fordism':

    | The | Deictic |
    | symbolic | Epithet (experiential) |
    | initiation | Classifier |
    | date | Thing |
    | of Fordism | Qualifier |

3. 'a period of global climate change':

    | A | Deictic |
    | period of | Numerative |
    | global | Classifier |
    | climate | Classifier |
    | change | Thing |

So far the examples have been nominal group structures where there is one Thing. The generic term for these structures is *complex nominal group*. But it is possible to have group structures where there are multiple Things, forming a *nominal group complex*.

'Stacking' Things: The Nominal Group Complex

This is a relatively simple phenomenon, in which Things are listed to form a unit comprising many Things. For example, members of a group can be listed, as in 'Wayne and Linda were living in Ryde'. Here the grammatical entity which has the role of Actor is the nominal group complex 'Wayne and Linda'. That they form a unit at the group rank can be readily seen if we apply a grammatical test such as the Mood Tag. We find that the reference of the pronominal is not to just one of the Things but to both (or all) of them.

Wayne and Linda were living in Ryde, weren't they?

The grammatical structure is actually that of a list of nominal groups, joined to form a *nominal group complex*.

Wayne   Thing
Linda   Thing

Each of these nominal groups could be extended to form a complex nominal group, as in 'Blond-headed Wayne'.

The phenomenon of forming nominal group complexes out of a lot of linguistic Things is quite common in narratives written for children. For example, there is a very interesting use in Jeanie Adams' *Pigs and Honey* (p. 3), in which the sense of a large group of people being together is built up economically through a nominal group complex:

There was Mum and Dad, my big sister and her baby, my younger sister, my young brother and his mate, Uncle and Aunty and their kids, . . . and Mum's old father and mother.

Here the nominal group complex is:

Mum and Dad, my big sister and her baby, my younger sister, my young brother and his mate, Uncle and Aunty and their kids, . . . and Mum's old father and mother.

In turn, it could be further analysed into complex nominal groups, such as 'my younger brother' and 'Mum's old father'.

Verbs as Things

The usual view of 'Things' at a commonsense level is that they are nouns, entities like prawns, soup, climates, Cairns and so on. But, in English, Things (in the technical sense) in a nominal group can be realised by verbs. For example, in the structure 'the killing of the whales' the action of killing is *nominalised* into a Thing. The structure of this group is:

the   Deictic
killing   Thing
of the whales   Qualifier

This is a very commonly used resource in English, basic to the construction of Western views of science. Halliday (1985a) argues that it is one of several forms of *grammatical metaphor*, in which the congruent (verb) form is shifted to play a new grammatical (Thing) role. The effect is to allow the language user to arrest the flow of experience, 'chunking' it as it were to make attributions to the segment. Thus in 'the running of the marathon was amazing' there is a nominal group 'the running of the marathon'. In the structure of the experiential meaning in the clause the nominal group becomes Carrier in a Relational: intensive: attributive clause, with 'amazing' as Attribute.

the running of the marathon	was	amazing
Carrier	Pro: rel: int: attr	Attribute

The nominal group can itself become a kind of agent, as in 'the running of the marathon caused them to review their training policies'.

These examples are relatively simple, but in scientific writing nominalised forms can require considerable unpacking. For example, think about what 'these periods of cooling' refers to in the *Dreamtime to Dust* brochure:

> The last 200,000 years have been a period of global climate change. Twice during this time the earth's climate cooled significantly and glaciers covered much of the northern hemisphere.
>
> During these periods of cooling, ...

With a structure such as 'budgetary funding provision' in 'budgetary funding provision for schools has been decreased', all three terms are metaphorical forms from, respectively, the verbs 'to budget', 'to fund' and 'to provide'.

Awareness of the structure of the nominal group is a very useful resource for practical teaching tasks. One immediate area of application is in assessing the potential difficulty of structures in texts, as we saw earlier with the Basic Skills Numeracy Test. Another important issue is the fact that nominalised structures often cannot be readily translated *directly* into a child's first language, and that therefore the language rather than the inherent complexity of a concept may be a source of difficulty for even third-phase NESB readers.

Similarly, many young children will not have experienced extensive use of nominalisation in written texts (Halliday 1990; Williams 1990) and will often need assistance in accurately interpreting such apparently transparent terms as 'rate' in a structure such as 'rate of population growth'.

That is one perspective, from the viewpoint of what readers have to do. From the perspective of writers, it is also important that as children move through the primary school they are progressively helped towards more abstract representations of arguments, reports and explanations within appropriate registers, through the use of grammatical metaphor. Abstract and technical terms are often coded through grammatical metaphors and they are not merely optional paraphrases within a register. Rather, they are crucial ways to access meaning and they can also, of course, be fascinating for young learners.

We return, now, to the grammatical structure of the clause to consider some of the resources through which interpersonal meaning is realised.

Clause as 'Interact': Interpersonal Grammar

The grammatical systems involved here at the clause rank are those of *Mood* and *Modality*. Interpersonal grammar is a particularly interesting and diverse area of the grammar, where again knowledge is useful for lots of practical teaching purposes. Using these analyses it is possible to describe features of classroom oral language interaction that can facilitate learning or cause difficulty for children, features which are not often clear from more global analyses of discourse (Hasan 1989). It is also possible to understand crucial aspects of 'interpersonal' differences between registers and genres, and to reinterpret some of the difficulties of relationships between English structures and meanings for NESB speakers. Cate Poynton's (1985) book, *Language and Gender: Making the Difference* will provide further useful information.

I will discuss just two aspects of the grammar of Mood: the function of components of the Mood element in a clause, and relationships between speech functions and the grammar of Mood.

John Burningham's book *Come Away from the Water, Shirley* provides a way of beginning informally. It is an example of the economical use of various resources in the interpersonal metafunction to build a particular tenor of relationship between Shirley (who never speaks) and her mother (who is the only character who speaks). Text 13 is the 'dialogue' from the first few pages, which is accompanied by illustrations of what Shirley is doing in her imagination while her mother is talking.

Text 13 *Excerpt from John Burningham*, Come Away from the Water, Shirley

Of course it's far too cold for swimming, Shirley.

We are going to put our chairs up here.

Why don't you go and play with those children?

Mind you don't get any of that filthy tar on your nice new shoes.

Don't stroke that dog, Shirley, you don't know where he's been.

That's the third and last time I'm asking you whether you want a drink, Shirley.

Careful where you are throwing those stones. You might hit someone.

Perhaps one of the strongest impressions from this language is the presumptiveness of the mother. The book opens with the words 'of course', indicating that the suitability of the weather is beyond question. The mother also issues commands, either in a familiar form such as 'Don't stroke that dog' or in a somewhat less obvious form such as 'we are going to put our chairs up here'. (As readers we can sense that this is not really a statement of information so much as a demand for a particular kind of action if we imagine the consequences of Shirley responding 'No we aren't'.) Even the question 'why don't you go and play with those children?' is a form of demand for Shirley to do something. Notice how different the interactive meaning is if the question is in a positive form: 'why do you go and play with those children?' So, in summary, the mother attempts to determine the action: she assumes a set of (self-evident) values, the primary role in organising activity and the right to regulate what Shirley does. In doing so she ranges across all of the major resources of the interpersonal metafunction in a consistent orchestration of features, which add up to the strongly polarised characterisation of adults which is so common in children's texts. Subsequently something of the detail of this orchestration will be unpacked.

Elements of Mood

Subject and Finite

The two key elements in the Mood structure are the Subject and Finite. Their presence and order in the clause strongly influence the exchange of information and goods and services. Additionally, there is a further important element in the Mood, the Mood Adjunct.

The *Subject* is the grammatical entity which is 'rhetorically' responsible in the exchange, the 'nub' of the exchange. Imagine three people discussing a tennis game:

> '*Boris* played well.'
> 'Did *he*?'
> 'No *he* didn't.'
> '*He* did, really.'
> '*Stephan* was better.'
> 'No *he* wasn't.'
> '*Boris* was much better.'

In each case the Subject is the element which has been italicised. It is 'batted' back and forth in a disagreement because it is the element in which the truth of a proposition is made to rest.

The Subject can readily be identified by adding a Mood Tag to form a question, as in:

> 'Boris played well, didn't he?'

The *Finite* does one of two things. On the one hand, it is the element which can indicate the 'location' in time of the clause relative to the speaker's 'now'. The Finite element, playing this role, has been italicised in the following clauses.

> They *were* going away for the weekend. They *had* been looking forward to the break for some time, and they *had* planned nothing very important.
> 'derivedWill we leave on Friday night?' he *was* asking.

> They *were* going away for the weekend. They *had* been looking forward to the break for some time, and they *had* planned nothing very important.
> '*Will* we leave on Friday night?' he *was* asking.

Notice the variation with respect to the writer's and character's 'now': past in the first clause, past-in-past in the second and third clauses, then future for the narrative internal speaker, and a return to the past for the writer.

Alternatively, the Finite may show the speaker's judgement of the likely truth of the proposition, or the degree of obligatoriness involved. In this case the element is referred to as the Finite modal.

'They *might* be.'
'They *could* be.'
'They *must* be.'
'They *should* be.'

The Finite can be identified using the same strategy as for the Subject. Add the Mood Tag and see which element in the verbal group is picked up.

'He has been reforming the economy, hasn't he?'

'He must be reforming the economy, mustn't he?

'He might reform the economy, mightn't he?

Sometimes the Finite element is not obviously present because the primary tense is indicated by the form of the lexical verb. Nevertheless, if the test of the Mood Tag is used, the form of the Finite can readily be interpreted, as in: 'She played well, *didn't* she?' The Finite is therefore 'did'.

Some of the words which are commonly used in the Finite modal role are:

Probability	*Obligatoriness*
can, may	must, ought to
could, might	has to

Halliday (1985a, p. 75) provides a list of temporal and modal operators, in the latter case categorised into high, median and low values.

Within various registers and genres the Finite will function differently to build a sense of tentativeness or obligatoriness. For example, in scientific report writing there are likely to be few modals of possibility: the interpersonal meaning tends to be 'this is the way the world is'. In

Text 14, written collaboratively by a Year 4 class, there is no use of Finite modals. All Finites are selections for primary tense.

Text 14 *Swans*

A swan *is* a bird.

The swan *has* snowy white feathers and a long graceful neck. In Australia there *are* black swans. In other countries they *are* white.

Swans (*do*) live in swamps and lakes.

They (*do*) eat worms, shellfish and the seeds and roots of water plants.

Baby swans *are* called cygnets.

They (*do*) fly in V-shaped flocks and (*do*) utter loud, trumpet-like notes while flying.

Swans *are* related to geese and ducks.

On the other hand, in discourses of persuasion and argument it is common to find patterns of Finite modals, as in 'it should . . .', 'it must be remembered . . .', 'it can be seen . . .', and 'it might be possible . . .'. The interpersonal meaning tends to be 'this is the way the world might be/ ought to be . . .'. Examples of the function of the Finite modal in these roles can be readily seen in bureaucratic texts. Here, for instance, are some of the key recommendations of a report on restructuring educational administration in New South Wales (New South Wales Government 1989):

'The reduced Head Office *should*, in future, become known as the Central Executive.'

'The Bridge Street building *should* be relocated . . .'

'North Sydney *could* become the node for a new Department-wide Human Resources Division . . .'

'Some former Head Office resources *would* be redeployed in the Regions . . .'

In fictional narrative, a reader's impression of a character can be influenced by the extent to which the character's speech is modalised. A change in the pattern of use of modality can also indicate a change in quality of the character, even a change in the gendered role.

In contemporary fiction the patterning of the primary tense encoded by the Finite can also be of interest, since authors often manipulate the primary tense element to prevent a simple reading of the narrative as a set of past events. Nadia Wheatley's *The House that was Eureka* is an example, in which the reader moves through many placements in time, most obviously between the era of the Great Depression and the reces-

Literacy Learning and Teaching

sion of the early 1980s but also subtly between placements within those periods.

In English the *polar element* is also closely associated with the Finite. The clause is assumed to realise positive polarity if negative polarity is not attached to the Finite. For example:

She *might* go
She *mightn't* go
Will he go?
Won't he go?

(It is important, though, in teaching to be aware that expressions of negative polarity may also be distributed through a clause in some dialects of English, not attached only to the Finite element. A structure such as 'I ain't never gunna do that again, never.' is an example.)

Selection of Mood and Speech Function

The ordering of Subject and Finite selects different Moods in English. For statements, the usual selection of Mood is the *declarative*, and the order is Subject followed by Finite. Thus:

Becker was defeated last night

Subject	Fi	
Mood		

For questions, the usual selection is the *interrogative* and the order is Finite followed by Subject.

Was Becker defeated last night?

Fi	Subject	
Mood		

For commands, the usual selection is *imperative*. Commonly no Subject or Finite is used, as in procedural texts which include structures such as:

|||Mix the lemon grass with the onion and garlic. ||| Fry gently, ||then add the prawns.|||

However, English does allow a choice of Finite in the imperative, and the effect is to build a contrastive meaning, 'do do it'. Thus:

Do go overseas as soon as possible

Fi	
Md	

248

Using Systemic Grammar

It is also possible to select 'you' as Subject, which is an emphatic, or the inclusive form 'let's', as in:

Let's	go overseas soon
S	
Mood	

These are the congruent forms in English, those which are the usual case. But one of the great complexities for non-native speakers is to understand the incongruent cases, where demands for goods and services, 'commands', are made through questions. As teachers, we see this phenomenon when little children first arrive at school and are asked, 'Would you please close the door?' The answer 'No' is not expected, since at this point the teacher is not actually wanting to engage in the exchange of information. 'I can't' would cause fewer problems! Shirley's mother uses an incongruent mood selection when she asks, 'Why don't you go and play with those children?' (an interrogative for a command) and when she says 'We are going to put our chairs up here' (a declarative for a command). Investigation of incongruence often reveals a good deal about classroom discourse and its covert purposes. Think, for example, about the speech function of a declarative such as: 'Perhaps it would be good to write about a thousand words on this topic.'

The third possible component of the Mood element is the Mood Adjunct. This element expresses a further aspect of interpersonal meaning, closely associated with Finite modals, and like these it varies significantly between registers. Mood Adjuncts also express meanings such as probability and obligation (perhaps, maybe, possibly). As well, they can realise other interpersonal meanings such as usualness (always, often), intensity (simply, never), inclination (gladly, willingly) and presumption (of course, clearly). Halliday (1985a, p. 82) provides a comprehensive list of items functioning as Mood Adjuncts.

In summary, the Mood of the clause can comprise three elements: Subject, Finite and Mood Adjunct. Some examples of analysis of structures which involve all three, with different Mood selections, follow:

He	is	just	making the dinner
S	Fi	MdA	
Mood			

Who	really	is	that?
S	MdA	Fi	
Mood			

249

Literacy Learning and Teaching

Are	you	really	going?
Fi	S	MdA	
Mood			

Definitely	do	finish it today
MdA	Fi	
Mood		

Other Aspects of the Interpersonal Metafunction

So far we have considered the potential structure of Mood, since its three elements are likely to be crucially involved in many aspects of educational work. It is only possible to mention other major components of the interpersonal structure of the clause.

Residue

In systemic theory the rest of the clause is called the Residue. It is made up of the Predicator (the rest of the verbal group after the Finite), Complement (an element which has the potential to become the Subject) and Adjunct (which commonly is adjunct circumstantial information). The complete analysis of the interpersonal structure of a clause, showing the elements of both Mood and Residue, is:

She	can	give	Ben	the book	tonight
S	Fi	Pred	Cmp	Cmp	Adjunct
Mood		Residue			

Vocative

One further element which is commonly important in interpersonal meaning is the Vocative. We have already seen an example of this in the title of John Burningham's book, in the use of 'Shirley'. These elements don't affect the Mood structure and they don't contribute to the meanings in the Residue, but they are interpersonally important in signalling qualities in the tenor of relationship between addresser and addressee. It obviously makes a big difference to interpersonal meanings in some contexts to use 'mate' or 'John' or 'kiddo'. Think, for example, of the range of vocatives you might use for your closest friend, depending on who else is present and therefore what aspects of your relationship can be revealed.

In educational work, with its heavy emphasis on conceptual learning and basic skills, interpersonal linguistic meanings are often placed in the background. The advantage of a theory of language which positions the interpersonal as simultaneously encoded with the experiential is that interpersonal meanings can be seen as equally central to interaction. It is not added-on meaning, but is as crucial in building up contexts as the experiential content. Technical analyses of this metafunction offer opportunities to reconceptualise how the interpersonal contributes to learning, though no educational linguist working from a systemic base would ever argue that such an analysis is an exhaustive description of the interpersonal.

Conclusion

As teachers, we have known for a long time that language is central to learning, both as a means for learning and as the means for making learning public even when the learning itself has been developed through other semiotic systems. Yet the actual patterning of language in various educational contexts has been peculiarly understudied, often because sufficiently sensitive techniques have not been available.

Here, as well as introducing some key features of the textual, experiential and interpersonal grammatical features, I have attempted to illustrate very briefly some of the ways in which thinking about texts grammatically can add to insights available from the perspective of discourse structure. The two perspectives are complementary to each other. To use only description at the level of discourse structure, such as the schematic structure of genre, is to run the risk of cutting genre descriptions adrift from their anchorage in the grammatical patterning of language, and therefore have them floating about in educational contexts, unrelated to their purposes in the living of life. Stages in a text are clusters of grammatical patterns, not just non-linguistic concepts or intentions in the head of the language user.

Traditional school grammar is of very limited value in practical situations partly for this very reason, that it does not provide ways of thinking about how grammatical patterns vary in different contexts of use. Multifunctional descriptions enable teachers to look at what learners have to be able to do in terms of organising messages, constructing experiential meanings and utilising appropriate interpersonal meanings. These are, of course, much richer perspectives than those available from traditional grammar or from grammars which consider experiential meanings exclusively.

But for this very reason systemic grammar often appears to be an extravagant grammar, making use of a large number of functional differentiations and, therefore, a large number of technical terms. However, one test of whether or not the description is unnecessarily extravagant is surely the usefulness of the descriptions in helping teachers organise effective, developmental programs for learners. Given the centrality of language to learning, it would not be surprising to find that careful description of how linguistic meanings 'work' is required for progress to be made in overcoming some of the learning difficulties created by current practices.

What systemic functional grammar seems to offer is precisely a sensitivity of technique, refusing global analyses of learning potential and learning difficulties and focusing attention on semantically important patterns of interaction in order to make learning accessible to many to whom it would otherwise be denied. It is an optimistic view of language and learning, and of the potential of technical linguistic resources to make a difference to educational practice.

References

Christie, F. (ed.) (1989) *Writing in Schools: Study Guide*, Deakin University Press, Geelong, Victoria.
Christie, F. and Rothery, J. (1989) 'Exploring the written mode and the range of factual genres', in *Writing in Schools: Study Guide*, Deakin University Press, Geelong, Victoria.
Derewianka, B. (1990) *Exploring How Texts Work*, Primary English Teaching Association, Sydney.
Halliday, M.A.K. (1976) *Language as Social Semiotic: The Social Interpretation of Language and Meaning*, Edward Arnold, London.
Halliday, M.A.K. (1981) Modes of meaning and modes of expression', in *Function and Context in Linguistic Analysis: A Festschrift for William Haas*, eds D.J. Allerton, E. Carney and D. Holdcroft, Cambridge University Press, Cambridge.
Halliday, M.A.K. (1985a) *An Introduction to Functional Grammar*, Edward Arnold, London.
Halliday, M.A.K. (1985b) *Spoken and Written Language*, Deakin University Press, Geelong, Victoria.
Halliday, M.A.K. (1988) 'On the language of physical science', in *Registers of Written English: Situational Factors and Linguistic Features*, ed. M. Ghadessy, Frances Pinter, London.
Halliday, M.A.K. (1990) 'Some grammatical problems in scientific English', *Australian Review of Applied Linguistics*, Series S, 6: 13–37.
Halliday, M.A.K. and Hasan, R. (1985) *Language, Context and Text: Aspects of Language in a Social Semiotic Perspective*, Deakin University Press, Geelong, Victoria.
Harvey, D. (1989) *The Condition of Postmodernity*, Blackwell, Oxford.
Hasan, R. (1987) 'The grammarian's dream: Lexis as most delicate grammar', in *New Developments in Systemic Linguistics*, Vol. 1, *Theory and Description*, Frances Pinter, London.

Hasan, R. (1989) 'Semantic variation and sociolinguistics', *Australian Journal of Linguistics* 9: 221–75.
Martin, J. (1989) 'Technicality and abstraction: Language for the creation of specialised texts', in *Writing in Schools: Reader*, ed. F. Christie, Deakin University Press, Geelong, Victoria.
Martin, J. (1992a) *English Text: System and Structure*, John Benjamins, Amsterdam.
Martin, J. (1992b) 'Types of grammar', Lecture to the Third Australian Systemics Summer School for Teachers, University of Sydney, 13 January.
Matthiessen, C.M.I.M. (1992) *Lexicogrammatical Cartography: English Systems*, Department of Linguistics, University of Sydney. Mimeo.
New South Wales Government (1989) *Schools Renewal: A Strategy to Revitalise Schools within the New South Wales State Education System*, Sydney.
Ong, W.J. (1982) *Orality and Literacy*, Methuen, London.
Poynton, C. (1985) *Language and Gender: Making the Difference*, Deakin University Press, Geelong, Victoria.
The Australian Museum (1988) *Dreamtime to Dust: Australia's Fragile Environment*, Sydney.
Wertsch, J.V. (1985) *Vygotsky and the Social Formation of Mind*, Harvard University Press, London.
Williams, G. (1990) 'Variation in home reading contexts', Paper read to The Fifteenth Australian Reading Association Conference, Canberra, 8 July 1990.

References to Children's Books

Adams, Jeanie (1989) *Pigs and Honey*, Omnibus, Adelaide.
Burningham, John (1977) *Come Away from the Water, Shirley*, Jonathon Cape, London.
Dahl, Roald (1974) *Fantastic Mr Fox*, Puffin, Harmondsworth.
Jennings, Paul (1986) 'One Shot Toothpaste', in *Unbelievable!*, Puffin, Melbourne.
Norman, David and Milner, Angela (1989) *Dinosaur*, Alfred A. Knopf, New York.
Wheatley, Nadia (1985) *The House that was Eureka*, Puffin, Melbourne.

Acknowledgement
For help in obtaining samples of text, the author thanks Robyn Cusworth, Louise Droga, Paul Dufficy, Linda Grundy, Carolyn MacLulich and Katina Zammit.

6
The Language of Social Studies: Using Texts of Society and Culture in the Primary School

Bill Cope, Mary Kalantzis, Peter Wignell

Contents

The Language of Social Studies: An Introduction to Some Linguistic Concepts 257

Doing Social Studies: What is the Discipline of Social Science About? 259

Learning About Environments: A Case Study of the Language of Social Studies in Action 260

The Relationship Between Social Studies Texts and Input Materials 264

Using Social Studies to Act on the World 271

What Makes 'Good' Social Studies Materials for Primary School? 274

Language and Social Studies Pedagogy 274

Texts That Tell 'Facts' and 'Truths' 276

Student Inquiry and the Texts of Progressivist Curriculum 281

Framing Texts in Social Studies 287

Conclusion 292

References
Appendix: Textbooks and Curriculum Materials

In examining the language of social studies, we want to look at social science as both process and product and examine the relationship between 'doing' the subject of social studies and the kinds of texts it is necessary to have control over in order to 'do' social studies effectively. After an introduction to some of the basic linguistic concepts that are used to discuss the discourse of social science, we will embark upon a detailed case study, examining the way language works to create meaning in a social studies unit dealing with the environment. On this basis, we move on to a broader discussion of the connections between language and social studies teaching methodology; looking at the different types of linguistic demands that are placed upon students in different methodological or pedagogical frameworks.

The Language of Social Studies: An Introduction to Some Linguistic Concepts

This discussion is based on a number of assumptions about language, the relationship between language and its social context and the role of language in constructing specialised knowledge. It is assumed that patterns of language choice found in any discourse are functional and have evolved over time to fulfil the needs of that discourse. Within particular discourses language is seen as a tool for acting on and interpreting the particular part of the world that that discourse concerns itself with. Thus we find different patterns of language choice in different discourses. For example, the discourses of science and the humanities are different because they are attempting to do, or explain, different things. Likewise, the discourse of social science is different from science and the humanities because it is doing different things. In broader terms, the social context in which language is found and the function of language within that context determine the kinds of language choices which will work in that context.

In the model of language and context used in this discussion it is assumed that context can be looked at in terms of two levels, register and genre. A schematic diagram of this is given in Figure 6.1 (Martin 1984).

The level of genre reflects the broader social context and represents the means by which cultures get particular jobs done through language. For example, if I want to buy something in a shop in Sydney, Australia, there is an identifiable sequence of steps that I go through to do it. Likewise there are particular, almost ritualised sequences of exchanges of words that accompany the process. If I were buying something at a street market stall in Bangkok, Thailand, the end result, receiving goods in exchange for money, would be the same but the nature of the transaction would be different. For example, I would be thought to be mad if I

```
┌─────────┐
│  Genre  │╲
└─────────┘ ╲
    ┌──────────────────────────┐╲
    │        Register          │ ╲
    ├──────┬──────┬────────────┤  ╲
    │Field │ Mode │   Tenor    │   ╲
    └──────┴──────┴────────────┘    ╲
                            ┌──────────────┐
                            │   Language   │
                            └──────────────┘
```

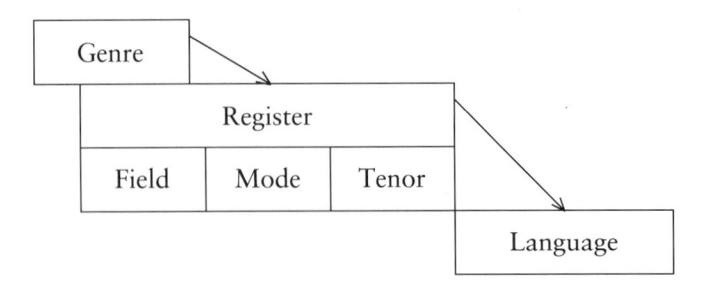

Figure 6.1 *A model of language in context*

criticised the merchandise and offered one-third of the listed price in Sydney. At a Bangkok market stall I would be thought to be mad, or stupid, if I didn't. What we have is the same social activity, buying and selling, but how it is negotiated differs according to the social and cultural context. In other words, different genres are employed.

The same kind of thing applies with the kinds of written text typically found in different subject areas in education. The texts are staged or structured according to the social purpose they are trying to achieve. They are functional in their context. The term 'genre' as it is used here refers to particular text types which have identifiable structures and patterns of grammatical choices which are functional in those texts achieving their social purpose. The terms 'report', 'explanation' and 'argument' used in this discussion are used as technical terms to refer to examples of different genres.

Similarly, the kind of language used differs at the level of register, which can be divided according to three variables, field, mode and tenor. Field relates to the social activity being engaged in. For instance, school curricula tend to be divided along field lines: mathematics, biology, physics, economics and the like. Field is most closely associated with what is generally called 'content'. Mode relates basically to the distance between language and its context. For example, the language of a face to face conversation will be different from the language of a textbook even if they are about the same field. Tenor relates to the degree of social distance between the people exchanging language. For example, the talk between a teacher and a student will be different from the talk between two students who are close friends even if the field and mode are the same.

Genre, field, mode and tenor are realised through patterns of language choice. This is particularly the case with written text. In a textbook, for example, the language (and accompanying pictures, graphs, etc.) creates the subject for the reader. In general, specialised discourses translate an area of experience into their own terms. For instance, science uses technicality to translate commonsense understandings of the world into understandings of a different kind. For example, by saying 'An ecosystem is that home or place in which an interacting community of plants and animals lives' (Sale *et al.* 1980), the word 'ecosystem' is introduced as a technical term which, in one sense, summarises its definition in one word, a kind of shorthand, and at the same time gives that term a specific meaning within the field. Now that the term is fixed, or has a specific meaning, it is possible to reorder commonsense knowledge by either introducing new types of ecosystems or dividing ecosystems into their component parts. As well as renaming the commonsense world science also reorders that world. It creates a different way of looking at and understanding the world.

Awareness of typical patterns of language in a subject and how they function in a subject or discipline are, therefore, important in selecting appropriate teaching and learning materials.

Doing Social Studies: What is the Discipline of Social Science About?

Broadly speaking, it can be argued that social studies is similar to science in that it attempts, through observation, analysis and interpretation to come to some understanding of some part of the world. Where it differs from science is that what the social scientist tries to understand is not necessarily some physical object or entity but usually a complex set of human activities or the result of human activities. The result of this is that the language of social studies does not simply duplicate the language of science. The language of social studies incorporates many of the features of scientific language but also adds another layer of complexity. In short, we can say that the language of science is by nature technical and that the language of social studies is by nature both technical and abstract.

This abstraction derives from the fact mentioned above, that the phenomena which social studies concerns itself with are by their nature abstract. Or perhaps it would be more true to say that while the phenomena observed are by and large tangible, the intellectual framework for making meaning of relationships between phenomena relies on generalisation and abstraction. It is in this generalisation and abstraction that the doing of social studies takes place. Without this there is no interpretation, only description, and in primary school, for example, in a local area study there is the real risk that the result will be a description of what everybody already knows. It is the language of interpretation in social studies, the language which constructs social studies, that will be concentrated on here.

Social scientific research uses all kinds of data. Data from just about any source and in just about any form can become the raw material for social studies. Data from sources such as direct observation, questionnaires, maps, graphs, interviews and other written texts, either other social science texts or material which does not itself pretend to be social science, are all used. The problem resulting from this is how to put information from all these disparate sources of data into a coherent framework. This will be discussed by looking in some detail at some typical social studies texts from primary school materials, and seeing how they function to create social science.

Learning About Environments: A Case Study of the Language of Social Studies in Action

To discuss these issues in detail as they relate specifically to teaching in the subject of social studies, we will take a sample piece of social studies curriculum, from one of the Social Literacy primary social studies units for Year Five: the book *Environments* (Kalantzis and Cope 1986). This book is not necessarily the 'best' available source but it is internally coherent, consistent in theme and uses a range of texts and activities typical of those involved in social studies within an integrated framework. We will discuss the sections of the *Environments* text as a case study of how language works in social studies. The step by step discussion of this text as an example of primary school social studies materials, is intended to show how the theoretical discussion of the language in this book, and of social science more generally, is of practical relevance to teachers in selecting and/or developing social studies materials for their classrooms.

The following discussion, in other words, focuses in a very concrete way on what is involved in 'doing' social studies, what kinds of texts might constitute both input for doing social studies and output of social scientific inquiry and some of the characteristic linguistic features of those social scientific texts. Figure 6.2 shows two pages from the Social Literacy *Environments* unit:

You will note that the unit begins with a focus question: What are human and natural environments? This question has the role of a research question. In other words, what are we looking at here? The focus question is followed by a short set of input data in the form of five pictures and an accompanying text.

These are followed by a section labelled 'analysis', which sets two tasks:

Analysis
1. Work out: Look at the other pictures of environments. Describe the things that make up each environment. Some things you can see in the pictures. But you might have to use your imagination a bit, too.
2. Look around you: What are the things that make up your environment at this moment? Who and what surrounds you? Give this environment a name.

The Language of Social Studies

FOCUS 1: What are human and natural environments?

Consider

Look at these five environments and consider all the parts that make them up.

1. A BIG TREE'S FOREST ENVIRONMENT.

2. A BIRDS' CITY ENVIRONMENT.

3. A FISH'S SEA ENVIRONMENT.

4. SUSAN'S HOME ENVIRONMENT.

5. TONY'S SCHOOL ENVIRONMENT.

Figure 6.2 *From* Environments, *Social Literary Series E, Book 4*

These tasks represent part of the process of 'doing' social science, observing one context and applying those observations to new contexts. The orientation here is still basically description although the task of giving the environment a name hints at what is to come.

Following these tasks is a section labelled 'main ideas', which consists of a very short but crucial text:

Main Ideas
Environments are surroundings. All the things that surround the tree are parts of its **environment**.

It is here that commonsense observations are beginning to be turned into social science. We find the term 'environment' introduced now as a technical term, and defined. Definition fixes an identity for that term in a particular conceptual framework. In a sense it says: 'as a social scientist, when I say environment I mean . . .'. In this particular definition the reader needs to refer both to the accompanying text and to the input material. It is necessary to go back to the data (the picture of the tree) to see exactly what things make up the tree's environment.

Another key feature here is the use of abstraction. The idea of an environment is itself an abstract concept; the things in it are tangible but the patterns of relationships which make it a whole are abstract. The term itself is a summary of countless things, activities and relationships. When we use the term 'environment' in the technical sense in which it is used here, all of these are implied in that term. The technical term is thus a kind of shorthand way of saying many things in one word.

The term itself is also defined through abstraction. The word 'surroundings' is an abstraction. It is a word derived through the process of nominalisation. It is an example of what Halliday (1985b) calls grammatical metaphor. It is an example of a noun derived from a verb. For example, in the preceding 'analysis' question 2 we find 'Who and what surrounds you?' In Halliday's (1985b) framework, 'surrounds' is classified as the congruent form. A distinction needs to be made here between the terms metaphorical and congruent. In congruent language we typically find people, things and objects realised grammatically as nouns, actions realised as verbs, qualities of things realised as adjectives, qualities of actions (or processes) realised as adverbs, and logical relations realised as conjunctions. This is typical of spontaneous, unselfconscious spoken language and particularly typical of the language of children.

In language containing grammatical metaphor we typically find people and concrete objects disappearing from prominent places in the text, 'process' type meanings grammatically coded as nouns, 'qualities' also coded as nouns, and logical relations coded as either nouns, verbs or prepositions. Grammatical metaphor is typical of written text. To make sense of much written text in education (apart from narrative text), control over meanings coded through grammatical metaphor is necessary. For example, compare the following two sentences (adapted from Eggins *et al.* 1987, p. 88 and originally from a CSIRO memo). The original, metaphorical, version is first (grammatical metaphors in bold, technical terms in italics).

> Without **technological change** the **lessening competitiveness** of *manufacturing industry* would **lead to** a **continued diminution** in the **overall wealth** and **employment potential** of the *economy*.

Now the more congruent version:

> Unless *technology* changes *manufacturing industry* will become less competitive so the *economy* will continue to become worth less and fewer people will be able to have jobs.

Notice also that while it is relatively easy to reduce the amount of grammatical metaphor in the text and still have it make sense, if the technical terms (which are themselves abstractions) were treated similarly the explanation of them would be particularly long-winded and the text would make less sense. For example, while it is relatively easy to unpack 'lessening competitiveness' to 'will become less competitive' how would *manufacturing industry, technology* or the *economy* be unpacked? Does the *economy* equal 'all the things that people do to make money or contribute to making that money and all the things that they do with that money once they have made it and all of the things that the people they give that money to when they buy things or invest it do with that money'?

Going back to the two versions of the short text above, it is clear that primary school students are unlikely to be able to understand the original version, most would, however, with a little explanation of the technical terms, be able to understand the second version. Some degree of abstraction is essential in social studies since in making general statements which are intended to apply not just to a given instance but to a whole class of instances it is impossible not to be a little abstract.

Halliday (1985b, p. 95) suggests that even very young children have little trouble in moving between the specific and general, that the ability to deal with abstraction comes later, at least after five, and that the ability to shift between the congruent and the metaphorical is unlikely to be present until about eight or nine. This is, however, a matter of degree. It is likely that a text as metaphorical as the first example cited above would prove difficult to decode even for many adults.

The data from a number of studies related to writing in schools (Martin and Rothery 1980, 1981; Martin 1984; Wignell 1987, 1988) show that children's writing is basically congruent and that where it does contain grammatical metaphor it is most often taken directly from source materials.

The difficulty faced by educators and materials writers is how to make something 'simple' enough for a relatively young child to understand without making it so simplistic that it becomes meaningless. That is, how do you rework what was originally usually a highly grammatically metaphorical discourse and at the same time make complex concepts accessible to younger readers?

The Relationship Between Social Studies Texts and Input Materials

Going back to the previous discussion on 'surrounds' and 'surroundings', we find that the abstraction 'surroundings' is directly traceable back to a congruent form 'surrounds' in the preceding 'analysis' question and that it can also be tracked back to the input data through the exercise of going back to the pictures and describing what 'surrounds' the observer. The word is also used in both a congruent and metaphorical form in the 'main ideas' text, in both cases in this text in conjunction with the term 'environment'. In the second instance 'surround' occurs in a grammatical location intermediate between the nominalised realisation and the congruent one. It occurs in congruent form (as a verb), but within an embedded clause (denoted by double square brackets) as a constituent of a nominal group: 'All the things [[that *surround* the tree]]'. This allows readers to track the term through a number of grammatical environments as well as to track it back to the source data.

This short text, generically a report (Martin and Rothery 1980), represents the beginning of the creation of a conceptual framework which can be used for the interpretation of social studies or, perhaps more strongly, to create social studies out of raw data.

One of the functions of the report genre is to establish technical discourse, or to provide a 'map' of the field. This genre is often where the technical framework of a discipline is presented. For instance, it is where technical terms are often introduced and defined and where the relationships among technical terms are established. The very short report discussed above introduces and defines one technical term. The following 'main ideas' section is also a report, or perhaps a continuation of the previous report. This text reads:

> **Human environments** are **environments** in which most of the things have been made by people. **Natural environments** are **environments** which have been made by nature, and which have not been changed much by people.

This text both introduces new technical terms, 'human environments' and 'natural environments', which represent different types of 'environment', and also defines them and establishes a relationship between the new terms and the term already known. The new terms are ordered as subclasses of the original. A taxonomy is being built.

If we take it that the two 'main ideas' texts are connected, the overall generic structure of this text(s) can be expressed as follows:

General classification + definition
 |
Subclassification 1 + definition
 |
Subclassification 2 + definition

The Language of Social Studies

It is through taxonomies that the relationships among terms are established. In this case the relationship is one of class to subclass, or superordination. The other possibility is for a taxonomy to be established on the basis of part to whole, or composition. Many of the activities in this book involve identifying the parts of the environment depending on which type of environment they are part of, for instance the activity shown in Figure 6.3 (Kalantzis and Cope 1986b, p. 12).

Inquiry

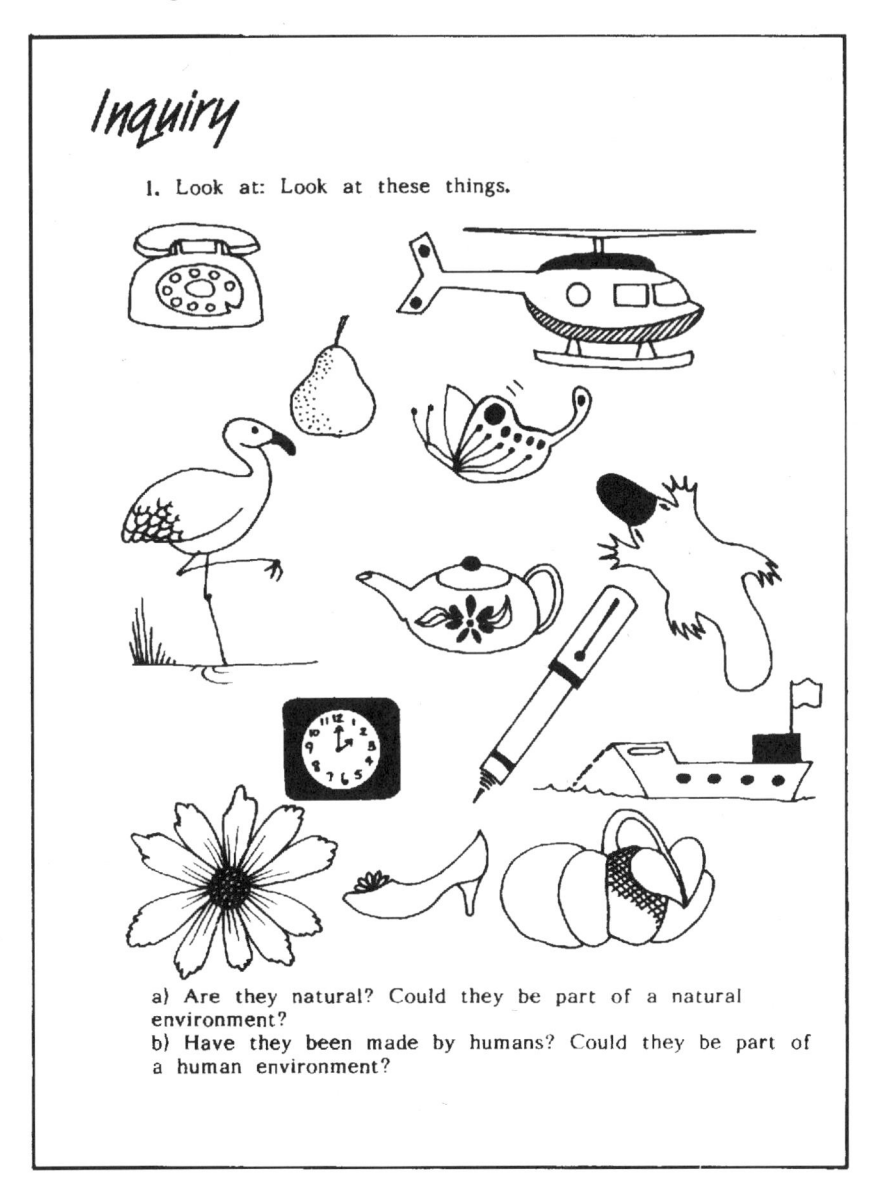

1. Look at: Look at these things.

a) Are they natural? Could they be part of a natural environment?
b) Have they been made by humans? Could they be part of a human environment?

Figure 6.3 *From* Environments, *Social Literacy Series E, Book 4*

FOCUS 2: How do natural environments work?

Consider

Environments work like groups or communities. The parts of environments are connected. Think about the connections in natural communities or natural environments. Consider the different parts of nature that make up the environment shown on the next four pages.

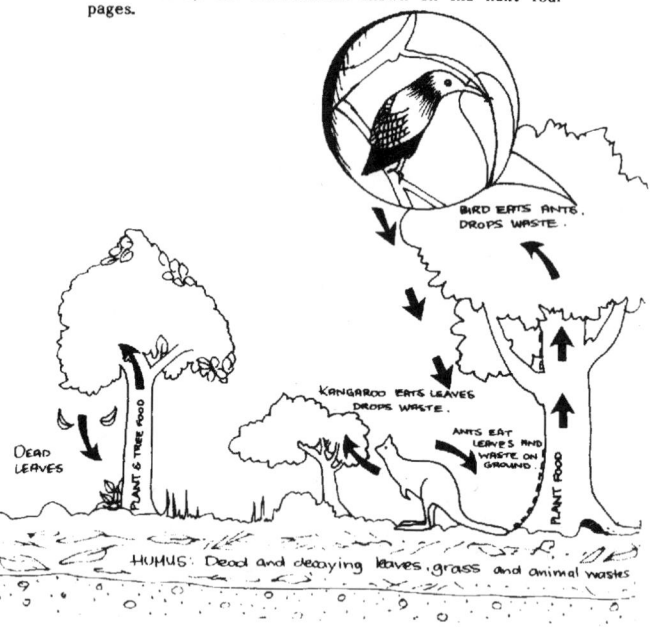

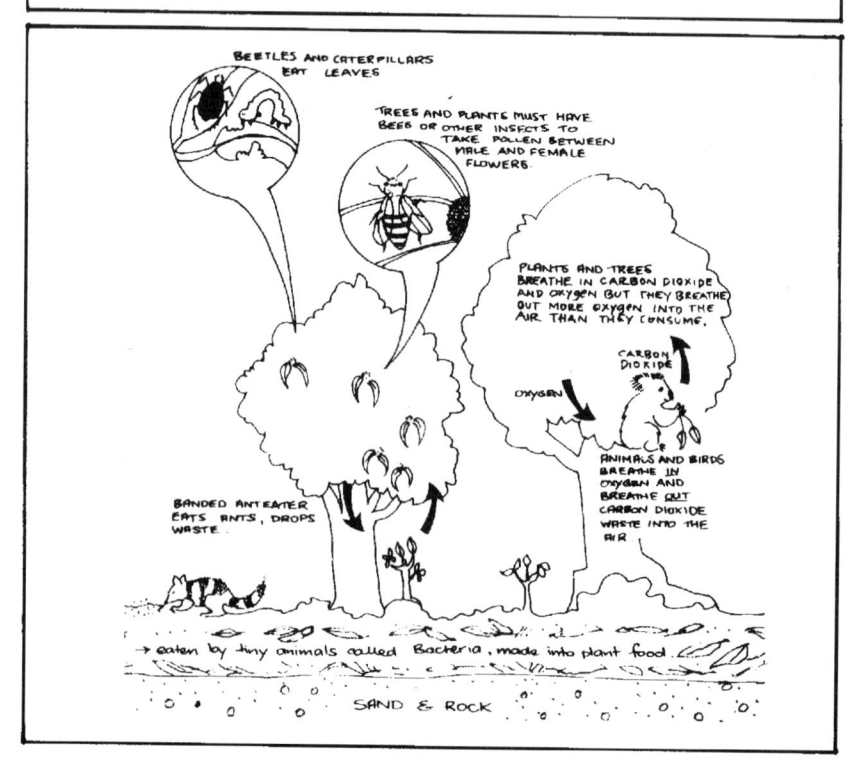

BIRD EATS ANTS. DROPS WASTE.

KANGAROO EATS LEAVES DROPS WASTE.

ANTS EAT LEAVES AND WASTE ON GROUND.

DEAD LEAVES

PLANT & TREE FOOD

PLANT FOOD

HUMUS: Dead and decaying leaves, grass and animal wastes

BEETLES AND CATERPILLARS EAT LEAVES

TREES AND PLANTS MUST HAVE BEES OR OTHER INSECTS TO TAKE POLLEN BETWEEN MALE AND FEMALE FLOWERS.

PLANTS AND TREES BREATHE IN CARBON DIOXIDE AND OXYGEN BUT THEY BREATHE OUT MORE OXYGEN INTO THE AIR THAN THEY CONSUME.

CARBON DIOXIDE

OXYGEN

ANIMALS AND BIRDS BREATHE IN OXYGEN AND BREATHE OUT CARBON DIOXIDE WASTE INTO THE AIR

BANDED ANTEATER EATS ANTS, DROPS WASTE.

→ eaten by tiny animals called Bacteria, made into plant food.

SAND & ROCK

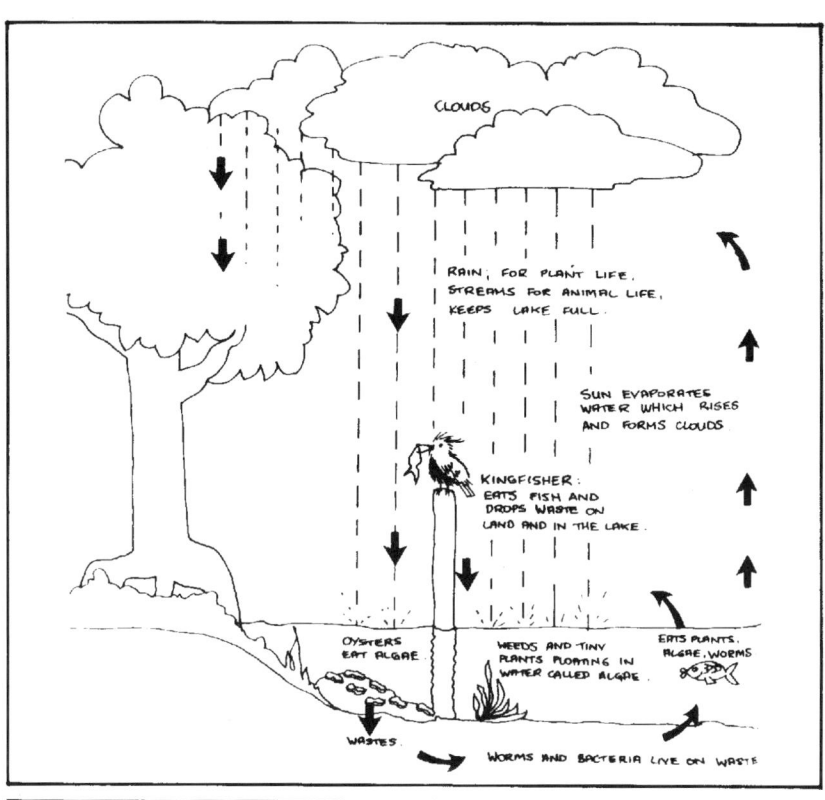

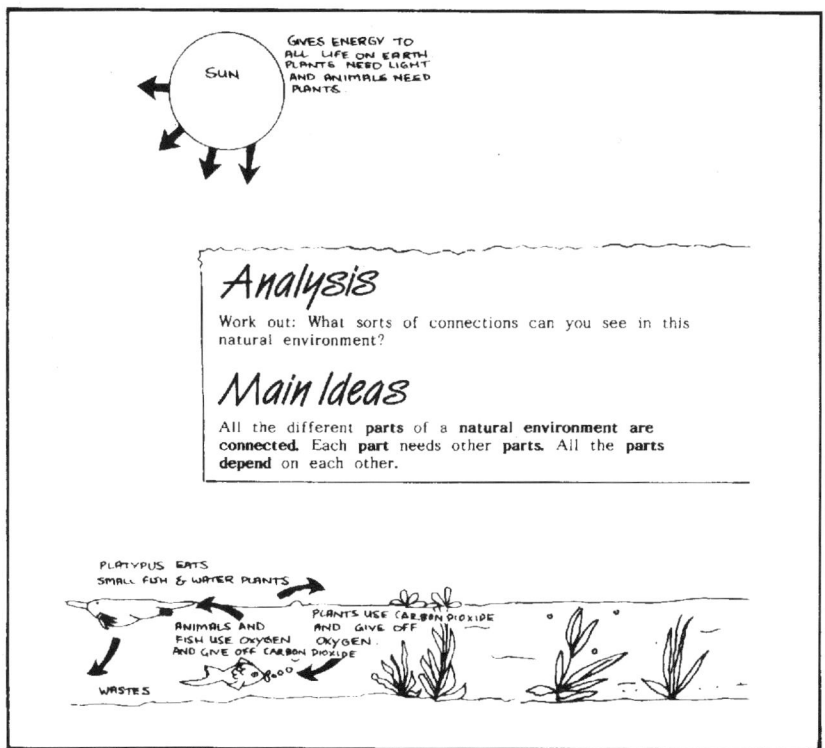

Figure 6.4 *From* Environments *Social Literacy Series E, Book 4*

The first focus question concludes here. Its job was to establish what it is that is being talked about and to show how the bits fit together. It does this through using genre and language choices. That is, for the reader the technical framework is created through these choices. It is not random. The language is the way it is because it is performing a particular function. The choice of genre and grammar here works for establishing what are essentially static relationships, relationships between things. That is one reason for nominalisation and abstraction. If we want to establish a static relationship, for example that something is something else, then this is easier to do if the object of interest is standing still. Just as a map is useful because it is a static representation of the location of things in relation to each other, likewise information coded in a report is there set out for later use. In English grammatically nouns are more static than verbs so if we want to hold something still it is useful to use the grammar to turn it into a noun. Nouns, even abstract ones, are much easier to order in relation to each other in taxonomies than are verbs.

Thus the function of this first 'focus' question has been to hold things still temporarily to see what they are and how they fit together and the language choices made reflect this function. Under 'Focus 2: How do natural environments work?' (Kalantzis and Cope 1986, p. 16), the emphasis changes from what to how (Figure 6.4). Here the input for the first 'main ideas' of this section is in the form of annotated diagrams and a short accompanying text.

In shifting the emphasis from 'what?' to 'how?' the language also changes. The concern shifts from a static representation of things to things in action. Things no longer 'are' as in the report texts but things now happen and animals and plants 'do' things. The switch is from a static to a dynamic representation of the world — from the map to the journey. For example, in the annotated diagram we find:

Bird *eats* ants, *drops* waste
Ants *eat* leaves on ground
Plants and trees *breathe* in carbon dioxide and oxygen

In the diagrams the connections between these events are represented by arrows.

Following this input there are a number of activities examining how things are connected, shown in Figure 6.5 (Kalantzis and Cope 1986, p. 20).

The Language of Social Studies

Inquiry

1. **Find out:** What do these words mean? Your dictionary will help you.
   evaporate
   decay
   pollen
   waste
   energy

2. **Draw:** What chains of connections can you see in the natural environment on the last two pages?
   a) Draw some of the chains of connections you can see.
   b) Label each of the parts of the chain.
   c) Draw the part inside each link.

3. **Work out:** How does each part of the chain depend on other parts of the chain?
   The word 'depend' explains the connections in the chain. Write a sentence about each connection. You should use the word depend in each sentence.

Figure 6.5   *From* Environments, *Social Literacy Series E, Book 4*

The input and activities are then summed up in a short 'main ideas' section:

> People need **nature**. We depend on **nature** for air, warmth, food, clothing, building materials and many, many other things. We are **connected** to **nature** in many important ways. Our **human environments depend** on the **natural environment**. Because we **depend** on the **natural environment**, we are also **responsible** for it.

This text represents a shift in genre from the 'main ideas' texts discussed previously. The shift is from report to explanation and this text represents a kind of transition between the two. This particular text, however, does not introduce any new technical terms or taxonomic relationships, using instead the ones already established. It draws on the technical framework already established and sets it into action. Having distinguished between human and natural environments, this text now brings them back together.

For example, the emphasis now is not on relationships between things but on relationships between processes, in this case 'needing' and 'depending'. We find this illustrated in the sentence 'Our **human environments** depend on the **natural environment**'. The type of process has also changed from mostly relational processes (which are about states of 'being') to processes which involve some kind of action. (For a discussion of process types see Halliday 1985a.) The text does not, however, explain how they come to be. Where this book differs from, say, science or geography is that the explanatory text does not really explain how things are connected.

For example, take the following short explanation from a junior secondary geography textbook:

> After flash floods, desert streams flowing from upland areas carry heavy loads of silt, rock and sand fragments. As they reach the flatter area of desert basins, they lose speed and their waters may also soak quickly into the basin floor. The streams then drop their loads, the heaviest materials first — the stones — then the sand and finally the silt. Choked by their own deposits, these short-lived streams frequently divide into a maze of channels spreading their load in all directions. In time fan or cone shaped deposits of gravel, sand, silt and clay are formed around each valley or canyon outlet. These are called alluvial fans. (Sale *et al.* 1980, p. 54)

This text outlines the sequence of events which leads to the formation of a particular natural phenomenon. The generic structure of this particular text can be expressed as:

Sequence of events (1–n)
|
Result

In the natural sciences, explanations such as this serve to state how things come to be. They are also used in the social sciences to explain how social phenomena come to be.

The Language of Social Studies

Many of the exercises in the focus question 'How do natural environments work?' rely on control of the explanation genre, even though this genre is not modelled explicitly. For example:

> 3. Explain: How does each human part depend on the next human part in the chain? Or, how does it depend on part of the natural environment? Write a sentence about each human part in the chain. Make sure you use the word depend in each sentence.

This type of question suggests an explanatory text, such as the one looked at above, as its response. It suggests a text which duplicates in words the dependency relationships expressed in the diagrams, that is, an explanation. It is the type of text a social scientist would be likely to produce in response to such a question. This genre typically focuses not only on action type processes but also on the logical links between them.

So far, we have looked at two aspects of social studies: first, creating a technical framework and second, using that framework as a tool for interpreting the world. The principal genre which it is necessary to have control over in the first instance is the report genre while the principal genre needed for the second activity is the explanation genre. It needs to be stressed that these are two of the genres social studies uses to act on information drawn from many other sources. Access to other genres is important in collecting data but the two mentioned above are crucial to making social studies out of those data.

Using Social Studies to Act on the World

Having covered briefly the 'what' and 'how' aspects of social studies, the next question to be addressed is 'why'. 'Why' is not used here in the metaphysical sense of 'why is it so?' It is used more in the sense of 'why should we?' That is, having constructed a social scientific framework for interpreting the world, what can we now do with it? Why bother?

In combination with other sciences, social studies research is an important input for many decisions which affect our daily and future lives, particularly in areas such as 'the environment'. As such the ability to use social studies to argue a case for or against a particular course of action is very important. In terms of written text, the key genre here is argument. This genre involves setting up a thesis or proposition to be argued for or against, and providing reasons and evidence in support of that proposition. For example:

> 9. b) Are we who live in towns and cities always thoughtful about the things we do? In what ways might our thoughtlessness be selfish? Prepare a talk or arrange a debate. (Kalantzis and Cope 1986, p. 51)

This question is clearly intended to generate argument. In this case, the word 'debate' indicates that an oral argument is what is called for. Although the proposition being argued might be the same, an oral and a written argument are structurally very different. Take the following two examples. The first is what is basically an oral argument written down and the second is a written version of the first. The answers are in response to the question 'Are governments necessary?'

1.
I think that governments like the Federal Government are necessary because they help to keep our economic system in order and if any problems occur to upset the economy the Federal Government will more or less straighten it out.

I also think that the State Government isn't necessary because there is the Local Government known as a shire or municipality to do jobs for the local environment and with Local Governments within every suburb there is hardly any use for the State Government because the Local Governments do all the work.

2.
In Australia there are three kinds of Government, the Federal Government, State Governments and Local Governments. Of these, two — the Federal Government and Local Governments — are necessary. This is so for a number of reasons.

First, the Federal Government is necessary because we need a Government big enough to look after the big things in the country. The economy for example. If any problems occur in the economy only the Federal Government can fix them up. The other types of Government are too small.

Furthermore, Local Governments are also necessary. They are there to do jobs too small for the Federal Government to do, such as local roads, garbage collection and jobs concerned with the local environment generally. There are Local Governments all over Australia. Every municipality has one.

On the other hand, State Governments are not necessary. This is so for precisely the same reasons as the other two types of Governments are necessary. If there is a Federal Government for the big jobs and Local Governments for the small jobs there is no need for a Government to do the middle sized jobs. State governments don't do anything that the Federal and Local Governments can't already do.

Therefore, for the above reasons, of the three types of Government currently in Australia, two are necessary and the other is not. So, in answer to the question, we can say that some governments are necessary. (Kalantzis and Wignell 1988)

Without going into the differences between spoken and written language, which are considerable, especially in more academic type texts, it is clear that the two examples above, while they are talking about the same thing, do it very differently. In reading, students are more likely to see texts similar to the second rather than the first.

(Question)
|
Thesis
|
Arguments (1–*n*)
|
Conclusion

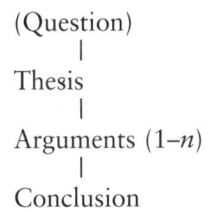

In *Environments,* the closest text to a written argument is:

People **depend** on the **natural environment**. But when they use the **natural environment**, they sometimes can spoil it. For example, if they want to take too much away too quickly, they can be **thoughtless** about the way they **change** the **environment**. They might not think about the mess they leave behind, such as rubbish and pollution.

People who are **thoughtless** about the **natural environment** spoil it for the plants, fish and animals who live there. They also spoil their own **human environment** by making it unpleasant and ugly. When they do this, they are acting **irresponsibly**, because they are not considering how they are **connected** with others.

This text is basically a written argument with an unstated thesis. If we were to add 'People should look after their environment for a number of reasons.' we would have a text structurally similar to the second example above.

Given that this is an argumentative text of sorts, how does it fit in with the rest of the framework developed throughout *Environments*? What it does is use the results of the previous investigations in formulating its argument. The terms natural environment and human environment are drawn upon and can be assumed from the previous material. The text also draws on the explanatory material. It discusses what happens when people abuse their environment and uses this to construct a case for social responsibility.

What *Environments* does on a small scale is replicate the processes of doing and using social studies. It provides input data from a variety of sources, sets tasks which involve engaging with those data and demonstrates how those data can be used to construct a social studies interpretation. It is through the 'main ideas' sections that the social studies is created and it is through these that readers and users of the book can see where they are being led to. Control over the kinds of meanings encoded in texts of this type is essential for transforming commonsense understandings into social studies. This applies most overtly at the level of genre and more subtly at the level of grammar.

In terms of genre the 'main ideas' texts are similar to the types of texts found in traditional textbooks (discussed later). However, the principal difference between these materials and traditional textbooks is the orientation towards 'doing' social studies/science as opposed simply to being confronted with the output of what social scientists have done in a prepackaged form. Students gain more power to critique and to use texts if the methods by which generalisations are formed and the mechanisms used to turn them into text are made more visible to them. This is superior to the simple presentation of 'facts'.

What Makes 'Good' Social Studies Materials for Primary School?

Based on the discussion of this case study text, several recommendations as to what makes 'good' social studies materials can be offered.

First, some kind of technical framework is inescapable for interpreting social studies data. You cannot really say that you are 'doing' social studies without it. And it is best if this framework is developed progressively over time and is constantly related back to the data rather than presented as a *fait accompli*. Through this process it is possible for students to see where the technicality comes from and to see where their research is leading. As well as being presented with a technical discourse they can, hopefully, see the purpose of that discourse.

Second, assuming that texts which contain a high degree of grammatical metaphor will be difficult, if not impossible, for relatively young children to understand, then texts which contain a low degree of grammatical metaphor will be preferable. Given also that a certain amount of abstraction is inescapable if one wants to generalise and interpret, and that abstraction is often achieved through grammatical metaphor, then those texts which show explicitly the congruent grammatical origins of the grammatical metaphor will be best. That is, texts in which it is possible to trace the grammatical origins of terms, thus making access to them explicit for readers, should be preferable to those in which it is not.

Third, given the relatedness of process and product, curriculum materials which involve both in a way which, through their use, shows how they are related will be best.

Fourth, awareness of how the language of the materials is working to construct specialised knowledge should provide teachers with additional criteria to apply in selecting materials.

Language and Social Studies Pedagogy

From this detailed analysis of the language of social studies, we now want to move on to a more general discussion of the different ways in which language is used in social studies, and in particular, the ways in which different approaches to teaching social studies will usually expose students to different types of text and create different types of expectations on students as makers of written texts. This broader view of the language of social studies is necessary because the teaching of social studies has changed dramatically in the past few decades, as, for that matter, has the teaching of literacy. Or, at least, teacher trainers and the people who make syllabuses for school systems would have us believe that things have changed a lot.

To take the case of teaching literacy first, the old spelling lists, traditional grammar, cloze activities and so on seem to have been discarded. We might call this older approach to becoming literate 'traditional' curriculum. In its place, there has arisen a new 'process' approach. The emphasis now is not on the formalities and rules of language conventions, for example, but on student motivation and the processes of self expression through written language. Writing for a purpose and enjoying writing is much more important than old-fashioned ideas of 'correctness'. If students write because they have something to say, this itself, together with the need to be understood, will lead them to pick up language conventions in use rather than through learning by rote. The key idea now is that learning needs to be 'natural' and 'child-centred' — not forced by authority structures, either in the institution of the school or the rules of language, or the need to repeat rigidly correct answers to succeed in examinations. This new kind of literacy pedagogy we might call 'progressivist'.

A very similar sort of change has occurred in the teaching of social studies. The traditional social studies curriculum was very much concerned with students learning social facts. It was authoritarian in its pedagogy. 'Learn these facts because they are good for you,' shouted syllabus and teacher and textbook, 'and see how well you can regurgitate them in the examination.' Through the sixties and seventies, however, a new approach to social studies began to emerge, also child-centred like the new approaches to writing. Again, the concern was with process rather than the formalities of content. Facts now seemed less important than the process of being a social scientist, of learning by inquiry, of the students finding things out for themselves about their social world. This would be the basis for producing knowledge and learning experiences truly relevant to the child, rather than their having to learn irrelevant, dry facts by rote for the examination.

Put side by side, the changes in social studies pedagogy and the changes in literacy pedagogy in the subject of English or 'language' add up to a major educational paradigm shift, from traditional to progressivist pedagogy. If we are to explain and handle many of the pressures and expectations placed upon teachers, both as social studies teachers and as language teachers, we have to understand the dimensions of the paradigm shift over the course of the lifetimes of many parents (and teachers' lifetimes for that matter). Parents might complain: 'Why can't my children spell? Why don't schools test spelling the way they used to?' Or they might ask 'Why don't my children learn facts and dates in social studies the way I used to?'. Perhaps we might want to be able to defend progressivist pedagogy. But if we do, we have to have a thorough knowledge of traditional pedagogy. It is also important to be aware, however, that there are incisive critiques of progressivism. Sometimes these come from the powerful lobbyists who recommend a return to traditional curriculum, often spearheading their attack with the slogan 'back to basics'. Other times, educational critics of progressivism do not necessarily advocate a return to the past, but nevertheless argue that there are significant shortcomings in progressivist curriculum. This is the position we will take. We have to know the pedagogical assumptions in both traditional and progressivist paradigms and the consequences of these assumptions for social studies, for language and for the role of language in social studies.

The paradigm shift in literacy learning and learning social studies is not just an interesting convergence. It is a central issue for the intersection of these two issues when it comes to the question of the role of language in the subject social studies. Our concern here is not with literacy in the subject of English or 'language' but with language in a subject which seems to be simply oriented to social issues and social facts — social studies. We use the word 'seems', not because social studies isn't about a real world of social issues and social facts outside of the classroom. It certainly is. But, as well as this, social studies is a figment of the language that happens in the classroom and in written social studies texts. Another way of saying this is that social studies is just as much the product of its own discourse as a discipline as it is a picture of the social world. It follows that every moment of teaching or learning social studies is also a moment of language teaching or learning. If we are to teach social studies well, we have to be good language teachers in every social studies lesson. Some of the details of the linguistic technology of social studies we have already described in some detail. We are now going to discuss the language consequences of different approaches to teaching the discipline of social studies, and the different text types that these approaches typically use.

Texts That Tell 'Facts' and 'Truths'

In the days of traditional curriculum, social studies was a matter of 'covering' subject matter. Students typically 'did' the states and the rivers of Australia in Year 4, for example. And one of the Year 6 topics in New South Wales in the fifties and sixties was 'Other Lands and Peoples', a topic which started with a study of the relationship of the 'Mother Country' to the members of the British Commonwealth of Nations. This is what the 1959 draft of the New South Wales Department of Education's Primary Social Studies Syllabus said the students should be 'covering' in this part of the course:

> Other Lands and Peoples
> This section should aim ... to give an appreciation of our British heritage and some understanding of the growing interdependence of nations.
> A. The Commonwealth of Nations: An introductory talk on the Commonwealth of Nations leading to the identification on the map of the United

The Language of Social Studies

Kingdom, Canada, New Zealand, South Africa, India, Pakistan, Ceylon, Malaya, Ghana and other nations that have become members of the Commonwealth.
(1) Our Mother Country.
    (a) Basic geography. A knowledge of the map: the general build, climate, principal industries and cities of the United Kingdom . . .
    (b) Cultural features: A description of two or three of the following interesting places and historic buildings: Universities of Oxford, Cambridge and Edinburgh; Stratford-on-Avon; Buckingham Palace, Westminster Abbey, Tower of London, St Paul's Cathedral, the Houses of Parliament; Edinburgh Castle, Carnarvon Castle. (New South Wales Department of Education 1959)

The tone was factual ('the general build, climate, principal industries and cities of the United Kingdom'). The purpose of the subject was to transmit contents and attitudes from the evidently all-knowing people behind the syllabus to unknowing children in the tutelage of the education system ('to give an appreciation of . . .'). And in a country a decade into a mass immigration program largely drawing on peoples of non-English-speaking background, it was a curriculum that was profoundly biased in cultural terms ('our British heritage'). But from the perspective of the nineties when it often seems process is all, perhaps the most remarkable thing about looking back at a document like this is just how little concern there seemed to be with the processes of learning, and with teaching methodology or pedagogy. It was as if students were empty vessels into which the education system could simply pour facts about the British Commonwealth and moral homilies about 'our British heritage'. Social studies teaching was almost exclusively about imparting social content.

In the same spirit, textbooks followed the syllabus, chapter and verse. The teacher almost need not have read the syllabus because the textbook 'covered' all the things that were supposed to happen in social studies. Here is an extract from G.T. Spaull's textbook for New South Wales schools, 'covering' the first bit of the 'Other Lands and Peoples' section of the syllabus:

Section IV
Other Lands and Peoples
Part 1
The Mother Country
Study 1
A Talk on the British Commonwealth of Nations

The British Commonwealth consists of a collection of countries, peopled by men and women differing in language, colour, religion and their way of life. Yet, although scattered about the world and divided by the oceans, they are held together by the same ideals — love of freedom and justice, a willingness to help one another in time of need and a desire to live in harmony and peace.

How, one might ask, has this peace been preserved in a world that has been so often torn by armed conflict? The answer is that Great Britain has, step by step, in the past, granted to the various peoples that were under her control, when the claim was made, the right to govern themselves.

The various nations belonging to the British Commonwealth are shown in the map on page 114. Some of them have already been mentioned, others will be dealt with more fully in later studies. Nearly all of them owe their present prosperity to the energy and enterprise of the British in the past. (Spaull 1960, p. 247)

The subheading, with its metaphor of motherhood, is a good indicator of the social 'answer' to any question there might be about the structure and nature of the British Commonwealth. Indeed, chapter headings and subheadings usually baldly state areas of fact or social answers of one sort or another. Fact: 'The various nations belonging to the British Commonwealth are shown in the map on page 114.' A social answer (following a question which is purely rhetorical in that a negative answer about the harmonious consequences of British imperialism is out of the question): 'The answer is that Great Britain has, step by step, in the past, granted to the various peoples that were under her control, when the claim was made, the right to govern themselves. . . Nearly all of them owe their present prosperity to the energy and enterprise of the British in the past.'

Finally, there was always a test to determine which facts and socially appropriate answers students had successfully imbibed. Gregory and Wicks wrote a textbook covering the same ground as Spaull's, and this is how they finished the section on the British Commonwealth (leaving a line between each question for the students to give relatively straightforward 'factual' answers):

Assignment
1. Where were the first English colonies made?
2. Who is often called the 'Father of British Colonization'?
3. What did all of the British colonies form throughout the world at one time?
4. In whose reign did these colonies reach their greatest height?
5. What right has since been given to many of these colonies?
6. Into what have all the British countries formed themselves now?
7. What do the British countries celebrate each year?
8. When is it celebrated?
9. What person is looked upon as head of this big family of nations?
10. Which nation is the mother nation? (Gregory and Wicks 1959)

Thus, traditional social studies curriculum was content-laden, and the contents of the texts with which children worked were dictated by the syllabus. This added up to a pedagogy of social prescription. The nature and purpose of social studies were determined by truths that were defined centrally, by the education system as an instrument of government. These truths were to be accepted and learnt by all. In this centralised curriculum structure, the teacher was locked, by the inspection system, and ultimately in the secondary school, by external examinations, into working to the same content and the same implicit pedagogy as the syllabus and the textbook. At the bottom of this pedagogy was the idea that the story of society could be told through just one, universalistic narrative (including the bit about the British Commonwealth of Nations and the virtuous historical role of the 'mother country'). The very idea of 'fact', quite strongly in evidence at the examination stage, reinforced this idea of universal truthfulness. Who can argue with a 'fact', after all? There was certainly no concession to students' diversity — be that the result of varying cultures of social class or gender or ethnicity, for example. What did 'our British heritage' mean if you were of Italian background?

As the sixties wore on, a progressivist critique of traditional curriculum became more and more insistent. Students might be able to learn facts and social values by rote to succeed in examinations, so the progressivist advocates of a new social studies argued, but this is hardly the best way of learning. Indeed, the whole emphasis of traditional curriculum on transmitting content had been at the expense of children learning how to learn or the processes involved in being a social scientist. Although they might be able to regurgitate the right answers about the 'mother country', this would hardly assist along a path where they might eventually become social scientists who were capable of making their own generalisations about the relationship of cultures. Indeed, far from the possibility of ever becoming a social scientist with an inquiring mind or ever being able to think creatively about social matters, the real message of traditional pedagogy was that students should be the passive receptors of knowledge whose 'factualness' and 'truthfulness' had been determined by someone else. It was a pedagogy, in other words, that actually worked against autonomous, critical or creative thought. Students of traditional social studies would not learn how to make their own knowledge, nor would they be getting an education that would ultimately give them the skills to innovate and adapt to a society that prides itself on constant technical and social change. If they did turn out to be innovators and adaptors, it was despite social studies rather than because of it.

As well as being less than useful because of its static, transmission model of pedagogy, traditional curriculum's universalism was more helpful to some students than to others. For some students, questions about the 'mother country' made sense. For others, getting this answer 'right' did not come so naturally. And more generally, the whole culture of schooling under the regime of traditional curriculum advantaged some students over others. Middle-class students, for example, were more culturally attuned to schooling as a competitive game where the rewards and credentials were worth struggling for. Formal examinations where facts had to be learnt by rote were a better measure of how well students had mastered examination technique than of what they really knew. Was it the case that whole schools in certain communities ended up 'failing' for lack of 'ability', or was there something wrong with a pedagogy which worked well for students from communities with particular sorts of cultural proclivities and not for others? Indeed, the ideas of 'failing' and 'ability' were rather convenient because they slated the problem back to the individual student rather than to the culture of the school and its pedagogy.

These broad philosophical questions might seem a long way away from the issue of the different types of text that students might encounter as they set about doing their social studies. And, you might respond, the days of traditional social studies teaching have well and truly gone. But it is still very important to have an understanding of the way traditional curriculum uses texts. First, many factual texts that students might encounter in social studies operate in the same way as traditional social studies textbooks. Indeed, there are still a lot of pedagogically traditional social studies textbooks around, notwithstanding the rhetoric of the new social studies syllabuses which demand student inquiry and the process approach. Second, texts never stand alone. They are always set into a curriculum frame that encourages one sort of a reading or another. Traditional texts do not have to be used in a traditional way, and the best teachers probably never used them that way. In other words, texts that would fit happily into a traditional social studies pedagogy might prove very useful provided they are not framed in the classroom in traditional ways.

To take the first point, when introducing a text into a social studies class, you need to ask, does this text, in the fashion of traditional curriculum, set out to 'tell' students social 'facts' and social or moral truths in such a way that they appear indisputable? It is not only old-fashioned textbooks that do this, but many other 'information sources' such as non-fiction information books and encyclopedias. In the natural sciences, the idea of 'fact' does have a reasonable amount of credibility, although even there 'fact' is to a significant degree a product of human interpretation and scientific theory. The facts of the world of Newtonian physics are very different from the facts of the world of Einsteinian physics. But in the social world, the notion of 'fact', or the idea that there is a single indisputable truth, is even harder to sustain. To a much greater extent than the natural sciences, the social sciences are coloured by the cultural and political perspectives of the scientist who produces the text. So, the first question one has to ask of any text that deals with the social world is 'what is the perspective of the author and does he or she present facts as truths which are in reality influenced by their own perspective?' Just what was the perspective of the author of the text about 'our British heritage', for example?

This is not to say that texts which pretend just to be factual and to tell one true social story should not be used in social studies. Indeed, it might even be a good idea to bring traditional textbooks into the classroom and use them in social studies, and this can be done without reverting to traditional curriculum. This brings us to our second point. The way social studies texts will be read is very much determined by the type of curriculum frame into which they are put. The purpose of traditional curriculum was to examine what students had learnt in terms of one, correct factual answer — to the question of 'our heritage', for example. This was the pedagogical frame for the Spaull text. But if we present students with this same extract from the Spaull text, and set it alongside a short story about a family of Italian background, the old text is framed in an entirely different way. It is evident that it is a product of the cultural intentions of the text's author (such as the cultural assimilation of non-English speaking background immigrants) or his monocultural view of the world. And there is some useful information we can extract about a time when Australia felt more British because of its historical links through the British Commonwealth. In other words, in a curriculum where texts are framed in such a way that students will not expect to find immediately 'correct', 'factual' answers staring them in the face every time they read a page, Spaull's social studies text might be a very useful thing. A curriculum which frames factual texts in this sort of way will assiduously ask questions rather than give answers. An important part of this process will involve the teacher exposing the students to texts which present different interpretations of the same phenomenon. So, don't throw out old books in order to expose students only to those that are 'ideologically sound' or 'politically correct'. And, if you want your students to become critical thinkers and good social scientists, do not impose 'correct information' on students in the manner of traditional curriculum and its textbooks; present them with different points of view and give them the opportunity to develop their own social scientific interpretations.

The most basic raw material for the framing of texts, moreover, should be the experiences of the students themselves. Texts do not simply communicate the conscious intentions or unconscious assumptions of the author. People do not read them for what they actually say. Sometimes readers resist what they are reading. Some student readers might get angry with a text about 'our British heritage' because it leaves them and their families out of the picture. Female student readers of a text that portrays men in traditionally male jobs and women in a domestic role might feel at least uncomfortable with the text, especially if their mothers are engineers or bus drivers. The way students read a text in social studies, then, might be as much a product of their interests or background as it is a reflection of what is actually in the text. This is an invaluable resource for a social studies curriculum which puts into question the simple factualness or truthfulness of social texts. In other words, students' experience should be used to help them develop a critical interpretative frame for reading social studies texts. Ask the students the following questions: 'Does this text make sense to you?' 'Do you agree?' 'What do you think?' 'What was the author trying to say?' 'Why?' 'How was he or she saying it?' 'Were you convinced or unconvinced?'

Student Inquiry and the Texts of Progressivist Curriculum

Armed with some very impressive educational arguments, progressivists have spent the last couple of decades trying to put a new shape to social studies. They said that the old textbooks had to be thrown away, never to be used again, because these books taught in ways that worked against students becoming creative thinkers or good social scientists. The key word for this new type of curriculum was 'process'. Social studies was no longer to be a matter of learning lots of content off by rote. Instead, students were to learn the processes involved in being a social scientist —

learning how to make one's own social knowledge, and learning how to learn rather than being told what to learn.

The new, progressivist social studies syllabuses that were put into place from about the mid-seventies could hardly be more different from the old, traditional syllabuses. Here is an extract from the introduction to the New South Wales Department of Education's 1983 Social Studies Syllabus:

> A unit structure offers an effective way of planning learning experiences in Social Studies. A unit should flow from the framework of the school social studies plan and be expanded to include:
> focus;
> objectives;
> questions;
> content samples;
> resources;
> evaluation strategies;
> teaching and learning activities
>
> from which inquiry will emerge. Teachers will select an approach to suit the needs of the group.
>
> Focus questions used to explore the content samples from the Personal, Social and Environmental areas encourage inquiry. Children are assisted to participate in framing the inquiry by co-operative planning of some contributing questions by the teacher. . . .
>
> In selecting and formulating focus questions consideration should be given to the interests and abilities of the children and the resources available. (New South Wales Department of Education 1983)

Whereas the old syllabus had been a list of social contents, the new syllabus had no content in it at all — no listing of areas of facts that had to be covered year by year. The inquiry syllabus laid out some general pedagogical principles about processes of learning and curriculum planning and implementation, but the content was up to the teacher. Content would develop according to the needs and interests of students, negotiated according to criteria of relevance to the particular students and school community. The old, universalist, singular storyline could no longer be imposed.

Indeed, with students as active investigators of their own social worlds, it was obvious now that there could be no single, true answer to any problem. Knowledge was a product of the individual perspective, cultural circumstances, subjective interests or personal needs. Active student learning based on principles of relevance, student motivation, student interests and inquiry learning — invariably multiple — superseded the old social monologues of traditional curriculum. At best, traditional curriculum had been truly relevant for only a few students. Relevance for progressivism really meant many different relevances, differing according to particular local community or cultural needs and interests.

The only way to realise this sort of relevance was school-based curriculum, which is why the new progressivist syllabuses did not even attempt to suggest content. This is why there could be no 'facts' that had to be learnt or cultural 'truths' that all students should end up accepting.

School-based curriculum (rather a misnomer in practice, actually teacher-based curriculum) started with the students' own experiences.

And with this shift of curriculum planning and design away from centralised authorities and onto teachers came a whole new institutional structure and set of work practices, not to mention a new jargon: 'inservice' training, release time to write 'programs', curriculum 'consultancy', curriculum 'resource centres' (in lieu of the textbook) and 'seeding grants' for innovative school-based curriculum development. The following is one such piece of progressivist curriculum, an example of what began to happen in social studies in the post textbook era. It is a social studies program for Year 7, developed at Riverside Girls' High School in 1984. The program was developed as the result of a 'seeding grant' for multicultural education, and because it was considered one of the best examples of the new social studies, it was published by the New South Wales Department of Education. Although a junior secondary school unit, it illustrates exactly the sort of program that the progressivist social studies syllabuses for primary social studies since the mid-seventies anticipated.

Unit 1: What is Our Heritage?
How has Ethnic Diversity Contributed to Our Heritage?
(Time allowed: 4 weeks)

KNOWLEDGE
Impact of different groups on
- food
- architecture/housing
- products
- handicrafts
- clothing/costumes
- music
- language
- family traditions
- festivals
- famous people

SKILLS
Group assignment — case study

ATTITUDES/VALUES
Appreciation that Australia's heritage is partly an outcome of ethnic diversity.

RELATED CONCEPTS
tradition
diversity
conserving
culture

TEACHING STRATEGIES
- Case studies — group work, lecturettes
- Carnivale Riverside — full form activity, including music, food, clothing, customs and other cultural activities
- Involvement of the school community

RESOURCES
Multicultural Education Materials kit (South Australia)
The Australians: Living in a Multicultural Society — kit

This program was all that individual teachers had to go by to teach social studies for four weeks. Compare this to the days of the old textbook which was in the students' hands. In the progressivist curriculum, the teacher immediately has an enormous job to do in giving substance to the program, and on top of this the issues are enormously complex, subtle and contested, at least in comparison with Spaull's uncontroversial presentation of the Anglo storyline. Perhaps ironically, and despite the pretensions to openness and inquiry in progressivist pedagogy, the social answer is just as preordained as it was in Spaull's time; a different answer maybe, but just as dogmatic: 'Appreciation that Australia's heritage is partly an outcome of ethnic diversity.' And also ironically, the sort of claim this sort of program makes on teachers' lives — now they are curriculum writers as well as teachers — all too frequently leads them into the photocopier curriculum in which old copies of textbooks like Spaull's are dragged out of the dusty recesses of the book cabinet and issued to students in bits.

Progressivism, moreover, was nothing if not ambitious. Perhaps it was unrealistically ambitious. And to make matters worse, it has run into hard times lately, in a very practical way. The structures intended to support teachers to make their own curriculum have been removed. If one takes a bleak view of the scene, one could argue that a poorly supported progressivism has led to social studies at best returning to the traditional model with its traditional discourse and at worst becoming eclectic and fragmented.

Assuming this kind of desperate or even rearguard traditionalism does not occur, what are the possible language demands of an eclectic, activity-based social studies? As we argued earlier in this chapter, there is a very significant difference between commonsense language and technical language about the social world. It is the job of social science not just to help students to know things about the social world, but to get them to think about the social world through a technical language capable of producing characteristically social scientific understandings which can do different things for us than commonsense understandings.

It is quite possible that the unit outlined above could have the students actively doing a lot of things that seem eminently multicultural — such as the 'full form' Carnivale experience that all too easily characterises a simplistic spaghetti and polka multiculturalism — without ever exposing them to the peculiar discourse that makes social science a different sort of linguistic event from chatting with one's friends whilst enjoying ethnic food or wearing national dress. Not that being with one's friends enjoying ethnic food or wearing national dress is a bad thing, nor that the language at work there is itself uncomplicated or uninteresting. It is just that, by itself, this is not social science. The unit outline lists as 'related concepts' the terms 'tradition', 'diversity', 'conserving' and 'culture', but beyond demonstrating to us that the students will be exposed to a lot of these empirical things, the program gives us no idea of how these will be

The Language of Social Studies

developed or technicalised as concepts into the linguistic–cognitive framework that is social science.

There are some indications of the sorts of texts that students might be exposed to in doing this unit of work. They might dip into the South Australian Department of Education's *Multicultural Education Materials* kit, for example, or *The Australians: Living in a Multicultural Society*. Kits like these, however, are almost always enormously complex texts, which move between the technical language of social science (a language, incidentally, which proves almost impenetrable for students as it is not introduced in an explicit or systematic way by the kit), recounts of family life, narratives such as traditional fairy tales, procedures such as recipes, and texts which involve subtle relation of visual and diagrammatic representations to the written word. If social studies teachers do not see themselves simultaneously as language teachers, if they do not discuss explicitly the various genres of text from which students might be expected to extract information of a social scientific nature, if they do not involve students in an examination of the structure of these different genres and link these linguistic–structural differences to differential social purposes, then many students will find it difficult to read the texts they encounter in the kits.

There is one indication of the sort of written text that students might be expected to generate as part of this unit: a 'Group assignment — case study'. Presumably this text would be synthetic of the students' various multicultural experiences, in much the same way that social science is characteristically synthetic of human experience. But there is no evidence that the students would be presented with models of synthetic texts that might be called 'case studies' or given explicit instruction about what a 'case study' is as a characteristic genre of social science, and how and why it differs from a story or a procedure or a map, for example. One suspects, in fact, that the injunction to produce a case study without explicit instruction involves such incredibly difficult expectations that students will need to have fancy headings and colour in their pictures really well to get good marks, but will still learn little of how a 'case study' works in the discourse of social studies. In an ironical sense, Spaull's textbook gave students more help to develop a language of social science. All the time students had a model in front of them (not too ambitious; there was just the one genre at work), which they could copy into their own words to get good marks. This is not to defend either the language of social science in Spaull's book (a dogmatic monologue), or copying as a pedagogy, but to point out that despite its high ideals and proper critique of traditional curriculum, a progressivism which gets students doing lots of things very actively can achieve even less in terms of the linguistic and cognitive demands of the discipline.

Take history, for example, a subdiscipline of social studies at the primary school level. We have seen the demise of old, unilinear, singly authored and singularly authoritative texts like Spaull's. Now, history is a matter of problems to be solved from the perspective of individual student historians, with their own perspectives, working with primary source documents. But however much one might be opposed to the form and contents of traditional curriculum, its virtue was at least to speak a theorising, technicalising language of social science. Process curriculum, in its very nature, need only be fragmented or eclectic because the aim of learning is to be an historian (the process of immersing oneself in the empirical matter of the past) rather than learning how to present a coherent world view through the discourse of history.

Progressivism, moreover, overstresses process at the expense of content. How could you expect to become an historian (the process) unless you can deal with a content by learning a methodology with which to handle that content? The preoccupation with process is at the expense of disciplined approaches to handling contents. This discipline more than anything else involves synthesis through learning the technical discourses of social science.

Then, when we come to the progressivist claim that diversified curriculum meets students' various needs and interests, we run into still more problems. That curriculum should be relevant is a disarming truism. Authoritarian, centralised, traditional curriculum indeed proved to be profoundly irrelevant to the needs and interests of most students. In fact, as we have already argued, for much of the time it was simply an institutional exercise in 'failing' particular social groups and then rationalising this as lack of individual 'ability'. But creating curricula which are diverse from school to school can end up being just as inequitable. Under the decentralised regime of school-based curriculum development, curriculum is devised in the name of 'relevance' in such a way that students in some schools, for example, get a multiculturalism of food and dance on the grounds that these are more appropriate for 'less able' or 'disadvantaged' students. Meanwhile, in more affluent, less linguistically and culturally diverse schools, school life goes on, perhaps with old fashioned textbooks and less influenced by progressivism, involving harder options which involve more difficult skills, skills which may even culminate in students writing reports or essays. One justification that is often offered for the new social studies course in disadvantaged schools is that 'relevant' programs will avoid placing the stigma of failure on students. But in reality the students in these schools do not end up being successful in terms either of the intellectual skills that social science learning is intended to develop or in the terms that will ultimately be measured by the conventional mechanisms for school credentialling that determine, to a large extent, life chances.

Linguistically too, progressivist social studies often places on students different expectations from those of traditional social studies. In much the same way that process writing encourages students to speak of personal experience, so progressivist social studies attempts to motivate students through personal involvement. When it comes to writing an extended piece of text, instead of writing a report on some matter of historical concern, it might be something like: 'Imagine you are ... [a Roman Centurion/an Aboriginal person experiencing the arrival of the first white people where you live/a soldier at Gallipoli].' There is nothing wrong with this sort of activity, but if the only generic expectations placed upon students involve the generation of recount or personal narrative, then students will never be able to generate the texts that are more characteristic of social science as a discipline or engage effectively with texts that are socially analytical. For example, students will not learn how to read or use grammatical metaphor which is a crucial part of technical languages.

To conclude, there is no denying that traditional curriculum is inefficient, discriminatory, boring and irrelevant to our society. The project of school reform is not simply to open traditional curriculum to a broader base. This would not only be very difficult, but a waste of resources. Yet, ironically, this would probably be more helpful than progressivism often is. Progressivism often ducks the educational issue for disadvantaged students. It reproduces educational inequity through deceptive, supposedly democratic arguments. All too frequently, 'needs', 'interests' and 'relevance' mean lowering expectations and not attempting to initiate students into the discourses of 'success', and thus attempting to avoid the invidious duty of failing students. It is centred on the self-expression of the individual child, which in practice restricts the genres of writing students produce. And in its own particular ways it is probably much more inefficient than traditional curriculum ever was, with teachers everywhere reinventing the same wheel in order to go through the pseudodemocratic ritual of school-based curriculum making.

So, having said all this, what can be done?

Framing Texts in Social Studies

As a way of working towards a concrete solution to the educational dilemmas that have emerged in the past few decades, we will now discuss the Social Literacy Project, a materials development project in which we have been involved, either as researchers (Wignell) or developers/researchers (Cope and Kalantzis). The goal of Social Literacy was to develop a social studies curriculum which addressed sensitive social issues newly considered to be crucial in education (such as multiculturalism, non-sexism and Aboriginal studies), and at the same time to come up with a working solution to the impasse between traditional and progressivist pedagogies. Our aim was to bring together the content in the new areas of social concern and the ideals of inquiry learning, without losing sight of intellectual rigour and academic skills.

Our starting point was the reality that we have already described, that traditional style textbooks, whilst being readily available, were not always relevant to the needs of all students. But school-based curriculum development tended to be fragmentary and often involved a slippage in educational goals. We wanted to bridge this gap between traditional and progressivist curriculum by producing materials that were cheap, accessible and easy to use, which included concrete learning strategies, and which emphasised academic skills (as did traditional curriculum) but which at the same time incorporated the new social issues, inquiry pedagogy and openness to locally relevant study (as did progressivist curriculum).

In terms of social studies methodology and framework, the Social Literacy materials set out to focus on social concepts. This meant that, as the materials are conceptually oriented (for example, 'What is community?'), rather than content oriented (for example, 'Who are the members of our community?'), teachers can refill the units with locally relevant content. The content to be found in each unit is only presented as a general example of teaching strategy. The core of the materials is the framework of concepts and the focus questions through which they are developed. Substantial content is simply introduced by way of example. New teaching methods and ways of addressing sensitive social issues in schools are best introduced by example. This is in order to give substance to the otherwise daunting idealism of the new syllabuses and social policy statements.

Not only were the Social Literacy curriculum materials innovatory in their approach, but the methods used in their making attempted to break new ground, too. Instead of commercially produced textbooks or school-based curriculum, the Social Literacy materials were developed through an extended process of consultation with a group of teachers, curriculum consultants and academics, followed by research and drafting, trialling in a variety of schools, and redrafting in the light of the trialling experience, using the feedback of students as well as teachers. Thus the initiative has been decentralised, but with systems support for substantial teacher-release for drafting and trial co-ordination.

All along, one of the main focuses has been on making curriculum change practical. The Social Literacy Project represented an attempt to educate the educators to new social issues and pedagogical techniques through responding to their immediate needs in the classroom. This is an important complement to the policy-syllabus/consultation model which, alone, is inadequate, inefficient and often counter-productive because it tends to spell out abstract principles rather than provide 'hands-on' materials like the old textbooks.

Beside principles of openness to local or particular cultural experience and inquiry learning, the Social Literacy Project also attempted to take a structured and explicit approach to learning. This operates at two main levels: a micro-level (the teaching/learning strategy within a lesson or over several lessons) and a macro-level (learning of social concepts structured over a year or years).

First, at a micro-level, the Social Literacy Project has developed the following teaching/learning sequence:

1. Focus question
2. Consider input
3. Analysis — critical activities relating to the input
4. Main ideas — concept naming
5. Investigation — social inquiry applying concept(s) to broader social context
6. Reflection — evaluation

We will move through each of these six steps, explaining what each involves, and contrasting it with the methods of both traditional and progressivist approaches.

At the first stage in the teaching/learning sequence, students are introduced to the point of the section in the form of a focus question. This can only be answered through abstraction and concept generalisation and will be addressed throughout subsequent steps in the sequence. An example of a focus question is 'What is community?' Traditional curriculum, in contrast, begins characteristically with a statement, in the form perhaps of a chapter heading, for example 'Community Life in Australia', or the teacher's introduction, 'Today we are going to learn about . . .'. Progressivist curriculum begins with an empirical question answerable in relation to personal experience and through the medium of recount or personalised narrative. An example is, 'What makes up my community?'

The next step in the Social Literacy sequence is an input to consider. This is never presented as a factual answer to the focus question (in the fashion of an inverted 'comprehension') but as a problem for the students to work with. This input varies considerably according to its medium (visual/textual) and linguistic genre. It could be a problem situation, a moral dilemma, conflicting points of view, factual information, an historical document, photos or drawings or a combination of different text types. Moreover, as the exercise is concept rather than content oriented, the inputs can either be used as they stand or serve as examples of the sort of material that might lead students to the concept generalisation. The input in other words could be drawn from students and local community experience. Traditional textbooks, on the other hand, simply present the author's monologue, with a closed, singular and opinionated content. In progressivist curriculum, teachers use whatever they can that will tell the students about the local community: maps, visuals, talks by community members or perhaps an excursion. Perhaps the teacher may photocopy some pieces of text and hand them out.

At the next point in the Social Literacy sequence, students work critically with the input they have received, analysing the problems it raises and having to make concept generalisations to solve those problems. One such generalisation might be: 'Communities satisfy basic human needs. One need they satisfy is the need for food. In our community we buy food in shops . . .' Meanwhile, in traditional curriculum students regurgitate the facts as presented in the authorial monologue, for example 'The Australian community is fed successfully because we have mechanised agriculture and because modern transport ensures quick distribution to shops.' Meanwhile, students of progressivist curriculum are recounting the details of what they found in their community: 'When we visited our local shopping centre we saw a Lebanese shop selling Lebanese bread, a Vietnamese shop . . .'

Then comes the 'main ideas' step in the Social Literacy sequence. This fourth step gives the concept being developed a technical name for the purposes of the unfolding macro-sequence. An example is: 'Humans live in groups and share the task of satisfying their basic human needs together. These groups are called communities.' Often the students have already been using this name in their analysis (step 3) of the input (step 2) in its commonsense vernacular form. There is no equivalent explicit step (the point of the whole exercise, though not an answer that can simply be learnt off by heart) in either traditional or progressivist pedagogies.

Step 5 in the Social Literacy sequence is investigation which involves active social research (being an historian, sociologist, anthropologist or geographer) and applying the key concepts, as much as possible to the students' immediate social environment. Part of this involves reconstructing the text types modelled in the inputs through application to the students' own social context. Students might construct a questionnaire to elicit information or write up a report, for example. At this point in the traditional academic curriculum knowledge is left abstract and distant, reproducing by copying (whilst trying not to appear to be copying) the textbook writer's singular narrative in the assignments or essays, and also copying the author's linguistic technology of abstraction and distancing. At this point in progressivist curriculum, knowledge is left empirical and diverse. Students produce commonsense recounts of the complexity and multiplicity of everyday life. There appear to be no overall ordering principles with which to comprehend society as a whole either at the level of social content analysis or at the level of the lexical and grammatical resources for generalisation.

Finally there's assessment and evaluation. In the Social Literacy reflection step, students assess themselves and teachers evaluate whether students can use the concept that was the point of the original focus question. The answer to this is not 53 per cent or 78 per cent. Essentially, for any individual student it is simply whether or not they can use the concept ably. This ultimately reflects the success of the teaching strategy in reaching the student. The reflection step involves two main questions. First, can the concept be reapplied? For example, when a student sees a community, other than the empirical, exemplary communities that have been studied, will he or she be able to generalise that this, too, is a community? And, second, can the concept be defined, for example 'A community is . . .'? Apart from the case when an answer is rote-learnt, the second question, especially in the case of abstract social concepts, is particularly difficult. The first question — which elicits information about competent use — is more critical. An ability to define the term adequately might develop further down the road of concept development. Meanwhile, students of the traditional social science curriculum regurgitate facts in essays and do get 53 per cent or 78 per cent, and for reasons that more often relate to the hidden curriculum of grammatical resources than the number of facts they manage to remember. And in so far as the assessment is on facts, it measures exam technique more than it does useful substantive knowledge because, as the saying goes, things learnt off by heart one day are forgotten the next. The knowledge tested in such exams, in other words, is unlikely to be useful to the constant reworking of technical and social knowledge we have to go through in a lifetime or to actively reading society and participating in it. Progressivist curriculum, in contrast, feels some reticence about grading students and passing judgement upon them. At best it evaluates differential, relative success. But 90 per cent in 'communication skills' is not usefully comparable to 90 per cent in traditional English literature. Students of progressivist social science, moreover, are frequently marked subjectively, on 'presentation', for example, or on 'performance' in relation to 'ability'. Much of this is very patronising to children who would on the whole prefer the dignity of having their work taken seriously and carefully critically appraised.

This description has, of course, involved simplifying lines of paradigmatic division for the purpose of clear argument. We will now extend this mode of argument to look at macro-structure, or discipline structure over a year or number of years. Each year's program in the Social Literacy materials is structured around the development of a framework of concepts, and that overall structure is ordered around principles of moving from the concrete to the abstract, from mechanical analogies to social reality, from the simple to the complex and from minor subconcepts to major complex and abstract concepts. So a *community* is a *group* of *groups* of people. *Groups* have *parts* or *members* which *share* something in *common* and which are *related* or *connected*.

The concept of *group* can be introduced in the concrete by set work: classifying things according to *common* characteristics. Students work out what a group is and does. The concept of *connections* can also be understood through concrete analogy. Take something apart. How does it work? What does it need to work? It needs all its *parts* and these need to be *connected* properly.

Then we move on to the social-abstract. Take a sports team, family or school class, for example: Who are the *parts/members*? What do they *share* in *common*? How do they need to *connect/relate* for the *group* to work? *Roles, rules* and *relationships* are key ways of describing *group connections*. Then how do individuals and small *groups* form *communities*? The language for this last general, abstract social concept has by now been systematically developed.

In any Social Literacy unit a quick read of only the 'main ideas' step in the sequence, each time it comes up, tells you exactly what the unit is about. Each whole year or series of units ranges from a total of a few hundred words of text and six or ten concepts at Year 4 level to several thousand words and a broader range of concepts by mid-secondary school. In form, therefore, the Social Literacy materials are explicit and highly structured. Yet they are deliberately packaged in such a way that they can be reprogrammed. In each year they consist of a series of between five and eight separate small books or units. Each series of units is self-contained. However, a mix and match approach to the materials, within or across different series, does require very careful programming by the teacher to ensure that there is systematic concept development and not bewildering jumps to concepts for which no groundwork has been laid. The materials are also open to modification in another, more important sense, mentioned earlier: to filling the concept structure with whatever content seems locally relevant or inherently interesting to students and teachers.

At this same overall level, traditional curriculum is structured in some quite different ways. Traditional history, for example, is arranged by chronology and narrative structure, telling of abstract social processes as they move through time. Traditional history textbooks are highly structured around these principles, which are represented as principles of content (the abstract truth or point of the history itself) and through the medium of the hidden abstracting language described by Eggins *et al.* (1987).

Progressivist social science curriculum, on the other hand, is eclectic and fragmented. Teachers are expected to 'program' the school-based curriculum of teaching/learning activities. But on top of having the job of teaching it is hardly possible even to achieve the systematic chronological and hidden linguistic coherence of, for example, history taught through traditional textbooks. So, progressivist 'programming' often really means a collage of themes (The Ancient Egyptians, the Australian Aborigines, the local community), without there being any deeper conceptual and linguistic ordering principle. Perhaps the photocopier might provide students with something from a traditional textbook every now and then, but this does not even add up to be a sustained text model from which students could learn, albeit slowly and inefficiently, by repeated copying.

It should be clear from this description of the way in which Social Literacy attempts to tackle the problems of traditional and progressivist pedagogy that the social science disciplines are not just subjects or disciplines in their commonsense definition of contents. (History is about the past, geography about humans and the environment and social studies about human interaction.) They are simultaneously specific discourses or technologies for reading and acting upon the world. In the Social Literacy Project we have tried to be explicit about this.

Conclusion

Clearly then, there is no going back to a supposed golden age when 'basics' reigned supreme, in the form of traditional academic social science subject areas. Traditional curriculum was inefficient, inequitable and involved select students copying discipline discourses which were not necessarily relevant to the social world of the late twentieth century. Yet, in an intuitive but poorly articulated, unimaginative and regressive way, the 'back to basics' people are correct about the failure of progressivism. What has happened to 'standards'? Do they measure up to expectations? Are some groups of students still unduly disadvantaged? What are the consequences of progressivism's eclectic and *ad hoc* mode of operation? We have tried to answer some of these questions and to point to some practical ways in which we can build on the strengths of progressivism whilst bringing structure and intellectual rigour back into the task of becoming literate in the social sciences. In particular, and to return to the point with which we began, we need to view social science both as a process of interacting with the world and a product: discipline knowledge and the text type in which that information is characteristically embodied. 'Doing' social studies effectively, in other words, is integrally related to attaining control over certain types of text. As teachers, we need to encourage students to be active inquirers into their social worlds and social experience. At the same time we must have an explicit and structured approach to content: the discipline of social science is a framework of concepts with which to make a certain sort of scientific meaning out of the world and the genres that typically carry those meanings.

References

Cope, B. (1986) *Traditional Versus Progressivist Pedagogy*, Social Literacy Monograph 11, Common Ground, Sydney.
Cope, B. (1987) 'Losing the Australian Way: The rise of multiculturalism and the crisis of national identity. A study of changing popular conceptions of Australian history and the construction of new cultural identities through Schooling', PhD Thesis, Macquarie University.
Cope, B. (1988) 'Facing the challenge of "back to basics": An historical perspective', *Curriculum Perspectives*, Vol. 10, No. 2, May 1990, 20–33.
Eggins, S. Wignell, P. and Martin, J.R. (1987) 'The Discourse of History: Distancing the Recoverable Past', in *Working Papers in Linguistics*, No. 5, University of Sydney.
Gregory, J.B. and Wicks, J.M. (1959) *Effective Social Studies*, Horwitz-Martin, Sydney.
Halliday, M.A.K. (1985a) *An Introduction to Functional Grammar*, Edward Arnold, London.
Halliday, M.A.K. (1985b) *Spoken and Written Language*, Deakin University Press, Geelong, Victoria.
Kalantzis, M. and Cope, B. (1986) *Environments*, Social Literacy Series E, Unit E4, Common Ground, Sydney.
Kalantzis, M. and Cope, B. (1990) 'Literacy in the social sciences', in *Literacy for a Changing World*, F. Christie (ed.), Australian Council for Educational Research, Melbourne.
Kalantzis, M. and Wignell, P. (1988) *Explain, Argue, Discuss: Writing for Essays and Exams*, Common Ground, Sydney.
Literacy and Education Research Network (1988) 'The fundamentals of literacy: Where will *Writing K–12* take us?', Mimeo.
Martin, J.R. (1984) *Language, Register and Genre*, Deakin University Press, Geelong, Victoria.
Martin, J.R. and Rothery, J. (1980) *Writing Project Report No. 1*, Department of Linguistics, University of Sydney.
Martin, J.R. and Rothery, J. (1981) *Writing Project Report No. 2*, Department of Linguistics, University of Sydney.
Martin, J.R., Wignell, P, Eggins, S. and Rothery, J. (1988) 'Secret English', in *Language and Socialisation: Home and School*, eds L. Gerot, J. Oldenburg, and T. Van Leeuwen, Macquarie University, Sydney.
New South Wales Department of Education (1959) *Special Studies Syllabus for Primary Schools*, Sydney.
New South Wales Department of Education (1983) *Investigating Social Studies K–6*, Sydney.
Sale, C., Wilson, G. and Friedman, B. (1980) *Our Changing World*, Longman Cheshire, Melbourne.
Spaull, G.T. (1960) *Studies for Sixth Grade*, William Brooks, Sydney.

Wignell, P. (1987) 'In Your Own Words', in *Working Papers in Linguistics*, No. 5, Department of Linguistics, University of Sydney.

Wignell, P. (1988) *The Language of Social Literacy: A Linguistic Analysis of the Materials in Action in Years 7 and 8*, Social Literacy Monograph, No. 41, Common Ground, Sydney.

Wignell, P., Martin, J.R. and Eggins, S. (1987) 'The discourse of geography: organising and explaining the experiential world', in *Working Papers in Linguistics*, No. 5, Department of Linguistics, University of Sydney.

Appendix: Textbooks and Curriculum Materials

Cope, B. and Kalantzis, M. (1987a) *Individuals and Groups*, Social Literacy Series F: Unit F2, Common Ground, Sydney.

Cope, B. and Kalantzis, M. (1987b) *Structure and Function*, Social Literacy Series F: Unit F3, Common Ground, Sydney.

Gregory, J.B. and Wicks, J.M. (1959) *Effective Social Studies*, Horwitz-Martin, Sydney.

Kalantzis, M. and Cope, B. (1986a) *Connections*, Social Literacy Series E: Unit E2, Common Ground, Sydney.

Kalantzis, M. and Cope, B. (1986b) *Environments*, Social Literacy Series E: Unit E4, Common Ground, Sydney.

Kalantzis, M. and Cope, B. (1986c) *Families*, Social Literacy Series E: Unit E8, Common Ground, Sydney.

Kalantzis, M. and Cope, B. (1986d) *Groups*, Social Literacy Series E: Unit E1, Common Ground, Sydney.

Kalantzis, M. and Cope, B. (1986e) *Making Choices and Decisions*, Social Literacy Series E: Unit E5, Common Ground, Sydney.

Kalantzis, M. and Cope, B. (1986f) *Prejudice, Stereotypes and Racism*, Social Literacy Series E: Unit E7, Common Ground, Sydney.

Kalantzis, M. and Cope, B. (1986g) *The World and Me*, Social Literacy Series E: Unit E3, Common Ground, Sydney.

Kalantzis, M. and Cope, B. (1986h) *The World in Australia*, Social Literacy Series E: Unit E6, Common Ground, Sydney.

Kalantzis, M. and Cope, B. (1987a) *Communication*, Social Literacy Series F: Unit F4, Common Ground, Sydney.

Kalantzis, M. and Cope, B. (1987b) *Connections: Social Literacy Series E Teacher Support Book*, Common Ground, Sydney.

Kalantzis, M. and Cope, B. (1987c) *Cultural Differences*, Social Literacy Series F: Unit F6, Common Ground, Sydney.

Kalantzis, M. and Cope, B. (1987d) *Human Needs*, Social Literacy Series F: Unit F5, Common Ground, Sydney.

Kalantzis, M. and Cope, B. (1987e) *Learning and Culture*, Social Literacy Series F: Unit F1, Common Ground, Sydney.

Kalantzis, M. and Cope, B. (1989) *An Overview: Teaching/Learning Social Literacy*, Common Ground, Sydney.

Kalantzis, M. and Wignell, P. (1988) *Explain, Argue, Discuss: Writing for Essays and Exams*, Common Ground, Sydney.

Kalantzis, M., Cope, B., Coleman, A. and Leonhardt, M. (1987a) *Co-operation*, Social Literacy Series D: Unit D2, Common Ground, Sydney.

Kalantzis, M., Cope, B., Coleman, A. and Leonhardt, M. (1987b) *Communities*, Social Literacy Series D: Unit D6, Common Ground, Sydney.

Kalantzis, M., Cope, B., Coleman, A. and Leonhardt, M. (1987c) *Needing People*, Social Literacy Series D: Unit D1, Common Ground, Sydney.

Kalantzis, M., Cope, B., Coleman, A. and Leonhardt, M. (1987d) *Relationships*, Social Literacy Series D: Unit D3, Common Ground, Sydney.

Kalantzis, M., Cope, B., Coleman, A. and Leonhardt, M. (1988a) *Rules*, Social Literacy Series D: Unit D4, Common Ground, Sydney.

Kalantzis, M., Cope, B., Coleman, A. and Leonhardt, M. (1988b) *Services*, Social Literacy Series D: Unit D5, Common Ground, Sydney.

New South Wales Department of Education (1959) *Social Studies Syllabus for Primary Schools*, Sydney.

New South Wales Department of Education (1983) *Investigating Social Studies, K–6*, Sydney.

Riverside Girls High School (1984) *Social Science Curriculum*, Sydney.

Sale, C., Wilson, G. and Friedman, B. (1980) *Our Changing World*, Longman Cheshire, Melbourne.

7
Choosing and Using Information Books in Junior Primary Science

Len Unsworth

Contents

The Interdependence of Learning and Literacy Development in Science Education 299
    Commonsense and 'Uncommonsense' Knowledge
    The Grammatical Construction of Scientific Knowledge
    Information Books and Learning: Accessing Text as Technology

Evaluating Factual Texts for Classroom Learning in Science 306
    Accuracy in Science Texts for Young Children
    A 'Childist' View of Science Texts as Comedy, Games or Puzzles
    Science Texts as Simplistic 'Readers'
    Factual Texts and Narrative
    Information Books that don't Inform

Negotiating Written Language: Text-based Teaching Strategies 326
    Getting into the Text
    The Reading–Writing Connection

The Language and Literacy Focus of Effective Science Programs 335
    Rocks in the Head
    Science as Ethnography

Conclusion 344

References
References to Children's Books

The Interdependence of Learning and Literacy Development in Science Education

Science education is frequently characterised as essentially involving pupils in investigating phenomena via their own direct experience. The role of language in developing scientific understanding is often taken for granted. Where explicit attention is given to language, it is usually in terms of negotiating technical vocabulary. In fact, teachers have been advised to avoid initiating children into the use of distinctively scientific language forms unless it is necessary (e.g. Victorian Department of Education 1981, p. 41). In practice this has meant that pupils have been given very little experience of reading factual books in learning science, and when they have been involved in writing in science, they have been encouraged to do so 'in their own words'. Underlying these practices is a view of language as an inert carrier or channel through which scientific understandings can be communicated. The meanings at stake are considered to be independent of the form of language which 'conveys' them, so everyday language is as effective as scientific language as long as the correct technical vocabulary is included where necessary. Such a view is grossly inadequate. In contrast, it will be shown here that meanings cannot be thought of as separate from the language forms through which they are realised. So learning in science is learning to control the language forms that construct meanings in science. As these meanings deal with ideas that extend beyond directly observable experience, the language forms consequently need to change from ordinary everyday language to the expert language of the scientist. Teaching young children science, then, necessarily involves initiating them into the spoken and written discourse forms that construct scientific knowledge.

Commonsense and 'Uncommonsense' Knowledge

> Educational knowledge is knowledge freed from the particular, the local, through the various languages of the sciences or forms of reflexiveness of the arts which make possible either the creation or the discovery of new realities (Bernstein 1971).

Scientific knowledge extends beyond commonsense knowledge. It is 'uncommonsense' or 'expert' knowledge in that it is more than the reconstruction of directly observable experience. Commonsense and science have different ways of looking at reality based on different organising criteria. 'Pumpkins for example are a kind of vegetable for cooks but fruit to a botanist' (Martin *et al.* 1988, p. 143). From the perspective of science, fruits come out of pollinated flowers but for the layperson fruits are sweet things that grow on trees and bushes. There are thus two different ways of talking about pumpkins. It is not that one is right and the other is wrong, it is just that science construes a different reality from that of the everyday or commonsense reality.

For everyday, commonsense purposes glass, rubber, plastic and air do not seem to constitute an obvious utilitarian categorisation. But from a scientific perspective, based on uncommonsense criteria, they do form an important category of 'non-conductors' of electricity or 'insulators'. The technical term is integral to the construction of the meaning of this categorisation. This essential technicalisation also occurs through compacting and changing the nature of everyday words. For example, marsupials are not just Australian animals like the wombat and the possum. From a biological perspective they are warm-blooded mammals that give birth to live young with no placental attachment and carry the young in a pouch until they are weaned; and they contrast with the two other groups of mammals, monotremes (egg laying) and placentals.

Scientific knowledge is concerned with an ordering of reality into taxonomic relationships based on 'uncommonsense' criteria and in the process involves the generation of explanations of the phenomenal world. However, quite fundamental scientific classifications are not learned by many children despite their experience of science teaching in the primary school. For example, biologists classify living things into two main groups (plants and animals, with some exceptions) but some research (Osborne and Freyberg 1989) indicates that 10 year olds, 13 year olds and 15 year olds did not understand this classification. Some suggested that a tree was not a plant — or at least 'it was a plant when it was little'.

> Other children suggested that a plant was something which was cultivated, hence grass and dandelions were considered weeds and not plants by some 13 and 15 year olds. Further, almost half the pupils interviewed considered that a cabbage and a carrot were not plants, they were vegetables. Over half of those interviewed did not consider a seed to be plant material. Despite considerable exposure to science teaching many of the 15-year-olds held similarly restricted ideas to the 10-year-olds (Osborne and Freyberg 1989, p. 7).

The findings in relation to the category of animals were similar:

> Many of the pupils considered only the larger land animals, such as those found on a farm, in a zoo or in the home as pets, as animals. Reasons for categorizing something as an animal or not doing so, included the number of legs (animals are expected to have four), size (animals are bigger than insects), habitat (animals are found on land), coating (animals have fur), and noise production (animals make a noise) (Osborne and Freyberg 1989, p. 30).

Similar commonsense interpretations were made in relation to concepts such as force, friction, gravity and energy (Osborne and Freyberg 1989, p. 8). Commonsense knowledge in this context is referred to by Osborne and Freyberg as 'children's science' and they indicate that it is the similarities and differences between children's science and 'scientist's science' (p. 13) that are central to the teaching and learning of science. Further, they emphasise that the scientific understandings constructed by children, and the extent to which such understandings are related to those intended by the teacher, are crucially dependent on accessing the forms of language which construct scientific knowledge (p. 33).

The Grammatical Construction of Scientific Knowledge

As scientists order and explain to build up a scientific perspective alongside that of commonsense they develop their own distinctive discourse. Technical terms are one important feature of this discourse, but to understand how the form of scientific English makes meaning, we need to look beyond the vocabulary to the grammatical structure of clauses and to the overall (generic) structure of the texts.

The generic structures that occur most commonly in science texts are report, explanation and procedure. Explanations are frequently embedded in reports and sometimes a report is embedded in an explanation. We will briefly examine some of the grammatical patterning in reports and explanations.

The report gives an account of phenomena as they are. Scientific reports take commonsense as a starting point and change this perspective on reality into one based on specialised knowledge. In so doing scientific reports build 'uncommonsense' taxonomical relationships. This entails the construction of new categories which are realised by technical terms. These technical terms both accumulate and change the nature of the meanings they translate into specialised knowledge. The technical terms are defined by identifying them with phenomena and distinguishing them from the terms which realise other categories.

THE GRAMMAR OF TAXONOMIC RELATIONS

There are two types of taxonomies that are frequently found in scientific reports: classification (kinds of) and decomposition (parts of). Technical classifications are built by starting with the most general or superordinate categories and progressively introducing criteria for correspondingly progressive subdivision of these categories into subclasses. The reports are often introduced by what Shea (1988) has called cue sentences. These can indicate the superordinate item, the number of subclasses and the criteria for establishing subclasses, although not all cue sentences contain all three pieces of information.

> There are two kinds of water wheel. An undershot wheel and an overshot wheel (McClymont 1987, p. 20).

> There are two main types of lavas — very dark basalt-type lavas which are usually found where the crust is splitting apart, and much stiffer light-coloured lavas which are found where crustal plates are coming together (Bramwell 1986a, p. 10).

Literacy Learning and Teaching

Our chart shows the four main types of reptiles that are alive today. Snakes and lizards are the largest group, with 5800 different kinds. There are 230 different kinds of turtles and tortoises. There are 22 different kinds of crocodiles and alligators. Our picture shows the tuatara, the only member of the fourth group (Bailey 1988, pp. 24–25).

Cue sentences in decomposition (part-whole) taxonomies are possessive clauses:

All microcomputers have five main parts.
Microscopes have two lens systems.

Although in some cases the possessive relation is a more abstract notion of containment:

A tooth is divided into three parts.
A complete flowering plant consists of two main parts.

The following extracts show the beginnings of reports dealing with a classification and a decomposition taxonomy respectively:

Snakes are reptiles (cold blooded creatures). They belong to the same group as lizards (the scaled group, Squamata) but form a sub-group of their own (Serpentes) (Derewianka 1990b, p. 54).

This report begins by locating snakes within a classification taxonomy. We could represent it as shown in Figure 7.1.

```
                              ┌── Serpentes (snakes)
                ┌── Squamata ──┤
                │              └──
Reptiles ──────┤
                │
                └──
```

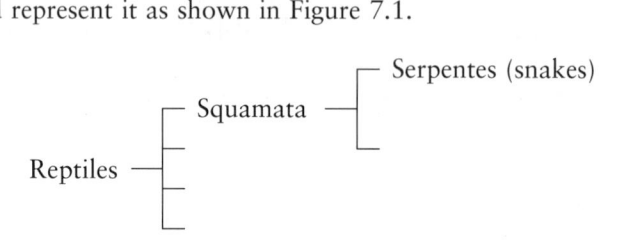

Figure 7.1 *Location of snakes in a reptile taxonomy*

Classification taxonomies are typically not accompanied by illustrations but decomposition taxonomies usually are. So the following report is accompanied by a labelled colour drawing:

A spider's body is in two main parts. The first part is a combined head and chest. It is joined to the back part, the abdomen, by a narrow waist. The mouth and jaws are on the underside of the head and the eyes are usually on the top. The legs are attached to the thorax, the chest, which contains the stomach. The abdomen contains the other major body organs (Bender 1988, p. 6).

DEFINITIONS
Technical terms are sometimes defined through elaboration of the nominal group containing the technical term. This is 'glossing' rather than defining and can be done by using parentheses as in the 'Snakes' report above. Other forms are the addition of a nominal group to elaborate the

Information Books in Junior Primary Science

technical term, for example 'When magma reaches the surface, it erupts from a hole or vent . . .' (Bramwell 1986a, p. 6), and the use of clauses 'embedded' within the nominal group containing the technical term. In the following clauses the embeddings are 'called the stopcock' and 'called pylons':

> Where the water enters the house there is a tap called the stopcock to turn the water on or off (McClymont 1987, p. 14).

> The electricity travels from the power station along thick wires. These are either buried below the ground so that they cannot be damaged, or they are held high in the air by tall metal towers called pylons (Clemence and Clemence 1987, p. 10).

At the clause rank the resource for defining is the Relational: identifying clause (Halliday 1985, pp. 112–128). It identifies a Token, which is usually a technical term, with its Value. This is the key feature of definitions although they also imply classification. Trimble (1985) described formal definitions as Term = Class + Differences; for example:

> The rock shale describes any fine grained sedimentary rock which breaks up into small pieces.

> Electricity which is made by using water is called hydro-electricity (McClymont 1987, p. 21).

> Metals which are not attracted are called non-magnetic metals (Fitzpatrick 1984, p. 8).

Not all Relational: identifying clauses incorporate all of these elements:

> The coloured ring in your eye is called the iris. The black hole in the middle of it is called the pupil (Thomson 1988, p. 14).

> The ends of a magnet are called the poles (Fitzpatrick 1984, p. 8).

Technical terms are frequently used to summarise processes. The technical term, as a summary, then, is the grammatical means of representing the sequence of processes as if they were a single entity or thing:

> The farmers have to take water from the nearest well or river to the fields. This is called irrigation (McClymont 1987, p. 24).

In this example, 'This' in the second clause refers to all of the first clause and the 'is called' therefore identifies all of the first clause with the single noun 'irrigation'. 'Irrigation' is a nominalisation — a 'thingised' realisation of the sequence of events in the first clause. The same grammatical resources have been deployed in the following examples:

> Where does our rain come from? It all begins with the sun shining on the seas, rivers, puddles or your wet clothes on the washing line. The water becomes warm and tiny bits of water, too small to see, rise into the air as water vapour. This drying is called evaporation (McClymont 1987, p. 8).

> As its speed slows, the river can no longer carry such a heavy load and so it starts to drop sand and mud on the river bed. This process is called deposition
> . . .
> The channel is usually kept open by the scouring effect of the river and tides, but some deposition does occur (Bramwell 1986b, p. 9).

EXPLANATION

When reports focus on processes, either to classify them or to use them for classifying things, definitions are longer than those that focus on things. These longer, step by step definitions form an implication sequence indicative of the explanation genre. In the 'deposition' example above, we can see how the grammatical resource of nominalisation is used to establish a technical definition and that the resulting technical term, 'deposition', is then used subsequently in the text to establish an extended explanation. The importance of this grammatical resource in scientific explanation is further illustrated through the establishment and use of the technical term 'lubrication' in the following extract:

> Friction forces in fluids are a great deal less than most of the friction forces between solid objects. If therefore we wish to make things slide easily over each other, one way is to introduce some liquid between the two.
> Liquids used in this way are called 'lubricants' and the whole subject of making moving parts slide easily over each other is known as lubrication . . .
> . . . If the piston is not to act like a file and wear away itself and the cylinder, the lubrication must be so good as to reduce the friction to a very low level indeed . . .
> . . . In very special machines where the forces of friction have to be reduced below those possible with liquid lubrication, gas lubrication is used (Laithwaite 1986, pp. 14–15).

In the following extract the final definition of a 'watershed' is dependent on the previously defined 'drainage basin' which is in turn dependent on the definition of a river and its 'tributaries'. The progressive summarisation of event sequences as technical nominalisations enables these to be used to build the extended explanation.

> As soon as rain falls on high ground, it starts to flow downhill. At first it flows in tiny streamlets called rills. As the rills come together, they form mountain streams, and these eventually join lower down the slope to form a river. The small streams are called tributaries of the river, and the whole area drained by a river and its tributaries is called a drainage basin. The line separating two or more drainage basins usually runs along the crest of a ridge. The ground slopes away on either side, draining away the rainwater, so the line is called a watershed (Bramwell 1986b, pp. 4–5).

The technical terms also facilitate the appropriate textual organisation of the explanation. This can be seen as newly defined phenomena, for example 'tributaries' occurring in the final position in a clause are incorporated and accorded prominence as 'given' information in the next clause within the initial or 'Thematic' position:

| The small streams | are called | tributaries of the river, |
| and the whole area drained by a river and its tributaries | is called | a drainage basin. |

This operates progressively so that the new information, drainage basin, occurs as given information in the next clause:

| The line separating two or more drainage basins | usually runs | along the crest of a ridge. |

The deployment of these grammatical resources does not always involve the explicit introduction of technical terms:

More things dissolve in water than in any other liquid ...
... But this ability to dissolve other substances makes it very easy to poison natural waterways (Bramwell 1986b, p. 14).

In this example the nominal group 'this ability to dissolve other substances' recodes the previous clause so that it is represented as 'Thing'. The grammaticalisation of science in this manner is integral to the construction of the field of knowledge and to the organisation of the textual information. This is not to say that there are no difficulties in scientific English which could be addressed by closer attention to linguistic form in science writing (Halliday 1990).

Accounts of the grammaticalisation of scientific knowledge extend well beyond the aspects that have been outlined here (for a more comprehensive discussion see Halliday 1988a, 1990; Martin 1989, 1990; for further examples of the grammatical features of report, explanation and procedural genres used in primary classrooms see Derewianka 1990b). This introductory discussion, however, indicates that knowledge in science cannot be thought of as separate from the forms of language which construct it.

Information Books and Learning: Accessing Text as Technology

There is evidence that many children have not developed basic scientific understandings from their primary school learning experiences (Osborne and Freyberg 1985). There is also evidence that the linguistic forms which realise such uncommonsense understandings are made explicit in certain science texts (Halliday 1988a; Martin 1989, 1990; Derewianka 1990b) and that improved use of textbooks in teaching science is an important factor in promoting conceptual change in science learning (Roth and Anderson 1988; Christie 1985, 1988). This implies that improvement in the teaching and learning of primary science needs to involve greater attention to the explicit teaching of the discourse forms that construct scientific understanding.

Christie (1988) has pointed out the need to initiate young children into this discourse and, in more general terms, Margaret Donaldson (1989) emphasised the importance of discourses of 'educational knowledge' in learning which she referred to as 'the language of systematic thought ... a sub class of the language of books'. Donaldson went on to point out that teachers of young children should see this as a major concern:

> The ability to deal with sophisticated impersonal prose of the kind we have been considering does not leap up suddenly when needed like the genie from Aladdin's lamp. It is the outcome of years of sustained direction towards an ultimate goal. If primary teachers do not see this they are failing to see the scope and reach of their own importance (Donaldson 1989, p. 25).

Much then depends on the quality of information books available for use in teaching science in the junior primary school.

Evaluating Factual Texts for Classroom Learning in Science

The teaching of scientific understanding to primary school pupils needs to be improved. Such teaching should include a greater emphasis on children's reading and writing of science texts from the beginning of primary school. Recent curriculum documents, the inclusion of more factual books in reading schemes and the increased availability of 'trade' books in the area of science for young children suggest a good deal of agreement thus far. However, when it comes to how science should be recontextualised in learning materials for young children, the form of available texts indicates vast disagreement or confusion. The variation in form in what counts as information books in science for young children is due to variation in the complex interaction of multiple factors that influence the texts' contexts of creation. These factors include the author's conceptualisation of the subject matter; his or her conception of the audience and the purpose of the book; the prevailing conventions of format and presentation for this type of text; and various constraints arising from the publisher's policies on such matters as number of pages, type of illustrations, etc. From the complex interplay of this multiplicity of factors influencing the form of each book, a few identifiable influences seem to have had an obvious impact on the range of text types available:

- An apparent acceptance of less than expert scrutiny of the scientific accuracy of information provided for young children.
- An ideology of childhood which sees children as more interested in play and make believe than exploring the reality they are growing up into. It therefore sees certain kinds of scientific knowledge as needing to be recast as entertainment through its presentation as comedy, games or puzzles.

Information Books in Junior Primary Science

- A theory of reading pedagogy which suggests that books for inexperienced readers need to contain only short simple sentences (and only a small number of these per page) which contain mainly short simple words and that the sentences should be highly repetitive and contain limited variation in vocabulary.
- A view of narrative as 'a primary act of mind . . . a basic way of organizing human experience' (Hardy 1977) which therefore considers narrative genres as appropriate to the organisation of curriculum area knowledge in primary school texts.
- A progressivist pedagogy which promotes individualist and child-centred learning in which the learner is to discover ideas through his or her own activity rather than be directly informed by the teacher or a textbook.

These influences and others have combined in various ways to produce the kinds of texts that relate to primary science curricula. Although many of the currently available books usually evidence a complex conjunction of such factors, each of the five listed above will now be discussed separately in relation to particular textual examples.

Accuracy in Science Texts for Young Children

Inaccuracy and confusion in the presentation of information may result from authors' lack of authority and/or currency in knowledge of the field; from a lax editorial procedure or from attempts to oversimplify the text.

One primary science series reviewed by Kwan and Riley (1982 pp. 138–139) contained inaccuracies such as references to 'tiny particles of electricity', confused the measurement of 'heat' with the measurement of 'temperature' and in its description of Saturn, failed to take account of information obtained in the Voyager missions.

A recent book entitled *Balancing* (Jennings 1989a, p. 12) contained the following text:

> William, Anna and David were playing in the park.
> They sat on the see-saw.
> William and Anna sat at one end of the see-saw.
> David sat at the other end.
> Did William and Anna balance David?

The illustration clearly shows that William and Anna are on the end of the see-saw very close to the ground while David is on the end which is up in the air. The text on p. 13 is as follows:

> David moved nearer the middle of the see-saw.
> Did the children balance now?

Unfortunately, the illustration shows that Anna and William were the ones who moved nearer to the middle of the see-saw and it is now in balance. One would not expect this kind of error to proceed past adequate editorial scrutiny.

A clear example of the way in which attempts at simplifying text can result in distortion has been pointed out by Stodart (1989):

> Honey Andersen has written an attractively repetitive book about how different garden animals breathe. Unfortunately she began the book, called *Breathing* with this sentence — 'All living things need air.' Now air is a particular mix of gases and a fish absorbing oxygen directly from the water is not using air. What is more, a young child who has caught tadpoles or fish knows only too well that air is the last thing they need. It kills them. How do we explain these complicated consequences of the statement that all living things need air? Was it worth the trouble of trying to avoid the word oxygen? (Stodart 1989, p. 5).

Stodart goes on to emphasise the need for expert advisors and informed editors and suggests that 'If a topic cannot be expressed for a young child simply and without too much distortion, it is better left to an older age, particularly in printed form (Stodart 1989, p. 5).

In some books the information is not inaccurate but the form of the texts constructs ambiguous meanings which could lead inexperienced readers to interpret a good deal of information wrongly. This is not to say that such books should not be used, but children need to be alerted to the ways in which the form of the text is making meaning so that explicit knowledge of semiosis can assist them to become critical resistant readers. To illustrate these kinds of issues we will examine some aspects of quite a useful book on spiders which is included in a popular, recently published reading scheme.

An Introduction to Australian Spiders (Cullen 1986) is described on its inside front cover as 'A book full of information about Australian spiders'. In its 24 pages it provides general information about spiders, referring to several different kinds, not all of which are peculiar to Australia. The book is intended for use in classrooms with children of about six to eight years of age.

The book contains no photographs. Most of the illustrations are coloured drawings, which on some occasions appear to be drawn to scale (e.g. bird eating spider and huntsman spider, p. 4) and sometimes clearly are not (e.g. triangular spider, p. 4; spitting spider, p. 6). There are also enlarged coloured drawings of parts of a spider (e.g. typical spinnerets, p. 11), a line drawing of a spider and a diagram of a cross-section of the body of a spider.

The ways in which the illustrations relate to the main text can be grouped into three main categories:

1. repetition of information pictorially equivalent to that in the main text;
2. augmentation of the main text through additional pictorial information;
3. exemplification of general information in the main text.

One example of augmentation and one of exemplification are discussed below to show how information could be derived wrongly due to the text form.

Information Books in Junior Primary Science

An example of augmentation is the use of the illustration entitled 'Typical spinnerets (enlarged)'. The role of spinnerets in the making of silk is not mentioned in the main text — or indeed anywhere else in the book. From the illustration showing the silk threads protruding from the spinnerets, young readers might infer that the spinnerets 'shoot' the silk out rather like a tube of glue!

Where exemplification of general information in the main text occurs in illustrations, in most instances the labels or captions clarify the exemplification but on one occasion this is not clear. On the last page of the book the main text is:

> Most spiders are too small to bite people but a few are known to be dangerous. It is a good rule not to touch any spider.

This page contains drawings of the following spiders: wolf spider, black house spider, red-back spider, trapdoor spider and funnel-web spider. It is not clear whether these are examples of dangerous spiders or those which are too small to bite people or both. The red-back is the smallest in body length — a mere 12 mm — and is the most highly venomous!

There is also a good deal of ambiguity in the naming and categorisation of spiders and their habits. In fact the text contains very little explicit development of a classification of spiders. It is mainly about what spiders do — material (action) processes dominate (75 per cent of process types). Although the pre-classifier 'different kinds of' cues a classification taxonomy this is not developed in the text. Illustrations of spiders are labelled using Classifier ^ Thing structures such as 'net-casting spider' and 'spitting spider' which seem to be names of particular spiders since they are juxtaposed with illustrations labelled 'St. Andrews Cross spider' and 'wolf spider'. But the main text also contains similar Classifier ^ Thing structures which name classes and not particular spiders:

> Most spiders have permanent homes but some hunting spiders wander about to different shelters (p. 8).
>
> Web-making spiders usually live in their webs (p. 10).

The only explicit references to a classification taxonomy which could clarify these relationships are two examples of nominal group apposition in labels accompanying illustrations: 'Flower spider (hunting)' (p. 8) and 'Flower spider (ambushing)' (p. 20).

Young readers provided with such minimal textual resources might well interpret the Classifier ^ Thing structures in the main text as names for particular spiders. But the lack of an explicit classification taxonomy causes further difficulty since knowledge of it is assumed if the reader is to understand the taxonomic relationships among the kinds of homes of different spiders:

> Most spiders have permanent homes but some hunting spiders wander about to different shelters.
>
> Trapdoor spiders and funnel-web spiders live in burrows in the ground. Wolf spiders also live in burrows but come out to hunt (pp. 8–9).

Literacy Learning and Teaching

Presumably this text is based on a habitat taxonomy as indicated in Figure 7.2. But to derive this understanding from the text the reader would have to assume that trapdoor spiders and funnel-web spiders are not hunting spiders and therefore do not wander about to different shelters. The reader would also have to assume that the wolf spider, in contrast to 'some hunting spiders' also does not 'wander about to different shelters'. Readers could only make such assumptions on the basis of prior knowledge. In the absence of explicit textual information, it is quite likely that readers would assume that trapdoor spiders, funnel-web spiders and wolf spiders are all examples of 'some hunting spiders' which 'wander about to different shelters' and hence locate 'burrows' as the different shelters that these spiders wander around to. Part of the difficulty is that while two categories of home are indicated in the clause complex on p. 8 of *Australian Spiders*, only the permanent homes are mentioned in the remainder of this section. No examples of the second category of 'different shelters' occur in the text.

```
                                    ┌─ Burrow
                  ┌─ Permanent home ─┼─ . . .
                  │                  └─ . . .
      Habitat ────┤
                  │                  ┌─ . . .
                  └─ Different shelter┼─ . . .
                                     └─ . . .
```

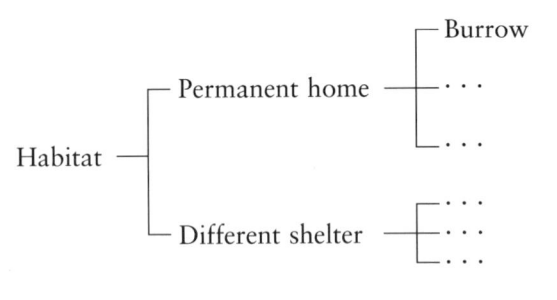

Figure 7.2 *Inferred spider habitat taxonomy*

The text could be rewritten to reduce such confusion:

> Most spiders have permanent homes. Trapdoor spiders and funnel-web spiders live in burrows in the ground. Wolf spiders also live in burrows in the ground but come out to hunt. Some (other) hunting spiders wander about to different shelters . . .

It would then be necessary to add an example or two of such spiders and the kinds of shelters they use. One possibility would be the huntsman spider which shelters under pieces of bark it comes across.

The kinds of problems found in the *Australian Spiders* text are not unusual in school textbooks. For example, Christie (1985, pp. 4–13) provides a not too dissimilar critique of *Beneath the Oceans* (Andrews 1972), a factual text for use in the upper primary school. This does not mean that such books have no value in the classroom, but they clearly need to be read critically and this means that teachers will have to show children how to read them critically by attending to the kinds of textual characteristics that have been discussed.

A 'Childist' View of Science Texts as Comedy, Games or Puzzles

Whose Toes and Nose are Those? What does the title of this book signal about its social purpose? What of its ideological positioning of the young reader? Would not most intending readers expect the prime function of the text to be light-hearted entertainment and also expect the text to be oriented to someone who liked to play games and complete puzzles for fun? Yet this genre is quite commonly included as a resource for curriculum area learning within the category of information books for young children in recently published reading schemes (*Animal Clues*, Drew 1987; *Whose Toes and Nose are Those?*, Vaughan 1986). These kinds of texts are popular with children and are similar to materials children might use for entertainment at home or to keep themselves occupied on journeys, etc. But when they are included in reading schemes they are accorded status and valency (which is not differentiated from other forms of information books) in constructing teachers' and pupils' views of what constitutes scientific inquiry.

Books dealing with aspects of physical science such as 'heat', 'balance' and 'floating and sinking' seem to be a major focus for the expression of childist ideology. It seems that natural science, especially when it is dealing with animals, is considered to be 'naturally' appealing to young children whereas physical science needs to be recast as comedy to maintain interest. This is done mainly by the illustrations. In some books the entire format is one of slapstick (Bolton 1986; Andersen 1986b). In the book entitled *Melting* the text simply sets up a series of oppositions:

> Heat from the sun makes some things melt
> but not all things.
> Butter melts in the sun but glass doesn't.
> Glass doesn't melt in the sun but chocolate does.
> Chocolate melts in the sun but paper doesn't.
> Paper doesn't melt in the sun but ice-cream does.
> . . .

Part of the problem here is the banality of the text — simply reconstructing what is very familiar to young children. But the illustrations show a clown-like character cavorting around balancing two plates of butter then standing on his head with empty plates balanced on his toes and the melted butter in a pool around his head. Similar slapstick routines accompany the melting of the chocolate and the ice-cream.

Another common technique is to incorporate a cartoon character as a gratuitous comic accompaniment to otherwise quite realistic representational illustrations. These characters permeate Oxford's *Into Science* series. In *Colour* (Jennings 1989d) a somewhat anthropomorphised, multicoloured worm/serpent appears mischievously among the drawings of experimental apparatus on every double-page spread. Similarly, in *Hot and Cold* (Jennings 1989b) a penguin appears throughout the book at times taking its own temperature with a thermometer, skiing down snowy slopes complete with wooden skis, scarf, etc. or eating dinner at a table with a knife and fork. Natural science books in the same series also incorporate this feature. In *Spiders* (Jennings 1989c) a somewhat anthropomorphised fly (?) makes irrelevant appearances throughout the book to display expressions of mischief, surprise, etc. The same technique is used in Gloucester's *Junior Science* series (e.g. *Floating and Sinking*, Jennings 1988) and in Viking Kestrel's *First Science Books* series (e.g. *What is Balance?*, d'Arcier 1986). The comic character in *What is Balance?* is a mouse and the final page of the book shows the mouse balancing on his tail and holding an umbrella with the accompanying text 'And how's that for a balancing trick!' Now this completely undercuts the main message in the text which is that balance is achieved by putting the heaviest components at the bottom. It also illustrates one more manifestation of childist ideology — the portrayal of science as magical or clever tricks. This is sometimes highlighted in the books' titles, e.g. *Science Surprises* (Waters and Round 1985a) and *Science Tricks and Magic* (Waters and Round 1985b). Not only is it unnecessary to try to augment the appeal of science by using such devices but it also constructs a very limited and inappropriate view of the kind of pleasure and satisfaction that is achieved through the development of scientific understanding.

Science Texts as Simplistic 'Readers'

Some books dealing with science topics, especially those included as factual texts in reading schemes, reflect a view that the language of information books for inexperienced readers should be simplified. This often means that the amount of written text is minimal; that short, simple repetitive sentences are favoured and that a limited range of vocabulary is used in any one text. Such books minimise technicality and limit children's development of a scientific perspective. This effect can be seen in comparing one such simplified text with a corresponding information book that provides a more appropriate scientific orientation. The following text is a 'simplifier' from the Bookshelf scheme called *Dinosaurs* (Collins 1988):

> Long long ago, before there were people, dinosaurs lived on Earth.
> [Full page colour drawing showing Muttaburrasaurus and Austrosaurus — labelled.]
> The word 'dinosaur' means 'terrible lizard'.
> [Double-page spread — colour drawing of Allosaurus — labelled.]
> Some dinosaurs were very small
> [Full page colour drawing of Compsognathus — labelled.]
> but other dinosaurs were very huge.
> [Full page colour drawing of Brachiosaurus — labelled.]
> Some dinosaurs moved on two legs but other dinosaurs moved on four legs.
> [Full page colour drawing of Aparosaurus and Camptosaurus — labelled.]
> There were even flying reptiles.

Information Books in Junior Primary Science

[Full colour drawing of Pteranodon — labelled.]
...
Some dinosaurs ate plants but others ate meat.
...

This series of discrete observations contrast with the following book called *A First Look at Dinosaurs* (Selsam and Hunt 1982). The text is one of *A First Look* series whose purpose is explicitly stated: 'Each of the nature books for this series is planned to develop the child's powers of observation and give him or her a rudimentary grasp of scientific classification.' The first few pages of the text are as follows:

Dinosaurs lived millions of years ago.
[Illustrated timeline of the age of dinosaurs — labelled.]
Some dinosaurs were giants and others were no bigger than turkeys. Some had long sharp teeth and ate meat. Others had teeth like pegs and ate plants. Some had bumps. Some had horns. Some had spikes. There were almost 1000 different kinds of dinosaurs. How do you tell them apart?
[Black and white drawings of four different types of dinosaurs — not labelled.]
One group of dinosaurs were meat eaters. They walked on their hind legs and had sharp teeth and claws. They came in different sizes.
[Black and white drawings of Tyrannosaurus, Megalosaurus and Compsognathus — labelled with phonic spelling in parentheses.]
Another group of dinosaurs were giant plant eaters. They walked on all four feet. They had very long necks and tails. Their legs were as big as tree trunks. Although they were all big, some were bigger than others.
[Black and white drawings of Diplodocus, Plateosaurus and Brontosaurus — labelled with phonic spelling in parentheses.]
Even though the meat eaters and the giant plant eaters looked very different, scientists found that their hip bones were the same. They looked like those of a lizard. The scientists called them lizard-hipped dinosaurs.
[Black and white drawing of the skeleton of a dinosaur with the lizard hip highlighted.]
Here are the bones close up:
[Black and white drawing of lizard hip.]
In lizard-hipped dinosaurs, bones 1 and 2 are wide apart, like this:
[Black and white diagram with bones numbered.]

The text goes on to discuss 'bird-hipped' dinosaurs and elaborate the classification. At the end of the text the full classification developed in the book is summarised in two pages.

Distinctly unhelpful are those texts which prostitute literary forms such as *The Bush Where I Walk* and *The Bulldozer Cleared the Way* (Sloan and Latham 1985). The latter is part of a series labelled 'Technology' and the following text appears under colour photographs:

> The bulldozer cleared the way (p. 1).
> The scraper scraped the road, but the bulldozer cleared the way (p. 2).
> The grader formed the road. The scraper scraped the ground, but the bulldozer cleared the way (p. 3).

The text form is dysfunctional for many reasons not least of which is that the sequence of events in reality, i.e. the building up of the road, is actually presented as being deconstructed by the order of events as sequenced in the text. Such texts are also extreme examples of the inappropriate imposition of a narrative genre which is clearly at odds with the context to which the text is intended to relate.

Factual Texts and Narrative

The most inappropriate use of story in teaching science is the pseudo-narrative which is frequently anthropomorphic and blends the real world with fantasy:

> He is the fastest swimming tiny tiny tadpole in the whole pond. But — look out! Here comes a hungry looking trout fish, and trouts like eating tadpoles.
> Quick!
> Zig-zag into those weeds. First one way then the other.
> Phew, that was a close shave!
> These green weeds are good food for tiny tiny tadpoles.
> (Todd 1982)

This is not to say that the real world and fantasy cannot be blended in very effective narratives where the central purpose is clearly to present an entertaining story — *James and the Giant Peach* (Dahl 1961) comes immediately to mind. Books like *Moggy's Hop* (Pigdon, N. 1987), however, create ambiguous contexts for interpretation. The text begins:

> In a pond, on a still dark night, the frog laid her tiny black eggs. The eggs were joined together with jelly-like stuff called spawn. They floated on top of the water.

We then learn that one of the eggs hatched into a tadpole called 'Moggy' and in the next 17 pages trace Moggy's development into a frog. The text then proceeds:

> She was very unhappy.
> When Grasshopper saw how unhappy she was, he asked her, 'What's wrong?'
> 'When I hop, I never quite reach where I want to go,' she answered. Grasshopper told her not to worry.
> 'I'll help you,' he said.
> 'When I was young I couldn't hop very far, either, and my friend Cricket helped me.'

Baker and Freebody (1989) have shown how such ambiguous contexts lead the teacher to adopt inconsistent frames of reference and confuse the children as to whether they should invoke the world of fact or the world of fiction.

> It appears to be the teacher who cues students to one or the other frame of reference, who can alternate between invoking the world of fiction or the world of fact from the same text. The problem for children, to decide which frame of reference is in play on some occasion of adult questioning (see also Mehan 1976), is in part produced through the provision of textual material which blends 'fantasy' with 'reality' (Baker and Freebody 1989, p. 269).

This kind of anthropomorphism also masquerades as factual text in popular magazines for young children. For example, an article entitled 'Animal Holidays' makes the following statements about humpback whales: 'These animals spend the summer months in the cold waters around Antarctica. In winter, they move to warmer waters near Australia to breed. That's a long way to swim for a holiday!' This is followed by a paragraph about eels (which 'enjoy their watery holiday') and then one about mutton birds (which 'like to have summer holidays all year round'). The next paragraph is about the locust:

> The locust looks very like a grasshopper. It is considered a pest when it moves in for holidays. The problem is that it brings all of its friends . . . millions of them. And they eat and eat and eat! Farmers are glad when locusts take their holidays somewhere else (*Lucky*, a magazine for young readers, Ashton Scholastic, 1986).

Many who would disapprove of these kinds of texts would nevertheless maintain that narrative form should be prominent in primary curriculum area learning. Traditionally primary education has valued fiction above factual texts and has preferred narrative genres. At least two major influences seem to have contributed to this. The first is a 'retreat from print' in the teaching of science and social studies under the influence of 'process' oriented curricula of the 1970s and 1980s. The second influence is an ideology of childism (noted above). Since this ideology treats children as being more interested in play and make believe than in exploring the reality they are growing up into, it therefore sees knowledge of the real world as best introduced to young children via puzzles and games and through narrative which encourages children's imagination. A related view is based on Barbara Hardy's (1977) proposal that narrative is 'a primary act of mind . . . a basic way of organizing human experience'. So narrative genres are still considered appropriate to the organisation of curriculum area knowledge in primary school texts. Consequently factual texts are sometimes evaluated in terms of their narrative qualities. For example, Stodart (1989) proposed a rewording of one factual text, commenting: 'We have also given the paragraph a little narrative structure. It now rises to a small climax. Narrative structure is something that I feel is not generally considered important in science books, although it should be.' The original extract is as follows:

> ... after a storm, coastal roads well above high tide level are often littered with pebbles and small rocks thrown there by powerful storm waves. This action, called corrasion, is one of the ways in which waves make coasts recede. Loose rocks hurled at the bottoms of cliffs by waves hollow out caves. This process gradually undermines the cliffs ... (Lye 1987).

As Stodart correctly points out, the problem is that 'This' refers to only part of the sequence of events which should be summed up by 'This action' because the definition of 'corrasion' interrupts the event sequence which it defines. Her rewording corrects this:

> ... after a storm, coastal roads well above high tide level are often littered with pebbles and small rocks thrown there by powerful storm waves. Loose rocks hurled at the bottoms of cliffs by waves hollow out caves. This process gradually undermines the cliffs. This action, called corrasion, is one of the ways in which waves make coasts recede (Lye 1987, quoted in Stodart 1989).

The text now provides the whole event sequence which is then summarised as 'This action', named as 'corrasion' and identified as 'one of the ways in which waves make coasts recede'. The modifications certainly improve the text but it is romantically superfluous to suggest that the new version 'now rises to a small climax'.

Stodart concedes that factual texts for the primary school child should also include 'the encyclopedic type in which facts are presented in an easily recognizable way' (1985, p. 252) but it is clear that she sees the narrative as pre-eminent:

> ... there will be those whose reading does not get past the exploration of facts, so that the encyclopedic type of book may be their only reading matter. Their eagerness to learn will allow them to read facts, but they will not readily progress to the greyer and more exciting areas of idea (particularly where there may be several conflicting ideas) and story (Stodart 1985, p. 252).

One can learn quite a lot from narrative whether it deals with fact or fiction. However, narrative is not an effective way of organising all types of factual writing. It is not prominent among the genres that are used to construct and exchange knowledge in the majority of areas of learning that are functioning within the culture, for example, economics, medicine, engineering, psychology, geography, computing, electronics, business administration, biology and linguistics. In these areas a range of genres is necessary according to the purposes for which written texts will be used. If children are to be effectively introduced to the forms of knowledge and understanding which are powerful in the culture, they need to be gradually introduced to the distinctive ways language is used to make meaning in these areas. Engaging with and learning to control the textual forms of reports, procedural texts, explanations, expositions, etc. is much more demanding and interesting than is suggested by any caricature which reductively describes these as 'the encyclopedic type in which facts are presented in an easily recognizable way' (Stodart 1985, p. 252). Convincing evidence of children's enthusiasm for engaging with these kinds of texts is provided in Heath's (1983) account of a fifth grade science unit on 'plant life' and in Derewianka's (1990a) account of a second grade science unit on 'rocks'.

Information Books that don't Inform

Books which recontextualise explanations of phenomena of physical science, such as sound, light, heat and balance, in information books for young children frequently reflect the pedagogy of 'discovery learning'. The emphasis is on instructing the reader to carry out activities and then questioning him or her about what is found. Typically, little information is provided in the text. The books are predominantly concerned with the reconstruction of directly observable experience, emphasising commonsense rather than technical knowledge.

Sound (Webb 1987) is a clear example of such texts. The tension in this book between its purpose in providing procedures for children to carry out and in explaining to them aspects of the phenomenon of sound is evident in the book's stated purpose:

> The activities and experiments suggested are simple enough for children to conduct themselves, with only a little help from an adult, using objects and materials which will be familiar to them.
>
> Children will gain most from the book if the book is used together with practical activities. Such experiences will help to consolidate knowledge and also suggest new ideas for further exploration and experimentation.

The second paragraph implies that knowledge is to be constructed from the text in the absence of performing the activities but that these would enhance learning. If the activities were not carried out, an adult would need to supply the answers to most of the questions in the text (see Table 7.1).

In text	In illustration	In procedure or from adult	From adult
1	4	17	1

Table 7.1 *Sources of answers to questions in 'sound' text*

The following are examples of questions for which the answers would need to be obtained by doing the activity or from an experienced co-reader:

- Does sound travel through the slack string of a yoghurt pot telephone?
- What happens if the string is stretched tight?
- What do you notice about the sounds the long and short nails make?

However, the only adult role mentioned is providing 'a little help' in 'using objects and materials'. The book therefore seems to assume that if activities are not carried out there will be an adult co-reader providing information but at the same time the role of this co-reader is very much understated.

The text's method of development is like a progression of activity-based quizzes. Direct explanation is minimised and procedures (commands) and questions are dominant (Table 7.2), combining with the photographs to suggest the construction of 'commonsense' knowledge based on direct observation.

Ranking clauses	Statements	Questions		Commands
		Wh	Yes/No	
63	26	17	6	14

Table 7.2 *Distribution of mood types in 'sound' text*

Explanation primarily involves the reader doing things. The text avoids the construction of explanations as sequences of events involving technical terms as participants. It interrupts and/or replaces such sequences with procedures in which the reader is Agent:

> How does someone's voice reach you?
> The sound travels through the air as sound waves.
> Throw a stone in a pool of water.
> Watch how the waves spread out.
> Sound waves move through the air in a similar way.

Even if a reader were carrying out the activities in the book 'with only a little help from an adult', it is unlikely that they would go out and throw a stone in a pool of water! (The accompanying photograph shows the waves in a pool in concentric circles.) Nevertheless the writer codes this text segment as a procedure. The next logical step in the implication sequence would be the sound waves entering one's ears but this must also be dealt with as the reader doing something:

> Cup your hands round your ears
> when you're listening to music.
> Does the music sound louder?
> You are catching more sound waves.

The fact that all of the illustrations are photographs reinforces this concrete, non-technical approach to explanation and that the child must 'discover' rather than be told directly.

This concrete, non-technical approach would seem to be further supported by the form the questions take and the fact that many of the questions are actually metaphorical expressions of commands. Questions dealing with feeling and hearing are modalised whereas the question dealing with seeing is not. That is, the former are presented in terms of possibility whereas the latter is presented as definite:

> What can you feel?
> Can you hear a sound?
> What do you see?

Information Books in Junior Primary Science

This is part of the grammaticalising of 'discovery learning', i.e. 'Is there a sound?' — not 'There is a sound and did you hear it?'

The motivation for this form of questioning is much more explicit in other sections of the book:

    42 Put your ear against one end of a plank.
    43 Can you hear
    44 if someone taps the other end?
    53 Can you hear
    54 if someone speaks through a narrow tube?

The questions do not ask the reader to confirm the known facts (e.g. that sound travels through wood) but rather constructs the situation as the child discovering this phenomenon.

The fact that the question in clauses 53 and 54 is a metaphorical expression of command is made clear in the following clause: '(55) Try it again with funnels stuck in both ends.' Several of the interrogatives throughout the text could be read as metaphorical commands:

    02 What sounds do these things make
    03 if you bang them?
    60 Which of these bottles will make highest
    61 if you bang them?

In this text learning about the physical world involves doing things. However, the grammar of the text suggests covert reservations about the adequacy of this over-reliance on discovery learning. Why are so many of the instructions realised metaphorically as questions? Why are the conjunctions between clauses like those above (2–3; 53–54) realised by 'if'? The use of the conjunction 'when' would be more consistent with the interpretation of these questions as metaphorical realisations of commands. There is an ambivalence here which invites a resistant reading by an experienced co-reader who might augment the text to produce a more technical explanation. However, such a reading would have to work hard against the multiple semiotic planes of the text which coerce a commonsense interpretation. This can be seen in the interaction between the illustrations and the questions in clauses 51–52 and 57. Clauses 51–52 are accompanied by a photograph showing a boy holding a 10 cm cylinder between his ear and a watch on a table:

    51 How can you use a tube
    52 to help you hear from further away?

Clause 57 is accompanied by photographs of a boy speaking into a cardboard megaphone and a girl with a scarf around her face:

    57 How can you make your voice sound
          louder . . . or more muffled?

A response from a co-reader in terms of directing sound waves would be highly resistant to the form of the text. The obvious answers are provided very obviously by the photographs and they once again involve physical activity by the children in the photographs with whom the child reader is aligned.

COMPARING TWO TEXTS

The two texts to be considered here are 'information' books intended for use with young children in the first years of school (approximately 5–7 years of age). Both books have the same title *Floating and Sinking* and both were published in 1986. The first (Andersen 1986b) is one component of a comprehensive, commercially produced set of reading materials for use in primary schools published by Ashton Scholastic and known as Bookshelf. The second text (Pluckrose 1986) is a hardcover book which is not part of a commercially produced 'school' reading scheme. It is 'designed for use in the home, playgroup, kindergarten and infant school'. Both books aim to provide children with a basis for determining independently which objects float in water and which objects sink.

> Which objects float in water and which objects sink? This book helps you to find out for yourself. (Andersen)

> Which of these things do you think will sink? Which do you think will float? (Pluckrose)

Despite their ostensible similarity, however, these texts construct different contexts for the development of understanding about floating and sinking and in fact they construct different kinds of understanding of the topic. In the Andersen text the language functions mainly to accompany action in the performance of experiments in the material situational setting whereas in the Pluckrose text the context of situation is constructed entirely by the language and illustrations in the book.

The Andersen text is highly controlling of the reader. The commands direct the child in carrying out the experimental procedures and account for a large proportion of the text as shown in Table 7.3. In contrast, the Pluckrose book directs the reader to experiment on the last page only and the procedures are realised by only two commands and the illustration there.

	Minor and non-finite clauses	Statements	Commands	Questions: Yes/No	Wh	Total
Andersen		10	16	17	4	47
Pluckrose	6	32	2	9	9	58

Table 7.3 *Mood analysis summary — 'floating and sinking' texts*

The Andersen text positions the reader as a highly dependent interactant whose responses, in nearly all cases, function simply to confirm what has been directly observed. The Pluckrose text, however, constructs a reader whose role is to contribute information from past personal experience, to infer from illustrations and experiential knowledge, to connect information from text and illustrations and to formulate explanations.

The common instructional purpose is clear in that the Andersen and Pluckrose texts contain 21 and 20 questions respectively. The form of the

Information Books in Junior Primary Science

questions, however, indicates that the nature of the instruction is quite different. The Andersen text contains a greater proportion of yes/no questions. Their role is to obtain an answer which will state explicitly what has just been directly observed and is also shown in the illustration:

> Put the table tennis ball and the rock into the water.
> What happens?
> Does the small object float or does it sink?
> Does the big object float or does it sink?

The four wh questions in the Andersen text are all repetitions of 'What happens?' They are also redundant in each case because the follow-up yes/no questions establish all possible response options.

The questions in the Pluckrose book do more than reconstruct immediate direct observations. The Themes in the wh questions in this text contrast with the repetition of 'What happens?' in the Andersen text: which toys; what; why; why; which of these things; which things; why; how. Language is being used here to probe personal experience: 'Which toys do you play with in the bath?'; to establish cause–effect relationships: 'What happens if the can fills with water? It sinks!'; to ask for reasons (why) and explanations (how) and to classify (which things).

In this text it can be shown that the selection of statements and questions and the illustrations work together to create an interactive reading context that enables the reader through interaction with the text itself to construct his or her understanding that air-filled objects float. In this sense the text itself is explicitly teaching.

> This glass bottle has a screw top.
> It is filled with air.
> Will it sink?
> [illustration of floating bottle]
>
> This glass bottle has no top.
> If it fills with water,
> will it still float?
> [illustration of submerged bottle with air escaping]
>
> This can is made of metal.
> It contains nothing but air.
> [illustration of floating can]
>
> What happens if the can fills with water?
> It sinks!
>
> Why do things float?
> [illustration of submerged can]
>
> Air helps things to float . . .
> like this rubber balloon,
> this buoy
> and this toy ship.

The form of the text operates to structure the child's learning from particular examples to the general principle. On the first page information is provided by the illustration and the two statements. The function of the yes/no question is to make the connection between these two information sources, i.e. to confirm that a sealed, air-filled bottle will not sink. Similarly on the second page the function of the yes/no question is to make linguistically explicit information that is provided in the illustration, i.e. that if the air escapes and the bottle fills with water it will sink.

The next double-page spread provides an opportunity for the reader to consolidate and extend this understanding by applying it to the example of the metal can. The information sources parallel the page showing the air-filled bottle — two statements describing the attributes of the object and the illustration showing that it floats. The yes/no question which 'scaffolded' the reader's connection of the two information sources on the first 'bottle' page is not included here. On the basis of the 'bottle' page the reader is likely to read the two statements about the can and predict that it will float. The illustration simultaneously confirms this prediction and, because of the position of the can in the water, anticipates the wh question on the following page: 'What happens if the can fills with water? It sinks!' This question and its answer are both highly predictable. The illustrations of the can and the experience of the previous 'bottle' example contribute to this predictability. The form of these wh questions assists children to verbalise their understanding of the general principle. The 'What happens if . . .' question provides the condition or cause and asks for the consequence or effect which is given in the answer. The next question — 'Why do things float?' — provides the consequence or effect and asks for the condition or cause. It is significant that the reader must turn the page to see the answer provided in the text. Before doing so, on the basis of the previous pages, the young reader might well formulate a response like 'because they are filled with air', or 'they float if they are filled with air'.

In the Pluckrose text the young reader is positioned so that he or she uses language to construct his or her understanding of this principle of flotation from direct observation to explanation.

Children who read the Andersen text are constrained to use language primarily to give expression to their direct observation in the 'here and now'.

Despite the similarity of topic in their common title, these books differ substantially in the meanings they develop. The Andersen text does not establish attributes of objects which might be related to whether they float or sink. The attributes occurring in this text are: small, big, round, flat; table tennis, plastic and drawing. The objects in the text are: objects, object, feather, stone, ball, rock, pin, toy, cork and the pronominals it and they. The meanings dealt with in the Andersen texts are insufficient to establish a general principle on which objects could be classified according to whether they float or sink. At the end of the text readers know whether the particular objects they have encountered float or sink; they know that big flat stones sink more slowly than small round stones; and they know that both big and small objects sometimes float and sometimes sink; but they have not established an explicit basis for predicting which objects will float and which will sink.

Information Books in Junior Primary Science

The Pluckrose text does develop explicit general principles upon which the reader may predict whether objects will float or sink. This text conveys the attributes of objects which are crucial to understanding whether they will float or not:

> It is filled with air.
> It contains nothing but air.
> . . . because they are lighter than water like these leaves.

The Pluckrose text provides a clear conceptual basis for predicting whether particular objects will float or not:

> Air helps things to float . . .
> like this rubber balloon,
> this buoy
> and this toy ship.
>
> All these things are hollow.
> If things are hollow
> they are filled with air.
>
> Some things float because they are lighter than water
> like these leaves.

In the Pluckrose text, the form of the language combines with the meanings realised by the illustrations to construct a reader whose active contribution to the development of explicitly stated understandings is respected. This can be seen in the following segment:

> This glass bottle has a screw top.
> It is filled with air.
> Will it sink?
> This glass bottle has no top.
> If it fills with water
> will it still float?
>
> This can is made of metal.
> It contains nothing but air.
> What happens if the can fills with water?
> It sinks!
>
> Why do things float? . . .

The way in which the form of the language positions the reader as an active, interpretive agent has already been discussed. In terms of the referential meanings at stake here, the 'air filled' characteristic of the objects is realised explicitly in the language. The causal link is then initially inferred from this information and that in the illustration showing the bottle floating. The same patterning occurs with the examples of the bottle and the can. The question 'Why do things float?' then encourages the reader to express the inferred reason directly. On the following page the answer is realised explicitly with 'Air' as the agent acting on the generalised 'things'. Air, now in first position in the clause, has thematic prominence as the reader's point of departure. The thematic organisation of the clauses reveals the method of development of this segment of the text.

The thematic progression is from specific to general and from concrete to abstract. There are two text segments, each on a double-page spread, where the thematic concern changes from 'object' to 'question on object' to 'condition of object' and then the themes are the more general 'Why' and 'Air' (Figure 7.3). The latter theme previously occurred as 'new' information at the end of the previous clauses. This kind of thematic development does not occur in the Andersen text. The thematic pattern for most of the text is:

>You
>Put (+ specific object)
>What
>Does (+ specific object)

This difference in thematic patterning draws attention to the ways in which reasoning is carefully structured into the Pluckrose text and is absent from the Andersen text in which the language functions to direct action and to confirm the observation of results of this action. This can be seen in the only two subordinate clauses in the Andersen text which are on the first two pages:

>Objects that float stay at the top
>when they are put into water.
>Objects that sink go to the bottom
>when they are put into water.

In the Pluckrose text, the subordinate clauses of condition are part of that text's reasoning about why things float; for example:

>. . . if they fell into the river.
>If it fills with water . . .
>If things are hollow . . .

Although both texts contain the same number of co-ordinated clauses, four of the five in the Andersen text are repetitions — does (specified object) float or does it sink? The alternative in the question is resolved by confirming that which matches direct observation. In contrast the co-ordinated clauses in the Pluckrose text contribute to the reasoning in the text because they contrast two situations, for example 'This boat is floating on the lake but boats full of water sink.'

The final clauses in these texts exemplify the different kind of understanding of the topic emphasised in each book:

Andersen	*Pluckrose*
Do some objects sometimes float and sometimes sink?	Why do some things float and some things sink and how does air help?

A significant proportion of primary school pupils are likely to encounter the Andersen book because it is part of a widely used comprehensive scheme of materials for the teaching of reading. I believe this book is educationally dysfunctional. It assumes a subordinate, dependent role for the reader and its construction of meaning amounts to no more than the

Information Books in Junior Primary Science

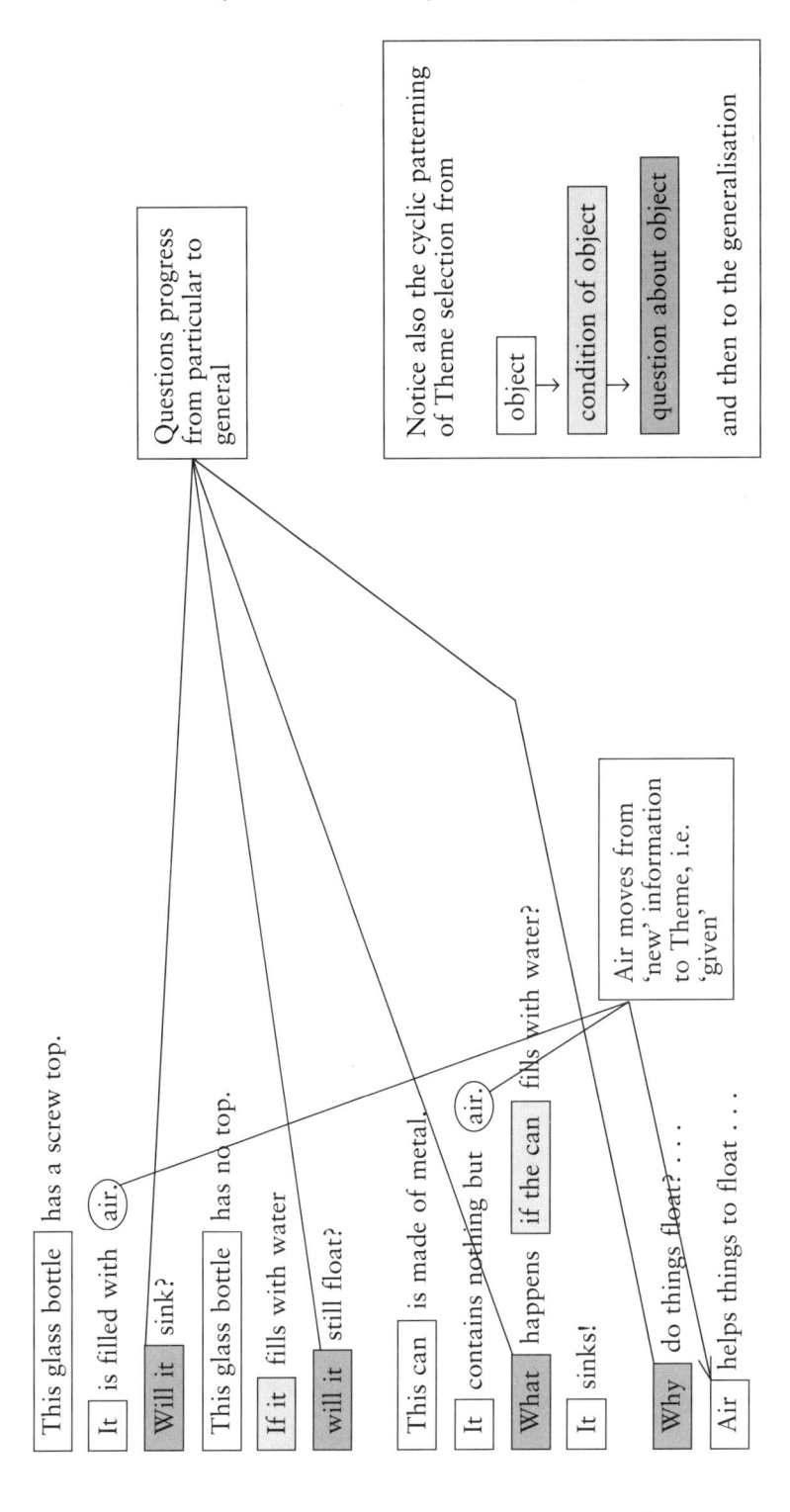

This glass bottle has a screw top.
It is filled with air.
Will it sink?
This glass bottle has no top.
If it fills with water
will it still float?
This can is made of metal.
It contains nothing but air.
What happens if the can fills with water?
It sinks!
Why do things float? . . .
Air helps things to float . . .

Questions progress from particular to general

Notice also the cyclic patterning of Theme selection from

object → condition of object → question about object

and then to the generalisation

Air moves from 'new' information to Theme, i.e. 'given'

Figure 7.3 *Thematic patterns in a segment of the Pluckrose text*

rehearsal of directly observable experience, failing to orient readers to the development of scientific principles. Significantly fewer children are likely to have access to the Pluckrose book. Although it includes some orientation to personal and local meanings, it extends beyond this and the form of the text simultaneously constructs a more active role for the reader and explicit knowledge of general principles related to flotation.

It should not be assumed that all information books in reading schemes compare less favourably with corresponding 'trade' books. Recent reading scheme material has included some very useful information books in science (e.g. *An Introduction to Frogs*, Tyler 1987; *Earthworms*, Pigdon and Woolley 1989) and the critique above has included a number of 'trade' books. What is clear is that the form of information books affects the construal of what counts as knowledge and understanding in the curriculum areas they relate to. At the same time information books are subject to very little in the way of critical review compared to the burgeoning critique of children's fiction. The improvement of the teaching and learning of science in primary schools must include greater critical attention to the choice and use of textual resources.

Negotiating Written Language: Text-based Teaching Strategies

> By appreciating the contrasts between students' everyday ways of thinking about natural phenomena and the explanations presented in science texts, teachers can begin to develop some ways of thinking about the use of the textbook that *will* help students make better sense (Roth and Anderson 1988, p. 140).

Firstly we need to find out how children are thinking about the topic to be dealt with. There needs to be opportunities for teachers and children to explore the existing experiential base of the learning to be undertaken. This involves direct experience through excursions or practical work in, for example, setting up an ant farm or making simple electric circuits with batteries and light bulbs. It can also involve vicarious experience provided through filmstrips, video, slides, etc. Crucial to all such activities is the opportunity for children to talk and make their current ways of understanding these phenomena explicit in an unthreatening learning environment.

The second step is to extend the dimensions of the children's understanding through their access to information and criteria beyond the scope of commonsense knowledge. Once again this may be achieved directly through experimentation and the use of technology or less directly by viewing demonstrations, illustrations of counter-examples or representations in the form of diagrams, etc. Talk accompanies these activities and it is in this context that the process of technicalisation in language begins as the teacher talks with pupils about the impact of new information on the ways in which their understanding is being extended.

As children's understanding is further extended to relate their new learning in this particular instance to the more general systematic frameworks into which the topic fits, there is a movement away from direct activity and the dominance of accompanying oral language interaction. Children now need to shift their focus away from the activity to its more general significance. In so doing they need to access the written forms of technical discourse if they are to construct and communicate their understanding of this more systematic, integrated, scientific perspective. Talk is still vitally important but it is now talk about text and its construction of uncommonsense knowledge. Closer attention to this 'getting into the text' phase could greatly enhance the teaching and learning of primary science.

Getting into the Text

We should extend 'getting into the text' to 'going beyond the text' as well, because we need to develop children's reading and also their writing in science. By selecting appropriate science books and explicitly teaching children the textual features of these books, teachers are equipping children with knowledge of text as a technology for learning and at the same time providing models for children's own writing. Getting into the text involves work on three levels:

1. the grammar and vocabulary within the clauses;
2. the cohesion or connections across clauses;
3. the genre or schematic structure of the text as a whole.

TALKING OUT THE TEXT
The grammar and vocabulary of scientific English is different from that of everyday spoken language and it is very different from the grammar and vocabulary of stories (Martin 1985; Christie 1986, 1989; Derewianka 1990b). Children's access to the grammatical forms of scientific English is via appropriate information books. But because the grammatical forms of these texts are so different from the oral or written story forms which children are used to, many will need to be shown how to read information books about science. Teaching science is also teaching reading (Davies and Greene 1984). Class time should be allocated to the reading of science texts. This should include occasions when the teacher makes use of overhead projection transparencies to engage in reading of factual material with children to show how the language constructs and organises meaning. This shared reading provides the opportunity for talk around text. The teacher can 'restate the unfamiliar in the more familiar and vice versa, helping to integrate the language of the textbook' (Lemke 1989a, p. 138). In the context of talking about the text, children can practise speaking the new language. They can 'make the text talk in their own voices, not by reading it, but by elaborating on it themselves,

building on it in their own words and making its words their own' (Lemke 1989a, p. 138).

Text-based learning tasks can be used to consolidate this process. A 'cloze' or masking procedure can be used to focus on the textual cues to the meanings of technical terms. In the following extract 'the Earth's pull' could be masked or deleted initially so that the children become more confident and familiar with the term 'gravity'. When this is felt to be the case on a subsequent occasion 'gravity' could be deleted.

> Gravity pulls like a big magnet,
> and normally the Earth's pull,
> or gravity, causes everything to
> fall to the ground (Durkin 1984).

A variation of this approach using short passages, especially with young children, is to ask the children to suggest a word to be erased or covered before they read the passage aloud as a group. Continue this procedure for several readings. The children become very confident in reading the gradually disappearing text and build familiarity with the grammatical forms. They also quickly learn which are the easiest words to suggest for deletion on the basis of remaining clues to such words in the text.

LEARNING TO MAKE CONNECTIONS THROUGH CLOZE ACTIVITIES

Oral and written cloze techniques can also be used to draw attention to the linkages across clauses (cohesion). The tracking of reference is important so that children know how reference functions to construct taxonomies and definitions. In the following example, children need to understand 'These' as referring to 'two groups'. Masking or deleting 'These' and requiring the children to reinstate an appropriate piece of text allows this kind of understanding to be confirmed.

> Although there are many different plastics,
> they can all be divided into just
> two groups. These are the 'thermoplastics'
> and the 'thermosetting plastics' (Whyman 1987, p. 10).

In a similar way children's understanding of definitions that rely on reference could also be confirmed by, for example, deleting 'this' in the following example:

> All these movements are driven by slowly churning currents in the mantle. This is a hot layer of partly molten rock. It lies just beneath the thin solid surface layer we call the crust (Bramwell 1986a, p. 7).

The same approach could also focus on reference in explanations. Note, for example, the importance of the several occurrences of the reference item 'this' in the following explanation:

> Now wheels are never perfectly round, for the pressure on their rims deforms them slightly. You can see this easily on car tyres, which have a small flattened area at the bottom where they are in

contact with the road. The expansions and contractions that are necessary as each point in turn becomes flattened causes some friction. This is known as rolling friction and is considerably less than sliding friction. This is why wheels are so useful (Laithwaite 1986, p. 16).

These activities should not be reduced to 'cloze' exercises or repetitive 'comprehension checks'. The purpose is to create a context for collaborative negotiation of written texts and discussion and clarification of the ways in which meanings are constructed.

DRAWING FROM THE TEXT: CLARIFYING SCHEMATIC STRUCTURE

Schematic structure of texts can be clarified during whole class or group shared reading of text segments, using overhead projection transparencies as suggested above. One approach is to mark and label the staging of the text as segmentations are identified through discussion with the children. Detailed procedures for doing this in secondary school science have been elaborated by Lunzer and Gardner (1984) and Davies and Greene (1984). Text segmentation and labelling to show the schematic structure and grammatical features of commonly occurring genres in primary school writing are illustrated in Derewianka (1990b). The use of this approach with Year 2 children in a classroom context is illustrated in Derewianka (1990a) and an example of such a 'marked up' text is shown in Figure 7.4.

Illustrations and diagrams sometimes accompany scientific reports and explanations in books for young children and where this is the case they can be used to facilitate the 'talking out' of the text in relation to schematic structure. If diagrams are not included, jointly constructing them with the children can help children to identify and become familiar with the text organisation of various genres. Children can then use diagrammatic summaries as they make use of information books. Figure 7.5 shows a simple diagram of the classification taxonomy in the following short report on plastics. This could be quickly constructed with children to link clearly the examples of plastics to their respective categories.

> Although there are many different kinds of plastics, they can all be divided into just two groups. These are the 'thermoplastics' and the 'thermosetting plastics'. Polystyrene, polyvinyl chloride (PVC) and polythene were the first thermoplastics to be developed and they are still widely used. More recently thermoplastics, such as Nylon, Perspex and Orlon have been produced.
>
> The common feature of thermoplastics is that they all melt when heated to high enough temperatures and set solid again as they cool. This means they can be reused. But thermosetting plastics do not have this property. They are resistant to much higher temperatures. For this reason they are often used to make saucepan handles and ashtrays. The first plastic ever made was a thermosetting plastic called Bakelite after its inventor Leo Bakeland (Whyman 1987, pp. 10-11).

How rocks are formed

Role of introductory (cue) sentence

There are **three** main kinds of rock, **igneous**, **sedimentary** and **metamorphic**.

1. **Igneous** or fiery rocks, form from **magma**. This is underground molten rock that oozes up through the Earth's crust, then cools and hardens.
2. **Sedimentary** rocks are formed from broken bits of rock or from the remains of dead plants and animals. In time, all pile up to form layers of mud, sand or shells. Then chemicals slowly change these layers to solid rock. *— sequence / formation*
3. **Metamorphic** or 'changed shape' rocks can start off as either igneous or sedimentary rocks. They **are** changed by baking or squashing **as a result** of underground heat or pressure. *— cause*

△ This diagram shows various stages in rock formation. 1 Magma forms igneous rock. 2 Weathering breaks up rock. 3 Rivers wash pieces to sea. 4 Particles pile up on sea bed. 5 These form sedimentary rock. 6 Heat and pressure can change igneous and sedimentary rock to metamorphic rock.

▽ This section through the Earth's crust shows where rock types may form. Movements in the crust may thrust some rocks high up as mountain ranges. Other rocks are forced far below the surface.

Role of captions and illustrations e.g. additional information summarising

Volcanic activity creates igneous rocks

Metamorphic rocks created in new areas of volcano activity

Fold mountains made of sedimentary rocks. They are thrust up by crust movements.

Sedimentary rocks forming from silt deposits

Figure 7.4 *Text segmentation and labelling*
(Source: Lambert, D. (1986) Rocks and Minerals, *Franklin Watts, London*)

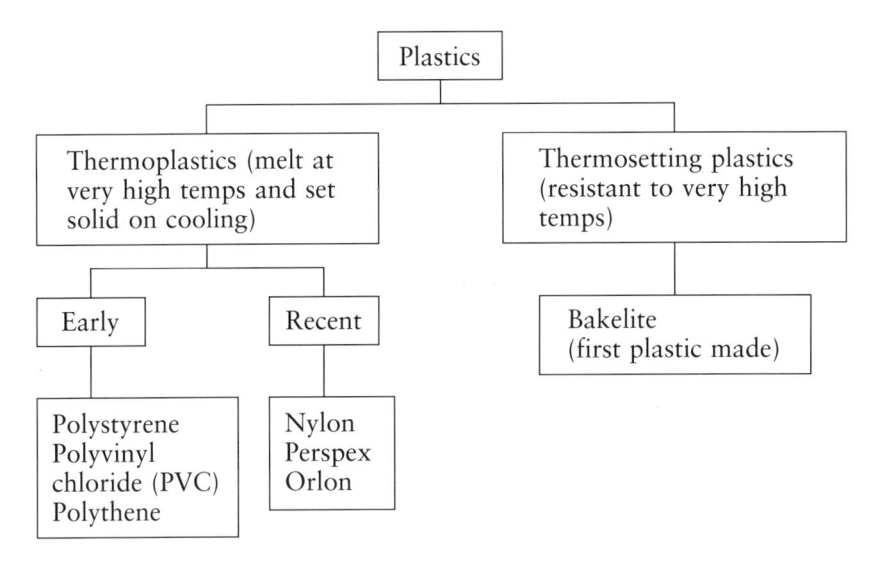

```
                        ┌──────────┐
                        │ Plastics │
                        └──────────┘
              ┌───────────────┴───────────────┐
    ┌─────────────────────┐         ┌─────────────────────┐
    │ Thermoplastics (melt│         │ Thermosetting plastics│
    │ at very high temps  │         │ (resistant to very  │
    │ and set solid on    │         │ high temps)         │
    │ cooling)            │         │                     │
    └─────────────────────┘         └─────────────────────┘
         ┌────┴────┐                           │
    ┌────────┐ ┌────────┐              ┌──────────────────┐
    │ Early  │ │ Recent │              │ Bakelite         │
    └────────┘ └────────┘              │ (first plastic   │
         │         │                   │ made)            │
    ┌──────────┐ ┌─────────┐           └──────────────────┘
    │Polystyrene│ │ Nylon  │
    │Polyvinyl  │ │ Perspex│
    │chloride   │ │ Orlon  │
    │(PVC)      │ │        │
    │Polythene  │ │        │
    └──────────┘ └─────────┘
```

Figure 7.5 *Diagram of a 'plastics' classification taxonomy*

For inexperienced readers of written explanations, the language which realises the causal relations sometimes seems opaque. This may be seen in the following simple explanation where a causal relation is realised by a non-finite clause — 'narrowing them'. The pattern of causal relations can be made accessible by the construction of a diagram such as that in Figure 7.6.

> Fatty substances in the blood can gradually become deposited on the walls of blood vessels, narrowing them and interfering with blood flow. For this reason, heart attacks and other diseases of the circulation are more common in people who eat large amounts of fat. In places like Japan and Africa, where little fat is eaten, heart disease is uncommon. But it is a killer in the Western World (Ward 1987, p.14).

Further detailed procedures and examples of the use of diagrams in teaching children to identify and use text organisation in curriculum area learning is provided in Morris and Stewart-Dore (1984), Lunzer and Gardner (1984) and Davies and Greene (1984).

'Text reconstruction' is another useful technique. Initially this should be carried out with familiar texts. For young children the text is cut up into sentences or clauses and the jumbled text is to be ordered and reconstructed. This can be done as a whole class activity with large format text or by children working in groups with duplicated copies of the original text which have been cut up and jumbled. Another way is to make several overhead transparencies of the text and cut these up. The children, working in groups, can reconstruct their texts inside a plastic sleeve and then put their versions on the overhead projector for class discussion. The task can also be set up as a computer-based activity where children are provided with the jumbled clauses on a data disk and use the word processor to reconstruct the text.

Literacy Learning and Teaching

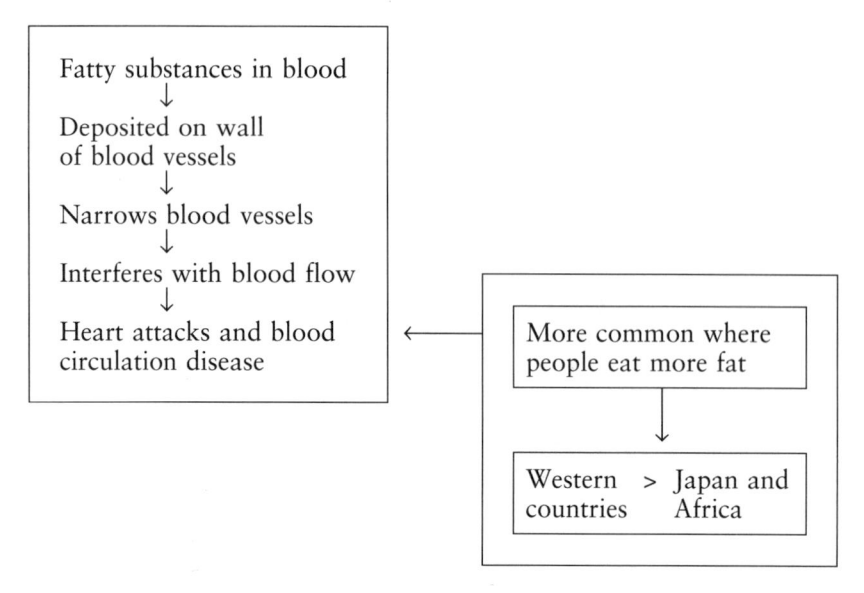

```
Fatty substances in blood
        ↓
Deposited on wall
of blood vessels
        ↓
Narrows blood vessels
        ↓
Interferes with blood flow
        ↓
Heart attacks and blood      ←——   More common where
circulation disease                 people eat more fat
                                              ↓
                                    Western    >  Japan and
                                    countries     Africa
```

Figure 7.6 *Diagram showing causal relations based on an excerpt from Ward (1987, p. 14)*

Another computer-based learning activity that is helpful involves the children in using data bases. In investigating a topic like reptiles, for example, the children build a data base with a record for each reptile that they find information about. Fields for each record could include appearance such as whether it has legs, type of skin and so on as well as habitat, food, etc. The sorting and report function of the program could then be used by children to explore the classification of reptiles and the criteria for categorisation. Alternatively the categories could be given and these could be the basis for sorting and reporting to explicate criteria and examples. This kind of learning task then provides a very useful reference for the children's own writing.

The Reading–Writing Connection

If children are to learn how to be active adult participants in the negotiation of social/scientific issues such as pollution, preservation of endangered species and *in vitro* fertilisation they need to learn how to compose and comprehend the forms of written texts (genres) through which the culture carries on such negotiation. This means learning to control the technical discourses that are used to construct and challenge knowledge in these areas. This is not something that can suddenly begin in secondary school because what children in their primary years understand science to be is shaped by the language of science teaching and learning. Effective use of appropriate science books from the beginning of primary school can help to initiate children into the discourses of specialised knowledge. But in learning how to organise informational content for writing, chil-

Information Books in Junior Primary Science

dren can also learn how authors use written language forms to construct and contest scientific knowledge. In so doing they are extending their strategies for comprehending the written texts they need to read.

Reports, explanations and procedures are the most common genres used to introduce students to scientific facts and research methodology. Exposition is a genre used to present arguments to justify a given position and 'discussion' is a genre which presents arguments for both sides of an issue and concludes with a recommendation based on the weight of evidence. Expositions and discussions are quite rare in science texts, especially those for young children, but they could be introduced into science programs via the teaching of writing.

The pedagogical practices of genre-based writing approaches build the reading–writing connection. A schematic representation of the teaching/learning cycle for a genre-based approach to writing (Macken *et al*. 1989, p. 42) is shown in Figure 7.7.

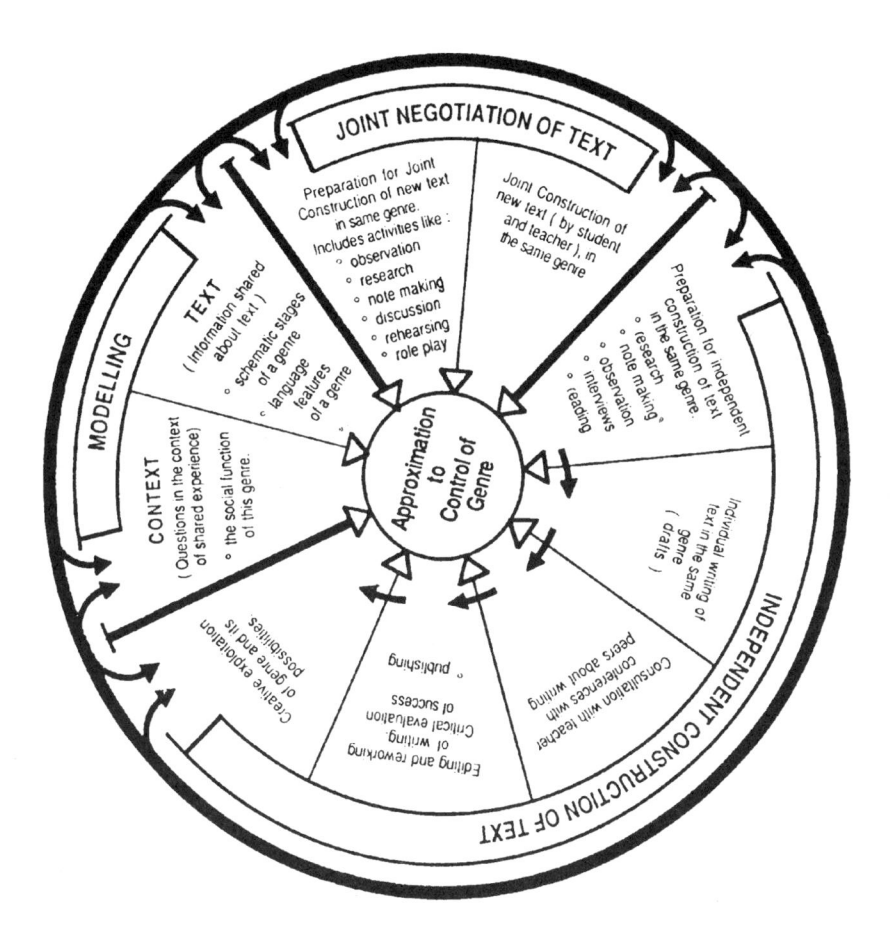

Figure 7.7 *Teaching/learning cycle for a genre-based approach to writing* (Source: *Macken* et al. *1989*)

In the modelling stage 'context' refers to the introductory exploration of the topic via direct and vicarious experience. Children's commonsense observations are the starting point which, via oral language interaction accompanying further probing of these experiences, is extended to more systematic understanding. During this phase the social purpose of the investigation is made explicit and hence the form of writing which will result. For example, if the investigation involves methods of keeping feral cats out of nature reserves, the appropriate genre to be negotiated is explanation.

The next phase of the modelling stage is the close discussion and 'deconstruction' of a model text. This could be an explanation of methods dealing with an analogous problem. The kinds of activities here would be those discussed above in 'Talking out the Text', 'Learning to make Connections' and 'Drawing from the Text'.

In the joint negotiation stage the teacher and children first decide what preparation will need to be done in order for them to collaboratively construct a text like the model they examined in the previous stage. They may need to gather more information, look more closely at pictures and diagrams they have found, etc. In the second phase of the joint negotiation the teacher scribes for the class/group and shapes the students' contributions into a text which approximates the genre (explanation, for example) which is under focus. This involves simultaneous shaping of Field and Mode, i.e. of the shift from commonsense to scientific knowledge and from everyday oral language to the grammatical forms of technical, written language.

During the 'independent construction of text' stage children are encouraged to write their own individual texts (explanations in this case) usually on a selected aspect of the broad Field under investigation (e.g. various methods of excluding a range of animal pests from reserves or farming areas). The role of the teacher is that of an experienced consultant who can provide help if required. The master–apprentice relationship between the teacher and pupil will persist until the pupil confidently controls the genre. A different relationship characterises conferences among students and their peers who are encouraged to share and discuss the progress of their work. During this stage some children may need more systematic guidance from the teacher and small groups may be convened for additional direct input. Other students may extend their work to creatively exploit the genre (e.g. an explanation scripted as a voice-over for a documentary video on the topic). Children should be encouraged to edit and 'publish' their work so that it becomes a resource for the classroom community and perhaps also for the community beyond.

The construction of effective contexts for science learning in primary schools includes opportunities for direct, 'hands-on' activities and oral language interaction in the exploration and discussion of phenomena of the physical and natural sciences. However, systematising and integrating the observations that children make into the frameworks of scientific knowledge necessitates a concomitant development of control over the forms of scientific discourse which construct such knowledge. The reading–writing connection is integral to the teaching of science.

The Language and Literacy Focus of Effective Science Programs

The implementation of two science units will be briefly outlined. The first was undertaken with a Year 2 class and the second with a Year 5 class. In both classrooms the teachers wanted to foster explicit understanding of how language functions in the learning process. In the case of the Year 2 class, the theoretical orientation for the program planning to achieve this was that of functional linguistic accounts of the relationship between language and social context (Halliday 1978b; Halliday and Hasan 1985; Martin 1984, 1989, 1990). A compatible orientation is evident in the Year 5 class although the program planning in this case did not derive directly from this functional linguistic perspective.

The oral and written texts which we engage with and produce have their particular linguistic form because of the social purposes they fulfil. To extend children's experience of language as a resource for meaning we need to understand how text form relates to its social context. The following outline account is derived from the model proposed by Martin (1984).

First, social context can be thought of in terms of two levels — genre, corresponding to the context of culture, and register, corresponding to the context of situation. Genres are the well-known meaning-making routines by which cultures deploy language in organised stages to achieve particular social goals. Making a dentist appointment, telling a joke, 'wanted to sell' advertisements, etc., as well as genres valued in schools such as explanation, discussion and exposition make their particular social meanings partly because of the characteristic steps or stages by which they achieve their goals. Genre networks are a way of accounting for the range of situation types which are found within a culture. So genres are realised by or given expression by particular combinations of the variables which define these situation types. The situational variables are known as Field, Tenor and Mode and the skewing of these variables within different contexts of situation makes meaning at the level of register (Figure 7.8).

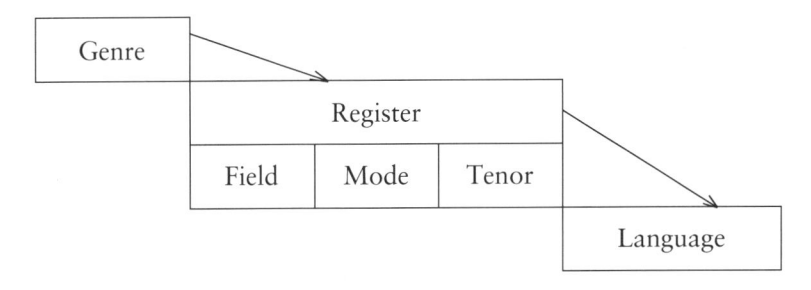

Figure 7.8 *Language, register and genre*

Contexts of situation differ from one another, broadly speaking, in three respects: first, the 'content' of what is actually taking place (Field); second, the relationships among those taking part (Tenor); and third, what part the language is playing (Mode) (for detailed descriptions see Halliday 1978b, p. 31).

Field is concerned with experiential meanings — the events, participants and circumstances of the social and phenomenonal world. Tenor is concerned with interpersonal meanings — the relative status of the participants, the nature of their social contact including their affective relations, their interactive roles and their personal perspectives and judgements. Mode refers to the role of language in a particular situation. It changes according to whether the language is accompanying some activity (e.g. a child giving commands to his or her team on the sporting field) or constitutes the activity (e.g. the child telling someone else about the game the next day). Mode also deals with the channel of communication (aural or graphic) and the medium (whether the grammatical form is closer to spoken or written language). Mode is therefore concerned with textual meanings — what makes a text coherent in a particular context of situation. This involves how linkages and emphases are achieved within the text itself taking account of its context.

Genre and register have been discussed as ways of thinking about meaning-making systems at the contextual levels of context of culture and context of situation respectively. Now, in indicating that the register variables of Field, Tenor and Mode are each distinctively concerned with particular kinds of meanings, i.e. experiential, interpersonal and textual, the interface between context and language has been introduced. This interface is part of a tri-stratal model of language, illustrated in Figure 7.9.

Semantics then is the interface between the social system and the grammatical system. It 'faces both ways' — it points 'upward' realising the meanings associated with each of the contextual variables Field, Tenor and Mode, which are construed as three very generalised functions or metafunctions:

1. the ideational metafunction which enables us to make sense of our world;
2. the interpersonal metafunction which enables us to participate in the world through interaction with others;
3. the textual metafunction which enables language to form into texts.

At the same time this metafunctionally organised semantic system points downward to, and is realised by, corresponding systems at the lexicogrammatical level.

Particular systems within the grammar realise the different kinds of meanings or metafunctions indicated above. The ideational meanings associated with Field are realised grammatically by the transitivity system. This includes the kinds of processes and participants involved. For example, the language of children on an excursion investigating rocks would include a lot of material (action) and mental processes with the children themselves as the Actors or Sensers and rocks as Goal or

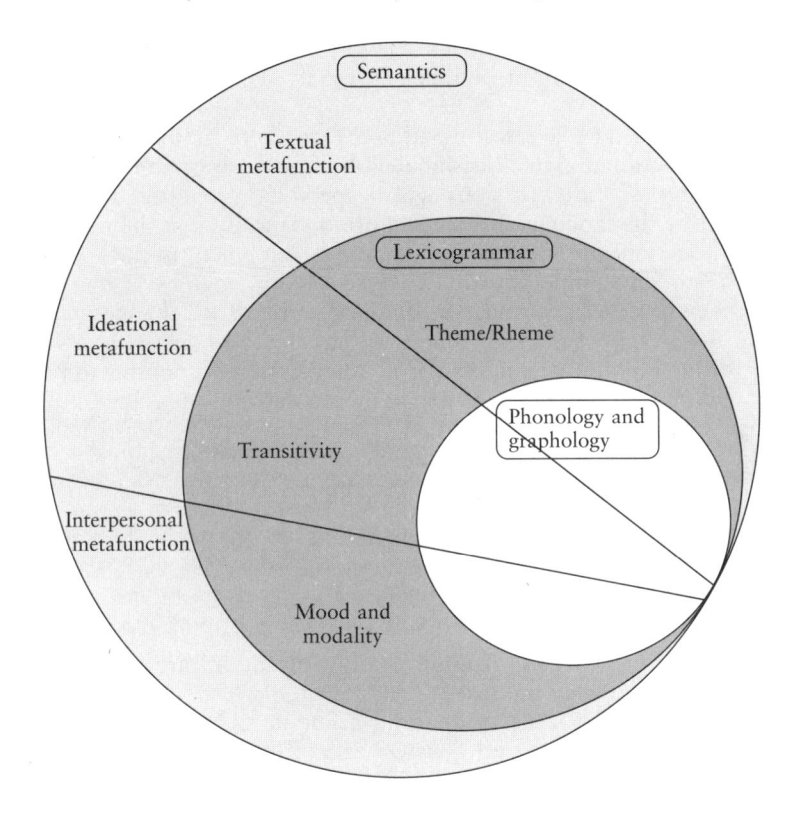

Figure 7.9 Tri-stratal model of language

Phenomenon: 'Can I break some of that black rock?', 'It probably came off the cliff', 'Can you see any?', 'Look at that smooth one'. As their knowledge of the Field develops and they use language to classify and define, they will use more technical terms as participants and the processes will more likely be relational (processes of being): 'The softest sample is sandstone', 'Basalt is an igneous rock'.

Interpersonal meanings relating to Tenor are realised grammatically by systems of Mood and Modality (the giving or demanding of information or actions). Notice that the questions, commands and statements of the excursion are appropriate to the interactive, exploratory nature of that situation. Indeed there will also be a good deal of questioning, commanding and responding with statements in the interactive learning of the classroom. But when the children later use language authoritatively to report their technical knowledge, they will make more use of statements to construct classifications and definitions.

The textual meanings associated with Mode are realised in part by the systems of cohesion and Theme selection. Notice in the second clause from the excursion, 'It probably came off the cliff', we can only know what 'It' is if we are present in the situation. Participants are identified by reference to the material setting, but in written language the participants are identified within the text itself: 'Sandstone is soft and easily cut up. It was therefore a common building material.' The 'It' clearly refers to 'Sandstone'.

Many of the Theme selections (i.e. the speaker's assumption of what is taken for granted, which is signalled by first position in the clause) in the language of the excursions will be personal references like 'I' and 'we'. But as the language becomes more distanced from the action, the Theme selections are more to do with the development of the topic as in the sandstone example above. The 'medium' of language being used is more like the written language medium of books. With changes in Mode (more toward the written medium) so that the language becomes more constitutive (i.e. not dependent for its interpretation upon being related to actual physical object or settings), nominalisation (discussed in 'Definitions' within the section entitled 'The Grammatical Construction of Scientific Knowledge') will become more prominent to enable the construction of technical explanation and reports.

> When volcanoes erupt molten magma is forced up to the earth's surface where it cools and hardens. These rocks created by volcanic eruptions are called igneous rocks.
> This diagram shows various stages in rock formation.

Nominalisations such as 'eruptions' and 'formation' are important resources for organising the text.

Of course there is much more to the grammatical systems of transitivity, Mood and Modality and Theme/Rheme than is indicated by the few examples indicated above. They simply illustrate that the grammatical systems are deployed in different ways in order to make appropriate meanings in varying social contexts. The relationship between contextual variables and grammatical systems is summarised in simplified form in Figure 7.10. Every text, whether spoken or written, simultaneously makes meanings which relate to the three aspects of register. Field, Tenor and Mode combine in different ways in different contexts of situation, i.e. values within each of the categories may vary with variation in social context. Consequently different selections are made simultaneously within each of the corresponding systems of the grammar. With register variation, therefore, there is a systematic variation in language form.

As children's learning in a particular unit of science develops, Field changes from everyday, commonsense observations to more explicit, systematic, integrated knowledge of the topic and how it relates to frameworks or paradigms of scientific inquiry. This involves a simultaneous change in Mode — the part language is playing in the learning situation. Mode initially involves language in the here and now — the oral language accompanying direct investigation of material objects in interaction with the teacher and/or peers. Then there is a gradual 'distancing' process as individual involvement in the detail of the material situational setting is replaced by a 'standing back', a more reflective, detached perspective where language is the sole means by which the topic is dealt with. This change in Mode means that the form of the language must change so that all of the relevant information is explicitly con-

Information Books in Junior Primary Science

Register variables	↔ Meanings of a text	↔ Metafunction	↔ Grammatical system
Field	Representation of experience	Ideational	Transitivity clause complex
Tenor	Interaction of participants' interpersonal perspectives	Interpersonal	Mood and Modality
Mode	Accompanying/ constituting activity; spoken/written; emphases; coherence	Textual	Theme/Rheme Cohesion

Figure 7.10 *Text/context relationships*

structed linguistically — the language is constitutive of, rather than accompanying, the situation. This gradual but simultaneous change in Field and Mode must be accompanied by corresponding changes in Tenor — the relationships among those involved. The social organisation of the learning situation must allow children to be able to use language to accompany direct investigation and to exchange meanings with the teacher and their peers in so doing. A highly authoritarian teaching approach precludes children from engaging in this kind of meaningful exploratory talk. At times, however, children will also need to be explicitly taught how to access certain technologies of scientific inquiry including the forms of written language by which the results of scientific inquiry are recorded within our culture. The teacher then needs to assume the role of authoritative (but not authoritarian) mentor. The roles of the children will also change. Whereas initially they may be interested participants or 'fellow travellers', ultimately they will take on more of the role of an 'expert' in relation to the topic. The teacher and pupils therefore enter into a variety of relationships, with differing attributions of power and status, which entail the use of a variety of forms of language in facilitating effective learning. Changes in the interrelated contextual variables of Field, Tenor and Mode during the development of the unit are related to variation in register and hence to children's experience of different forms of language in learning in science. A general schema for the way in which forms of language result from interrelationships of genre, register and lexicogrammar is shown in Figure 7.11.

The register variations which children experience in their science work will also be related to the different social purposes they have. Particular patternings of register variables will be associated with particular genres such as recount, report, procedure, explanation, discussion, exposition (see Martin 1984 for the relationship between register and genre). Children need to become aware of register and genre if they are to control the

Literacy Learning and Teaching

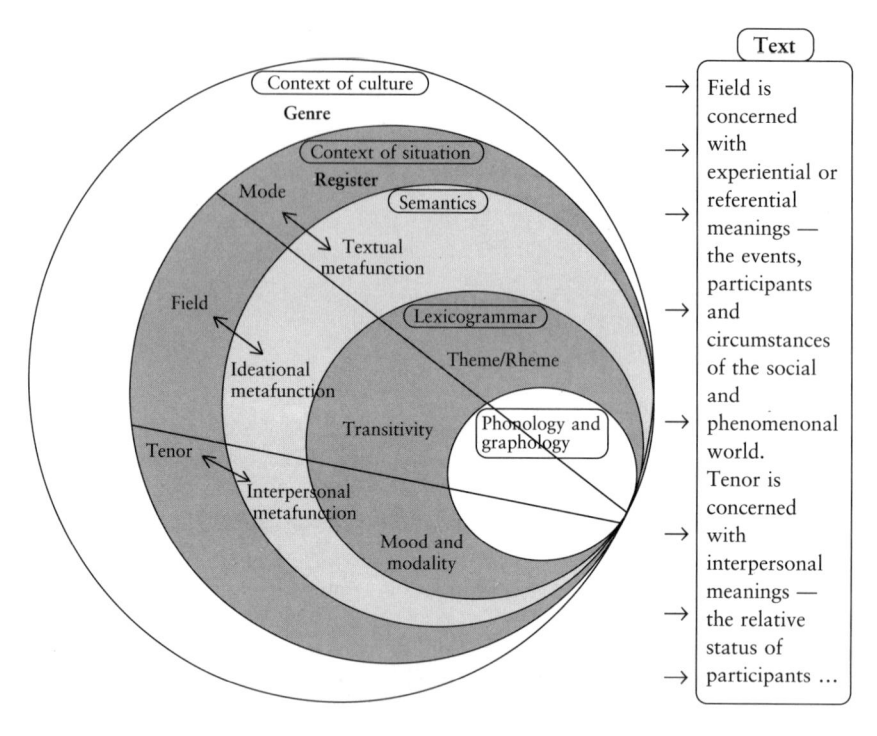

Figure 7.11 *Language, context and text*

varieties of language that are appropriate to different uses. For example, in learning science, they must learn the form of language appropriate to contexts which range from language associated with observation, the collection and discussion of data to the language of directions, reports, explanations and textbook expositions.

The following programs emphasise the interconnectedness of social and linguistic contexts as integral to the teaching and learning of science.

Rocks in the Head

In this program Derewianka (1990a) worked with a teacher to devise and implement a unit of work for a Year 2 class on the theme 'Why We Study Rocks'. The learning context was consciously structured in terms of Mode, Field and Tenor:

- the Mode ranged from oral/active to written/reflective as the unit progressed;
- the overall Field involved an ever-increasing knowledge of 'rocks', deliberately introducing an awareness of relationships through comparing, contrasting, classifying, etc.;
- the Tenor reflected the various roles and relationships engaged in by teacher, children and parents.

Information Books in Junior Primary Science

A diagrammatic summary of the program is provided in Figure 7.12 and a more detailed descriptive account follows.

The unit began with an excursion to the surrounding countryside visiting sites where children observed and noted the characteristics of rocks in their natural state or rocks that had been used for construction. The language was mainly oral, accompanying the children's exploration of the sites, but some brief 'field notes' were taken by the children to act as 'memory joggers'. The relationship between the adults and the children had an 'equal status' quality with the children, their parents and the teacher exploring as co-learners. Field at this stage was a mixture of everyday knowledge and some technical terms which were introduced in context in response to the children's inquiries.

Back in the classroom the experiences were shared in a joint oral recount. Language was now somewhat distanced from the actual activity and there was some putting of things in perspective, selection of signifi-

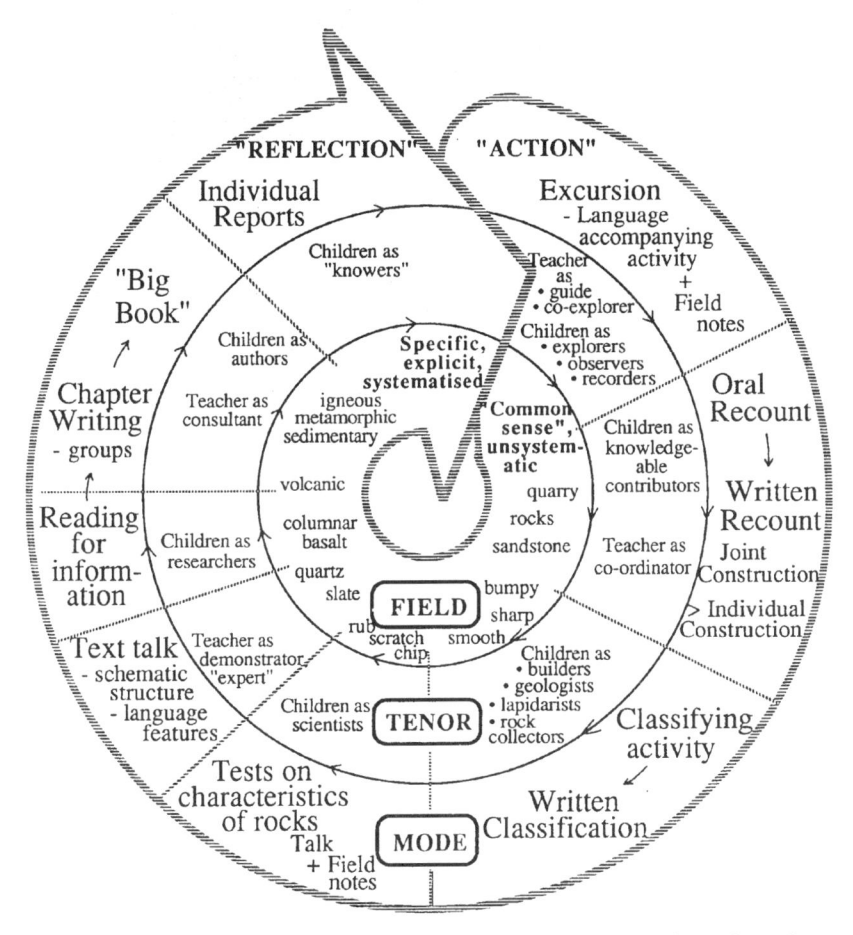

Figure 7.12 *A diagrammatic description of the unit of work 'Why We Study Rocks'*
(Source: Derewianka 1990a)

cant aspects and ordering of events in time. The Field included the children's recollections of the trip and their observations. There was still a mixture of mainly commonsense with some technical information including the names of rocks like 'basalt' and some categories like 'igneous'.

The next classroom activity was a classification of the rock samples the children had collected so the Mode shifted again back a little toward language accompanying action as the children discussed their groupings of the rocks. The pupils' roles were specifically structured for this activity with different groups of children taking on the roles of lapidarists, geologists, builders and rock collectors. The children looked for characteristics of the rocks that would be of interest to the roles they adopted. In terms of Field the children learned a lot about the process of classifying but were frustrated by their lack of more detailed knowledge of the rocks and their attributes.

This led to the next class activity of carrying out 'tests' on the rocks such as scratching, rubbing, chipping, etc. The language was mainly oral, accompanying action again with some written notes of results as groups dictated their findings to a group scribe. The peer relationship was one of knowledgeable equals negotiating collaboratively to carry out their tasks. As the children worked on these tests they regularly compared their samples with those in a labelled rock collection so their control of Field was becoming more systematic.

At this point the teacher started to exploit the resources of written mode to construct a more explicit scientific perspective. The class were to construct a 'Big Book' about rocks and groups of children within the class worked together to produce a chapter on their topic. The teacher chose a simple factual text about rocks, made an overhead transparency of a relevant section and guided the children to engage with the text through a shared reading during which she drew attention to various features such as schematic structure, major participants, use of exemplification, as well as formating features like headings, illustrations, captions, glossary, etc. This helped the children to see how to locate information in such texts and also served as a model for their own writing. A copy of such a text segment used was shown in Figure 7.4. In this activity the teacher assumed the role of 'expert'; however in her authoritative role she maintained a supportive relationship with the children so that they were active contributors to the exploration and discussion of the text. The text presented the Field in an organised manner — filling in gaps in the children's knowledge and developing an explicit classification taxonomy.

As the children worked in groups to prepare their contribution to the 'Big Book' they located and read information books about rocks, took notes, drafted, redrafted, edited and finally published their 'Big Book' chapters. They were now in control of a good deal of systematic uncommonsense knowledge of the Field. Although oral language was important in the discussion and preparation of their jointly constructed texts, they were now well into the writing process and the negotiation of written mode took precedence as they researched factual texts and wrote their own texts.

Science as Ethnography

This science unit (Heath 1983) was undertaken with a fifth grade made up of almost entirely black boys who experienced extreme difficulty with reading and were considered the lowest science class. They began a unit on plant life with a film about life in a Latin-American village and then a discussion with Heath about her anthropological research in that village. The pupils were then keen to undertake their eight week unit on plant life as ethnographic researchers.

> ... the students were told to imagine they had just been set down as strangers in their own community. They were scouts or early arrivals of a group which would set up an agricultural resource center in the area. Most of the children were familiar with this idea, since there had recently been several highly publicized research projects in the area promoting new approaches to soybean production and the substitution of soy products for meats. As employees of the imaginary center, they were to have the task of learning as much as possible about the ways of growing foodstuffs currently used by the local people. They had only the local residents to learn from as they participated, observed, interviewed, collected documents and artifacts, took photographs, and collected histories in the area. At the end of their preliminary stay, their task would be to advise the agricultural resource center on ways in which the local people's folk concepts were like or different from 'scientific' approaches. In other words, for their bosses, they would have to translate knowledge into scientific knowledge and answer the questions of whether or not science could explain why local folk methods either worked or did not work (Heath 1983, p. 317).

It was decided to focus on a minimal number of initial questions in the ethnographic work:

- What were the foodstuffs most commonly grown in the area?
- Who were considered the best farmers and what were their methods?

The answers to these questions had to come from at least two sources — one oral and one written. The pupils interviewed throughout the neighbourhood and analysed their data to determine the most popular responses to both questions. Verification by written sources was more difficult. One boy brought in a local newspaper clipping of a farmer who had grown a pumpkin exceeding 100 lbs. The article said he often produced vegetables of immense size and was well known for his good garden year after year.

> After this first breakthrough, the boys collected back issues of the weekly newspapers distributed in the textile mills in which their parents worked. These carried local features, many of which focused on gardening or cooking talents. The class also asked the local newspaper for back issues of October and November editions, many of which featured harvest articles etc ...
> To provide written verification of foodstuffs that were most frequently grown in the area, the boys — at the suggestion of a local minister's wife — checked through recipe books produced by local church groups. The recipes often depended on local vegetables and seasonings and the vegetables for which the greatest number of recipes were offered were sure to be those grown locally (Heath 1983, p. 318).

The boys collected life histories and artefacts. The life histories of the 'best farmers' were summarised, involving listening to tapes over and over in order to make a suitable written condensation. They were then typed and placed in the 'science book' with photographs of the informants. Comparative charts translating and/or explaining folk concepts through scientific reasons were hung around the room. In preparing these, the boys drew on information available from science books in the classroom and in the library. In essence, the culmination of the unit's work was a book written by the class, similar to a chapter on gardening in a traditional ethnographic study.

> By the end of the eight weeks, the standard unit test of the textbook was given: twelve boys scored above 90%, eight scored in the 80's, and three in the 70's. Of the twenty three boys in the class, none failed the test. Their cumulative folders indicated that none of these boys ever passed a standardized unit science test in his school career. Average attendance during earlier units of the year which had been approached through traditional teaching methods had been 68%; average attendance during the two months of this unit was 92%. Six parents visited the school, sharing information or demonstrating techniques of gardening; eleven family members sent information or artifacts to the school. Prior to this unit, only two family members had contacted the teacher regarding matters other than discipline or failing grades (Heath 1983, p. 320).

This unit took into account the fact that knowledge, thought, language and learning are intrinsically social and collaborative. It also took into account the relationship between commonsense and uncommonsense knowledge and the need to provide contexts for learning which dealt explicitly with the initiation of children into the discourse forms that construct uncommonsense knowledge. The pupils were tested at the end of the unit, but their collective effort was also tested. Their book had to meet their demands — those of the teacher and the pupils — for a genuine resource that could be useful to the next year's fifth class. The collectiveness of pupil–community–teacher knowledge and effort is a radical deviation from the privileging of pedagogical procedures in classrooms which emphasise independent, individual-student and teacher-dominated approaches to learning, and the explicit attention to the linguistic construction of scientific understanding is a departure from the taken for grantedness of language in science teaching.

Conclusion

To improve the teaching and learning of science, teachers and pupils will have to work toward a much clearer grasp of the function of language as technology in building up a scientific picture of the world (Martin 1990, p. 115). Right from the beginning, children's learning of science in the primary school must involve a simultaneous apprenticeship to the linguistic forms that construct scientific understanding if children are to progress beyond their 'children's science' by the time they finish their primary school education (Osborne and Freyberg 1989). 'Hands on' learning experiences and accompanying oral language interaction are not sufficient. These activities need to be extended and augmented by explicit teaching of the forms of written language that construct scientific knowledge. Children's main form of access to the written mode is through reading. Appropriate information books are therefore a crucial resource as they also provide the models of the genres children need to learn to write. Indeed what counts as science in primary school classrooms is indicated by the form of the texts to which the children are introduced in the science program. Hence the need to critique science texts in terms of their effectiveness in inducting into scientific discourse children at various stages of reading development throughout the primary school. This kind of critique involves knowledge of science and knowledge of text as technology. These are also the resources that teachers can use to enhance programming and classroom management of science learning as they develop units of work such as 'Rocks in the Head' based on an emerging linguistic theory of learning.

References

Baker, C. and Freebody, P. (1989) 'Talk around text: Constructions of textual and teacher authority in classroom discourse', in *Language, Authority and Criticism: Readings on the School Textbook*, eds S. de Castell, A. Luke and C. Luke, Falmer Press, London.
Bernstein, B. (1971) 'On the classification and framing of educational knowledge', in *Knowledge and Control: New Directions in the Sociology of Knowledge*, ed. M. Young, Collier-Macmillan, London.
Christie, F. (ed.) (1985) *Reading Curriculum: Study Guide*, Deakin University Press, Geelong, Victoria.
Christie, F. (1986) 'Learning to write: Where do texts come from?', *Proceedings of the Twelfth Australian Reading Conference*, Australian Reading Association, Perth.
Christie, F. (1988) 'The construction of knowledge in the junior primary school', in *Language and Socialization: Home and School*, eds L. Gerot, J. Oldenburg and T. Van Leeuwen, Macquarie University, Sydney.
Christie, F. (1989) *Writing in Schools: Study Guide*, Deakin University Press, Geelong, Victoria.
Davies, F. and Greene, T. (1984) *Reading for Learning in the Sciences*, Oliver and Boyd, Edinburgh.
Derewianka, B. (1990a) 'Rocks in the head: Children writing geology reports', in *Knowledge about Language and the Curriculum: The LINC Reader*, Hodder and Stoughton, London.
Derewianka, B. (1990b) *Exploring How Texts Work*, Primary English Teaching Association, Sydney.
Donaldson, M. (1989) *Sense and Sensibility: Some Thoughts on the Teaching of Literacy*, Reading and Language Information Centre, University of Reading, Reading.

Halliday, M.A.K. (1978a) 'The significance of Bernstein's work for sociolinguistic theory', in *Language as Social Semiotic*, Edward Arnold, London.
Halliday, M.A.K. (1978b) *Language as Social Semiotic*, Edward Arnold, London.
Halliday, M.A.K. (1985) *Spoken and Written Language*, Deakin University Press, Geelong, Victoria.
Halliday, M.A.K. (1988a) 'On the language of physical science', in *Registers of Written English: Situational Factors and Linguistic Features*, ed. M. Ghadessy, Frances Pinter, London.
Halliday, M.A.K. (1988b) 'Language and the enhancement of learning', Paper presented to the Post World Congress Symposium: Language and Learning, University of Queensland.
Halliday, M.A.K. (1990) 'Linguistic perspectives on literacy: A systemic-functional approach', Paper presented to the Inaugural Australian Systemics Network Conference, Deakin University, Geelong, Victoria.
Halliday, M.A.K. and Hasan, R. (1985) *Language, Context and Text*, Deakin University Press, Geelong, Victoria.
Hardy, B. (1977) 'Narrative as a primary act of mind', in *The Cool Web: The Pattern of Children's Reading*, eds M. Meek, A. Warlow, and G. Barton, The Bodley Head, London.
Heath, S.B. (1983) *Ways with Words*, Cambridge University Press, Cambridge.
Kwan, T. and Riley, J. (1982) 'Curriculum reviews: Holt elementary science', *Science and Children* 19: 38–40.
Lambert, D. (1986) Rocks and Minerals, Franklin Watts, London.
Lemke, J.L. (1985) 'Ideology, intertextuality and the notion of genre', in *Systemic Perspectives on Discourse: Selected Theoretical Papers from the Ninth International Systemic Workshop*, eds. J.D. Benson and W.S. Greaves, Ablex, Norwood, New Jersey.
Lemke, J. (1989a) 'Making texts talk', *Theory into Practice* 27(2): 136–41.
Lemke, J.L. (1989b) *Literacy and Diversity*, Language in Education Conference, Murdoch University, December 1989.
Lemke, J. (1989c) 'The language of science teaching', in *Locating Learing Across the Curriculum*, ed. C. Emihovich, Ablex, Norwood, New Jersey.
Lunzer, E. and Gardner, K. (1984) *Learning from the Written Word*, Oliver and Boyd, Edinburgh.
Martin, J. (1984) 'Language, register and genre', in *Children Writing: Study Guide*, ed. F. Christie, Deakin University Press, Geelong, Victoria.
Martin, J. (1989) 'Technicality and abstraction: Language for the creation of specialised texts', in *Writing in Schools: Reader,* ed. F. Christie *et al.*, Deakin University Press, Geelong, Victoria.
Martin, J. (1990) 'Literacy in science: Learning to handle text as technology', in *Literacy for a Changing World*, ed. F. Christie, Australian Council for Educational Research, Melbourne.
Martin, J. (1985) *Factual Writing: Explaining and Challenging Social Reality*, Deakin University Press, Geelong, Victoria.
Martin, J., Wignell, P., Eggins, S. and Rothery, J. (1988) 'Secret English: Discourse technology in a junior secondary school', in *Language and Socialization: Home and School*, eds L. Gerot, J. Oldenburg and T. Van Leeuwen, Macquarie University, Sydney.
Macken, M., Martin, J., Kress, G., Kalantzis, M., Rothery, J. and Cope, W. (1989) *A Genre-based Approach to Teaching Writing*, Literacy and Education Research Network and Directorate of Studies, New South Wales Department of Education, Sydney.
Morris, A. and Stewart-Dore, N. (1984) *Learning to Learn from Text*, Addison-Wesley, Sydney.

Information Books in Junior Primary Science

Mehan, H. (1976) 'Assessing children's school performance', in *The Process of Schooling*, eds M. Hammersley and P. Woods, Routledge and Kegan Paul, London.
Osborne, R. and Freyberg, P. (1989) *Learning in Science: The Implications of Children's Science*, Heinemann, Auckland.
Roth, K. and Anderson, C. (1988) 'Promoting conceptual change: Learning from science textbooks', in *Improving Learning: New Perspectives*, ed. P. Ramsden, Kogan Page, London.
Shea, N. (1988) 'The language of junior secondary science textbooks', A thesis submitted in partial fulfilment of the degree of Bachelor of Arts (Honours), Department of Linguistics, University of Sydney.
Stodart, E. (1985) 'Wings of fact: Non-fiction for children', in *Give Them Wings: The Experience of Children's Literature*, eds M. Saxby and G. Winch, Macmillan, Melbourne.
Stodart, E. (1989) Some notes on writing about science for children, *Reading Time* 33: 4–7.
Trimble, L. (1985) *English for Science and Technology: A Discourse Approach*, Cambridge University Press, Cambridge.
Victorian Department of Education (1981) *Science in the Primary School*, Vol. 3, Department of Education, Melbourne.

References to Children's Books

Andersen, H. (1986a) *Breathing*, Martin Educational and Ashton Scholastic, Gosford, New South Wales.
Andersen, H. (1986b) *Floating and Sinking*, Martin Educational and Ashton Scholastic, Gosford, New South Wales.
Andrews, K. (1972) *Beneath the Oceans*, Macdonald Educational, London.
Bailey, D. (1988) *Reptiles*, Macmillan, London.
Bender, L. (1988) *Spiders*, Gloucester Press, Sydney.
Bolton, F. (1986) *Melting*, Martin Educational and Ashton Scholastic, Gosford, New South Wales.
Bramwell, M. (1986a) *Volcanoes and Earthquakes*, Franklin Watts, Sydney.
Bramwell, M. (1986b) *Rivers and Lakes*, Franklin Watts, Sydney.
Clemence, J. and Clemence, J. (1987) *Electricity*, Macdonald, Sydney.
Collins, M. (1988) *Dinosaurs*, Martin Educational and Ashton Scholastic, Gosford, New South Wales.
Cullen, E. (1986) *An Introduction to Australian Spiders*, Martin Educational, Sydney.
Dahl, R. (1961) *James and the Giant Peach*, Puffin, Harmondsworth.
d'Arcier, M.F. (1986) *What is Balance?*, Viking Kestrel, Melbourne.
Drew, D. (1987) *Animal Facts*, Methuen Australia, Sydney.
Durkin, P. (1984) *Satellites in Space*, Young Australia Reading Scheme, Thomas Nelson Australia, Melbourne.
Fitzpatrick, J. (1984) *Magnets*, Hamish Hamilton, London.
Howes, J. (1987) *Down, Roundabout and Up Again: The Life of a River*, Macmillan, Melbourne.
Jennings, T. (1988) *Floating and Sinking*, Gloucester Press, New York.
Jennings, T. (1989a) *Balancing*, Oxford University Press, Oxford.
Jennings, T. (1989b) *Hot and Cold*, Oxford University Press, Oxford.

Jennings, T. (1989c) *Spiders*, Oxford University Press, Oxford.
Jennings, T. (1989d) *Colour*, Oxford University Press, Oxford.
Laithwaite, E. (1986) *Force,* Franklin Watts, Sydney.
Lambert, D. (1986) *Rocks and Minerals*, Franklin Watts, London.
Langley, A. (1987)*Trees*, Franklin Watts, Sydney.
Latham, R. and Sloan, P. (1985) *The Bulldozer Cleared the Way*, Methuen, Sydney.
Lye, L. (1987) *Coasts*, Wayland, Hove.
McClymont, D. (1987) *Water,* Macdonald, Sydney.
Petty, K. (1986) *Trucks*, Franklin Watts, London.
Pigdon, K. and Woolley, M. (1987) *River Red*, Macmillan, Melbourne.
Pigdon, K. and Woolley, M. (1989) *Earthworms*, Macmillan, Melbourne.
Pigdon, N. (1987) *Moggy's Hop*, Macmillan, Melbourne.
Pluckrose, H. (1986) *Floating and Sinking*, Franklin Watts, London.
Pollock, J. and Pollock, Y. (1986) *Trucks*, Martin Educational and Ashton Scholastic, Gosford, New South Wales.
Selsam, M. and Hunt, J. (1982) *A First Look at Dinosaurs*, Scholastic, New York.
Sloan, P. and Latham, R. (1985) *The Bush Where I Walk*, Methuen, Sydney.
Thomson, R. (1988) *Eyes*, Franklin Watts, Sydney.
Todd, H.E. (1982)*The Tiny Tiny Tadpole,* Carousel Books, London.
Tyler, M. (1987) *An Introduction to Frogs*, Martin Educational and Ashton Scholastic, Gosford, New South Wales.
Vaughan, M. (1986) *Whose Toes and Nose are Those?*, Martin Educational and Ashton Scholastic, Gosford, New South Wales.
Waters, G. and Round, G. (1985a) *Science Surprises*, Usborne, London.
Waters, G. and Round, G. (1985b) *Tricks and Magic*, Usborne, London.
Ward, B.R. (1987) *Diet and Nutrition,* Franklin Watts, Sydney.
Webb, A. (1987) *Sound*, Franklin Watts, London.
Whyman, K. (1987) *Plastics*, Gloucester Press, Sydney.

8
Resourcing Children's Learning

Keith Pigdon and Marilyn Woolley

Contents

Introduction 351

Classroom Planning and Organisation 354

People and Places as Resources 362
 Visit to a Retirement Centre
 The Zoo
 A Market
 Simulated Historical Settings

Video and Film Resources 374
 The Lorax
 See it My Way
 The Other Facts of Life

Pictures and other Visual Print Resources 386
 The Changing Countryside
 Niki's Walk

Computer Resources 395
 Application Software

Books as Resources 400
 Factual Text

Conclusion 409

References
Resources for Children

Introduction

When we think of exemplary classroom practice we consider the combination of rich resources, challenging and inclusive teaching strategies and an appropriate analysis of children's learning behaviours and outcomes. In attempting to achieve improvement, our emphasis is on the selection and use of quality resources in classrooms because we believe this has an important impact on teaching and learning for critical literacy. We would argue that what counts as knowledge and understanding in classrooms is determined very largely by the range of resources that are available to children, the status which is assigned to these resources in classrooms, and the kinds of learning activities undertaken in connection with them. The comments of Katherine, aged eight, on the quality of factual texts used in her classroom support this point of view:

> We have read a lot more books in Grade 3. We take books home and learn at home. We do lots of writing at home. It's good. We need more non-fiction books to be written for us to read. If you learn about animals you can go out and say I know what sort of animal or bird or fish that is. It helps you in your life on the weekends.
>
> When you're reading you learn about writing and when you're writing you're thinking about reading. You can read other people's writing and learn from them. I also like the back page recommendations.

In this statement Katherine highlights the crucial connection between her classroom literacy learning and her daily life experiences. We believe that this is an important indicator of achievement, the linking of in-school and out-of school learning. Katherine also demonstrates that she has developed the essential skill of linking her reading and writing experiences.

Katherine and her peers operate in a classroom where literacy functions in a context of challenging curriculum content alongside a program of rich children's literature. In selecting texts, the teacher has asked different questions of them according to her specific teaching purposes. Such questions include: What key ideas about . . . (a given topic) do these books contain? Or what ideas about the structure and function of language do these books contain?

A balanced literacy program will contain factual texts demonstrating a range of genres, and fiction texts including high quality rhymes, poems and stories. Christie (1990) argues that literacy pervades all aspects of contemporary life and social practice; not only is the volume of books, newspapers, journals and magazines today greater than it has been in the past, but the very nature of what constitutes literacy has been transformed by the appearance of the microfiche, the computer and the word processor. These changes have forced us to reconsider what we mean by 'literacy' and what we mean by 'text'.

Selection of Resources or Texts

The concept of text needs to be examined carefully. Several people concerned with the study of language and literacy tend to restrict notions of text to spoken or written language. For example, Christie states: 'Language is for negotiating meaning, building understanding and relationships, and the activity of using language for any purposes always involves what is technically called a text — a stretch of language which is coherent and meaningful. Texts may be either spoken or written' (Christie 1987, p. 208). Such a view overlooks many of the ways in which children construct meanings about the world using the texts and visual images of direct experience, pictures, drama, dance and television or film. Smith (1977) has extended Halliday's (1973) uses of language to include many 'non-language' alternatives. Selected resources need to reflect all the instruments or semiotic systems used by people to build, create, realise or communicate meaning. Additional to language texts should be film, video, music, dance, drama, animation, painting, photography or various combinations of these.

Text is made of meanings which are expressed in words, structures, sounds or visual and written symbols and images. Text 'is a form of social exchange of meanings' (Halliday and Hasan 1985, p. 11) and therefore demands a multidimensional view of literacy or a conceptualisation of multiple, critical literacies within social practice. We have, therefore, categorised different types of resources which enable children to build meanings. These include places, people, pictures, computers and books, and such resources can be viewed as examples of cultural texts which provide the information from which children construct their ideas about the world.

Redressing Imbalance through Variety

The selection of resources requires particular consideration if teachers are to implement an inclusive curriculum which redresses previous imbalances with regard to gender, ethnicity, people with disability and older people. In spite of a decade which has seen the development of equal opportunity legislation, resource units and materials, more needs to be done to raise teachers' awareness of the implications of curriculum decisions and grouping strategies which aim to increase the participation of girls, Aboriginal people and children from non-English-speaking backgrounds.

This is not to deny the achievements of particular groups and programs with regard to resource development. For example, Batchelor College's Remote Area Teacher Education Program (RATE) operates throughout the Northern Territory and has developed community-based teacher training programs and literacy production centres to publish local literacy resources and video materials. Unfortunately, the benefits of many such initiatives have yet to impact on mainstream curriculum guidelines, resource development or published books; and education about the community, in the community and for the community remains the exception. So the dominant ideology of the white, Anglo-Saxon, middle-class, nuclear family prevails at the expense of cultural diversity.

In addition, the emphasis on the use of fiction has perpetuated cultural and gender stereotypes with the result that: 'Almost without exception, books studied in schools have been seen to rely upon cultural stereotypes of girls and women, to offer few adult female role models for girls and to have portrayed a world which is predominantly peopled and organised by men' (Gilbert 1989, p. 73). Moreover, Gilbert argues that the gender of the author is no guarantee that the fiction will resist gender stereotypes.

Our concern is to examine the ways in which teachers can select and use curriculum resources which allow for the sharing of information together with a variety of learning outcomes, and which reflect cultural diversity and gender balance. This examination also raises issues about how we define and evaluate learning.

Evaluating and Measuring Learning

Effective and successful learning entails far more than a knowledge of process or the skills of inquiry. Learning is measured also by one's ability to gather, organise, interpret, apply, synthesise and explain important social and scientific ideas, read critically, sustain arguments and undertake social action. Such competence involves mastery of particular skills and the capacity to handle new information in challenging ways.

We can only measure learning growth holistically in terms of demonstrated behaviours and quality outcomes, products or artefacts. Christie (1990) argues that in the act of using language, either spoken or written, one necessarily engages both in process and in product, and that we cannot separate form and content, form and function. Therefore we need to address seriously the forms of knowledge learnt in primary school, the ways in which this knowledge is gathered, shared, refined and represented. Careful use of resources will assist this in a well-contextualised curriculum program.

Contextualising Literacy, Learning and Classroom Literacy Practice

The following statements summarise the essential arguments and assumptions put forward so far and provide a framework for the structure and content of the following sections.

1. Our selection and use of resources provide the additional information from which children construct their ideas about the social world (in terms of class, gender, ethnicity, age and disability) and the scientific world (in terms of natural and physical science, health/personal development, environmental education) and demonstrate the ways we define knowledge. More attention to selection and use of resources could help us to redress the imbalances in the current material as well as assist children in critically reading, examining and resisting ideologies, attitudes, values and stereotypes presented in the popular media.
2. Children's literature as currently defined does not encompass the range of functional literacy texts which children must deal with in their everyday lives.

3. To be literate in the contemporary world requires an understanding of the diverse range of written forms or text types so that successful participation in community life and fulfilment of aspirations, ambitions and independence can be achieved.
4. Children need to move *beyond* their current idiom and knowledge in order to understand the uses of language in our society, to function in society and work towards changing it.
5. Oral and written modes of language are used for different purposes and occur in different contexts.
6. The purposes for effective oral language use in classrooms can include giving instructions, reporting information, clarifying ideas or sequences, asking for detail, justifying opinions and arguments, recounts of personal experiences, conversations.
7. Written language is used for more permanent records for future use (later today, tomorrow, next week, month, year). Such records can be read, and reread by writers or other readers.
8. The use of exemplary models in schools is crucial. Rather than leaving children to find out for themselves, exemplary models are used to develop literacy competence by making explicit the qualities of effective writing. These models explicate the role of the teacher or published writer as the master craftsperson and the children as apprentices who study and analyse the achievements of others, experiment with the models and work towards developing new ones.
9. Assessment of achievement in literacy requires an examination of content, purpose, audience, use of language and organisation and presentation of information.
10. Evaluation of effective classroom practice involves an examination of the use of resources and teaching strategies together with an analysis of both children's learning behaviours and learning outcomes.

Classroom Planning and Organisation

A FRAMEWORK FOR USING RESOURCES
The treatment of specific resource types will be dealt with through a framework designed to assist teachers with a systematic approach to planning and evaluation. An overview of the framework is set out below and specific examples of strategies we have used with such resources follow in later sections.

Step 1: Documenting Major Understandings
In selecting curriculum resources, teachers need to consider the essential ideas about the world which children might construct from the information contained in them and the particular focus that is intended for the work being planned. Suggestions about focus might originate from the

children, the teacher or a school level decision but it is likely that the teacher will select the resources. It is helpful if teachers make their intentions about the topic or field explicit by writing a set of generalisations which are referred to here as major understandings. Curriculum guidelines in science, social education and personal development or health usually set down such statements and will assist in this process. These written understandings are helpful to teachers in that they provide clear purposes for the selection and evaluation of resources and activities. Examples of possible understandings are provided with each resource outlined in later sections.

Key Concepts and Generalisations Underlying Resources
Concepts are what we think with, and therefore concept development is synonymous with thinking development (Novak 1988). The intention in planning to use concepts or generalisations as a content focus is an attempt to honour holistic learning which can be used or applied in the exploration of other issues, problems, systems or contexts rather than as mere items of knowledge or objects of mastery.

Among curriculum developers throughout Australia there is wide agreement about the types of conceptual understandings or ideas about the world which primary school children need to consider. These understandings relate to the areas of social education, science, and health or personal development and are published in curriculum guidelines (see, for example, Ministry of Education (Victoria) (1987a, b, c) *Frameworks* documents). Social education draws on the disciplines of sociology, history, geography, anthropology, politics and economics. Science draws on the natural and physical sciences together with fields such as health or personal development and environmental education. Curriculum guidelines also suggest topics through which children can share, explore and refine their understandings about the world. These guidelines in the relevant subject areas normally specify topics considered appropriate. The topics and the understandings appropriate to them can form the basis of teachers' planning and their selection and use of resources.

Step 2: Tapping Learners' Prior Knowledge
Activities which assist children to summarise their existing knowledge, focus on an area for investigation or develop questions for exploration will significantly increase the effectiveness of the resource. The investment of time on this component will prove to be very worthwhile as children will approach the resource with enthusiasm and specific purposes in their minds.

Children operate in their daily lives with knowledge of the world gained from their personal experiences. They therefore continue to develop understandings of family, transport, institutions, community, weather, environment and living things. These understandings must be acknowledged as the source of prior knowledge which will significantly influence curriculum outcomes. However, children are limited to this experiential base unless the school provides experiences which will take them beyond their existing knowledge, challenge their existing ideas, interests and beliefs and thus allow them to refine their understandings of the world. This is, after all, one of the essential purposes of schooling, to provide the contexts which will ensure growth; and the extent to which the school extends the experiential base of the children is a major curriculum evaluation question. Rich and diverse school experiences also provide the range of social contexts in which language use can be demonstrated and employed. This in turn facilitates another important measure of literacy achievement: the child's ability to employ the widest possible repertoire of literacy practices.

When discussing a particular field or topic, children will initially rely upon their own commonsense ways of expressing their knowledge and understandings. It is important that this knowledge is valued and acknowledged as the starting point of new learning. Such acknowledegment can take the form of group and class records of statements, lists and questions on large charts which can be displayed or stored for future reference and modification. This record keeping will also provide the basis of important evaluation strategies.

Step 3: Using the Resource as a Shared Experience

Curriculum resources in the form of direct and vicarious experiences become the vehicle for introducing new information about the world, thus broadening the experiential and knowledge base of the learners. The way these resources are used will in part determine their effectiveness. The resources enrich the curriculum content but the processes of gathering, organising, interpreting and drawing conclusions from the information and using it as valid evidence are critical to the learning outcomes. Children must be seen as investigators who act on their insights, make decisions, form conclusions, defend their point of view, negotiate their knowledge with peers and teachers and communicate this knowledge in a variety of forms. The skills fostered in using these resources should enable children to more critically read, examine and resist ideologies, attitudes, values and stereotypes presented in other material, including the popular media.

Step 4: Gathering Information from the Shared Experience

In sequencing a range of resources for use within a curriculum unit, teachers have some critical decisions to make in order to assist children in their investigations. The findings of the Bullock Report suggest that there are four distinctive ways in which primary age children can gather information (Bullock 1975, p. 190):

   i. finding out from observation and first hand experience.
   ii. finding out from someone who will explain and discuss.
   iii. finding out by listening to a spoken monologue on a radio program or cassette.
   iv. finding out by reading.

The Bullock Committee also reported that these information-gathering options form a hierarchy from the easiest (first hand experience) to the most difficult (reading). These findings do provide some guidance for the sequencing of resources within a unit. The principle suggested is that one should normally begin with the more direct sources of information gathering:

- excursions
- classroom observations of various kinds (including bringing animals, plants, artefacts and visitors to the classroom)

and then move to the more vicarious forms of experience:

- film and videotape
- audiotape
- reading

Concepts, Facts, Generalisations
In addition to the hierarchy of information *sources* outlined above, there is also a sequence of information *types* to consider in curriculum planning (Anderson 1991). Having chosen or negotiated an area or formulated a focus question (using prior knowledge), children's investigations usually begin with the gathering of facts, those critical items from which we derive our understandings of the world. These facts are gathered as children interact with the resources available to them. In processing the information in a variety of ways (through art, drama, role play, movement, mathematics and language) the factual knowledge is transformed into key concepts. When children draw conclusions from their investigations they formulate generalisations which explore links between those concepts. Thus the information types dealt with move from the smallest unit (facts) through concepts to the largest unit (generalisations).

Facts → Concepts → Generalisations

Step 5: Processing the Information Gathered
When children process information they organise it, ask questions of it, represent or reconstruct it, interpret the meanings behind what they find, and where appropriate, communicate their findings to others. They do this by making lists, classifying, making tables or charts, dramatising, visually representing, graphing and generalising. As they carry out these tasks, they employ language (talking, listening, reading and writing) appropriate to these contexts and apply skills developed in many areas of the curriculum including art, drama, movement, mathematics and language.

A range of groupings will allow learners to be actively engaged individually or as part of a small group or a large class. In planning these strategies, teachers need to move children from their own commonsense understandings to more refined, technical understandings and language associated with the topic or field of study.

Initial Language Activities
Heath (1986) has argued that over time children have been encouraged to talk less and less and that their progress has been measured increasingly through the written mode. This has resulted in a preoccupation

with reading and writing rather than with talking. Dalton (1986) and Hill and Hill (1990) have, through their promotion of co-operative learning, revitalised the role of talk in classrooms; but there has been little attempt to designate growth points of effective and efficient oral communication or discourse.

We believe that oral language is a powerful medium for children to use in constructing meaning. Accordingly we have selected those areas of curriculum which foster oral language, namely art, construction and drama to provide the initial activities. In most instances, these activities would be conducted before children are asked to write. Such activities need to be structured to increase participation within paired or small-group contexts.

Role Play and Practical Problems
In developing understandings about the world, children need to explore the consequences of human activity on the physical environment and within social relationships. Role play and the discussion of practical problems enable learners to understand the complexity of particular issues, competing perspectives and interests and the cumulative effect of certain factors and actions. Role play and discussion also demonstrate that interpretation of events does involve personalised perspectives: 'Practical problems (if they *are* genuinely practical and not merely technical problems or applications of theory) necessarily involve subjectivity. Their resolution requires personal knowledge, critical skills and value judgments, not just the "objective" methods of the sciences and the technologies' (Gough 1987, p. 59). Questions used by teachers in these contexts therefore should, according to Gough, include both planned scientific inquiry (e.g. How is sunlight energy transformed into chemical energy?) and values questions, (e.g. What sort of heating system should you choose for your home?) or technical questions (e.g. How can household energy consumption be decreased?) (Gough 1987, p. 58).

Teachers can often structure a simulated situation in which all three types of questions and interaction can be employed. Examples of these are provided in our later discussion of particular resources. Another effective form of simulation has been developed through Incursion Theatre programs, which bring aspects of the physical or natural environment or particular social issues into the classroom. An example, Vox Bandicoot, a conservation theatre company, has been working in primary schools for some years on a range of environmental concepts and issues. Earth Education (camp nature programs in the United States of America) began this educational innovation. Its aim was to help learners build a sense of relationship — through both feelings and understandings — with the natural world (Van Matre 1979, p. 5), with an emphasis on direct sensory experience and on sharpening learners' perceptions of their environments, thus assisting them 'to interact more directly with the fascinating array of living things around them' (p. 7).

Written Language Activities
The limitation of oral language is that it exists only for that moment. Learners need to understand that if we need to refer to the ideas or issues

arising from shared oral language encounters we need to keep more permanent records — lists, charts, graphs. Written language can be composed individually or collaboratively. It can be planned, edited, drafted and revised, and perhaps published to make the message or meaning clear. It can be read and reread by the author(s) or other readers. It has to make sense in another time or place and perhaps to an unknown audience.

Written Text Construction and Analysis
Teachers' knowledge of good published models will serve as a starting point for explicit analysis of an author's craft in presenting information in a written form. Joint construction of similar forms of writing is an acknowledgment of children's contributions and a way of localising particular content or issues. Some individuals or small groups of children will need further exposure to other published models or explicit instruction about particular aspects before they can independently transfer the knowledge and skills to their own writing endeavours.

Big Books
Well-written 'big book' models of factual texts can be used explicitly to show the reading strategies to be adopted in consulting reference books of various kinds. Thus they can provide an excellent vehicle for showing students how factual texts work.

> Students will need guidance in handling the table of contents, the indexes at the back of the books, the various chapter headings and subheadings within chapters, and the points at which, perhaps, matters are summarised in different parts of the book. All these aspects of the genres of scientific textbooks are worth explicit discussion in the classroom, not only to produce efficient readers who can 'find their way' around the books, but also because students will learn something of the ways in which those who provide scientific information organise it into the various discourse patterns of science (Christie and Rothery 1990, p. 190).

Some big books integrate visual and verbal information in making the author's message clear. They also allow for an analysis and discussion of the text and the illustrations, using a format fully visible to both teacher and children. This involves a process of deconstructing or reconstructing a text in order to make explicit the structure of the text, the patterns of language appropriate to the text and the organisational devices employed. Children also need to know what types of questions to ask or answer in order to write the text forms related to the content areas. Big books can provide easily accessible, appropriate models of these text forms for children to explore the decisions the author has made and the issues which have been considered (Woolley and Pigdon 1984).

Step 6: Drawing Conclusions
After children have gathered and organised their information, they should be encouraged to draw conclusions or make generalisations and express them in writing. If these generalisations are written on large charts they

can be checked by other children for accuracy of content, clarity of meaning and patterns of language. This allows for an appropriate discussion of the need for technical language and forms the basis for future writing of reports, explanations or expositions.

The generalisations also serve as a valuable tool for evaluation. By referring to statements previously recorded during activities concerned with prior knowledge, learners can engage in a process of refining and extending their statements and thus concretely demonstrating their learning. At the same time they are engaging in a process of self-evaluation as records of their developing knowledge are updated. Teachers are also provided with an opportunity to compare the children's statements with the major understandings they drafted in documenting their planning intentions.

Grouping Strategies
Compared with typical school tasks, engaging students in problematic inquiry leads to situations demanding ambiguity and uncertainty, autonomy in decision making and judgements, and the confidence and insight to challenge conventional wisdom (Newmann 1987). Inquiry also requires many opportunities for intensive interaction between individuals in paired or small-group settings. Further, it requires provision for the sharing of technical and scientific perspectives alongside personal subjective and practical knowledge forms.

Within the learning cycle the teacher will have a predictable routine of movement from large class to small group, individual or paired activities depending on the teaching purposes. Sometimes the composition of these groups will be negotiated according to friendship, or interest; at other times the groupings will be randomly structured to increase communication, feedback and modelling, or structured according to a specific teaching need. Learners will feel comfortable with these routines so long as they are made explicit and are sufficiently flexible to allow for child choice, responsibility and control. It is important for children to know when they have input into the learning program, and when the teacher has planned certain activities for particular purposes.

Negotiated curriculum
The very notion of negotiation implies that the parties involved will have knowledge or skills with which to negotiate. In any social setting such as a classroom there will also be non-negotiable elements. Some of these will relate to expectations and procedures, others will relate to socially defined curriculum knowledge as set out in guidelines or frameworks. This means that there will be the opportunity for children's interests and prior knowledge to be valued and used but that there is also a requirement to take children beyond their current idiom or repertoire of knowledge and skills.

Whilst understanding the need for a negotiated curriculum with teachers and children both having a real investment in the learning process, the ultimate responsibility for planning lies with the teacher whose experiences, understandings and expertise makes this an appropriate locus of responsibility. The concept of negotiation in a classroom does not relieve teachers of their responsibilities and the requirement to provide input at points of need. Making sense of the classroom, the children and their needs entails a joint effort between teacher and children. The assumption here is that the role of the teacher is not just to transmit knowledge, but to help students take increasing responsibility for their own learning

Britton has made the point that the maximum effect of the educational system on the child is the classroom (Britton 1987, p. 19). Thus the teacher is in the best possible position to enable action to occur that will best realise the potential of the teaching and learning processes and provide an important element in the transaction of language learning between home and school contexts.

Within a classroom language learning context the teacher takes on many roles. Some of these include that of instructor, which involves explicit teaching and exposition or demonstration, or that of facilitator, which involves encouraging the learner to take risks and increasing responsibility for their learning. Knowledge of how language functions in social contexts is one of the critical aspects of curriculum which learners must develop. Such knowledge is empowering in that it can provide opportunities for access to information and active participation in social action: '. . . people who have not mastered expository writing cannot change the world, nor can they work effectively to keep it from changing in ways they don't like' (Martin 1985, p. 50).

Everyday Essential Resources
Certain resources are essential to all classrooms because of their utilitarian value. They need to be accessible to children at all times as there are so many possible opportunities for their use. The major ones are discussed below.

The Globe. Understanding Australia's position on the globe will enhance children's understanding of the nation's history, its physical features, rainfall patterns, concepts of distance and its relationship with other world states or concepts of the global village.

Globe maps also assist in children exploring ideas about the earth's relationship with the other planets of the solar system and that system as part of other systems, along with the physical distribution of land and ocean around 'the globe' (Tinkler 1989).

Wall Maps and Atlases. Maps and atlases are indispensable in locating nations, states, capitals, cities, suburbs or local municipal areas.

Street Directories. Street directories enable learners to locate particular addresses and places of interest, and demonstrate devices such as the use of keys, abbreviations and colour codes.

Aerial Photographs of Localities. Often the area and the size of the enlargement can be decided by the school community. These photographs can highlight changes over time in the school ground, settlement patterns, suburban or town facilities including transport routes.

Popular Media. Television programs and commercials, daily newspapers, magazines provide a profusion of scientific, social and environmental concepts, generalisations and problems.

In the following sections we explicate some approaches and strategies associated with the use of particular resources in classrooms and some of the possible learning outcomes.

People and Places as Resources

In any given community people in various capacities will be able to make a significant contribution to the development and refinement of children's knowledge of the world. Using people as resources seeks to achieve a more thoroughgoing integration of school and community through the greater involvement of the community in school life and through an expansion of in-community learning opportunities. In curriculum terms, the major contribution that the use of people can contribute is a context for the use of oral language in a variety of social practices. It enables a realistic application of language use in terms of the social relationships and roles they represent. Thus children's experience of language use in particular contexts may be broadened and in the process their knowledge of the world and of language is enriched. Interactions with people in these settings are often accompanied by the use of artefacts. These artefacts give powerful insights into the cultural and social construction of what counts as knowledge in given communities or the wider society. This allows for explicit discussion and analysis of both the artefacts and the patterns of language use.

Visit to a Retirement Centre

This example was devised for younger learners (Year 1) but could easily be modified for middle or senior primary students.

Major Understandings
1. In their retirement, some people in our society choose to live together in a community setting.
2. There are similarities and differences in the types of games played today to those played 60–70 years ago.
3. The type of equipment used in modern classrooms is very different from that used 60–70 years ago.

4. The availability and choice of food is different now from what it was 60–70 years ago.
5. The types of childhood illnesses, diseases and accidents which were serious problems 60–70 years ago are different from those causing most concern today.
6. The way people use time and space is different today.

Prior Knowledge
1. Preparing for the Interviews
Provide some focus questions so that children can think about particular aspects of their lives to share with the older people. For example:

- What do you like about our classroom?
- What do you enjoy most about your life?
- What types of equipment do we have in our classroom?
- What types of food do you like best?
- What do you do mainly on the weekends?
- What do you do mainly after school?
- What do you do on your birthday?
- What types of games do you like playing?

The above questions were used in a Year 1 classroom to allow the children to share personal experiences and rehearse the types of questions they would ask old people. It resulted in a class list of questions as shown in Figure 8.1.

WHAT DO WE WANT TO ASK?
1. What books did you enjoy reading?
2. What games did you play?
3. Where did you play these games?
4. Did you like your teachers?
5. Did boys play with girls?
6. How many brothers and sisters did you have?
7. Did you have jobs to do?
8. Did you get sick and have to go to hospital?
9. Did you have birthday parties?
10. What did you do when you couldn't go to McDonalds?
11. What did you sleep in?

Figure 8.1

This list was then used as the basis for a letter to elderly citizens in which the children introduced themselves, sent a photograph and asked them to look for photos or think about the answers to the questions. The letter to the old people was developed through a jointly constructed text which was later duplicated and accompanied by an individual introduction from each child.

2. Preparing a Tally Sheet

Ask children in small groups to discuss places that they might spend long periods of time in after school or on the weekends. Ask one child from each group to report back to the rest of the class. As the reporting is being carried out, make a class list. From this list prepare a tally sheet so that children can draw on their own experiences to complete it and then compare this information with that offered by their older partner (see Figure 8.2).

Sample Tally Sheet

Place	Weekday		Weekend	
	Me	Old Person	Me	Old Person
In home (chores)				
In home (reading playing, radio, TV)				
Garden				
Friend's home				
Playground or park				
After school care				
Street				

Figure 8.2

3. Jointly Constructed Texts

Ask children to generate statements about what they have learned from their communication with the elderly citizens. Use these statements as the basis of:

- A report on a particular topic, e.g. games, schooling.
- An explanation of why we now eat different foods.

The Zoo

This example was devised for Year 3/4 children.

Major Understandings
1. Zoos allow people to observe many different species of animals which can't easily be observed in the wild.
2. Animals have different needs in terms of their diet, shelter and environmental conditions.
3. Many animals are able to reproduce successfully in zoo environments.
4. Some zoos allow people special access for the observation of the young of certain animals.
5. Zoos provide a means by which many people can observe and learn more about endangered species.

Prior Knowledge
1. The Needs of Animals in Zoos

- Children, in small groups, collect pictures from magazines of all creatures they would expect to find in a zoo. They then decide how they wish to group these creatures together. The pictures are then pasted on large sheets of paper, labelled and displayed around the room.
- Each group then chooses one animal and discusses what they think it needs to survive. This could include food, weather, habitat, protection from predators, conditions which help them to reproduce.
- Ask the children to think about the needs of that animal living in zoo conditions. How would some of their needs be provided? Would they need protection from people or would people need protection from them? Children might illustrate the kind of enclosure they think would be appropriate for that animal in a zoo setting.

2. The Needs of People at Zoos

- Place children in small groups and ask them to consider the range of signs that might be displayed around the zoo and what purposes these fulfil (see Figure 8.3).
- Pose the question 'Why do you think we have zoos?' Children in groups of three discuss their ideas and choose from this discussion three important reasons in response.
- Ask a reporter from each group to contribute their reasons and compile these on a large sheet. The teacher lists a range of responses on newsprint and keeps this for future reference.

Sign	Purpose
Where to go	Find the animals Find our way around
About the animals	What they eat What family they belong to
What not to do	Don't feed the animals Don't put your hand in the cage Don't tap on the glass

Figure 8.3

Shared Experience — Zoo Excursion
A day at the zoo can be an exhausting experience for teachers and children alike. It is important to limit the focus of the experience by concentrating on those areas which yield the greatest potential to connect the children with the understandings you seek to develop. Some enclosures provide more obvious insights into the needs of the animals they contain (e.g. nocturnal animal houses, seal enclosures) or the needs of the people visiting the zoo (the large cat enclosures). If consideration of these matters is one of the major purposes of the experience, plans should be made for these areas to have priority over other areas. It may be educationally better to see less than to attempt to cover everything on one visit.

Processing the Information
1. *Retrieving and Organising Information*
Place the children in small groups and set the following tasks for different groups:

- Group 1 — make a visual representation and reconstruction of the physical layout of a part of the zoo. This might include roads, buildings, enclosures, etc.
- Group 2 — make an enclosure using the sand tray, icy-pole sticks, lego and Plasticine.
- Group 3 — make a different enclosure using collage.
- Group 4 — design and make a better enclosure for an animal which you felt wasn't in a good enclosure.

2. *Recount*
Ask children to recall the major events, and make a rough draft for future reference as they, in pairs, make a mural of the zoo excursion. Once the mural is assembled, ask children to provide appropriate descriptions of each event, so that a *wall story* is compiled.

3. Text Analysis

Choose sections of an appropriate text such as *Animal Jigsaws* (Howes 1987) which provides a good model of report writing about animals. Read through the text and divide it with line breaks between the major sections of information.

Write the passage on the chalkboard, newsprint or on an overhead projector transparency so that all the children can see it. Read the first section to the children and ask them what kind of information that section gives. Make a note at the side of the section (Figure 8.4).

Example:

The Crocodile

1. The crocodile has a large tail which it can use in two ways. *Physical features*

2. When the crocodile is in the water its tail curves from side to side like a huge paddle and pushes the crocodile quickly through the water. *How it moves, where it lives*

3. When the crocodile is hunting in the water it usually grabs its prey in its powerful jaws. Then it uses its tail to do sideways rolls or somersaults under the water. This makes it almost impossible for the captured animal to escape and it usually drowns. *How it captures its prey*

Figure 8.4

This text analysis should include aspects such as structure, patterns of language, and the use of layout and graphic devices. This session should be followed by further analyses of other reports or explanations which use different structures from the one initially chosen for analysis. Through this process children can come to understand the options which writers of factual material have in constructing their texts. The subject matter and the audience may both influence the structure and sequence. Over time children will come to see the alternatives and make better decisions about how they structure their texts.

4. Graphing

- Encourage children to use information provided in records around the room, for example pictures, charts, visual representations, lists and books to classify and organise data about animal body coverings. They could use symbols or make lists of the alternatives, skin, scales, feathers or fur.

- Divide the class into four groups and ask each group to take the responsibility for compiling a record on a particular body covering type, for example scales.
- Make a class graph showing the number of animals in each category.

Ask children to look for patterns in their findings and to express these in statements; for example, What can we say about the body coverings of zoo animals?

5. *Further Analysis*

Ask the children to reconsider their findings by looking for further patterns and/or relationships:

- Tracing the relationship between body covering and animal size.
- Considering other places where people keep animals and the conditions under which they are kept, for example farm animals, pets.

6. *Concept Attainment*

Prepare a list of animals which are herbivores. Introduce children to the concept through the use of a game called *Join My Club*. Draw up a chart with two columns, one for the Yes category and one for the No category (Figure 8.5).

JOIN MY CLUB

Yes	No
Giraffe	book
kangaroo	wolf
parrot	rock

Figure 8.5

Write a Yes example (e.g. giraffe) and a No example (e.g. book) (see Figure 8.6). Write two more Yes and No examples and invite the children to test their understanding of the concept by providing additional Yes examples. They are not permitted to say what they think the concept is but must participate by giving Yes examples. Confirm or reject the example by writing it in the Yes or No column. The No category does not need to have a relationship with the Yes category, for example rock is just as good an example of a No as is wolf. When enough children seem to have grasped the concept invite some to state what they think it is.

COMPLETED CHART

Yes	No
Giraffe	book
kangaroo	wolf
parrot	rock
cow	lion
elephant	cat
hippopotamus	spider
grasshopper	tree
Herbivores	**Non-herbivores**

Figure 8.6

Children can then be encouraged to devise their own examples using different concepts, for example carnivores, mammals, birds. As children become accustomed to the games examples with more than one attribute can be demonstrated, for example mammals which are found in Antarctica. Young children have demonstrated to us that they can operate with several attributes.

A Market

This example was devised for Year 5/6 children.

Possible Major Understandings about Markets
1. Markets involve the exchange of goods and services (usually in exchange for money).
2. Most of us rely on the market system for our food needs.
3. Australia exports and sells some products overseas to earn money and imports and buys products from other countries.
4. Many forms of transport are involved in the delivery and purchase of goods at markets.
5. Prices of some items can be affected by profit levels, costs and shortages of supply.

6. There are many controls needed to ensure that markets operate fairly, with minimum standards of hygiene and in an orderly manner.
7. Many kinds of work are involved in markets.

Prior Knowledge
The investment of time into a range of activities designed to increase curiosity, raise questions and review existing knowledge about markets will make any visit to a market far more effective. Many children have experienced some kind of market in connection with their regular family activities and as a result will have something to contribute to these activities. A range of activities will help to ensure that children have the opportunity to move beyond their present understandings. The nature of the activities will depend to some extend on the age and experience of the children. The following have been used by us with junior and middle primary children.

1. Provide a General Focus Question
An example is: What do you want to find out about the market?

Children can be placed in pairs or small groups for discussion and a range of questions could be recorded by the children or the teacher. Recording the child's name after the question can be useful.

2. Provide Specific Focus Questions for Different Groups
- Group 1: What types of things can you buy at the market?
- Group 2: How do people and goods get to the market?
- Group 3: What kinds of rules are needed to run a market?
- Group 4: What signs would you find around a market?
- Group 5: What types of work do people at markets do?

After the groups have explored these questions conduct a share time to allow the class to become aware of the range of items which could be examined on the visit to the market.

Groups could consider which information they would like to gather and what they need to prepare beforehand in order to collect their data. For example, tally sheets might be helpful for the goods and service group (Group 1) and the transport group (Group 2) if they wish to collect quantitative information. Rules and signs groups would need to find a suitable method to record their information (a polaroid camera, videotape, scribes copying down the rule or sign). Lists of the types of work observed would also need to be recorded.

3. Thrifty Shoppers
The purpose of this exercise is to compare the prices of a given parcel of goods at the market with some other location and/or the

family shopping for the week. Initially, this requires children to consider what to include in the parcel (and their reasons for doing so). All of the class could be involved in this exercise, using a small-group format. Ask each group to prepare a list of their items (written or illustrated) and give verbal reasons for their choices. A class decision would then be necessary in order to determine the contents of the parcel. Such a debate is bound to reveal cultural and economic differences together with those stemming from values.

Ask the children to consider how they will gather the information they require from the different sources. Tally sheets, lists or whatever should then be prepared for the excursion and for use in the home.

The Shared Experience
The activities listed above will ensure that children have lots to observe, record and think about during their visit to the market.

Processing the Information
1. *Art and Construction*
Some of the groups could prepare to present their findings through collage, construction with 3D materials and posters.

2. *Graphing*
A number of groups may prefer to provide a visual presentation of their findings by using various types of graphs. Line graphs, bar graphs, pie graphs and picture graphs would all be appropriate depending on the particular group. These graphs could clearly show the comparative information about prices which the children have compiled.

3. *Written Language*
This may be the preferred medium for some children.

Note: A combination of forms could be another option.

Simulated Historical Settings

A GOLD RUSH SETTING
The purposes of visiting such settings are to give children insight into and empathetic understanding for the lives of others; knowledge about values and value judgements in human activity and events; and to enable children to make reasoned judgements and explanations of particular historical actions and intentions.

Such visits also enable children to use reference skills to gather, check and organise specific items of information, analyse and interpret this information, evaluate the source material, recognise gaps in the evidence, detect bias, draw inferences, reason cause and effect, make propositions or hypotheses and attempt explanations or comparisons.

> This example was devised for Year 5/6 children.

Possible Major Understandings
1. The discovery of gold affected people's lives in a variety of ways.
2. Many people left towns and settlements in Australia in search of gold.
3. Large numbers of people emigrated from many different countries, providing a foundation for future immigration policies.
4. The discovery of gold resulted in a boost to the economy and changes in production and consumption patterns.
5. Conflict between people on the goldfields and the authorities arose from the licensing system.

Ideally, this study could be followed by one of modern immigration which could help to reinforce that most of us are recent or fairly recent immigrants through raising with children the question Where was your family in 1787?

Prior Knowledge
1. Pose questions to find out what children already know about gold and non-Aboriginal settlement of Australia. For example:

- What are the special features of gold?
- Where did gold come from?
- How do people feel about finding gold?
- What do we know about the European settlement and development of Australia?
- Who were the people involved?
- What dates and events come to mind?

Preparing for the Shared Experience
1. Simulation of Family Tree
Ask individual children to simulate a family tree on their mother's side. Begin by asking each child to assume the role of someone living in 1850. Margaret Simpson (1980) has documented a unit and strategies to demonstrate how this can be done. Children provide the name, age and sex of their historical characters and

investigate aspects of their lives in the 1850s. In constructing their case studies, children are learning how to use historical evidence from primary sources (documents, letters, accounts, maps, charts).

The questions in Figure 8.7 will help them work backwards historically and develop understandings of overlapping ages within a family tree.

1850

Question	Response
What is your name?	My name is Emma Campbell.
How old were you in 1850?	In 1850 I was 20 years old.
When were you born?	I was born in 1830.
If Emma Campbell was born in 1830, what was her mother's name?	My mother's name is Elizabeth.
How old was her mother when Emma was born?	She was 22 when I was born.
When was her mother born?	She was born in 1808.
If Elizabeth was born in 1808 what was her mother's name?	Elizabeth's mother's name is Anne.
How old was her mother when Elizabeth was born?	She was 18 when Elizabeth was born.
When was Elizabeth's mother born?	She was born in 1790.
Anne was born in 1790.	
Her mother, Susan, was a convict with the first fleet.	
Look at a map of Britain and decide where she came from.	

Figure 8.7

Children can compare their simulated family tree with their own.

2. *Mapping*
Using the decision about where Anne's mother came from, children can develop a map of Britain with the names of towns, distances

from London, distances of journeys to Sydney town and to other parts of Australia.

3. Timeline
This information can then be transferred to a timeline of major events from 1789–1850.

4. Different Forms of Writing
Discuss with the children how the historical information can be compiled into a factual report and how this form of writing differs from the autobiographical account of one person's experience.

5. Analysing Evidence
In these reconstructions, children are confronted with different sorts of evidence, and they should be encouraged to analyse these in a variety of ways. Sometimes the evidence will be biased, incomplete and contradictory. For example, children should examine several accounts of bushrangers' 'hold ups', or newspaper articles about the Chinese on the goldfields and assess these for accuracy. This can be used as the basis for jointly constructed texts which attempt historical explanations showing that causal factors tend to work collectively rather than singularly and that progress is not assured just because things change.

6. Then and Now
Divide the children into a number of groups and ask them to compare life in the 1850s with life today. You can do this by negotiating particular aspects as a focus, for example protective clothing, cooking appliances, housing, means of transport. Synthesise each group's contributions onto a retrieval chart.

Video and Film Resources

The latter half of the 20th century has seen a profound development in the film/video area. Australians quickly took on the film/video culture as the home video recorder became an economic reality for the majority of households. The video shop quickly became an adjunct to the local milk bar or deli as demand for video hire created another form of retailing. New patterns of family and group lifestyles accompanied this phenomenon and this was seen by some as having deleterious consequences for community values, literacy attainment and schooling.

Community response has taken a wide variety of forms. Overwhelmingly, critics have attacked television as the destroyer of language (for some one could substitute *civilisation* for language) and corrupter of children. One of the principal concerns is that on so many issues, television is the major source of information upon which people form their conclusions and make their judgements. Given commercial imperatives and the power of the few program makers and others who decide what we will see, this is a legitimate concern. Yet television has a good case to make for its contribution to our understanding of the world, particularly in some areas. In a recent article in *The Age* Dennis Pryor put the following proposition:

> What people all over the world have seen on television has been our most single source of information in matters of the environment. The present strength of the environmental awareness is largely the product of television, which has influenced and informed much more profoundly than the posturing, shouting, slogan-waving, demonstrating and lying in front of bulldozers by ecopaths and Gaiamaniacs (Pryor 1991, p. 12).

The actions of environmentalists do not constitute a separate event from television, they are very much a part of it, but what Pryor refers to here is the impact of people such as David Attenborough and others who have made television their medium and who have certainly heightened our awareness of some of the major issues through television. Television has been able to popularise the great moments of history, so defined. Events such as the lunar landing and the accompanying image of the planet earth as a spark of colour in an ocean of blackness, flashing across the screen, creates a special perspective for viewers (Greig, Pike and Selby 1987).

Concerns about television's impact on our children generated the notion of children's television ('kid vid') as organisations attempted to address the 'quality' issue in ways similar to those which had been undertaken by various professional and community groups which engage in the review and critique of children's literature. The Australian Children's Television Foundation commissioned manuscripts from established children's authors which were published as books and simultaneously produced for television. In the 1980s the ABC as the major provider of television for schools broadened the range and type of programs available. An attempt was made to bring out-of-school and in-school television closer together.

The overseas trend to popularise best selling children's literature led to the production of *Storm Boy*, *Playing Beattie Bow* and other Australian classics. Studies of Australian authors such as Robin Klein, Colin Thiele and Ruth Park have provided children with televised insights into the writers' craft. In these and other ways links between film and television and literacy for children are well established.

These events have tended to conceptualise television as fiction. This is essentially scratching the surface of this powerful medium. Television has the power to inform children about their world and in so doing demonstrates important uses of language (to inquire, etc.). In looking at the critical social or scientific ideas in particular programs we can give an additional emphasis to the use of these resources.

Literacy Learning and Teaching

The focus here is on three programs which are available to schools and are appropriate to use as a key shared experience within a curriculum unit:

The Lorax (CBS Television 1972), *See it My Way* (ABC Television 1980), *The Other Facts of Life* (Australian Children's Television Foundation 1985).

The Lorax provides an animated version of the popular Dr Suess picture book. The narrative is enriched by the use of rhyme and rhythm in the language, by the use of powerful graphic images to generate meanings and by the creative use of a range of music styles appropriate to the various contexts. The program appeals to a very wide age range: it engages pre-schoolers through to adult viewers.

See it My Way aims to demystify the processes which underly all film and television by making explicit the producers' craft relating to editing and shooting. The power of the few to persuade the many is clearly demonstrated in this program. The depiction of the crossing of Sydney harbour by a Manly ferry from two opposing points of view visually parallels the construction of a complex text in quality literature.

The Other Facts of Life provides a visual medium for questioning many of the assumptions upon which Western culture is based. The actions of Ben as he works through some of these issues and responds in a variety of ways challenges the values of the audience and provides a context for the analysis and clarification of values positions.

The Lorax

This program is conceptually dense, yet the cognitive complexity still allows different audiences to participate in their own way. Such multilayering is similar to that achieved in particular types of literary texts which allow readers to take as much or as little as they are ready for (Saxby 1987, p. 14).

This example was devised for Year 3/4 children.

The Major Understandings in the Program
1. People change the environment for their own purposes/needs.
2. People develop, produce and market products which are designed to create human 'needs'.
3. Modern urban communities organise their work in ways which produce a highly specialised division of labour.
4. Large companies sometimes have very diversified business interests.
5. The earth's resources are finite.
6. Our economic system is connected with our ecosystem.

7. Humans must accept some personal responsibility for the environment which supports all forms of life as we know it.

Prior Knowledge
1. Visual Representation
Ask children to discuss their favourite tree or plant. Ask them to illustrate their tree or plant and add any special features — where it is found, flowers or seeds, birds or insects which use them.

2. Class Synthesis
In groups of six children can assemble their trees or plants to make a garden or streetscape or a park. They might now add people who might be found near these trees or plants and show how the plants could be important to people.

3. Tuning in to the Lorax Themes
Read *The Giving Tree* (Silverstein 1964) to the children. Place the children in small groups and ask them to talk about the main ideas in the story. Have each group report back to the whole class and list the main ideas which are presented for future use. Use the synthesis to introduce the videotape of *The Lorax*.

The Shared Experience
Show the video/film.

Processing The Information
1. Visual Representation — Mural
Divide the class into three groups. Ask each group of children to make a mural that will contribute to a larger mural — one group focusing on *Before the Oncler Came*, another group on *After the Oncler Came* and another on *The Future*.

2. Uses of Language
Ask each of the groups to make signs and labels for their mural.

3. Point of View
Move around the class and give each of the children a number from 1 to 4. Have character cards prepared: 1, The Lorax; 2, The Oncler; 3, The Workers; 4, The Animals.

Group the children with the same number together and ask each group to rewatch the video focusing on the particular point of view of their character. Ask each group to provide a report to the class which outlines their point of view about the events which take place in the video.

4. *Modelling an Explanation — Jointly Constructed Text*
Ask the children to help you write an explanation of how and why all the trees were lost in the town.

5. *Modelling a Letter — Jointly Constructed Text*
Ask the children to help you and the child at the end of the video construct a letter. One of the purposes of the letter would be to propose some appropriate future social action.

6. *Needs or Wants?*
Prepare a number of retrieval charts so that children can categorise the products created by The Oncler. Place the children into small groups and ask them to discuss what they believe are the differences between needs and wants. Replay the section of the tape which shows the development of the business of THNEEDS Inc. and ask the groups to list all of the products. Get the children to go through their lists and categorise each item (Figure 8.8). Compare each group's response and discuss the differences.

Needs	Wants

Figure 8.8

See it My Way

This program is part of a series produced by ABC television for schools. The series can be commended alone for its overriding objective in setting out to show how television programs are constructed. Given the power of television's visual and audio images which are a fundamental part of our contemporary culture, there is a real need for the audience to be aware of the production values and techniques which influence what we see on our screens. *See it My Way* has a clear, unequivocal message — *what we see on television is what someone wants us to see.*

The capacity of the director to use the medium to persuade the audience to take a given perspective or apply a specific interpretation is demonstrated admirably through a range of techniques. The use of sound and images to 'fool' us is exposed by recording an audience viewing of the finished segment with discussion of the meanings and exploration of possible interpretations. Viewers are then shown exactly what happened as the segment was filmed including the director's instructions and how post-production techniques were used to achieve the desired effects. The demonstration is crystal clear and children can easily see how a program can be constructed by the director in ways which misrepresent what actually happened.

> This example was devised for Year 4/5 children.

Major Understandings in this Series
1. What we see on television is what somebody wants us to see.
2. Very few people are involved in deciding what we see on television.
3. Most television programs are paid for by advertising.
4. People advertise their products and services on television so that they will sell more.
5. Commercials try to create particular images for their products.
6. We need to consider carefully the claims made in commercials, promotions and programs on television.

Prior Knowledge
1. Group children into threes and ask them to think about ways in which television or film is made so that the audience is 'tricked' into thinking something has happened when it has not. After giving them time to clarify their ideas through oral language ask them to choose one or two ways that they know of and to record that method on paper so that others will come to see how it might be done. Question them about forms of presentation and a range of media so that clarity of the presentation is emphasised.
2. Give each group the opportunity to present their findings to the rest of the class.
3. Ask the children to look over the various methods used to create effects and put them into groups, for example scenes involving substituting another person (usually a stuntperson), using time lapse and so on.

The Shared Experience
Introduce the videotape. Tell the children that it has been made in order to help them understand how television works. Be prepared

to stop the tape in order to give the class the opportunity to exchange and clarify impressions.

Processing the Information
1. *Analysing the Content*
Place the children in small groups and ask them to discuss then list the devices which the director used in the program to give the audience particular impressions.

Compile a class list of the responses the children provide. Ask them if they can think of another program they have seen where the same device has been used.

2. *Applying the Knowledge to Another Visual Text*
Using existing videotape stock select a range of program excerpts which contain editing, sound effects, stunts, chromakey and other visual effects.

Show the tape to the class and ask them to note examples of devices which the director has used to create images and sounds which are designed to suggest particular points of view to the audience. Prepare a retrieval chart which lists the program, the device and how the particular effect is achieved (Figure 8.9).

Program	Device	Technique

Figure 8.9

Such experiences are vital to informed television watchers. They may be helpful in assisting children to understand the fundamentals of television and thus become more critical and informed viewers. *The Media* series was used in a study of children's perceptions of television and advertising (Pigdon 1985). The study was conducted in a working class school in Melbourne. When interviewed after seeing parts of this series children offered some interesting responses in relation to the relevance of the curriculum to their social contexts and the connection between school and family. 'I told my dad about the media, how commercials were made, and he said it was good. Somethings I told me mum she didn't even know.' (Hanna, in Pigdon 1985, p. 4).

The study revealed some interesting conceptions which children held about television advertising and news. The children were unanimous in the view that they, and people generally, believe television news more readily than that which comes from the newspapers or radio. Most gave reasons similar to that expressed by Dean: 'Because you can see what's happening. Like the *Herald*, you just see a photo, but the T.V. you see what's happening, what they are doing.' (Dean, in Pigdon 1985, p. 61). Such evidence and that of Novak (1988) highlight the necessity of addressing children's conceptions about the world in the selection of appropriate curriculum resources.

The findings of this study suggest that the videotapes provided a valuable curriculum resource in terms of their capacity to demystify the production process. Findings in relation to this aspect were:

1. The use of production techniques to manipulate an audience made the greatest impression on the children.
2. The idea that few people are involved in decisions about television programs was the least understood and made the least impact on the children.
3. The children demonstrated in their responses that they had become more critical television viewers, particularly with respect to advertising. However, their view that news items are consistently factual and that the coverage of news is comprehensive was not challenged by the unit.

The importance of selecting resources appropriate to the curriculum purposes chosen was also endorsed by the children in the study. They confirmed the soundness of using television to study television and that this had also enhanced the effectiveness of the limited books available for this topic.

Findings in relation to the appropriateness of the choice of resources were:

1. Videotape was favourably regarded by the children in terms of accessibility to the whole class, relevance and quality.
2. The available books were viewed as the least reliable and least interesting sources of information.
3. It was apparent that information on videotape had helped the children make sense of the information in these books.
4. Children indicated that demonstrations were very powerful and effective sources of learning.
5. The children demonstrated that the unit was successful in arousing their curiosity about television and provided a sensitivity for future learning and refinement of ideas.

The Other Facts of Life

This program is part of The Australian Children's Television Foundation series titled *The Winners*. The initial production involved eight one-hour-long dramas commissioned from leading Australian script writers. After the scripts were completed, the stories were produced as paperback novels. They deal with a range of social issues through comedy, science fiction, historical drama, adventure, fantasy and social realism. Their production in both video and print form provides opportunities for cross-media analysis. Unsworth has cited Meek (1982) in endorsing the value of such dual productions: '. . . the security of the "known text" and the attraction of repeatedly "revisiting" favourite stories has been shown to provide the recurrent contexts which extend very young children's reading development' (Unsworth, this volume, p. 157).

> This example was devised for Year 5/6 children.

Major Understandings
1. People have different points of view about what the world should be like and how it should be run.
2. When there are conflicts over these issues people respond in a variety of ways.
3. Attempting to force people to reconsider how they see things can take the form of individual action or socially organised protest.
4. Our knowledge of local, national and global issues stems largely from the mass media.
5. People's involvement with issues may change over time.
6. People's attitudes to issues are influenced by their interests, values and beliefs.

The program constructs points of view from multiple perspectives though the views held by the son Ben are central. At 12 years of age Ben becomes highly engaged with global issues — two-thirds of the population of the world are starving, people are dying every few seconds, nuclear war seems imminent and political prisoners are increasing in number. Local concerns such as battery hens and fur clothing also trouble him and he is dismayed at how people around him can ignore the gravity of these problems. His parents' inability to deal with the issues leads to protests which take the form of acute embarrassment of his family and their friends and business acquaintances. This element also provides the basis of the humour of the program. It is important that children consider the differing perspectives held by the characters in the narrative and are given the opportunity to discuss and analyse these.

Prior Knowledge
Ask the children, in pairs, to discuss and share the social issues which most concern them. The pairs then consolidate into fours and list the issues discussed and classify them into groups. Groups then appoint a reporter to outline the issues and the reasons for the classification they have used. Examples of possible issues are:

- Issues to do with the environment
- Issues to do with war
- Issues to do with families
- Local issues
- National issues
- World issues

Draw the children's attention to the range of perspectives which have been canvassed in this short discussion. Pose the following question to them: If we were to ask our parents or grandparents about these issues would they feel the same way?

Introduce the video by stating that they are about to see a program which deals with many important social issues and that there are different points of view presented.

Shared Experience
Show the program in its entirety.

Processing the Shared Experience
1. Analysing Point Of View

- Ask the children (in small groups) to share their responses to the video and highlight the parts they liked most.
- Provide focus questions which assist children in considering the range of perspectives.
- What do you think Ben's father was concerned about?
- What do you think Ben's mother was concerned about?
- What do you think Ben's sister was concerned about?
- How were Ben's concerns different from theirs?

2. Making Connections
Prepare a retrieval chart to synthesise class views about the characters in terms of the items in Figure 8.10.

3. Comparing Formats and Text Constructions
Provide multiple copies of the novel version of *The Other Facts of Life*. After a sufficient number of children have had the opportunity to read the book, ask them to compare the book with the film.

- What is similar about the two formats and what are the main differences?

- Are these generally what you find when something is produced in both formats or are the differences more to do with the nature of the particular narrative?

In books the writer can say what the characters thoughts and feelings might be, whereas in video the actors and the director interpret the writer's words and convey this through gesture, body language and intonation. Ask the children to find examples in the book of a particular character's thoughts and feelings. For example:

'You know the meat business,' said Ron. 'Bloody murder.'
Ben laughed. This was one of Dad's jokes and Ben always did the right things and laughed. Except today it didn't come out right so he changed it to a cough. He wondered what was going on. (p. 11)

'She's better fed. They probably get more rain in West Africa.' He looked at Di sadly.
Di smiled weakly, suddenly concerned that Ben shouldn't realise he was a late developer and get neurotic about it. She made a mental note to give him more meat. (p. 22)

'Can I talk to you now Dad?' he said. Ron's shoulders sagged. 'Not tonight mate,' he mumbled wearily. 'It's nearly midnight. Some other time, eh?'
He ruffled Ben's hair, stepped past him and plodded up the stairs, hoping with his last glimmer of energy he wasn't being a bad parent. (p. 29)

They might then like to see the video once again to find the corresponding section for comparison.

4. *Studying the Writer*
Morris Gleitzman writes regularly for film and television. His scripts include *Doctors and Nurses*, *Norman Gunston*, and *Son of Alvin*. Ask the children to research and consider the type of writing he portrays and the issues his screenplays depict.

5. Studying Other Texts
Choose a range of novels which construct point of view in different ways, for example *The Great Gilly Hopkins* (Paterson 1981), *The Secret Diary of Adrian Mole* (Townsend 1982) *Playing Beatie Bow* (Park 1980), *Penny Pollard's Diary* (Klein 1983).
Encourage children to share their responses to these books and make comparisons with *The Other Facts of Life*.

Resourcing Children's Learning

Character	Interests	Beliefs	Attitudes to Ben's Beliefs	Actions
Ben's father				
Ben's mother				
Ben's sister				
The aged protester				

Figure 8.10

Pictures and other Visual Print Resources

The use of visual material for picture chats or focused discussions has been a traditional curriculum or language activity. Like a good book, visual material can be used for sustained learning, small-group discussion and a focus for art, drama and mathematics. Visual materials lend themselves to the organisation, interpretation and presentation of information in concrete ways that promote oral language. They also provide rich cultural texts for analysis of social role, values and factors associated with changes in our society or the environment.

They differ from video in their potential to be used as a static display for intense observation and analysis. Pictures allow for a concrete comparison of images or text or interpretations. Billboards and visual displays have increasingly presented themselves as sources of literacy in our everyday lives. In addition access to the camera has provided most people with a medium for capturing aspects of their personal experiences. We seek to explore ways to use this factor in curriculum terms. Children will be better served if they develop the facility to become critical readers of all forms of information, and in particular those presented in advertisements in the popular media.

This section focuses on two examples which are available to schools and are appropriate to use as a key shared experience within a curriculum unit.

The Changing Countryside

This unit is based on *The Changing Countryside* (Muller 1973). This work provides a visual documentation of change through seven pictures which the artist has painted at a specific geographic location over an extended period of about 20 years. Though the artist's point of view about the changes witnessed is unmistakable, the pictures allow for a wide range of interpretations, explanations and speculations and the viewer can be encouraged to examine events from the various perspectives of those involved. The work is dense in its graphic representation of the physical, technological and social change taking place and intense observation helps to extract the critical patterns and themes.

This example was devised for Year 5/6 children.

Major Understandings in these Pictures
1. The consequences of change are difficult to predict.
2. We have greater awareness of rapid change than of slow, gradual, long-term change.
3. Changes to one part of an environmental 'system' may have detrimental effects on other elements in that system.
4. Technology increases both the rate and the scope of change.
5. The attitudes of people towards change are influenced by their values and their interests.
6. The benefits of change may not be shared equally by all the groups affected.
7. Some groups are able to influence the direction of change more than others.
8. Changes in the weather bring about changes in work and leisure activities.

Prior Knowledge
A rich visual text of this kind offers possibilities for intellectual engagement to 'readers' of widely varying experience and backgrounds. Indeed, using these pictures frequently provides concrete evidence of how the meanings constructed by the reader are shaped by the knowledge brought to the text. This was clearly demonstrated to us on an occasion when we used *The Changing Countryside* with an adult audience. One of the activities involved estimating a date for the first and the last picture and seeking evidence in the illustrations for the particular choices. A member of the group identified the motorcycle in the final picture as a four cylinder model and also knew the date that these were first released (1970 as we recall). Thus, in one learner's mind 1970 becomes fixed as the earliest possible date for this particular picture. Other learners who did not use this piece of prior knowledge may decide on other possible items of evidence.. Similarly, children will bring their developing knowledge to a text of this type without any fears of intimidation from the 'unknown information' in the illustrations with which more sophisticated or experienced persons may be operating.

Before introducing a picture set such as *The Changing Countryside* to the class it is helpful to use a strategy designed to focus the children's attention on changes in their own lives and thus explore connections between their personal experience and the issues raised in the pictures. This can be done in several ways.

1. Group the children into threes or fours and ask them to think about important changes in their lives. If appropriate, some of the ideas could be recorded on newsprint for later sharing. Move around the groups and tune in to the discussions. You might throw in some questions where appropriate. For example:

- Has anybody moved house recently?
- Are there any new people living with you?
- Have there been any big changes in the area close to where you live which have changed things for you?
- What about other changes such as coming to school, people you know and like moving away, deaths?

2. Tell the children that you are about to show them a set of pictures titled *The Changing Countryside*. Place them in small groups and ask them to predict what they think will happen (this could be done visually through paint or other illustrative media). Share the group responses with the whole class and save for comparison with the picture set.
3. Display picture 1 and ask the children to make predictions about what will happen in the future. You may need to set time-frames for this. Again, this could be recorded in writing or illustrative form and shared with the class.

The Shared Experience

Display the pictures around the walls of the classroom or in an adjacent corridor. Care needs to be taken about the display. Each picture should be clearly numbered and sufficient space left between pictures to allow children appropriate access. You may prefer to group the pictures in pairs to help children make comparisons. These observations are the crucial data collection component and the capacity of the resource to raise critical questions about the world is dependent on the effectiveness of this strategy.

1. Set the Task

I want you to look carefully at the pictures displayed around the walls. They were painted by an artist who went to the same spot every so often to record in pictures the changes taking place in this village. Your task is to look over the pictures and make notes about what has changed. You can start and finish wherever you like.

Group children into groups of three with one child recording examples of change and the other two observing. Ask each group to appoint a reporter.

2. Share the results

Starting at picture 2 move from group to group asking for one example of change. Make sure that groups listen carefully to the responses so that repetition does not become a problem. (*Note*: There is an incredible number of changes between the pictures from more global things such as the seasons and the time of day and the vast changes in the landscape to what the cats are doing.)

Move to picture 3 and continue sharing the findings. Ask a particular group to lead the discussion and then call for contributions from the others. Continue for pictures 4, 5, 6 and 7.

3. Estimation
Ask the groups to look over the pictures and make an estimate of the number of years between picture 1 and picture 7. 'How long would it take for these vast changes to take place?' If appropriate, you could also ask the children to estimate the year for picture 1 and the year for picture 7. Tell the children you are very interested in why they chose particular time spans or dates. 'What is there (evidence can you show) in the pictures which supports your estimates?'

Processing the Information
1. Visual Representation
This is a very powerful strategy through which children can clarify, refine and articulate their responses to the events they have observed in a picture set or other visual resource. A great deal of oral language accompanies such experience, particularly when small groups share the responsibility of generating and articulating a response. You could apply this strategy to *The Changing Countryside* in the following way.

Ask the children to think carefully about the changes they observed in the village and choose one which they would like to represent through art. Provide a range of media — paint, collage materials, coloured paper, construction materials such as plastic blocks, multi-link materials, oil pastels and large sheets of paper. Tell the children that they have three decisions to make:

(a) Which idea/s do I want to represent?
(b) Which materials will I use?
(c) Will I work alone or with others?

Set an appropriate time limit and foreshadow a share time to conclude the session. Groups may need to organise a presenter for this purpose.

Conduct the share time. At the conclusion ask the children to identify the main ideas which were represented in the art work. You might wish to record these yourself or ask some children to write these down on newsprint for future reference.

2. Drama or Role Play
The value of a structured role play as a form of response to a picture set such as *The Changing Countryside* lies in its capacity to allow children to develop a human perspective on the physical changes to that environment. In a sense, the effects of large-scale changes on the lives of the various people involved in the situation are not very explicit in the illustrations, yet we can easily identify possible consequences and responses if we focus on the point of view of those involved. Role play allows us to do this.

(a) To begin with, some of the characters in the pictures need to be identified. You could do this yourself or you might wish to involve the children in this process. Some of the characters are quite explicit (the illustrator, the family who own the big house and farm the land) and others need to be flushed out (a property developer, a government official, business and industry leaders, church leaders, migrant workers, etc.). You may need to return to the pictures for this purpose.

Identify about five characters who will be involved in discussions about the future of the community. This works best when there is a fixed topic which can be identified in the pictures, for example a proposal to demolish the old house to construct a new shopping complex. On the chalkboard, list the characters involved in the meeting and give each a number.

> 1. An old lady who owns the big house
> 2. A government minister
> 3. The owner of the supermarket
> 4. A migrant worker
> 5. The artist

(b) Set the classroom furniture up to accommodate the number of roles chosen (5). The next stage is the allocation of roles to the children. There are many ways of doing this, from random allocation by giving every child a number from 1 to 5 to allowing some individual or group choice. Random allocation is sometimes helpful in that it may force children to adopt a point of view with which they may not be in personal agreement. Tell the class that each of them will have a role to play at a meeting which is to be held soon.

(c) Place all of the participants in their role (expert) groups (see Figure 8.11). All of the house owners meet together, as do all of the property developers, etc. Set a manageable time limit for this activity (15–20 minutes, depending on the class). Each group then considers the situation or proposal together from the point of view of the role they have been allocated. Some teacher assistance may be needed in situations where the work or interests of the particular role are not well understood (e.g. a property developer). You may prefer to provide some lead time for children to investigate the nature of their roles. A collective response is then generated within each group based on the perceived interests of the person/s they represent. Ask one of the groups to take responsibility for chairing the meeting.

(d) Children then move into their meeting groups so that each role is represented in each meeting. In a class of 30 there will be six meetings of five people going on simultaneously.

Expert Group Meetings

1. Owners of the house

2. Government ministers

3. Supermarket owners

4. Migrant workers

5. Artists

Meeting group

1. House owner

5. Artist

2. Government minister

4. Migrant worker

3. Supermarket owner

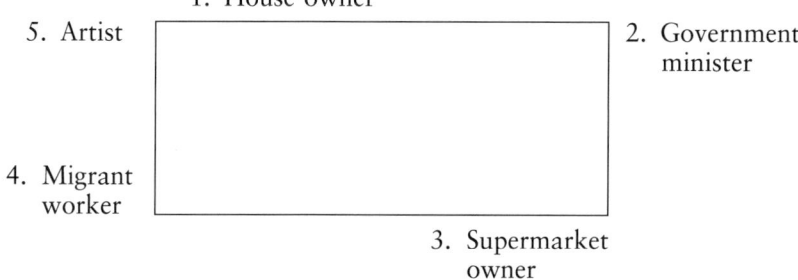

Figure 8.11

(e) Set a realistic time limit which will provide an opportunity for all points of view to be presented (15 minutes) and give directions if you want a decision to be taken by vote or some other outcome or action plan.
(f) Conduct a debriefing session so that children shed their respective roles. Discuss how they felt about the role they were allocated, which points of view surprised them, what decision they made and why and so on.
(g) At the conclusion ask the children to identify the main ideas which were represented in the art work. You might wish to record these yourself or ask some children to write these down on newsprint for future reference.

Niki's Walk

This unit is based on *Niki's Walk* (Tanner 1987). In the work, an established illustrator, Jane Tanner, was commissioned to provide a realistic depiction of a particular inner city neighbourhood and some of its facilities and daily activities. The pictures highlight many contemporary issues related to multiculturalism, concepts of work and leisure and urban lifestyles and land use. In curriculum terms, a focus on these particular issues is more appropriate than using the pictures for a discussion of the personal point of view depicted through the character Niki. Intense observation, categorisation and interpretation are required as well as the use of knowledge arising from learners' everyday lives. The book is produced in large and small formats to facilitate different types of use.

This example was devised for K/P/Year 1 children.

Major Understandings
1. Human settlement has changed the environment.
2. People from many cultural backgrounds live in particular inner city areas.
3. There are different means of transport used in the inner city.
4. A shopping centre provides for a range of employment, goods and services.
5. Over time, some materials used in building construction have changed.

Prior Knowledge
Before introducing a pictorial resource such as *Niki's Walk* it is helpful to use strategies which focus children's attention on their own experiences and knowledge of living in a neighbourhood.

1. Where We Live
Ask the children to work in small groups and individually draw a picture of where they live and discuss what the building is made of, other people who live with them and other flats, houses or buildings near them. These drawings can be displayed and information used as the basis of a class graph showing types of places children live in. The book *How We Live* (Harper and Roche 1977) could be shared to stress diversity of lifestyles and housing.

2. Partner Discussion
Ask the children to choose their two favourite shops. They can draw the shop, write the names of the types of shops, add any special signs and symbols, draw things in the window, make a sign to tell people what time each shop opens and closes.

3. Small-group Discussion
In groups of six, children put their shops together to make a streetscape. In doing so they will need to decide the order of the shops, the numbers they will have and any other signs which may go outside their shops such as street name, parking signs or meters, pedestrian crossing.

The Shared Experience
Introduce the book and tell the children that Jane Tanner has painted one neighbourhood she lives near. Discuss the title so that the children can see that the character is walking around this neighbourhood for a particular purpose.

Skim for general information by showing the children the pictures and asking individuals to predict what they think Niki might see in the different parts of the neighbourhood (houses, shops, recreation facilities, transport).

Processing the Information
1. Retrieving and Organising Information
Prepare a retrieval chart and ask the children in small groups to give examples of each category depicted in the pictures. Design for each group a particular list to complete with words or illustrations (Figure 8.12). Copies of the small-format book will assist them with this activity.

What people are doing	What houses and buildings are made of	Things that move	Things that don't move

Figure 8.12

2. *Reporting Back — Large Class*
Ask each group to appoint a reporter to share what the group listed. The children can compare this neighbourhood with the information previously collated about their own neighbourhood.

3. *Uses of Language*
Ask the children to make the signs they observed in the pictures. Classify their signs under headings (Figure 8.13).

4. *Modelling a Report — Jointly Constructed Text*
Ask the children to focus on how people live. For example:

> Some people live in small houses.
> Most small houses are made of ———.
> Some people live in big houses.
> Most big houses are made of ———.

5. *Modelling a Procedure — Jointly Constructed Text*
Tell the children that they are going to help write a set of instructions for Niki so that he can get to the park by himself. The title is: *How to Get from Niki's House to the Park.*

6. *Estimating, Using Time and Number Concepts*
Ask the children to predict how long it took Niki to go for his walk. Encourage them to give reasons for their responses.
  Ask them to estimate the time of day that Niki went for his walk. Encourage them to look for evidence in the pictures to justify their response.

7. *Health and Safety Concepts within Neighbourhoods*
Ask the children to share knowledge of safety house zones, protective behaviour, safety procedures in their own neighbourhood.

8. *Comparing Texts*
Collect other related literature for comparison, for example *My Place* (Wheatley 1987), *Window* (Baker 1991), *What Doesn't Belong?* (Long 1987), *How We Live* (Harper and Roche 1977).

Computer Resources

Computers have now been in our schools for a considerable period of time though their potential as a curriculum resource remains largely untapped. In many cases schools have placed the emphasis on learning about computers and the aspect of learning through computers has been

Signs that tell us what to do	Signs that advertise things

Figure 8.13

neglected. Approaches focusing on learning about computers tend to concentrate on the development of computer-related skills and learning how computers work or, in a small number of cases, how to program computers.

A study of computer applications in Australian schools showed that schools, parents and teachers ranked the use of computers as an information source as the main advantage in introducing computers (Fitzgerald *et al.* 1986, p. 30). The development of language and writing skills through word processing was also accorded a high priority by teachers and schools. Interestingly, parents gave the teaching of programming a much higher ranking than did schools or teachers! This suggests that parents would prefer a greater emphasis on teaching about computers.

The focus here is on the computer as a resource. Such an approach assumes that the computer should be considered in a similar way to other resources presented in this book. The capacity to organise and present information in multiple ways, thus facilitating interpretation and explanation, is probably the greatest strength of computers as a curriculum resource. Computers can be used in highly interactive ways, allowing for a balance between 'hands on' and 'hands off' activities which allow learners to sustain their explorations and develop and refine their understandings in systematic ways. In selecting application and other software it is important to consider whether the computer provides more effective ways of achieving the intended curriculum purposes or whether some other resource such as print or videotape might be more effective. Software falls into a number of clear categories. This work focuses upon application software which is largely underutilised in our schools.

Application Software

These are packages which are designed for the user to provide the data. In the main they include word processing packages, desktop publishers, spreadsheets and data bases. Word processors are now well understood by many teachers who use them for their own writing purposes and for writing and publishing in their classrooms.

Word Processing and Jointly Constructed Text
One of the problems in effectively producing a jointly constructed text in a classroom setting is the difficulty in manipulating the text (changing its sequence, inserting, deleting and correcting errors) in ways which allow all of the participants to see what is going on. Visual access to text changes is essential if children are to use this strategy to learn more about how writers construct different text types and about the processes involved in writing and publishing. Computers can demonstrate these things brilliantly, but the size of the display limits the participants to a very small number. As the unit cost of large visual display devices such as Kodak's Datashow (which can display the output of the computer through an overhead projector) comes down, the use of word processing packages

for jointly constructed texts with larger groups of children becomes a reality.

Technology of this kind has been used in senior primary classrooms with great success. In the context of a unit of work where children were studying sea creatures as part of their science curriculum, children were introduced to report writing. This was necessary as the children needed to write in this genre in order to document their investigations. The introduction was initially provided through the analysis of a suitable text. The text was broken up into chunks which contained the major elements. Each chunk was read with the children and discussed. The children were then asked what kind of information was being provided. Their responses were recorded in a column beside the piece of text (Figure 8.14).

Example: The Polar Bear   (*Title*)

Polar bears are mammals.   (*Type of animal*)

They have a thick coat of fur.   (*Features*)
They need this coat to survive the freezing temperatures of the Arctic.

Polar bears are predators.   (*Behaviour*)
They hunt seals by waiting at holes in the ice where the seals come to breathe.

Figure 8.14

The structure of this report was then used as the basis for the joint construction. The children chose whales as their topic and everyone agreed to find out something about whales for the following day.

The computer, Datashow and overhead projector were set up prior to the session. Children were asked to provide sentences for their report on whales. These sentences were typed into the word processing package as they were provided and the children could read the text as it was typed in a large font and displayed through the overhead projector. Sentences were simply entered as they were given without any editorial changes. After children were satisfied with the amount of information, they were asked to consider the structure of the report using the model derived from the analysis of the previous day.

They began by selecting a title. This was followed by a general statement about whales which located them in their scientific classification as mammals. Sentences describing their appearance were then cut and pasted in the order decided by the children. There was considerable debate over some sequences. Finally, the information about behaviour was discussed and sequenced.

Having satisfied themselves that the sequence was reasonable, the children began to look at aspects such as cohesion, the variety of sentence beginnings and repetition or redundancy in their text. There was no difficulty in maintaining interest as the large display allowed children to follow and read the text at all times and thus contribute to the structure and suggest amendments to the sequence and patterns of language. The computer made it a simple matter to change these items and children were able to generate many alternatives, consider them as they were visually displayed and confirm or reject them. The process was much more effective on the computer than previous attempts with newsprint or acetate sheets. The cost of this technology has decreased markedly in recent times and its availability to classroom teachers in the immediate future seems assured.

Spreadsheets
These applications allow users to enter their own information and complete a wide range of operations on the data. In terms of school uses, spreadsheets allow users to enter formulae in cells which can add, subtract, multiply, divide and calculate percentages. Many spreadsheets have a chart feature which uses the data entered to draw graphs. These can be drawn very quickly and the range of types available (line, bar, column, pie, scatter, even three-dimensional versions) means that the user can experiment with the output in order to find the most effective presentation form. Such experimentation is incredibly time consuming using paper-based graphs but can be achieved and printed out in a few minutes with a spreadsheet. Any investigation involving the collection of quantitative data could be a suitable candidate for presentation through a spreadsheet. Opportunities for their use occur regularly in classrooms.

Data bases
Data base applications allow users to store, sort and retrieve information in ways which are not possible with books. Information about community, neighbourhood, country, environment, leisure, people, plants or animals could be the basis of a data base.

In the context of studying the features of vertebrates, children could construct a data base which could allow them to compare various types of vertebrates and identify the distinguishing characteristics.

1. The first step is to identify the characteristics which children want to compare. Children could discuss these in small groups and a class list of their suggestions could be made. After further consideration finalise the list. These become the field names for the data base. Animal, type of vertebrate, body covering, food, habitat, country, size and features would be useful fields.
2. The field names and details about the type of information to be included (alphabetical/numerical) are then entered into the data base.
3. Now individual records can be entered. Children would need to gather this information systematically. Children would need to identify animals they wish to research and collect the information required for the data base. Their investigations may take some time. Data can be added as it is collected or when convenient and could

continue throughout the year. Some reconsideration of the fields is sometimes necessary as the data entry proceeds.

Once the records are entered the data base can be sorted in various ways. Sorting alphabetically by the 'Type' field would group the vertebrates together by class — birds, fish, mammals and reptiles. This would allow them to compare other features (such as body covering) to discover whether there were any common features. Fields such as habitat, food, country and size could also be sorted or searched to identify particular characteristics (Figure 8.15).

Application software has provided the focus of this section as it is seriously underutilised in our classrooms. Visits to schools suggest that quite extensive use is made of some packaged software and adventure games and simulations do seem to receive a great deal of attention in some classrooms. These can be valuable curriculum resources when used judiciously for specific purposes and children clearly benefit from exposure to a good adventure game when it is used appropriately. The advantage of application software such as spreadsheets and data bases lies in the capacity of users to shape the data in a way which conforms to their own needs and purposes.

Books as Resources

The treatment of fiction material and children's literature in schools has received much attention (Johnson and Louis 1985; Nicoll and Unsworth 1989, 1990; Chambers 1985; Meek 1982; Saxby and Smith 1991). Less has been written about appropriate ways of dealing with factual books though the systemic linguists (Christie 1985; Martin and Rothery 1985; Wignell and Martin 1987) have certainly focused on this category of published books. This section provides a model for the treatment of a factual text, *Earthworms*.

Factual Text

EARTHWORMS
This unit is based on *Earthworms* (Pigdon and Woolley 1989) which is available in 'big book' and small book formats.

Major Understandings in this Book
1. Earthworms play an important role in improving soil conditions for other living things.
2. Earthworms are part of the food chain of other animals.

Sample vertebrate data base

Animal	Type	Body covering	Food	Habitat	Country	Size
Giant panda	Mammal	Fur	Bamboo	Mountains	China & Tibet	75–150 kg
Wolf	Mammal	Fur	Meat	Grasslands, forest	Europe, North America, Asia	45–55 kg
Gorilla	Mammal	Fur	Bamboo, roots, leaves	Jungle	Africa	200 kg
Cheetah	Mammal	Fur	Meat	Grasslands (dry)	Africa	45–65 kg
Peregrine falcon	Bird	Feathers	Birds	Grasslands	Most	0.57–0.65 kg
Fairy penguin	Bird	Feathers	Fish, krill	Ocean, beaches	Southern Australia	1 kg
Emu	Bird	Feathers	Grass, roots, insects	Grasslands, desert	Australia	55 kg
Estuarine crocodile	Reptile	Scales	Meat, fish	River estuaries	Australia, South East Asia	1000 kg
Boa constrictor	Reptile	Scales	Birds, small mammals, reptiles	Mountain forests	Central & South America	60 kg
Blue-tongue lizard	Reptile	Scales	Snails, mice, insects	Coastal plains and hills	Eastern Australia	0.4 kg
Tiger shark	Fish	Scales	Meat and fish	Most waters	All	1000 kg
Manta ray	Fish	Scales	Plankton	Tropical waters	Tropical countries	2000 kg
Bream	Fish	Scales	Crabs, shrimps, small fish	River estuaries, reefs, surf beaches	Australia	1.5 kg

Figure 8.15

3. Earthworms have an interesting life cycle which is quite different from most other species.
4. Earthworms have very specific requirements which must be met if they are to live and breed successfully.

Prior Knowledge
1. *Worm Investigators*
Tell the children that over the next few weeks they are going to find out and share a lot of ideas about a special creature. Introduce a sheet headed *Worm Investigator* and ask the children in pairs to go away and find out as much as they can about earthworms. You might question the children about possible sources — parents, older siblings, books, etc. The responses in Figures 8.16 and 8.17 were provided by six year olds.

Caleb and Anna have responded using the everyday commonsense knowledge one would expect to find about earthworms in our community (Figures 8.18 and 8.19).

Megan and Adrian have taken a different approach. Megan begins by telling the reader some of the things earthworms can't do. Her final sentence reveals that she has discovered something fascinating about earthworms. Adrian has investigated earthworms by looking in books for information.

Make a list, using one contribution from each pair of children (Figure 8.20).

Place children in small groups to discuss earthworms. Provide the focus question: 'What do we now want to find out about earthworms?'

Record some of the questions for future use. A Year 1 class provided the responses shown in Figure 8.21.

2. *Observing and Gathering Information about Earthworms*
Tell the children that they are going to make a worm farm so that they can watch how earthworms grow and what earthworms do. This provides a context for following written instructions. Refer to the big book model and turn to the section entitled Making a Wormery (p. 23). Use the instructions to build a wormery in a jar or a glass aquarium.

The Shared Experience
Using the big book version, read the text to the class. This can be done in one session or over several sessions, using a few chapters each time, depending on your purposes and the group of children.

As you read the book, take advantage of its large format to demonstrate some of the features of a factual text to the class. These might include:

1. Using a table of contents, for example p. 1. This feature can be used to highlight the differences in the way we read a factual

Resourcing Children's Learning

text as compared with a story. We can begin to answer our questions by going to a specific chapter, for example 'Where Earthworms Live'. You don't have to start at the beginning!
2. Examining the illustrations before reading the words, for example pp. 4–5. Illustrations on these pages provide a detailed cross-section of an earthworm's head and enlargements are used to show minute detail of the bristles and muscles.

Worm Investigator   Name *Caleb*

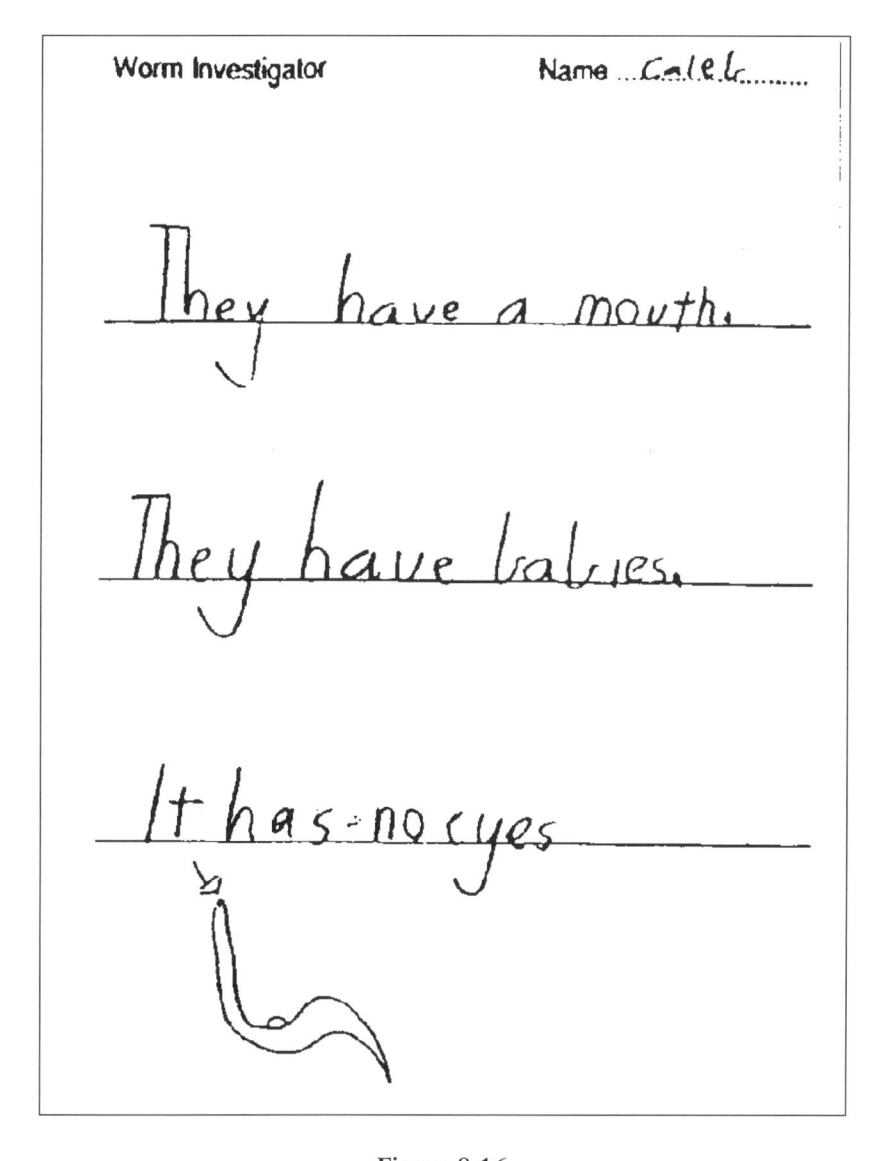

They have a mouth.

They have babies.

It has no eyes

Figure 8.16

Literacy Learning and Teaching

> **Worm Investigator** **Name** Anna
>
> Worms are found in the ground.
>
> They give the soil vitamins.
>
> you can use them as bait for fish.
>
> They wiggle all around when you hold them.

Figure 8.17

3. Moving from commonsense to public/scientific knowledge, for example p. 6, the introduction of the term *organic material* in a context where children can easily grasp its meaning.
4. Using brackets (parentheses) to introduce technical terms, for example p. 13: 'Each earthworm is both male and female. (Creatures which are male and female are called hermaphrodite.)'
5. Relating the information to the life of the child, for example p. 7. Compare the daily intake of an earthworm with the equivalent daily intake by a seven to eight year old.

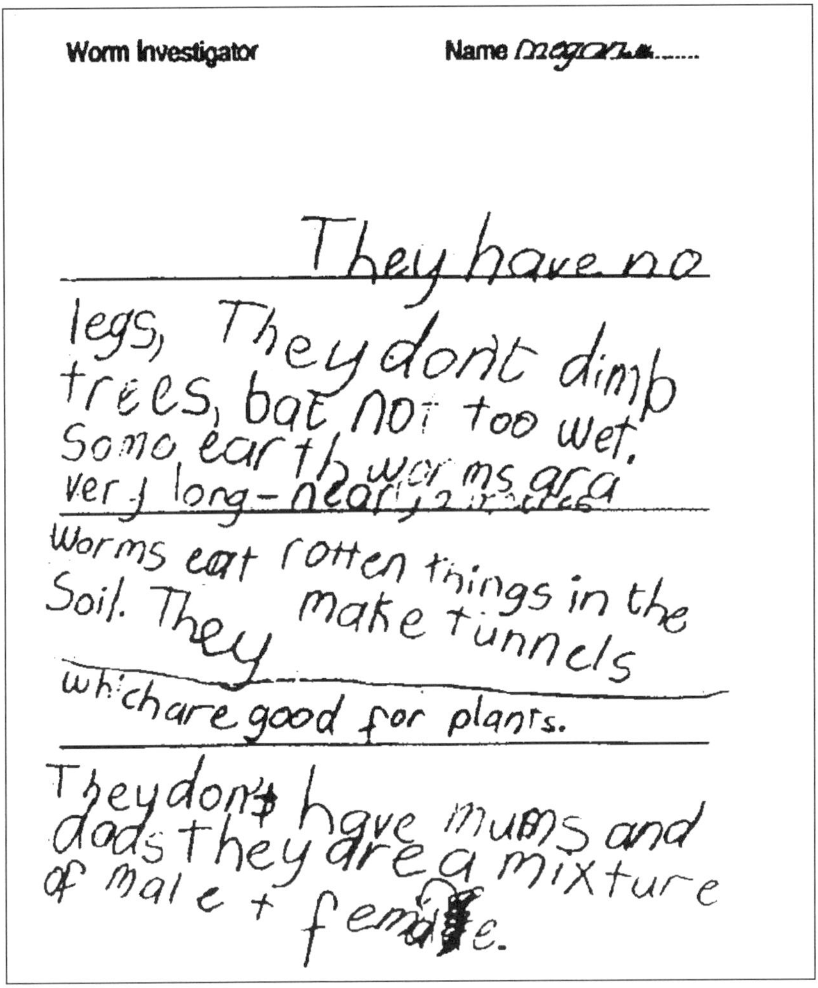

> **Worm Investigator**   Name *Megan...*
>
> They have no legs. They don't climb trees, but not too wet. Some earthworms are very long – nearly 2 inches.
>
> Worms eat rotten things in the soil. They make tunnels which are good for plants.
>
> They don't have mums and dads, they are a mixture of male + female.

Figure 8.18

6. The use of visual devices to show:
   (a) relativity of size and shape, p. 14.
   (b) time concepts, pp. 15 and 18.
7. Using an index to locate specific information and as a spelling checker, p. 24.

Processing the Information
1. Synthesis of Additional Information
Refer to previous records and ask the children if they see any reason to change any of the statements or answer any of the questions they raised earlier. Compile a new list of statements if necessary (see Figure 8.22).

Literacy Learning and Teaching

> **Worm Investigator** Name **Adrian**
>
> Earthworms are the gardeners friend.
> They mix, aerate and break up the soil.
> They feed by swallowing soil digesting animal and plant food in it.
> Worms do not have lungs.
> They absorb air through their skin.
> Their skin must be kept moist or they may die.

Figure 8.19

Worm Investigators
What we found out about earthworms   Some earthworms grow very big — 15 metres. (Erica, Joel)   They cover themselves with dirt. (Marissa, Megan)   Earthworms help our soil. (Stacey, Karen)   They live under the ground. They help the plants to grow. (Emily, Sandra)   They move very slowly. (Sara, Nicole)   Earthworms do not climb trees. (Erica, Megan)   Earthworms wiggle and squirm under the dirt. They eat leaves. (Ben, Adam)   If you cut an earthworm in half, it bleeds a lot. (Adrian, Daniel)   If they are split in half they are still alive. (Jason, Caleb)

Figure 8.20

> **Our questions about earthworms**
>
> Do earthworms eat leaves? (Karen)
> Do eagles eat them? (Sara)
> Do they like eating lily pads? (Ben)
> Do earthworms eat the soil? (Brooke)
> Do they like it under the dirt? (Meaghan)
> Can earthworms swim? (Stacey)
> If their heads are chopped off are they still alive? (Chris)
> What eats earthworms?
> Can they break rocks underground? (Mrs Furhmann)
> Do earthworms like light? (Mrs Furhmann)
> Can people eat them? (Nathan)
> Do they like Nectar? (Adrian)

Figure 8.21

> **What we now know about earthworms**
>
> All earthworms can have babies.
> The babies are inside the egg sac for two weeks.
> They have five pairs of hearts.
> Lots of animals are dangers for them.
> Birds eat earthworms.
> Earthworms can die from poison.
> They can drown or dry up.
> They don't like light.
> They have tiny bristles to move with.
> They eat growing things.
> Sometimes lots of them live together in the one place.
> They eat a lot of dirt for their size.

Figure 8.22

2. *Going Beyond the Text*
(a) Refer to pp. 9 and 10. Study the illustrations done by Sadie and Suzanne Pascoe and discuss the range of places you might find earthworms. Ask the children what is similar about all these places. Prepare a retrieval chart so that children can research other books to classify animals which live in dark places and animals which live in light places (see Figure 8.23).
(b) Refer to the retrieval chart, Comparing Creatures, on p. 24. Prepare a similar chart and ask the children, in pairs, to choose a creature to add down the list and then to choose another category, for example food, to add across the list. Again en-

courage the children to research other factual books to locate this information or use information from appropriate television programs.

Animals which live in dark places	Animals which live in light places
Echidna Platypus Bat	Kangaroo Koala Giraffe

Figure 8.23

Investigating Language Use
1. *Constructing the Text*
Discuss with the children the authors' craft using the following focus questions:

- What did the authors need to know about earthworms in order to write this book?
- How would the authors find out this information?
- What decisions about the information did the authors make?
  — what to select for the book?
  — how to use the information?

2. *Analysing a Report*
Write up parts of the text in front of the children to show them that there are particular patterns of language used in report writing and that information can sometimes be organised under headings.

EARTHWORMS

Features

Earthworms *are* interesting creatures.
Their long, thin bodies *are covered with* damp skin.
They *have* a saddle which is used for laying eggs.
They *also have* a mouth, a brain and five pairs of hearts.
Earthworms *move by* pushing themselves along with their tiny bristles.

Feeding

Earthworms *like to eat* anything that was once alive and growing.

> **Living Together**
>
> Earthworms *live together* in very crowded conditions.
>
> **Dangers**
>
> Insects, frogs, lizards, birds and lots of other creatures *eat them*.
>
> Using the above structure of text organisation and patterns of language, encourage the children to construct their own report about an animal or creature they know a lot about.
>
> *3. Analysing Language Patterns and Uses*
> 'Big book' formats allow you to return to particular sections of the text to demonstrate the author's employment of particular patterns and uses of language. This strategy provides a meaningful context for the refinement of children's language knowledge through discussions of specific features of language used by writers in texts which have been previously read for other purposes. *Earthworms* provides the following examples:
>
> (a) Descriptive patterns of language: interesting creatures (p. 2); long, thin bodies (p. 2); damp skin (p. 2); tiny bristles (p. 5); amazing appetites (p. 7); enormous amounts of food (p. 10); food is ground up very quickly (p. 8); Normally only one worm ... (p. 15).
> (b) Time concepts: Once a week (p. 3); Every two or three weeks (p. 15); As soon as they are born (p. 17); Three months old (p. 8); Before they become adults (p. 19); After a few days (p. 23).

Conclusion

This work has proposed a careful consideration of the resources on which curriculum is constructed. The content of the resources used in classrooms defines for children the essential ideas about the world in which schooling will attempt to engage them. Differences in learners arising from gender, ethnicity, culture, class, experience, knowledge, learning styles, interests and needs should inform the selection of resources. Imbalances and stereotypes in resources previously used with children is a further consideration.

The approach adopted stresses the importance of science, social education, environmental education and health as the key areas for defining curriculum content. Hence the starting point for the analysis of any resource will be: What ideas about the world can this resource introduce children to? This has implications for the types of texts which children will be expected to discuss, read and write in these contexts. In other curriculum contexts (literature workshops) different texts should be considered and used.

The model provided proposes documentation of major understandings to be investigated, and the use of a variety of ways to enable children to work through the information gathered from the resource. In this process children analyse, interpret and categorise information in order to generate new understandings or refine their existing ideas.

Resourcing children's learning in these ways provides different perspectives on children's language needs. The approach advocated views literacy as social practice and requires a reconceptualisation of what counts as literate behaviour in contemporary society and redefines what constitutes an essential reading and writing repertoire in the primary school. Access to new fields of factual information about the world can be provided through the curriculum resources selected by teachers. Quality resources, used appropriately, will extend children's individual personal experience and move them beyond their existing knowledge. This we consider to be a major objective of schooling.

Note

The authors wish to acknowledge many teachers and students who have contributed (sometimes unwittingly) to this work. In the process of demonstrating units of work and teaching strategies, we have learnt a great deal from their questions, their responses and their interpretations.

Special thanks are accorded to the following teachers and schools who allowed us to work with their children and gave freely of their time and expertise: Lesley Wing Jan and Carol Furhmann (Eltham East); Glenda Gauntlett and Linda Ratcliffe (Anderson's Creek); Sue Trounson (Alphington); Peggy Giochas (Reservoir East); Paul Molyneaux, Sally Dayton, Barbara Flattley and Marta Cesnik (Boundary Road, North Melbourne).

References

Anderson, R. (1991) 'Planning social studies units', in *Teaching Social Studies* (2nd edn), ed. C. Marsh, Prentice-Hall, Sydney.
Heath, S.B. (1986) 'Literacy and language change', in *Language and Linguistics: The Interdependence of Theory, Data and Application*, eds D. Tanner and J. Alatis, Georgetown University Press, Washington DC.
Britton, J. (1987) 'A quiet form of research', in *Reclaiming The Classroom: Teacher Research as an Agency for Change*, eds D. Goswami and P. Stillman, Boynton Cook, USA.
Bullock, Sir A. (1975) *A Language for Life*, HMSO, London.
Chambers, A. (1985) *Book Talk: Occasional Writing on Literature and Children*, The Bodley Head, London.
Christie, F. (1985) 'Learning to mean in writing', in *Writing and Reading to Learn*, ed. N. Stewart-Dore, Primary English Teaching Association, Sydney.
Christie, F. (1987) 'Factual writing in the first years of school', *Australian Journal of Reading* 10 (4) November: 207–216.
Christie, F. (1990) 'The changing face of literacy', in *Literacy for a Changing World*, ed. F. Christie, ACER, Melbourne.
Christie, F. and Rothery, J. (1990) 'Literacy in the curriculum: Planning and Assessment', in *Literacy for a Changing World*, ed. F. Christie, ACER, Melbourne.
Dalton, J. (1986) *Adventures in Thinking*, Nelson, Melbourne.
Fitzgerald, D., Hattie, J. and Hughes, P. (1986) *Computer Applications in Australian Classrooms*, Australian Government Publishing Service, Canberra.
Gilbert, P. (1989) 'Stoning the romance: Girls as resistant readers and writers', in *Writing in Schools* (B.Ed. Course Reader), Deakin University Press, Geelong, Victoria.
Greig, S., Pike, G. and Selby, D. (1987) *Earthrights*, Kogan Page, London.
Gough, N. (1987) 'Learning with environments: Towards an ecological paradigm for education', in *Environmental Education: Practice and Possibility*, ed. I. Robottom, Deakin University Press, Geelong, Victoria.
Halliday, M.A.K. (1973) *Explorations in the Functions of Language*, Edward Arnold, London.
Halliday, M.A.K. (1981) 'Three aspects of children's language development: Learning language, learning through language, learning about language', in *Oral and Written Language Development Research: Impact on the Schools*, eds Y. Goodman, M. Haussler and D. Strickland, International Reading Association, Newark, Delaware.
Halliday, M.A.K. (1985) *An Introduction to Functional Grammar*, Edward Arnold, London.
Halliday, M.A.K. and Hasan, R. (1976) *Cohesion in English*, Longman, London.
Halliday, M.A.K. and Hasan, R. (1985) *Language, Context and Text: Aspects of Language in a Social Semiotic Perspective*, Deakin University Press, Geelong, Victoria.
Hammond, J. (1990) 'Is learning to read and write the same as learning to speak?', in *Literacy for a Changing World*, ed. F. Christie, ACER, Melbourne.
Hill, S. and Hill, T. (1990) *The Collaborative Classroom: A Guide to Co-operative Learning*, Eleanor Curtain Publishing, South Yarra, Victoria.

Houston, C. (1986) *English Language Development Across the Curriculum,* Division of Special Education, Department of Education, Queensland.
Johnson, T. and Louis, D. (1985) *Literacy Through Literature.* Methuen, Sydney.
Lemke, J. (1985) *Using Language in the Classroom,* Deakin University Press, Geelong, Victoria.
Lemke, J. (1988) 'Towards a Social Semiotics of the Material Subject', in *Working Papers,* Vol. 2, Nos 1–2, ed. T. Threadgold, Sydney Association for Studies in Society and Culture, Sydney.
McNamara, J. (1989) 'The writing in science and history project: The research questions and implications for teachers', in *Writing in Schools* (B.Ed. Course Reader), Deakin University Press, Geelong, Victoria.
Martin, J.R. (1985) *Factual Writing: Exploring and Challenging Social Reality,* Deakin University Press, Geelong, Victoria.
Martin, J.R. (1990) 'Literacy in science: learning to handle text as technology', in *Literacy for a Changing World,* ed. F. Christie, ACER, Melbourne.
Martin, J.R. and Rothery, J. (1985) *Factual Writing: Exploring and Challenging Social Reality,* Deakin University Press, Geelong, Victoria.
Meek, M. (1982) *Learning to Read,* The Bodley Head, London.
Ministry of Education (Victoria) (1987a) *The Social Education Framework P–10,* Government Printer, Melbourne.
Ministry of Education (Victoria) (1987b)*The Science Framework P–10,* Government Printer, Melbourne.
Ministry of Education (Victoria) (1987c) *The Personal Development Framework P–10,* Government Printer, Melbourne.
Morris, A. and Stewart-Dore, N. (1984) *Learning to Learn from Text: Effective Reading in the Content Areas,* Addison-Wesley, Sydney.
Newkirk, T. (1989) 'Archimedes' dream', in *Writing in Schools* (B.Ed. Course Reader), Deakin University Press, Geelong, Victoria.
Newmann, F.M. (1987) 'Higher order thinking in the high school curriculum', Paper presented at the Annual Meeting of the National Association of Secondary School Principals, San Antonio, Texas.
Nicoll, V. and Unsworth, L. (1989) *Dimensions Teachers' Book Level I,* Nelson, Melbourne.
Nicoll, V. and Unsworth, L. (1990) *Dimensions Teachers' Book Level II,* Nelson, Melbourne.
Novak, J. (1988) 'Learning science and the science of learning', *Studies in Science Education* 15: 77–101.
Pigdon, K. (1985) *Children's Perceptions of a Collaborative, Inquiry Based Approach to Teaching and Learning in Social Studies: A Unit on Television and Advertising,* unpublished M.Ed. thesis, La Trobe University, Melbourne.
Pigdon, K. and Woolley, M. (1980) 'Developing integrated curriculum units for social studies: A planning model', *MANSOC 5* (1).
Pigdon, K. and Woolley, M. (1984) *Developing Integrated Curriculum Units: A Planning Model for Social Studies,* In-Service Education Centre, Melbourne College of Advanced Education, Melbourne.
Pigdon, K. and Woolley, M. (1988) 'Eltham East research study', unpublished paper. University of Melbourne.
Pryor, D. (1991) *The Age,* 13 May, *Extra,* p. 12.
Reid, I. (1987) *The Place of Genre in Learning: Current Debates,* Deakin University Press, Geelong, Victoria.
Saxby, M. (1987) *Give Them Wings,* Macmillan, Melbourne.
Saxby, M. and Smith, G. (1991) *First Choice: A Guide to the Best Books for Australian Children,* Oxford University Press, Melbourne.

Simpson, M. (1980) *Australian Studies — Gold*, Victorian Association of Social Studies Teachers, Melbourne.
Smith, F. (1977) 'The uses of language', *Language Arts* 54 (6): 638–644.
Street, B. (1984) *Literacy In Theory And Practice*, Cambridge University Press, Cambridge.
Tinkler, D. (1989) *Social Education for Australian Primary Schools*, Macro View Educational Publications, Melbourne.
Van Matre, S. (1979) *Sunship Earth: An Acclimatization Program for Outdoor Learning*, American Camping Association, Martinsville, Indianna.
Wells, G. (1989) Foreword, in *Teachers and Research: Language Learning In The Classroom*, eds G. Pinnel and M. Matlin, International Reading Association, Newark, Delaware.
Wignell, P. and Martin, J. (1987) *Writing Project Report, Working Papers in Linguistics*, No. 5, Department of Linguistics, University of Sydney, Sydney.
Woolley, M. and Pigdon, K. (1984) 'Getting "inside the author's head"', in *Towards a Reading–Writing Classroom*, eds A. Butler and J. Turbill, Primary English Teaching Association, Sydney.

Resources for Children

ABC Television (1980) *See it My Way, The Media Series*, Sydney.
Australian Children's Television Foundation (1985) *The Other Facts of Life, The Winners Series*, Melbourne.
Baker, Jeannie (1991) *Window*, Julia McRae, London.
CBS Television (1972) *The Lorax*.
Harper, Anita and Roche, Christine (1977) *How We Live*, Kestrel Books, Harmondsworth.
Howes, Jim (1987) *Animal Jigsaws*, Macmillan, Melbourne.
Klein, Robin (1983) *Penny Pollard's Diary*, Oxford University Press, Melbourne.
Long, I.B. (1987) *What Doesn't Belong?*, Macmillan, Melbourne.
Muller, Jorg (1973) *The Changing Countryside*, Atheneum, New York.
Park, Ruth (1980) *Playing Beatie Bow*, Puffin, Harmondsworth.
Paterson, Katherine (1981) *The Great Gilly Hopkins*, Penguin, Harmondsworth.
Pigdon, Keith and Woolley, Marilyn (1989) *Earthworms*, Macmillan, Melbourne.
Silverstein, Shel (1964) *The Giving Tree*, Harper and Row, New York.
Tanner, Jane (1987) *Niki's Walk*, Macmillan, Melbourne.
Townsend, Sue (1982) *The Secret Diary of Adrian Mole*, Methuen, London.
Wheatley, Nadia (1987) *My Place*, illus. by Donna Rawlins, Collins Dove, Melbourne.

Index

Aborigines and Islanders 5, 19–20, 47–8, 29–30, 31, 57, 65, 352
Adams, Jeanie 65, 242
adjectives 201, 262
adverbs 262
Allen, Pamela 69–70, 122
alphabet 10, 11
Armstrong, William 65

Baillie, Allan 57, 62, 63, 73–4, 80, 82, 165, 169
Baker, Jeannie 66, 134
Ball, Duncan 68, 71
basal readers *see* children's readers
Blume, Judy 33, 73
Blyton, Enid 28, 58
Bolton, Barbara 68
bookclubs 80, 81
books
    children and 62–84, 75, 95, 153, 155
    big 359
    banned 33
    information 75, 280, 305–45
    picture story 61, 62, 66, 68, 69–70, 74, 75, 76, 96, 100, 112, 134, 150, 151, 158, 174
    text 306–34
    see also children; literature; readers
Briggs, Raymond 69, 153
Browne, Anthony 61, 70, 98, 134, 151, 153, 158–9, 174
Bruce, Mary Grant 67
Byars, Betsy 164
Burningham, John 61, 98, 116, 127, 159, 169, 244

Carle, Eric 61
Carr, Roger Vaughan 57
Carrol, Lewis 60
cartoons 27, 38
Caswell, Brian 64
Chambers, Aidan 72, 74–5, 150, 153, 158, 163, 167, 171, 190–1
child-rearing and gender participation 30
children's, literature 18, 19, 20, 28, 33–41, 47, 57–60, 62–84, 95–9, 112, 147–53, 154–69, 192, 351, 353, 400
    and adventure 63
    and character 63–5, 82, 148, 222
    and humour 62, 68–9, 76–7, 164
    and language 148–9
    multilayering of 38, 61, 112, 148, 153
children's readers 33, 35–41, 58, 61, 78, 148
    pictures in 102
classroom management 46–8, 81–4, 112, 148–50, 154–69, 288, 353–62
    and grouping 154–5, 156, 159–62
    practical 21–2, 31, 32, 41–5, 77, 343–5, 351
    programs 16, 113–35, 170–92
    theoretical 6, 7, 112
    see also literacy
classroom talk 32, 41–5, 244, 357–8
clauses 201, 202, 203–4, 218–52
    clause complexes and 204–6, 240, 241
    embedded 206–7, 216, 240, 241, 264
    finite and non-finite 207–8, 214–15, 245–8
    group division of clauses 235–43
        adverb 236
        nominal 236–43
        verbal 236
    meaning and 208, 210, 216, 219, 228, 236, 242–3, 246
    mood elements in 244, 245–51
    the nominal group in 236–42
    polarity and 248
    Process elements in 218–36
    Rheme elements in 208, 216
    structure of 201, 218–43, 301, 327
    Theme elements in 208–217, 227–8, 337
    see also metafunction; mood and modality; Process; Theme
Cleary, Beverly 72, 159
cloze activities 275, 328–9

414

Index

Coerr, Eleanor 57
cognitive development 14, 152, 200
comics 28
composition activities 16
comprehension 16, 29
computers 395–400
concepts 8, 75, 200, 217, 233, 243
   abstract 262, 263
   development of 59, 61, 355, 357
   of framing 156, 159
   of morality 60
   textual 211, 352
   of time 59
   see also genre; grammar; linguistics
context *see* language
conjunctions 210–11, 212, 262
conversation 23, 101–2
Crew, Gary 57, 62, 66, 72
cultural
   change 200
   hegemony 38
   patterns 8, 62
   symbols 189
   traditions 3, 10, 20, 26, 28–31, 38, 46, 48, 77–9, 133–4, 234, 352–3
   see also ideology; knowledge
culture 3–4, 5, 7, 48, 149, 257
   Australian 13, 18, 76–77, 352
   patriarchal 30, 37
curriculum 3, 16, 32–5, 46–8
   development 4–5, 18, 20, 113–33, 133–5, 218, 275–6, 352, 353, 354–62
   evaluation 356
   guidelines 33, 352, 355–6
   processes 281–7, 289, 292
   traditional 276–81, 282, 285–6, 287, 289, 291

Dahl, Roald 33, 68, 73, 220
dance 352
Dann, Max 64
Dekker, Midas 67
discourse structure 201, 203, 251
Dickinson, Peter 58, 159
Digdy, Desmond 76
Dolch list 151
drama 352

education 7, 8, 16, 31, 200, 287, 355–6
   equality and 4–7, 17

grammar and 199–200
   resources 350–410
   standards 3–4, 7
   systems 18, 276–81
   and testing 16, 32, 201
Ende, Michael 61

Factor, June 76, 134
Fadiman, Clifton 57, 64
fairy tales 27–8, 47–8, 57, 61, 62, 70, 76–9, 84
fantasy 67, 79–80
fiction 15, 58, 62–9, 95, 148, 351, 353
   imagination and 80
   meaning and 148
   science 79–80
   stereotyping and 64, 65, 353
Fienberg, Anna 68
'fill in the blanks' 16
film 352, 374–85
Fleischman, Sid 69
Flynn, Rachel 72
folk tales *see* fairy tales
Forster, E.M. 62
Fox, Mem 68, 122
Frances, Helen 63
French, Fiona 70
French, Simon 63, 64, 71, 74, 75, 167–8

Garner, Alan 75, 159
gender 6, 9, 15, 23, 29, 30, 35–41, 47
   stereotypes 37, 62, 65, 352–3
genre 10, 14, 16, 21, 46–8, 75, 335, 340
   concept of 200
   definition of 335, 336
   literary 11, 29
   schematic structure 201, 203, 251
   register and 244
   speech 22, 77, 244, 257, 258
   written 9, 11, 201, 212–13, 216, 246, 251, 258, 266, 273, 316, 327, 333, 345
Gillilian, Strickland 57
Gleeson, Libby 63, 64, 71, 72, 74, 169
Gleitzman, Morris 68, 82
Godden, Rumer 57
grapho-phonics 111, 116
Graham, Bob 74, 75

415

Index

grammar 36, 38, 116, 148,
    197–252, 266
  concepts of 200, 201, 211, 217,
    233, 243, 251, 262
  definition of 201
  functional 199, 200, 201–3
  interpersonal 244–52
  literature and 148
  meaning and 203, 208, 209,
    218, 219, 227–8, 243
  metaphor and 262, 263, 274, 287
  parsing and 202
  science and 301–5, 327–9, 338
  semantics and 219, 233, 234,
    336–7, 340
  structure of 38, 199–203,
    218–52, 301–5, 327, 335–40
  systemic functional 197–252
  taxonomy and 301–6
  traditional school 199, 201–3,
    251, 275
  transformational 199
  see also speech; writing

handwriting 3
Hathorn, Libby 65, 68, 78
Hautzig, Esther 63
Heide, Florence Parry 61
Heyer, Georgette 58
Heylen, Jill 77
Hoban, Russell 61
Hope, Laura Lee 58
Hughes, Shirley 97
Hughes, Ted 61, 153
Hunt, Nan 67
Hutchins, Pat 40, 61, 96, 113–19,
    122, 131, 153

ideology 4, 6, 31, 32, 46
  cultural 352
imagination 77, 79, 83, 84
information, gathering of 356–8
  see also books
in-service programs 5, 35
intonation 32, 81
irony 69–70, 76
Isaacson, Phillip M. 76

Jellett, Celia 77
Jennings, Paul 68, 73, 237
Johns, Capt. W.E. 58
Joyce, James 60

Kelleher, Victor 61, 62, 80
Kemp, Gene 65, 166, 167

Kidd, Diana 65, 71
King-Smith, Dick 69
Klein, Robin 64, 65, 71, 72–3, 78,
    157, 159, 167, 175
knowledge 6, 8, 12, 13, 17, 18,
    21, 32, 41, 46, 362
  commonsense 344, 356, 357
  existing 355–6, 360–1, 363
  factual 357
Konigsburg, E.L. 64

language 5, 6, 8, 19, 133–4, 148,
    149, 199, 201
  Aboriginal 19–20
  Arabic 12
  children and 8, 14, 23–6, 48,
    101, 149–50, 262, 354
  codes 8, 148
  community 33
  congruent 262, 263, 264
  context and 8, 102, 111, 149,
    151, 152–3, 192, 199–200,
    203, 258, 338, 339–45,
    353–4, 356, 357, 361, 362
  Creole 29–30
  definition of 148, 352
  development of 22–6, 77, 83,
    148–9, 200, 209, 213,
    218–36, 339–45, 357
  function of 219, 257, 335,
    344–5, 351, 361
  meaning and 8, 149, 257,
    258–9, 299–300, 316, 335,
    352, 360
  model of 257, 258, 355–7, 340,
    341
  observation and 340, 343
  patterns of 57–8, 76, 77, 78,
    98, 148, 153, 208–9, 212,
    213, 218, 251, 257, 258–9,
    359, 360, 362
  signs and symbols of 8, 111
  social context in 257, 258, 335,
    361, 362
  socialisation and 22–6, 31, 149,
    257–9
  society and 354
  structure of 199–251, 351–2
  theory of 199, 251, 260
  see also oral; science; social
    studies
Lurie, Morris 74, 165
Lear, Edward 76
learning 7, 57–60, 111, 149, 192,
    218, 275, 288

collaborative 149–53, 155, 157, 159, 168–9, 356
computers and 331–2
difficulties 200–1
evaluation of 353, 356
group 112, 114, 116, 154–69, 360
independent 100–2, 105, 112, 113, 149–53, 158, 161, 168, 351, 355–6
measurement of 353
by observation 100–2, 356
theory 151–2, 275–81, 345
see also literacy
Lewis, C.S. 60, 62, 161–2, 165
lexical repetition 38
lexicogrammar 10, 39, 337, 339–40
linguistics 199, 200–1, 203, 218, 335
  codes 8, 105, 111
  concepts of 200, 257–9
  development of 58, 62, 81, 149, 338–9
  meaning and 111, 202–3, 251
  patterns in 150, 199
  processes 149
  systemic 200
  theory 15, 345
Lisson, Deborah 66
listening 356
literacy 5, 7, 15
  classroom 4, 7, 16, 31, 32, 34, 41–5, 77, 81, 82, 84, 112, 113–32, 133–5, 148–53, 154–69, 170–92, 275, 351–2, 353–4
  codes 8, 11, 105, 157
  communal 8, 22–5, 26–32, 46
  conventions 78, 148, 165
  cultural 8, 19, 27, 29, 77–9, 133–4, 149, 200
  development 6, 16, 30–1, 58, 62, 95–9, 111, 112, 113, 133–5, 148–53, 154–69, 192, 199, 356
  function of 9–10, 16, 157
  home 22–5, 26–32, 41, 95, 100, 102, 351
  ideology and 5, 6, 7, 11, 18, 20, 22, 28, 46, 48
  learning and 5, 12, 112, 151, 155, 163, 200, 275, 351–2, 353–4, 356
  memory and 9

men and 10, 11–12, 20–1
morality 27
mythology 61, 70, 77, 79
myths 3, 5, 151
power and 4, 6, 8, 11, 15, 16, 29, 31
religion and 10, 12, 26, 28–9, 67–8, 80
skills 4, 5, 356
social 4, 5, 7, 8, 10, 31, 32, 46–8, 287–93, 352, 354
social construction of 6, 11, 82
techniques 69–75
universal 12, 13
values 6, 8, 11, 21–2, 29
women and 10, 12, 13, 20, 29, 33
literature 20–1, 57–60, 75–7, 148
  aboriginal 20, 31, 65
  introduction to 76, 99–102, 111–12
  meaning and 148–9
  migrant 20, 27, 31, 33
  multiculturalism in 65, 78, 133–4, 352–3
  setting 62, 65–7
  symbolism and 61
  theme 62, 67–8, 82, 105, 148, 158–9, 169
  traditional 77–9, 84, 98, 134
  see also children; meaning-making
Little, Jean 68

McAfee, Annalena 61
Macdonald, Caroline 63
MacLachlan, Patricia 84
MacLeod, Doug 76
Magorian, Michelle 68
Mahy, Margaret 73
Mappin, Alf 77, 134
Marryat, Capt. 65
Marsden, John 72
Mason, Sophie 59
meaning-making 8, 15, 37, 58, 75, 95, 98, 99, 100, 102, 104, 105, 111, 112, 116, 150, 153, 155, 156, 192, 199, 202–3, 208, 237, 262
  abstract 216–17
  experiential 216, 251, 336, 243, 244–51, 336
  group 236, 237
  interpersonal 219, 243, 244–51, 336
  literature and 148–9

417

Index

meaning-making — *contd*
  oral language and   358
  science and   299, 300–1, 327
  textual language and   336, 337, 352
  see also clauses; grammar; language; linguistics; literacy
media   353, 356
  electronic   7, 134
  print   7, 8, 13, 102
  technological   134
  visual   7, 72
Meek, Margaret   61, 96–9, 102, 111, 112, 150, 153, 154, 155, 157
Meredith, Louisa Anne   67
metafunction
  experiential   218–22, 336
    ergativity   218
    transitivity   218, 227–8
  ideational   336–7, 339, 340
  interpersonal   219, 244–52, 336–7, 339, 340
  textual   336–7, 339, 340
mood and modality   209, 241, 244–51, 337, 338, 339, 340
music   352

narrative   70–3, 76, 77, 95, 100–2, 167, 192, 213, 222, 316
Nash, Ogden   76, 134
Needle, Jan   65
non-English speaking backgrounds (NESB)   209, 213, 234, 240, 243
  relationship between English structures and   244
non-fiction   75–6, 351
Norman, Lilith   66, 164
Nostlinger, Christine   62
nouns   242, 262, 266
novels   62–75, 150, 152, 158, 167
  action and conflict in   63
  formula to   62–3
nursery rhymes   57, 61, 76

Oakley, Graham   70
oral language   6, 11, 12, 22, 24–6, 29, 76, 95, 103, 104, 111, 112, 148, 157, 244, 334, 341–2, 354, 358–9, 362
  visual material influence   386
  text and   352

painting   352
Park, Ruth   59, 66, 67, 68, 80, 157, 169

paragraphs   215
Paterson, Katherine   64, 68
Pausaker, Jenny   71, 74
Pearce, Philippa   164
Pedley, Ethel   67
personal development   81, 355–6
Phipson, Joan   60, 63, 65, 165
phonics   38, 111, 116
photography   352
plot   82–3
  structure of   62–3
poetry   11, 76–7, 83, 95, 152, 158, 351
Potter, Beatrix   57, 58, 69, 100–1
Prelutsky, Jack   77, 134
Process   218–36
  material   219–20, 222, 224–8, 234
  participants   219, 224–7, 233, 234
  relational   219–20, 222–3, 228–33, 270
  Second-order
    mental   220, 223, 233–4
    representation   220, 233, 234
    verbal   220, 223–4, 234–6

Rawlins, Donna   59
readalong tapes   157–8
reading   4, 5, 8, 14–15, 26–30, 32, 48, 62–9, 80, 192, 356
  ability   150–3, 154
  aloud   81, 95, 99, 103, 150, 158
  close   82–3
  collaborative   115, 151, 157, 168
  completion   103–4
  co-operative   103–4
  cues   111, 116
  decoding and   157
  definition of   30, 61
  development   6, 7, 10, 28–9, 62, 63, 81–3, 95–112, 113–32, 133–5, 148–53, 154–69, 170–92, 218, 236, 240, 340–1, 345, 358
  extension activities and   116–17, 151, 155, 157, 170–92
  fluent   103–4, 111
  groups   154, 159–62
  guides   162
  meaning and   148–9
  miscues   110
  mumble   103–4
  patterns   62, 77, 96–8, 103
  practices   14, 29, 41–5, 77, 81, 95, 99, 100, 102, 192, 327, 358

Index

prediction 78, 111
programs 55–74, 80, 81, 83, 112, 113–32, 133–5, 147, 150–3, 156–62, 170–92
  schemes 61, 95, 148, 150, 151, 306, 312, 326
  science 327–8
  shared 95, 99–102, 105–10, 111, 112
  television and 157
  theories of 32, 150
  visual knowledge and 111
  wide 82–3
register 257, 258, 335
  concept of 200
  definition of 335, 336
  field 258, 336, 339, 340–2
  genre and 244
  mode 258, 336, 337, 338, 339, 340–2
  tenor 244, 258, 336, 339, 340–1
resources
  books 400–9
  computer 395–400
  curriculum and 354–409
  everyday essential 361–2
  film and video 374–85
  people as 362–4
  pictures as 386–95
  places as 365–74
rhymes 76, 351
  see also nursery rhymes
rhyming 25
Richards, Frank 63
Rockwell, Thomas 69
Rodda, Emily 62, 63, 71
role playing 357, 358
Rubinstein Gillian 62, 63, 72, 73, 82, 157, 169, 173, 177–92

satire 70, 76, 77
Scholes, Katherine 62
schools 3–4, 7, 12, 14, 17, 19, 46, 81, 355–6
science
  text books 306–34
  education and 299, 305–10, 339–45, 353, 355
  language and 258–9, 299–305, 326–34, 338, 339–45
  reading and 327–8
Scieszka, Jon 70
Scott, Bill 77
Scott-Mitchell, Clare 77

semantics 26, 37, 111, 219, 233, 234, 336–7, 340
  see also grammar
Sendak, Maurice 62, 75, 116, 153, 165
sentence structure 38, 58, 98, 202, 204, 213
sequencing 356–7
Sharpe, Margaret 65
Smith, Doris Buchanan 68
social
  change 200
  class 6, 9, 10, 13, 15–17, 47, 201
    middle 31
    working 5, 10, 16, 31, 47
  conditions 7
  history 20, 201
  power 4, 8, 9, 14, 41, 46
  processes 112, 135, 149
  relations 8, 11, 25–6, 149, 358, 362
  structure 6, 135, 149, 199
  values 31
  see also literacy
Social Literacy Project 287–92
social studies 18, 257–92, 353, 355–6
  language and 257–92, 356
society 3–4, 5, 7, 65, 351, 354
  inequality in 4, 6, 13, 17
  see also language
Southall, Ivan 64, 150, 157, 159, 173
speech 22–3, 32, 237, 272
  conjunctions and 210–11
  development 23, 149
  grammar and 202, 203, 205, 210, 244, 262, 336, 338
  patterns 23
spelling 3, 14, 275
  patterns 10
Spence, Eleanor 66
Spenser, Herbert 21
Stevenson, R.L. 60
Stewart, Maureen 64, 72
stories 47–8, 61, 351
  bedtime 26–8, 30
  development of 101
  structure of 35–41, 78, 96–9, 100–2, 105, 153
storying 27, 32
Stow, Randolf 70
Stowe, Harriet Beecher 65–6
Stretton, Hesba 67
syntax 10, 37, 111

talking 23, 357–8
  patterns 33
  see also classroom talk
Taylor, Mildred 65
teachers 34, 46, 77, 149, 155–6, 159–60
teaching 46–8
  strategies 3–5
  techniques 113–35, 154–69
television 38, 134, 157, 352, 374–85
texts
  cultural 352
  definition of 352
  selecting 157
  structure of 262, 336–7
Theme 208–17, 337
  development of 211–12, 216–17
  grammatical 208, 217
  Interpersonal (Vocative) 215–16, 244–52
  Marked 210, 211, 212
  and meaning 210, 216–17, 323–4
  patterns of 323–6
  principles of 209–11
  Textual 210–11, 215, 216, 217
  Transitivity and 227–8
  Topical 211, 212, 215, 216
Thiele, Colin 60, 64, 77, 157
Torres Strait Islanders see Aborigines
transitivity 227–8, 337, 338
Turner, Ethel 67, 71
Twain, Mark 64

Umansky, Kaye 70

Van der Loeff, Rutgers 63
verbs 102, 203–8, 218–22, 228, 242, 262, 266
  see also process

verse 76–7
video 157, 352, 374–85
visual images 148, 352
vocabulary 10, 57–8, 101, 102, 151, 218, 327
Voigt, Cynthia 64, 150

Wagner, Jenny 61
Wakefield, S.A. 68
Weld, Ann 70
Wheatley, Nadia 59, 65, 72, 169, 247
White, Mary 80
Wignell, Edel 66
Wild, Margaret 57, 68, 72
Willmott, Frank 72
Winch, Madeleine 60
Wittgenstein 23
Wrightson, Patricia 60, 65, 66, 75, 83, 157
writing 3, 5, 8, 11, 32, 48
  conjunctions and 210–11
  development of 6, 7, 111, 149, 151, 200, 205–17, 218, 236, 332–45
  expository 216
  grammar and 148, 199–251, 337–8, 339, 340
  process 286
  practices 14, 41–5
  report 216–7
  structure of 212–13, 235–6, 237
written language 7, 8, 9–10, 21, 26, 102, 105, 111, 112, 116, 157, 205, 262, 272–3, 275, 326–34, 337–45, 354, 357–9
  development of 149–50
  text and 262, 352

Zimnik, Reiner 75